Building Effective Sentences

Grammar, Punctuation, and Writing Techniques

Judith L. White

Davenport College
Kalamazoo, Michigan

GLENCOE

Macmillan/McGraw-Hill

New York, New York   Columbus, Ohio   Mission Hills, California   Peoria, Illinois

White, Judith L.
    Building effective sentences : grammar, punctuation, and writing
techniques / Judith L. White.
        p.   cm.
    Includes index.
    ISBN 0-02-800883-9
    1. English language—Sentences.   2. English language—Rhetoric.
I. Title.
PE1441.W48   1993
428.2—dc20   92-40028
                                                                  CIP

**BUILDING EFFECTIVE SENTENCES: GRAMMAR, PUNCTUATION, AND WRITING
TECHNIQUES**

Copyright © 1993 by Glencoe Division of Macmillan/McGraw-Hill School Publishing
Company. All rights reserved. Except as permitted under the United States Copyright Act,
no part of this publication may be reproduced or distributed in any form or by any means, or
stored in a database or retrieval system, without the prior written permission of the
publisher.

Send all inquiries to:
GLENCOE DIVISION
Macmillan/McGraw-Hill
936 Eastwind Drive
Westerville, OH 43081

ISBN 0-02-800883-9

Printed in the United States of America.

1 2 3 4 5 6 7 8 9   POH   99 98 97 96 95 94 93

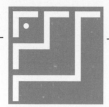

C O N T E N T S

UNIT 1 BUILDING PHRASES AND CLAUSES　　1

UNIT 2 CONSTRUCTING SENTENCES 178

UNIT 3 MAKING WORD CHOICES 277

UNIT 4 CONNECTING SENTENCES   352

INTRODUCTION

This is your first look at the text for your English class. Some of you have had a good background in English usage. Your previous schooling offered much study in the proper use of the language. Still, a class in English usage with an emphasis on writing techniques can be a good refresher course for you. Proper usage is a learned skill, honed by practice.

Others of you know that you need additional work with your usage of grammar, punctuation, and writing techniques. You may not have had any formal study of English usage since high school or even elementary school. Some of you may have been out of school for some time. You may have lost confidence in your ability to use the language correctly.

All of you have enrolled in college to further your education because you know that your success in your vocation or profession depends on the quality of your preparation for it. You want to succeed at what you do, or you will not be happy in your chosen career.

Although it is not "fair," people do judge each other on their usage of language. To some, poor usage seems to indicate poor education generally. Bright, capable people have lost job opportunities because of poor language habits. On the other hand, people who have good usage habits have enhanced their careers. Developing your language skills can add to your confidence, and that added confidence can help you succeed in any career.

This book is designed to help you improve your English language skills. While a general review of grammar and usage practices makes up parts of the text, particular attention is called to writing techniques that will add much clarity, conciseness, and variety to your style. You will learn varied ways to present your ideas, using differing grammatical forms. You will learn a step-by-step technique for composing a well-developed paragraph. You should leave this class knowing more sophisticated writing methods. You should gain much more confidence in your ability to write and punctuate sentences and short essays.

Each chapter introduces concepts, explains them, offers a self-check review after each section, and then has varied exercises for the needed practice to really learn the concepts. There will be some necessary memorization suggested to assist your learning. Many of the exercises will give you practice in writing your own sentences as well as those which have you proofread other writing. These are in addition to the usual exercises to assist in the learning of the grammar and structure principles.

This textbook assumes that you have had English usage courses in the past and that you are somewhat familiar with the common grammatical terms. However, an overview is presented of the parts of speech before Chapter One, and each chapter gives detailed definitions with illustrations of the grammatical concepts to be covered in that section.

Parts of Speech

The parts of speech are categories into which words, phrases or clauses are grouped based on their functions in sentences.

ADJECTIVE: Any word, phrase, or clause that tells WHICH, WHAT KIND OF, or HOW MANY about a noun or pronoun.
Example: *Any unnamed* bug could be *a poisonous* one.

ADVERB: Any word, phrase, or clause that tells WHEN, WHERE, WHY, HOW, or HOW MUCH (to what extent) about some action verb, adjective, or other adverb in a clause; an adverb clause often modifies another entire clause.
Example: *Nowadays* people *usually easily* travel long distances.

CONJUNCTION: Any word or word group that serves to connect two or more other things; conjunctions can connect words, phrases, or clauses.
Example: Any teacher *or* counselor can call you *and* give you the date.

INTERJECTION: Any word that shows an emotion and can convey a complete thought by itself.
Example: Oh! Wow! Stop!

NOUN: A word, phrase, or clause that names such things as these: person, place, object, idea, activity, or quality. The named item is not necessarily tangible.
Example: Your *mood* can be a *detriment* to your *attitude*.

PREPOSITION: Any word or word group that connects a noun or pronoun to some other word in the sentence. A preposition does not act alone but begins a phrase that ends with the noun or pronoun called its object.
Example: *During working hours* a book *about computer games* will be *on the desk.*

PRONOUN: A word that is used to replace a noun.
Example: *Anyone* is welcome to present *his* or *her* point of view.

VERB: A word or word group that either names the main action of the idea or is used to link a subject to something stated about it. This linking-type of verb can be called the State of Being verb.
Example: When Mary *is* tired, she *falls* asleep anywhere.

U N I T 1

Building Phrases and Clauses

Phrases and Clauses

OVERVIEW

- **Phrases**
- **Clauses**
- **Punctuation: An Introduction**
- **Punctuation Points: Commas With Phrases**

Grammar is nothing more than the organization and naming of the patterns of language. Early people spoke before they wrote; children speak before they learn to read and write. Spoken language is, however, somewhat different from written. When speaking, you can always immediately clarify your meanings by acting on your listener's puzzled facial expressions or voiced questions. Writing requires that you state your message clearly as you choose and combine the words you put on paper. Your "listener" has only these written symbols to use in interpreting your intended meaning.

By electing to prepare for an advanced career, you have committed yourself to developing your communication skills as well as your other job skills. You likely will be called on to use both written and oral communication. You will want to represent yourself and your employer in the best possible way. One important way to do so is to become more proficient in your use of language. One good way to begin is to differentiate between phrases and clauses.

 **PHRASES**

Although a word is the basic element of language, a word alone seldom transmits a thought. Words are joined into groups, the smallest of which is called a phrase. A phrase is a group of related words that gives a part of an idea but which lacks the two basic elements of a complete thought, the subject and the verb.

DEFINITION A **phrase** is a group of related words without a subject and a verb. A phrase does not express a complete thought.

(*Note:* Subjects and verbs will be defined and discussed in depth in Chapters 2 through 4.)

The English language uses many different types of phrases. Often, the name of the phrase tells what type of word starts the phrase. For example, a prepositional phrase begins with a preposition, an infinitive phrase with an infinitive, a gerund phrase with a gerund, and so on. This chapter will focus on prepositional phrases; you will learn about other kinds of phrases in other parts of this text.

Prepositional Phrases

A prepositional phrase is a word group without a subject and verb. The phrase contains at least two words, the first of which is called a preposition.

DEFINITION A **prepositional phrase** is a group of related words without a subject and verb but which starts with a **preposition** and ends with an **object of the preposition.**

These little phrases usually add extra information to the main ideas of a sentence by telling <u>where</u>, <u>when</u>, or <u>how</u> something occurs. They may also describe something named, telling <u>what kind of</u>. Notice how each phrase in the following sentences adds information to the main idea.

1. Where?

   Henry walked *to his office.*

2. When?

   Joy played golf *in the afternoon.*

3. How?

   Marcie does her income tax return *with ease and confidence.*

4. What kind of?

   The box *of candy* costs $4.29.

Did you notice that the prepositional phrase in the third sentence contains two objects? Both *ease* and *confidence* tell how and act as objects of the preposition *with. Ease and confidence* is a compound object.

The English language allows for many parts of sentences to be compounded, that is, to have more than one part. However, a connecting word must be added to make the compound element. The most common connecting words are *and, or,* and *nor.*

Notice that although the example phrases contain at least two words, these phrases would not give meaning without being part of a main idea.

Prepositional phrases are said to modify—to change or add to—the main idea. In fact, phrases often contain their own modifiers (such as *his* in *to his office*), which add to the idea within the phrase. The phrase begins with the preposition and ends with the object, often with one or more modifiers in between. The preposition acts as the connector that shows how its object is related to the rest of the sentence.

SELF-CHECK 1-1

The Self-Checks throughout this text are designed to help you gauge your understanding of the concepts in each section. In the following sentences underline the prepositions and put parentheses around each of the prepositional phrases. To find out where each phrase stops, say the preposition along with the word what *or* whom. *For example, if the preposition is* of, *ask* of what? *or* of whom?

1. The office of the President is on the second floor.

    Of whom?   On what?

2. Everyone except the office clerks went to the meeting at the Regency Hotel.

    Except whom?   To what?   At what?

3. Without Ms. Cady our office team would not have won the bowling tournament in Dallas.

    Without whom?   In what?

4. Mr. Jones gave the letter to Ms. Smith and Ms. Halsted for proofreading.

    To whom?   For what?

5. Please put the chair by the window in the bedroom.

    By what?   In what?

Before you continue, turn to p. 169 to check your answers.

Once you understand the concept of prepositional phrases, your next task is to become familiar with the most common prepositions. Until you learn the list of prepositions, you will not be able to locate prepositional phrases.

One hint you may have already learned for recognizing prepositions is to think of a preposition as showing "where a mouse can go." This hint helps because so many prepositions tell where. If you think of a mouse in relation to a room, it could be *in* the room, *on* the floor, *under* the table, and so on. Look at the list that follows to see how many other words can relate the mouse to the room. This example should show you how prepositions do act as words that relate their objects to other elements in the main idea.

Common Prepositions

about	before	concerning	off	to
above	behind	down	off of	toward
across	below	during	on	up
after	beneath	except	over	upon
against	beside	for	past	under
along	besides	from	regarding	underneath
amid	between	in	respecting	until
among	beyond	into	since	with
around	but (meaning	like	through	within
as	"except")	of	throughout	without
at	by			

Prepositional Word Groups (the two or more words act together)

apart from	devoid of	in place of	next to
as for	from beyond	in reference to	on account of
as regards	from out	in regard to	to the extent of
as to	in accordance with	in spite of	with regard to
by way of	in addition to	instead of	with respect to
contrary to			

Although you may already recognize some of these words, try to become familiar with all of them before moving on to the next chapter. Learning the complete list will make locating prepositional phrases much easier for you.

As your study of grammar continues, you will discover that the words listed here as prepositions do not <u>always</u> act as prepositions. Depending on how they are used in sentences, they can also function as other parts of speech. This is true of most parts of speech. You recognize a word for how it functions in the sentence, not for some permanent label. Most words can function in more than one way. To be sure that one of the listed words is being used as a preposition, simply verify that it is the start of a phrase and that it has an object. A word cannot function as a preposition unless it is part of a phrase.

You will learn about other kinds of phrases in other parts of this text, but a good recognition of prepositional phrases will make the rest of your study much easier.

Answer the following questions:

1. Can you list ten prepositions on a piece of paper? Twenty? Jot down as many as you can.

2. What is a prepositional phrase?

3. Is a prepositional phrase a complete thought?

4. Could you find a subject or a verb in a prepositional phrase?

5. Is any word listed as a preposition always a preposition?

Before you continue, turn to p. 169 to check your answers.

TRY IT OUT: **Complete Exercises 1.1 and 1.2, p. 11, to practice working with prepositional phrases.**

 ## CLAUSES

Although phrases add bits of extra, sometimes quite important, information to your sentences, the bigger ideas will be written in clauses.

DEFINITION A **clause** is a group of related words with a subject and a verb. A clause may or may not give a complete thought by itself.

Notice that the definition of a clause is similar to the definition of a phrase. Pay particular attention, however, to the differences between the two grammatical forms.

	Phrase	Clause
Has subject and verb	No	Yes
Is mandatory in sentence	No	Yes
States major idea	No	Yes
Contains complete thought	No	Yes or No
Makes sentence by itself	No	Yes or No

Thus, you can see that phrases and clauses are very different. The most important difference is that a clause must have a subject and a verb. A phrase can have neither. Although phrases alone will never make up a sentence, a lone clause could.

You will learn more about clauses in the next three chapters. There are two basic types of clauses, and not all clauses can stand alone as sentences. Chapters 2 through 4 will teach you to recognize clauses by introducing you to subjects and verbs. Locating the verb is the first step you must take to identify clauses.

┌ᴸ SELF-CHECK 1-3

1. What is the main difference between a clause and a phrase?

2. Is every clause a sentence?

3. Does every sentence have at least one clause?

4. What two elements must be present to have a clause?

5. Which of these elements must you locate first?

Have you been jotting down your answers before you look them up in the answer section? Doing so should really help you to learn the material before you go on to new material. Before you continue, turn to p. 169 to check your answers.

PUNCTUATION: AN INTRODUCTION

Spoken language came before written; but after language began to be written, another need became apparent. When a person speaks, he or she "punctuates" spoken language with facial expressions, gestures, and changes in the tone and pitch of voice. The listener uses these audio and visual cues to help interpret what is being said.

The listener can also stop the speaker and ask questions to clarify a point or can show a lack of comprehension by puzzled looks, shrugs, and other body language.

In written language punctuation marks were created to function in place of the audio and visual cues of speech. A standardized set of marks and rules for their use make certain that the marks mean the same thing to all speakers and readers.

Punctuation rules are just one part of a system of rules about the English language and its accepted usages. This standard set of rules, which has evolved over centuries, is what makes our communication possible, what makes for clarity and conciseness. All told, this is Standard English, the language widely recognized as acceptable wherever English is spoken. It is the language you hear in the mass media, in the business world, in the academic community.

Where appropriate, this text will cover the accepted ways of using marks of punctuation along with the discussion of grammatical structure.

This will allow you to apply your new knowledge to both your written and your spoken language.

Canyouimaginereadingsomethingthatisnotpunctuatedatallbyspacesbetweenwords?

You can see that even spacing can be a way of punctuating. Margins, indentations, underlining, capitalization, and the various marks of punctuation all provide clues to the meaning, intent, and emphasis of the written word. Read this sentence.

After eating the dog a member of the family started barking.

Sound unusual? What if you read it this way:

After eating, the dog, a member of the family, started barking.

That makes more sense, doesn't it? The words are actually the same, but the commas provide a guide as to how to read the sentence. That's what punctuation is for.

Start your study of punctuation by debunking an often-heard "rule" about commas. Many students have been taught to put commas wherever they might pause while speaking. That too-simple rule would have you missing some very important commas and placing others in the wrong places. Start now to learn the accepted rules for punctuation.

PUNCTUATION POINTS: COMMAS WITH PHRASES

The punctuation for prepositional phrases is simple: Prepositional phrases are seldom set off by commas.

Look for prepositional phrases as you read magazines, newspapers, or other textbooks. Prepositional phrases that support a main idea by telling where, when, how, or what kind of do not have commas on either side of them—unless the comma is needed for other constructions nearby. Information in this type of prepositional phrase is usually so closely related to the main idea and gives such important detail that no commas are called for. Look at these examples.

Several *of the first-quarter reports* must be completed *by next Thursday.* [Without the two phrases you would not know what should be done by when.]

Put everything *except the case of stationery in the storeroom.* [Without these related phrases not much would be known.]

Some *of the environmentalists* seek a solution *to the problem of landfill overflows.* [Without the phrases you would not know who is seeking a solution to what.]

There are a several instances where commas are used with prepositional phrases: (1) after long introductory phrases, (2) when a sentence might be misread without the comma(s), and (3) to set apart transitional phrases.

Long Introductory Phrases

Some writers like to give their readers a pause after two consecutive phrases or a very long phrase if these come <u>at the beginning</u> of a clause. A comma in this situation is optional, as shown by the brackets.

In the long history of Native Americans [,] there is much tragedy recorded.

After his first enthusiastic but halting steps [,] the year-old boy raced from place to place.

At the time announced in the convention program [,] the leader stepped to the microphone to begin the announcements.

Easily Misunderstood Phrases

Sometimes the comma after an introductory phrase is needed for more than a pause. In certain sentences the reader may have to reread the sentence several times to avoid misunderstanding the construction if there is no comma after the introductory phrase. Look at the following examples.

To an avid sports fan like Jean, Johnson was more than just another basketball player. [Without the comma the reader likely would read *Jean Johnson* as a person's name.]

In making the presentation to my sister, Hanna listed her many volunteer services to the community. [Without the comma the reader may at first assume that *Hanna* and *sister* are the same person.]

In the final scene of the third act of the opera, Carmen Santiago sang the first solo of her career. [*Carmen* is the title of an opera, but here *Carmen Santiago* is the name of a performer.]

After all, the money had been spent. [Without the comma this seems to be an incomplete idea indicating that something would result from the spending of the money.]

Transitional Phrases

Unlike prepositional phrases that modify the content of the sentences to which they are attached, another type of prepositional phrase acts in a different manner. This type of phrase guides the reader to follow the same train of thought as the writer. These phrases do not answer the usual questions—where, when, how, and what kind of—and can be removed without changing the meaning of the clause to which they are attached. These nonessential phrases are often called **interrupters** or **transitional expressions** and are set out with commas.

Mr. Johnson, *on the other hand,* liked the rewritten ad.

The new product, *for example,* does fulfill your need.

Did the students, *as a rule,* do well on the weekly quizzes?

I am, *in other words,* very angry about the decision!

Here are some prepositional phrases that can function as interrupters. In most cases you would set out these phrases from your clauses using commas. For a complete list see pp. 241–242 in Chapter 9.

as a matter of fact	in fact
as a rule	in my opinion
at any rate	in other words
by all means	in the first place
by the way	of course
for example	on the contrary
in brief	on the other hand
in contrast	

SELF-CHECK 1-4

Put in any commas needed to set off the nonessential phrases.

1. My boss by the way gave me the afternoon off.

2. The Stevenses' file is in the third drawer.

3. In other words you cannot help me.

4. He tried to put it in other words.

5. On Monday Mr. Scott submitted his resignation.

6. Mr. Scott by the way submitted his resignation on Monday.

7. We hope for example to double the Snapp account.

8. The fire happened as a result of carelessness.

9. We decided to ban smoking as a rule of the association.

10. Ms. Kozlowski as a rule is very generous with her praise.

Before you continue, turn to pp. 169–170 to check your answers.

TRY IT OUT: **For more practice go to Exercises 1.3 and 1.4, p. 12. Exercise 1.5, p. 12, will provide more challenge.**

⊡ Chapter 1: Phrases and Clauses

● E X E R C I S E   1 . 1

Underline the preposition and put parentheses around the prepositional phrase. Notice that when you read each sentence without the prepositional phrases, you still have a basic thought; however, the thought becomes completed with these phrases.

1. All of the accountants are going to the convention on Saturday.

2. The study of English grammar is necessary for an understanding of correct writing.

3. Mr. Johnson from Des Moines will be arriving at the airport at three o'clock.

4. Underneath the stack of files you will find the memorandum concerning the Delta account.

5. In addition to your original please type three carbons.

6. Between you and me we should have five people doing this job instead of four.

7. Since yesterday Ms. Robinson has called five of the applicants for interviews.

8. Everyone but Mr. Armour will be seeking the answer to this problem.

9. The typewriter beside Peggy's desk has been broken for three days.

10. We will have our meeting on the first day of April.

● E X E R C I S E   1 . 2

Put parentheses around each prepositional phrase; underline the preposition once and the object of the preposition twice. Remember that there can be a compound object.

1. During your lunch hour will you please see that Miss Franks gets a copy of our data.

2. Anyone in our offices is entitled to the use of our copy machines.

3. In spite of the holiday we should still have time for the completion of this project.

4. Around Easter our retail sales increase by leaps and bounds.

5. There are several good reasons for our hesitation concerning a starting date.

6. Mrs. Fredericks wants a cup of coffee with cream and sugar.

7. I drove to the center of the city in seven hours.

8. Send the invoice to the Joneses at the address on their letterhead.

9. The new computer is designed with an eye toward economy.

10. The cartons from Brown Company were misplaced behind the shipment from Webster and Smith.

Put commas around any nonessential prepositional phrases.

1. Several of the sales representatives have gone over their quotas this year.

2. By the way have we received a letter from the Brown Company yet?

3. She said in fact that you were to complete the contract yourself.

4. After January 1 our new health insurance policy will cover dental care.

5. The manuscript on the table should be retyped by Friday.

On a separate sheet of paper, write fifteen sentences that contain prepositional phrases. Underline each phrase and put commas around those that act as interrupters and are not closely related to the main idea. At least five of your phrases should be interrupters.

Rewrite this paragraph on a separate sheet of paper, adding prepositional phrases where there are blanks. If you use any of the transitional expressions, be sure to add commas.

The other day _____ I saw a car full _____. I could hardly believe my eyes! Who would expect to see a car full _____ driving _____. Maybe you'd at times expect to see them _____, but as a rule you would never expect to see them _____, would you? I pulled my car _____ to catch my breath, and I noticed another car _____ which was also full _____ parked _____. I stared and stared _____ and then drove _____ hurrying home to tell my family _____. They became excited and wanted to see the car full _____ themselves. We drove quickly back _____ and were able to see them. This time they not only filled the car, but the car was pulling a trailer that was overflowing _____.

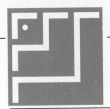

CHAPTER 2

Verbs and Verbals

ACTION VERBS

Most people think of a verb as a word that shows action. This concept is incomplete, however, and can cause a great deal of misunderstanding. There are actually two types of verbs, the action verb and the linking verb.

The most common verb is an action verb.

DEFINITION An **action verb** is a word or words that show what happens in a clause.

Words like *sell, hit, jump, write,* and *swim* are easily seen as action words. You can make a mental picture of someone or something doing the named activity. You can see someone *sell* or *hit* or *jump.*

Many other action verbs, such as *want* and *think,* are less easily pictured. As these words show, action verbs can express mental activities as well as physical activities. An action verb may even represent a combination of activities, with both mental and physical aspects. For example, the verb *sell* often means more than a simple exchange of money and property; it also means "convince to buy." Other words like this are *manage* and *succeed.*

Perhaps you could think of action verbs as words that show someone or something expending energy.

In an action verb clause the activity often moves from the front to some person or object later in the clause.

The salesperson *sold* twelve typewriters.

Hortence *smiled* at her sister afterwards.

The lazy cat *flinched* during its nap.

LINKING VERBS

Very often, a writer isn't reporting an activity but is, instead, giving some description about a named subject. Because no action is being described, another type of verb—a linking verb—is needed.

DEFINITION A **linking verb** is a word or words used when nothing actually happens but some statement is being made to show some condition of the subject of the clause. These verbs link the statement to the subject. These verbs are also called "state of being" verbs.

Be Verbs

The most common linking verbs are the various forms of the verb *be.* Because these *be* linking verbs are more difficult to find, you should memorize them for quick sight-recognition.

am	was
is	were
are	be (been, being)

Be aware that verbs can consist of more than one word; thus, the *be* verb could also be *could have been, might be, is being,* or *shall be.* (These added words, called helping verbs, are discussed later in the chapter.)

As you look at this list of verbs, you can see that no action is being reported; for instance, can you "is" anyone, or did you ever try to "was" something? No, you cannot <u>do</u> these words. They are rather like equal signs between the subject and whatever is being said to describe it.

The salesperson *is* my brother.

Hortense *has been* in her office all day.

The lazy cats *are* under the table.

In these linking verb clauses the words after the verb reflect back to describe the subject. Notice that nothing is said about what the salesperson, Hortense, or the cats are <u>doing</u>. The sentences report only the condition or existence of the subject at the time indicated by the clause.

Versatile Verbs

In addition to the various forms of *be,* several other words can be linking verbs. These words are linking verbs when they show no action by the subject. They could be replaced by some form of the verb *be* without appreciably changing the meaning of the clause.

appear	look	smell
become	prove	sound
feel	remain	taste
grow	seem	

You should probably memorize this short list of verbs as well as the forms of *be* so that you can easily recognize these words as verbs in clauses.

Many of these verbs, you will notice, relate a sensory perception, such as sight or hearing. This clue may help you to remember some of the non-*be* linking verbs.

The unique thing about these few verbs is that most can be used as either type of verb—action or linking. (*Seem* is always linking.) How each is used in its clause will determine its type. To distinguish the difference, you must be able to locate the subject of an action verb, thus this definition.

DEFINITION The **subject of an action verb** is a naming word (a person, place, thing, or idea) that is the doer of the action of the verb.

Although subjects will be covered more completely in Chapter 4, learning this definition now is necessary for you to distinguish between action and linking verbs.

Decide whether each verb in the following pairs shows action (AV) or just replaces a linking verb (LV) form of *be*. The subjects are underlined once, the verbs twice to help you locate them. You can tell if the verb is an action verb by determining whether the subject is the <u>doer</u> of the verb in the clause.

1. a. <u>Mr. Read</u> <u>grows</u> many plants in his office.
   b. The <u>time</u> <u>grows</u> late.

2. a. The bakery <u>products</u> <u>smell</u> very good.
   b. <u>I</u> could <u>smell</u> the furniture polish as I came into the office.

3. a. The <u>advertisements</u> <u>look</u> professionally done.
   b. Did <u>Mr. Cooper</u> <u>look</u> at the advertisements?

4. a. Mary stayed home today because <u>she</u> <u>feels</u> ill.
   b. <u>Mary</u> <u>feels</u> each part to check for flaws.

Examples 1b, 2a, 3a, and 4a contain linking verbs. The verbs in the other sentences are action verbs because someone or something is doing the action.

⌐• S E L F - C H E C K   2 – 1

Underline the verb twice, the subject once in each of the following sentences. On the blank tell whether the verb is action (AV) or linking (LV).

_____ 1. The shelf paper remained clean for a year.

_____ 2. Einstein proved his theory of relativity.

_____ 3. I tasted the mushroom carefully.

_____ 4. The mushroom tasted strange to my palate.

_____ 5. Your idea sounds like a good one.

Before you continue, turn to p. 170 to check your answers.

A very few other verbs could, on occasion, act as linking verbs, although they ordinarily serve as action verbs. Notice the use of *act, get,* and *make* in these sentences. Each could be replaced by a *be* verb.

The dog acts sick. [He isn't really "acting" as a stage performer would.]
This verb usage gets somewhat tricky. [A usage can't really "get" anything.]
Elsie makes a good chairperson. [She actually "is" the chairperson.]

TRY IT OUT: Complete Exercises 2.1 and 2.2, p. 25, to practice finding verbs and identifying them as action or linking verbs.

▛ VERBALS

Chapter 3 will go into much more detail about verbs, but before that you should know this important principle: <u>Not every action word or linking word is a verb</u>. Remember, a word becomes a certain part of speech only because of how it acts in its own word group. Recognizing when words are not verbs is as important as recognizing when they are.

Notice the action or linking words in the following examples. Although each example contains only one verb, you'll also recognize other words as action or linking words. All these words are italicized, but they are not all verbs in these sentences.

1. Mr. Rohm *jogs* to *remove* his tensions.
2. *Driving* a company car, our sales representative *travels* thousands of miles each year.
3. *Flying* on commercial flights, Mrs. Luscomb *is* able to *arrive* at her *meeting* on time.

Without an understanding of verbs, a person could be confused by this variety of verblike words. The verblike words result when a good writer combines ideas into one sentence instead of writing two or more sentences. The careful writer keeps the most important idea in the main clause and uses modifying phrases to add the less important ideas. These less important ideas are often expressed in verbals.

DEFINITION A **verbal** is a word that looks like a verb (action or linking) but that acts more like another part of speech—a noun, an adjective, or an adverb—in its current use.

You don't have to know whether a verbal is functioning as a noun, adjective, or adverb to be able to identify it (you'll become more familiar with these parts of speech as you continue in this text). To find out if an apparent verb is really a verbal, just apply the following three hints.

HINT 1: Any "verb" preceded by the word *to* is not a verb but a verbal. This type of verbal is called an **infinitive.**

In the preceding Example 1, "Mr. Rohm jogs to remove his tensions," *to remove* cannot be a verb because it begins with the word *to*. It is instead an infinitive; therefore, it does not tell the most important idea of the sentence.

In Example 3, "Mrs. Luscomb is able to arrive at her meeting on time," *to arrive* is not the verb; it is an infinitive, only a modifier of the main idea.

You will learn more about how infinitives act in clauses and how to punctuate them in Chapter 8. For now it is enough to be aware that infinitives do not function as the verbs in their clauses but as verb forms used as other parts of speech.

TRY IT OUT: **For practice in recognizing infinitives, do Exercises 2.3 and 2.4, p. 26.**

HINT 2: Words that end in *-ing* can be either verbals or parts of verbs. If an *-ing* word is a verb, it must have some form of the *be* verb as a helper (to tell the time) as well as a doer subject. Without both of these elements the *-ing* word will not be a verb but a verbal—a participle or a gerund.

Look at the word *driving* in the earlier example sentence about the sales representative.

> Driving a company car, our sales representative travels thousands of miles each year.

Driving is not the verb in this sentence. It does show an action, but it has no helping verb; therefore, it is not the verb. It is a verbal. It simply adds an extra idea to this sentence. The main idea is that the sales representative travels thousands of miles each year.

If the main idea were meant to be that the representative drives a company car and not that he or she travels so far, *driving* would have been given a helping verb and would have been the verb.

> The sales representative is driving a company car.

In this sentence, *is driving* is the verb; it has a helping verb and a doer of the action named. Do you see how the emphasis changed when the verb changed? It is now more important that the sales representative is driving a company car.

Note also that *flying* and *meeting* in Example 3 don't have helping verbs.

> Flying on regularly scheduled commercial flights, Mrs. Luscomb is able to arrive at her meeting on time.

You now know that neither of these *-ing* words acts as the verb in this sentence because neither has a helping verb preceding it. These *-ing* words are verbals in this sentence. (The verb is the word *is*.)

HINT 3: A verblike word that ends in *-ed* is not necessarily a verb. To be a verb, the *-ed* word must show the main action done by the subject.

Contrast the word *headed* in the following examples:

1. *Headed* home, Mr. Burns *was* glad the day was over.
2. Mr. Burns, *headed* home, *was* glad the day was over.
3. Mr. Burns *headed* home, glad the day was over.

Can you see how in Examples 1 and 2 the *headed home* just adds to the idea that Mr. Burns was glad the day was over? The phrase is not the main action. In Example 3 the main idea is that Mr. Burns headed home; thus, only in Example 3 is *headed* the verb. In the other two examples *headed* is a verbal, acting as the less important idea.

Also, if a verblike *-ed* word is preceded by a linking verb, the *-ed* word is not the verb. The linking verb is. Thus, in the following sentence the verb is *was*, not *headed*.

The Board of Directors was headed by a woman.

Note that the subject (Board of Directors) is not the doer of the action.

Later, in Chapter 8 on verbals, you will learn more about participles and gerunds, which are what *-ing* and *-ed* words are when they are not acting as verbs. For now, just be aware that to be verbs *-ing* words must have helping verbs and doers and that *-ed* words must show the main action done by the subject. Otherwise, you must look someplace else in your clause for the verb.

▣ Verbal Phrases

An important point regarding verbals is that they are often, although not always, a part of a small, related word group. Because grammatical groups are named by the words that begin them, these verbals and their related words are called **verbal phrases,** more specifically infinitive phrases, gerund phrases, and participle phrases.

A verbal phrase is a word group that starts with a verblike word. Within the phrase there will be no doer of the action. There is no subject and verb. The verbal phrase simply adds an extra idea to the main idea. Actually, the use of verbal phrases is one writing technique that the more sophisticated writer uses to combine ideas. You will learn how to use these phrases in your writing as you study Chapter 8, but the study of verbs is not complete at this point. To successfully incorporate verbal phrases into your language, you must first understand clauses.

The italicized words in the following examples are verbal phrases. These phrases only add to the main idea and cannot stand alone. The verbal word is not the verb because the writer did not intend the main message to be stated in the verbal phrase. The writer placed the more important idea in the main clause—where the verb is. (The examples throughout the text will use abbreviations for the parts of sentences. Here S = subject; V = verb.)

         S   V

The briefcase, *bulging with papers,* spilled all over the floor.

                  S   V

To play tennis well, Darren practiced daily for six hours.

  S ⌐—V—⌐

Ike has been retired for six months *after working for forty years for Stern and Company.*

          S   V

The mayor, *sickened by the damage,* called a meeting of all affected people.

             S   V

Nearing home, Frances, *tired as could be,* stopped at the grocery for milk.

Underline the verbals and verbal phrases in the following sentences. The first three sentences are examples from the text to get you started.

1. Mr. Rohm jogs to remove his tensions.

2. Driving a company car, our sales representative travels thousands of miles each year.

3. Flying on commercial flights, Mrs. Luscomb is able to arrive at her meeting on time.

Continue to underline the verbals and verbal phrases in these next sentences. When you're through, go back and mark a V over the verb in each sentence.

4. To win the account, Mr. Howard called on the customer for several weeks.

5. Mr. Howard wanted to win the account.

6. Dave Johnson, winding up the meeting, called for a vote.

7. Driving, Mr. Ellsworth could cover 200 miles of his territory in one day.

8. Called EXEL, the new product certainly proved its name.

Before you continue, turn to p. 170 to check your answers.

TRY IT OUT: **Go to Exercise 2.5, p. 26, for more practice in recognizing verbals. Exercise 2.6, p. 27, should help you to see if you can distinguish verbals from verbs. Remember as you do these exercises that any grammatical part can be compounded as long as a connecting word (*and, or, nor*) joins the parts.**

HELPING VERBS

Not all verbs consist of only one word. That is because verbs tell not only what happens but also the time of the happening or under what conditions something occurs. For this reason, many verbs need helping verbs to denote more accurately that action and its time or condition.

DEFINITION A **helping verb** consists of one or more verbs placed before a main verb to aid in telling time or to add emphasis or conditions to the verb.

You have already learned that *-ing* words need helping verbs to complete them as verbs. Without these helping verbs the *-ing* words could not perform one of the functions of a verb—to tell time. Words like *walking* or *selling* couldn't be verbs alone. If a sentence said "Tom walking back to his office," no time would be apparent. However, the sentences "Tom is walking back to his office" and "Tom will be walking back to his office" state the time clearly.

Whereas some helping verbs tell the time, others such as *might, could,* and *ought* make the verb true only under certain conditions. Other helping verbs can add emphasis, such as *must* and *do,* as in "I *do like* your suit."

Notice the helping verbs (underlined) in the following sentences.

Joan *was* working on her report.

Denise *is* helping with the project.

Ms. Carter *could have* done the program by herself.

Our office *did* earn a bonus last year.

I couldn't tell, but Mr. Ellis *must have been* working on the statistics.

Once these helpers are added to the main verb, all of the words now act together as the verb. The main verb plus its helper is called the **complete verb.**

The following is a list of helping verbs that you should learn to recognize. When you see these words placed in front of a verb, you will know that the verb is not a simple one-word verb but that there is a complete verb in the clause, consisting of more than one word.

can	am	will	do	has	could
may	is	shall	did	have	should
	are			had	would
	was				must
	were				might
	been				ought

If any of these words appears alone in the clause, not in front of another verb, then this word is the main verb in the clause. One of these words becomes a helping verb only when it precedes another verb.

main   Jacob *has* ten dollars with him, but he *has paid* as much as twelve for past lunches.   *helper*

main   Gwen *was* good in the role of Scarlett.

helper   Scarlett *was treating* her husbands badly.

By tomorrow my tooth *will have been hurting* for a week.   *helpers*

helper   I *do need* a haircut, but I just *had* one three weeks ago.   *main*

Occasionally a writer will insert one or more modifiers between the helper and the main verb.

I *could* easily *stay* here all day.

1. What is a clause?

2. What is a verb?

3. What are the two types of verbs?

4. Can *seem* show action?

5. Name the six common forms of the linking verb *be.*

6. How do you know if an action word is the verb of the clause?

7. How can you tell an infinitive from an prepositional phrase beginning with the word *to?*

8. Can verbs or verbals be compound?

9. Is every *-ing* word a verb?

10. What is a complete verb?

Before you continue, turn to p. 170 to check your answers. Review the chapter if you have difficulty with these questions.

TRY IT OUT: Complete Exercise 2.7, p. 27, to practice recognizing helping verbs. Exercises 2.8 through 2.11, p. 28, will give additional practice. Exercise 2.12, p. 29, is the Challenge exercise for the verb usages in this chapter.

WRITING HINT: PARALLEL STRUCTURE

Does there seem to be something wrong in the following sentence?

I like football, basketball, and oranges.

Don't you expect, once you have started reading about athletic activities, to have the third item in the series also relate to athletics?

That is the way our minds work—we group like things together. In writing, this is called parallelism.

DEFINITION **Parallelism** is keeping the items in a pair or a series alike in form.

By looking at these examples of faulty parallelism (in italics), you should be able to see the problem.

1. The water was everywhere—in the basement, in the kitchen, and *filling the window wells.* [The italicized phrase is *not a prepositional phrase.*]

2. Helga disliked grocery shopping, cooking, and *to do dishes.* [The italicized phrase *is not an -ing form.*]

3. Before you leave, you should turn off the machine, shut off the lights, and *the alarm should be activated.* [The italicized phrase does not contain *an action verb for the subject you.*]

As the examples show, errors in parallelism often occur with the use of verbs or verbals.

Repairing nonparallel structures is easy. Just select the grammatical form and stick to it. Here are the revised examples.

1. The water was everywhere—in the basement, in the kitchen, and in the window wells. [These are *all prepositional phrases.*]

   or

   The water was everywhere—seeping into the basement, edging along the kitchen floor, and spilling into the window wells. [These are *all -ing phrases.*]

2. Helga disliked to grocery shop, to to cook, and to do dishes. [These are *all infinitives.*]

   or

   Helga disliked grocery shopping, cooking, and doing the dishes. [These are *all -ing forms.*]

3. Before you leave, you should turn off the machine, shut off the lights, and activate the alarm. [These are *all action verb forms for the subject you.*]

Underline the part of each sentence that is not parallel. Rewrite each sentence to make it parallel.

1. She was nervous, jumpy, and acted as if she could panic.

   _____

2. Hating quiet, Theron always had the radio playing, the television set blaring, and he played the CDs on the upstairs machine.

   _____

3. Deciding to return to school, to take a part-time job, and quitting his full-time job, Mark was ready for September 12 to arrive.

   _____

4. The hunters packed their guns, put the dogs in the car, and their suitcases were stored in the trunk.

   _____

5. You may do one or the other: Take 16 credit hours next term or graduation will be later than you had planned.

   _____

Before you continue, turn to p. 171 to check your answers.

TRY IT OUT: Do Exercises 2.13 and 2.14, pp. 29–30, for more practice correcting faulty parallelism.

▣ Chapter 2: Verbs and Verbals

●EXERCISE 2.1

Tell whether each verb is an action verb (AV) or linking verb (LV). If it could be either, write E *on the blank.*

_____ 1. learn   _____ 8. has been   _____ 15. represent

_____ 2. touch   _____ 9. appear   _____ 16. smell

_____ 3. are   _____ 10. replace   _____ 17. am

_____ 4. seem   _____ 11. is   _____ 18. continue

_____ 5. feel   _____ 12. was   _____ 19. remain

_____ 6. read   _____ 13. taste   _____ 20. become

_____ 7. locate   _____ 14. fly

●EXERCISE 2.2

Underline the main verb in each of the following sentences. You will find your task easier if you put parentheses around the prepositional phrases first. Remember, prepositional phrases do not contain verbs.

_____ 1. Do these photographs look too dark?

_____ 2. Mr. Leonard brought flowers for his secretary for National Secretaries' Week.

_____ 3. Fred Stolz has been with this company for twenty-seven years.

_____ 4. All of our men's wear is on the second floor.

_____ 5. Our new product needs more testing.

_____ 6. The Board of Directors passed the motion yesterday.

_____ 7. The students smelled smoke before the alarm.

_____ 8. My assistant laid those papers on my desk.

_____ 9. Our company became Number One last year.

_____ 10. Our new distributor joined our firm on November 1.

Now go back to the underlined verb. Write on the blank whether it is an action verb (AV) or linking verb (LV).

● EXERCISE 2.3

Tell whether each of the following is a prepositional phrase (P) or an infinitive phrase (I). (Hint: An infinitive phrase has an action or linking word in it.)

_____ 1. to sell machines   _____ 6. to collect

_____ 2. to town   _____ 7. to practice

_____ 3. to Chicago   _____ 8. to have become

_____ 4. to be   _____ 9. to the study

_____ 5. to Mary's house   _____ 10. to study hard

● EXERCISE 2.4

Underline only the simple infinitive (not the infinitive phrase) in the following.

1. To win, competitors must show their best to the judges.

2. Harold Green went to Los Angeles to learn about marine life.

3. The President tried to conserve energy in our company.

4. Helen wanted to try to be a bookkeeper.

5. To get to Kalamazoo, turn left at this corner and take I–94 to the proper exit.

● EXERCISE 2.5

Underline the verbals and complete verbal phrases in each of these sentences.

1. On her vacation Peggy wanted to get a good tan.

2. Typing for three hours, Mr. Brown was able to complete his quotation.

3. Miss Francis was exhausted.

4. Mr. Ells, locating the problem, finished the model in time for the display.

5. Ms. Fritz read the remarks and voted after studying the question.

6. Being an accountant, Mr. Zeddies saw the error in the figures immediately.

7. The Union Company produces several tools with which to garden.

8. You study this course to write, to speak, and to think more clearly.

9. We created a new manual to replace the original.

10. The dresses, marked down to half price, sold in the first three hours of the sale.

● **E X E R C I S E   2 . 6**

Now underline the verb in each of these sentences.

1. On her vacation Peggy wanted to get a good tan.

2. Typing for three hours, Mr. Brown was able to complete his quotation.

3. Miss Francis was exhausted.

4. Mr. Ells, locating the problem, finished the model in time for the display.

5. Ms. Fritz read the remarks and voted after studying the question.

6. Being an accountant, Mr. Zeddies saw the error in the figures immediately.

7. The Union Company produces several tools with which to garden.

8. You study this course to write, to speak, and to think more clearly.

9. We created a new manual to replace the original.

10. The dresses, marked down to half price, sold in the first three hours of the sale.

● **E X E R C I S E   2 . 7**

Underline the complete verb (main verb plus helpers) in each of the following sentences. You will notice that occasionally another word or words come between the helping verb and the main verb.

1. Your staff members are coming to our meeting.

2. Are you coming to the meeting?

3. You will be happy to know that our new insurance plan covers dental work.

4. Could we have the luncheon meeting at Normandy's?

5. The speaker at the seminar talked about the new trends in merchandising.

6. The invoice must have been lost in the mail.

7. May we deliver these to your warehouse?

8. Last year we did manufacture pistons but do not make them anymore.

9. Atlas will be closing its New Orleans office in June.

10. Will you wrap and ship these parts this afternoon?

Underline the complete verb in each sentence and tell whether it is an action (AV) or linking (LV) verb.

_____ 1. Please reply before June 27.

_____ 2. He was working in the stockroom during the storm.

_____ 3. He was in the stockroom during the storm.

_____ 4. You will hear from us before next Friday.

_____ 5. Did Ms. James collate and staple the copies of the minutes of the last meeting?

_____ 6. Mr. Wooten is being unreasonable about the reaction to his project.

_____ 7. The warehouse report has been on my desk for three days.

_____ 8. You might be surprised to learn our new sales figures.

_____ 9. To be salable, a product must demonstrate adaptability.

_____ 10. The blender must have been lying under the counter all this time.

Label each of the following as a verb (V), infinitive (I), or neither (N).

_____ 1. to win   _____ 6. pizza

_____ 2. helping   _____ 7. to share

_____ 3. is helping   _____ 8. simplify

_____ 4. find   _____ 9. had been

_____ 5. to me   _____ 10. appear

Write ten sentences and underline the complete verb in each. Write AV over each action verb and LV over each linking verb.

Choose five of the verbs that can be either action or linking verbs. Write two sentences with each verb. In the first sentence, use the verb as an action verb; in the second, use the same verb as a linking verb.

● E X E R C I S E   2.12   CHALLENGE

Underline the verbs in the following. Watch that you don't identify any verbals as verbs.

Jacoby, Smith and Brown is a new law firm in our community. At one time, Mr. Jacoby was with another firm but decided to begin his own firm when he became interested in specializing in real estate.

Their new offices are located on Palmer Street next to the Gumby Corporation. Mr. Jacoby bought this building last year and hired many people to restore it. He has incorporated all of the newest devices into his offices, including the most recent automatic typewriters and dictating equipment.

Ms. Smith and Mr. Brown are recent graduates from the Detroit College of Law. Both had been interested in the legal matters concerning real estate while they were in school. Ms. Smith studied private real estate holdings, whereas Mr. Brown worked more with commercial law.

Because our city has not had a legal firm that specializes in real estate, we are extremely pleased to see this new office. We wish the partners a successful future in their new location.

● E X E R C I S E   2.13

Add a parallel element to complete each of the following.

1. You can find "shy" insects under rocks, in the long grasses, or _____.

2. To act, to sing, and _____ are the skills needed to make it on Broadway.

3. I don't like to see children hitting each other, couples sitting at dinner not speaking, or

_____.

4. Marlene took off the dog's collar, put him into the washtub, and _____.

5. An ambitious employee will finish her own task, help a colleague with his or her work, and

_____.

Cross out the nonparallel element in each of these and write a parallel part to replace it.

1. Arlene turned on the bath water, was checking the thermostat, and took off her clothes.

   _____

2. Children are generally cheerful, want to behave well, and curious. _____

   _____

3. Although the weather report was good, I checked the sky for clouds, listened to the radio, and was

   preparing for possible thunderstorms. _____

   _____

4. The semi truck was new, shiny, and it cost very much. _____

   _____

5. Carlos wanted to earn a good living but not working weekends and nights. _____

   _____

6. He spoke forcefully, confidently, and with no hesitation about the project. _____

   _____

7. When she swam, she dove, she did the crawl, and was swimming without getting tired out.

   _____

8. Macklyn is a student, a wife, and has two children. _____

   _____

9. The final report was double-spaced, bound in a folder, and it had to be sent Express Mail.

   _____

10. I prefer vacations that are in a warm place, not many people around, and that have nothing more

    rugged than paper bath mats instead of cloth. _____

    _____

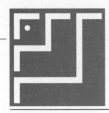

More About Verbs

OVERVIEW

- **Verb Tense**
- **The Three Simple Tenses**
- **The Three Perfect Tenses**
- **Progressive Tenses**
- **Irregular Verbs**
- **Active Voice and Passive Voice**
- **An Unusual Use of** *Were*

Correct verb usage is essential to good writing. Because verbs both show time and indicate singular or plural usage, there are many forms of verbs to master. You will want to do so, however, because misused verb forms are as obvious to most people as spelling errors. Misused verb forms are as readily apparent in your spoken English as in your written language, where Standard English is expected.

Although written English seems to demand more exact usage than "everyday" or slang spoken usages, you would be wise to use Standard English in both your speaking and your writing. If you do not, you may get careless and fall back into making the same errors you were making before your present study. You should now be trying to "tune up" your ear so that what "sounds right" is right.

Do these sentences sound right to you?

I seen him at the store.

I done my homework.

I have went to that office before.

You can probably spot the misused verbs right away. However, haven't you heard these misused verbs before? An "educated" ear hears these errors; unfortunately, if a job applicant makes such an error during a phone inquiry or an interview, the applicant may be disregarded for English usage alone. Certainly this is not fair, but it is oftentimes true.

Consequently, this chapter will concentrate on the study of the correct parts of verbs as they change with the change of tense.

 # VERB TENSE

DEFINITION The **tense** of a verb indicates time. As the time of action or being changes, the form of the verb often changes as well.

Notice these examples of the verb *do* as it changes tense.

I *will do* the assignment. [No work has been completed. It will happen sometime in the future.]

I *do* the assignments. [The assignments are consistently done. Some have been done already; some will be done in the future. The writer can be counted on to do the work.]

I *did* the assignment. [The assignment is completed.]

Other forms of the verb *do* could tell that "I *have done* the assignments" or "I *had done* them, but I lost them."

All of these statements differ in meaning, yet everything but the verb tense remains the same. The verb changes spelling or form to indicate different tenses. Verbs can be classified as regular or irregular, depending on how they change tenses.

DEFINITION A **regular verb** is one that changes form in a standard way: It adds *-ed* or *-d* as it changes from present to the other tenses.

Regular verbs come from the Germanic language base from which English is derived. These words all follow the general rules that this language has developed over its centuries of use.

The trouble with English is that it is not a pure language. Many other peoples have lived among English-speaking peoples, and words from other languages have become part of the English language. These borrowed words have added variety and color to the language but have also produced irregularities that pose a problem for the student of English language usage: Every rule has exceptions.

A basic rule often applies only to English-based words; words derived from other languages often follow their own rules.

DEFINITION An **irregular verb** is one that can change into as many as three forms as it changes from present to the other tenses. Because these verbs are irregular, though, they are <u>not</u> consistent in their ways of changing.

Compare the forms of the regular verbs *walk* and *raise* to the forms of several irregular verbs.

Regular		**Irregular**	
walk	walked	go	went, gone
raise	raised	do	did, done
		cut	cut, cut

All verbs can be used to designate six basic tenses. The following chart lists these six tenses and the times expressed by each of the six tenses; it also gives examples of regular and irregular verbs, showing how the verbs change as they move from one tense to another. The changes in form described in the chart will make more sense after you read the following sections on verb tenses.

Tense	Time	Form Change	Regular Verb (*walk*)	Irregular (*go*)
Present	Now or permanently true	Add *-s* or *-es* for singular	S: walks P: walk	S: goes P: go
Past	Completed or over with	Add *-ed* or *-d* for regular; various changes for irregular	S, P: walked	S, P: went
Future	Is yet to happen	Add *will* to present form	S, P: will walk	S, P: will go
Present Perfect	Started in past and is still true up to now	Add *has* for singular or *have* to plural; use *-ed* for regular verb form; use the 3rd form of irregular	S: has walked P: have walked	S: has gone P: have gone
Past Perfect	One thing was completed before the next was completed	Add *had* to the *-ed* form of regular or 3rd form of irregular	S, P: had walked	S, P: had gone
Future Perfect	Will be over and completed by a deadline set for future time	Add *will have* to *-ed* form for regular or 3rd form of irregular	S, P: will have walked	S, P: will have gone

S = singular subject; P = plural subject

As you study this chart, you see that each tense tells a specific time for the action of the verb. With a linking verb the tenses report the time of the described situation, such as "Ms. White is a teacher" or "Ms. White was a teacher."

THE THREE SIMPLE TENSES

The three simple tenses can be called the regular tenses because they are less complicated than the three perfect tenses. These regular tenses each tell only one general time.

The Present Tense

DEFINITION The **present tense** of a verb is the form of the verb that tells about the present time or about something that remains the same.

The form of the verb in the present tense is the **infinitive form,** or **first form,** that is, the form listed in the dictionary. You add -*s* or -*es* to make the verb singular. Here are some examples.

walk, walks do, does plan, plans

(*Note:* Two pronoun subjects, *I* and *you,* do not use a verb ending in -*s,* even though *I* and *you* are singular.)

The present tense can also show that something is permanently true—a fact that does not change. Notice the times shown in these examples.

Mr. Nino *is* in his office. [He is there now.]

That author *writes* with a flourish. [The author does so consistently; this statement is permanently true.]

Robert Fulton *is* the inventor of the commercial steamboat. [This fact will not change; it was true in 1807, is true now, and will remain true.]

Writers who overlook the "permanent truth" of a statement can produce some funny sentences. You can see in the following examples that if something is permanently true, the present tense must be used even though some aspect of the event may have occurred in the past.

I can't remember what the name of yesterday's visitor *was.* [Did the visitor change names?]

The census showed that Los Angeles *was* the largest city in the United States. [If another city became larger, why didn't the census show that city as the largest?]

As I told you in last Friday's interview, honesty *was* my best quality. [Is this applicant no longer honest?]

1. "Verb tense" means _____.

2. Verbs that add *-ed* to form some tenses are called _____ verbs.

3. Because some verbs came from other languages, these verbs change

   form in different ways and are called _____ verbs.

4. The number of verb tenses is _____.

5. The present tense shows either of two times, now or

   _____.

Before you continue, turn to p. 171 to check your answers.

▣ The Past Tense

DEFINITION The simple **past tense** is the form of the verb that relays the message that something has already happened. The action or state of being is completed.

Regular verbs add *-ed* or *-d* to the infinitive form to make the verb show past tense. This **past tense form** of a verb is that verb's **second form.** Following are some spelling guidelines that can help you to write these verb forms correctly; you will not have to check your spellings so often if you learn these rules. The rules concerning the addition of *-ed* also apply to the addition of other suffixes (word endings).

Spelling Rules for Adding *-ed* or Other Suffixes

1. A <u>one-syllable</u> word that ends with <u>one</u> consonant with <u>one</u> vowel in front of the consonant doubles the final consonant before adding *-ed* or any other suffix that begins with a vowel. (*Note:* Words adding *-ing* follow this rule.)

can	canned	swim	swimming
wrap	wrapping	fit	fitted

   Following this rule, you would <u>not</u> double the consonant if the consonant was preceded by two vowels (*suit = suited; ruin = ruining*) or by another consonant (*melt = melted; hand = handed*). You also would not double the final consonant of an appropriate word if the suffix began with a consonant instead of a vowel (*fit = fitness; cup = cupful*).

The only letter combination that does not follow this principle is *qui*.
Note the spelling of *quitter* and *equipped*.

2. A <u>two-syllable</u> word that ends with <u>one</u> consonant preceded by <u>one</u> vowel doubles the consonant only when the accent (emphasis) falls on the <u>second</u> syllable. (Your voice will rise on an accented syllable and will drop on an unaccented syllable.)

oc·cur′	occurred	o·mit′	omitted
re·fer′	referred	re·mit′	remitted
al·lot′	allotted	trans·fer′	transferred

Do <u>not</u> double the final consonant if the accent is on the <u>first</u> instead of the second syllable.

of′·fer	offered	hap′·pen	happening
to′·tal	totaling	la′·bel	labeled
tra′·vel	traveled	dif′·fer	differed

In keeping with this rule, you would <u>not</u> double the final consonant of any word with <u>three or more syllables</u> (*ben·e·fit = benefited*).

3. Words that end in *-y* preceded by a vowel simply add the ending, keeping the *-y*. If there is a consonant before the *-y*, change the *-y* to *-i* before adding a suffix other than *-ing*.

survey	surveyed	carry	carried
play	played	embody	embodied
convey	conveyed	study	studied

If adding *-ing* to words that end in *-y*, always keep the *-y* and add the *-ing* (*studying; playing*).

⌐ SELF-CHECK 3-2

See if you can correctly spell the past tense forms of these verbs when adding -ed.

1. admit _____   6. appeal _____

2. slip _____   7. refer _____

3. weary _____   8. offer _____

4. attack _____   9. convey _____

5. benefit _____   10. permit _____

Before you continue, turn to p. 171 to check your answers.

Writing Hint: Dropped -ed Endings

Because English is so often carelessly spoken, sometimes word endings are left off. This carelessness can cause a problem in writing certain past tense forms. Be aware that the following words do end in *-ed,* even though they are not always carefully pronounced: old fashion*ed,* us*ed* to, bak*ed* beans.

Watch that you don't make this error with other past tense forms. Remember, most verbs undergo some change to switch from present tense to past tense.

Writing Hint: Unnecessary Tense Shifts

Get in the habit of proofreading your writing to check that you are consistent in your verb tense usage. Don't shift from one tense to another in a sentence or paragraph unless you have a specific reason to do so.

Here are examples of a tense shift made in error.

I *saw* the freighter on the horizon. It *has* its lights on. [Probably not at this time, but it *had* lights on when I saw it.]

We *were* walking back to the car. Suddenly, Melanie *hears* a noise behind the bush. [All of the story occurred in the past—she *heard* the noise as she walked back to the car.]

Of course, expressing several ideas may require changes in verb tense to show the time relationship in the ideas. Just be careful that you have a reason for a change.

Last year I *was* afraid of the water. However, this year, I *am* no longer afraid because I took swimming lessons. [Two different times are reported.]

TRY IT OUT: Do Exercise 3.1, p. 51, to practice forming the present and past tenses. Exercise 3.2, p. 52, will give you practice in avoiding unnecessary tense shifts.

The Future Tense

DEFINITION The **future tense** is the form of the verb that shows that an action or condition has not occurred yet but that it is still to come.

The exact time that the act will be completed is not apparent in the simple future tense. Although Standard English usage used to dictate that *shall* be added if the subject were *I* or *we,* it is now commonly accepted to add *will* to the first form of the verb to denote future, no matter what the subject.

Present	Future
select, selects	will select
intend, intends	will intend

THE THREE PERFECT TENSES

The three perfect tenses differ from the three simple tenses in that the perfect tenses tell more specific times than do the simple tenses. Actually, each perfect tense tells two times rather than one. These tenses denote completed—or perfected—action.

Each of the perfect tenses adds a helping verb to the form of the verb called the **perfect participle form,** or **third form.** In regular verbs the perfect participle ends in -*ed.* In irregular verbs it is the third form of the verb as it is conjugated. The three forms of irregular verbs have become fixed over the centuries of usage and must be learned. The irregular verb forms are listed later in this chapter.

This third form, the perfect participle, is used in all of the perfect tenses but cannot stand alone as a verb. To be used as a verb, this third form always needs a helping verb. Each of the perfect tenses has its own helping verb or verbs to help denote the correct time. Without the helping verb, this third form is only a verbal—a participle. The name *perfect participle* describes two functions, a perfect tense verb or a participle.

The Present Perfect Tense

DEFINITION The **present perfect tense** is the form of the verb used to show an action or condition that started in the past (thus, part of it is past) and has continued up to the present.

This verb tense differs from the simple past in that although some of the action is over, all is not completed by the present time. The present perfect tense actually shows a series of actions. Notice the difference in these two sentences.

1. Mrs. Sparks worked here for twenty years.
2. Mrs. Sparks has worked here for twenty years.

Do you see that Example 1 shows a completed event? It seems to say that Mrs. Sparks no longer works here. Example 2 shows that she worked here for twenty years but also that she is still here. It leaves open the idea that she may continue to work here, although the present perfect tense doesn't predict anything about the future.

The present perfect tense shows that a past action is not completely finished. The action or condition can touch the present or can be a part of a continuing series.

Decide which verb you would choose in the following sentences.

Our company (has been, was) in business for thirty years. [If your company is still in business, you would choose *has been.* If your company is now closed, *was* would show that the condition is over.]

We (traded, have traded) with the Wilson Company many times. [If you no longer trade with the company, you would choose *traded,* the simple past tense. If you still do trade with Wilson and plan to continue this "series" of events, you would choose *have traded.*]

Notice that these present perfect verbs combine either *has* (singular) or *have* (plural) with the participle to form the present tense. You must always use one of these helping verbs, or you will not be indicating the present perfect tense.

One common misuse of the present perfect tense occurs because of carelessly spoken forms of this tense. This error occurs when the so-called conditional helping verbs are paired with the present perfect. The conditional helping verbs are *would, could, should, might,* and *must.* The helping verb now seems to run together in some careless speech to *of* instead of *have.* Don't write any of the following forms when you mean to use the present perfect tense.

Error	Correct
I could *of* done it.	I could *have* done it.
He should *of* been there.	He should *have* been there.
I would *of* gone there.	I would *have* gone there.
You must *of* known better.	You must *have* known better.
We might *of* referred him to you	We might *have* referred him to you

SELF-CHECK 3-3

See if you can answer these questions about what you have studied so far in this chapter.

1. Tense means _____.

2. Verbs have how many tenses?

3. To form the future tense, add _____.

4. Any perfect tense uses the third form of the verb called the

   _____.

5. All perfect tense verbs need helping verbs: (True, False).

6. Which word is singular, *has* or *have*?

7. If something is always true, which verb tense would you use?

8. Many singular present tense verbs end in -_____.

9. Past tense regular verbs end in -_____.

10. *Should of studied* is a correct verb phrase: (True, False).

Before you continue, turn to p. 171 to check your answers. Review the chapter if the questions seemed difficult.

The Past Perfect Tense

DEFINITION The **past perfect tense** is the form of the verb that shows that a past action or condition was completed before another event was completed.

The past perfect appears to be "past the past." Unlike the simple past, it shows two past actions. To form the past perfect tense, you add *had* to the perfect participle form of the verb.

Study these examples that illustrate the use of the past perfect tense.

1st *2nd*

> I *had sealed* the envelope before I remembered to enclose the check. [Notice that two events happened: I remembered and I sealed the envelope. However, one was done before the other. The first to occur must be written in the past perfect tense.]

2 events

1st *2nd*

> The bus *had left* before we arrived. [Both of these events occurred in the past, but the one happened (*the bus left*) before the other happened (*we arrived*).]

Try to choose the correct verb for the following sentences. Remember to check to see if one event was finished before the other event occurred.

> He (studied, had studied) the night before he took the test. [Did he do two things, one before the other? Yes, he studied first; thus, *had studied* is correct.]

> When the carpet installer arrived, I (painted, had painted) the room. [It's likely that the painting was done by the time the carpet was to be installed. If so, *had painted* would be correct.]

TRY IT OUT: **Do Exercise 3.3, p. 53, for practice in choosing between the past, the past perfect, and the present perfect tenses.**

The Future Perfect Tense

Just as the past perfect tense tells of two events happening, one before the other, the future perfect tense also tells of two times.

DEFINITION The **future perfect tense** is the form of the verb that indicates that an action will be completed (not simply begun) at some specified point in the future.

The future perfect tense differs from the simple future in that the future perfect tells when the action will be finished, whereas the simple future just indicates that it will occur at some time after the present. The future tense does not indicate when the action will be completed. To form the future perfect, the helping verbs *will have* are added to the third form, the perfect participle.

Notice these two examples:

1. Don't worry; I will correct these exams. — *action completed*

deadline set
2. By class time tomorrow, I *will have corrected* these exams.

Which statement would a student prefer to hear after taking an exam? Example 1 gives no time for the completion of the grading. The time could be today, tomorrow, or next year. Example 2 promises that the action will be completed by class time the next day.

Can you choose the correct verb in these sentences? See if a specific deadline is given for the action to have been completed.

By next Friday I (will earn, will have earned) at least $200. [If the money will be earned by the end of Thursday, choose *will have earned*. Otherwise, the person will have to work Friday as well to earn the $200.]

At five o'clock Mary (will finish, will have finished) these letters. [To leave at five, Mary will have to have already completed the letters; otherwise, the sentence should say *will finish*, which means that Mary will still be typing at five.]

┏ S E L F - C H E C K 3 - 4

Can you now answer these review questions with no hesitation? If so, you have a good grasp of the material.

1. How many verb tenses are there?

2. What is the verb form used in the perfect tenses called?

3. What helping verbs are added to this form to make a verb present perfect?

4. What is added to the participle form to make the past perfect?

5. What are the helping words for future perfect?

6. What two times are shown in the present perfect tense?

7. What two times are told in the past perfect tense?

8. What condition is shown by a future perfect verb?

Before you continue, turn to p. 171 to check your answers.

TRY IT OUT: **Complete Exercises 3.4 and 3.5, pp. 54–55, for practice in choosing the correct verb tenses.**

PROGRESSIVE TENSES

You will remember from Chapter 2 that not all words that end in *-ing* are verbs. An *-ing* word is a verb only if it is part of a clause that has (1) a *be* helping verb and (2) a *doer* of the action named by the *-ing* word.

When both a helping verb and doer are present, the resulting *-ing* verb is a progressive tense verb.

DEFINITION   **Progressive tense** verbs denote an incomplete action or condition, one that is still in progress, hence the term *progressive*.

Rather than thinking of the *-ing* verbs forms as separate tenses, this text will view them as showing unfinished action in any of the six basic tenses.

Progressive tense verbs are not linking verbs; they do show action. Look at the progressive forms of the verb *walk*.

Tense	Progressive Form
present	am walking, is walking, are walking
past	was walking, were walking
future	will be walking
present perfect	has been walking, have been walking
past perfect	had been walking
future perfect	will have been walking

In each progressive form the verb is preceded by one of the *be* helping verbs. These helping verbs indicate the time of the progressive form; the *-ing* form can tell no time. The sentence "Mr. Jefferson *was* walking his dog" shows that he was walking his dog during a specific interval in the past, but he is no longer doing so. "Mr. Jefferson *is* walking his dog" shows that he is presently walking his dog. The helping verb made the difference.

You'll recall that the spelling rules given for adding *-ed* also apply to the *-ing* ending. Here are some additional spelling tips.

Spelling Rules for Adding *-ing* or Other Suffixes

Any word ending in *-e* usually drops the *-e* before *-ing* is added. This rule is true for almost all suffixes that begin with a vowel. Two unusual exceptions are *canoeing* and *tiptoeing*.

hope	hoping	arrange	arranging
improve	improving	receive	receiving

Remember also that any word ending in *-y* keeps the *-y* as well as the *-ing*.

try	trying	carry	carrying
vary	varying	identify	identifying

If a suffix beginning with a consonant is added, the final -*e* is kept on the base word, with three exceptions: *duly, truly,* and *wholly.*

| hope | hopeful | arrange | arrangement |
| sincere | sincerely | improve | improvement |

TRY IT OUT: **As you complete Exercise 3.6, p. 56, apply these spelling rules so that your answers will be correctly spelled.**

IRREGULAR VERBS

Although most verbs are regular verbs with -*ed* or -*d* added for the past tense form and the perfect participle form, many verbs create their other two forms in unusual ways. There are some patterns, but there are enough inconsistencies that no real rules emerge.

Most of these irregular forms are learned through early drill in school, but everyone seems to misuse some forms. Look over the list that follows to see if any of these forms are unfamiliar to you. Mark these and learn them. Some of the more commonly misused verbs in the list are starred.

Remember that each verb has three forms—often called principal parts. The first form, the infinitive, can stand alone to form the present tense or join with the helping verb *will* to form the future tense. The past tense form is used only for past tense and should have no helping verb. The third form, the perfect participle form, combines with the helping verbs *has, have,* or *had* in the three perfect tenses. You will see, in Chapter 8, that this perfect participle form can also function as a describing word. When not a verb, this type of word is called a **participle.** Often, a participle will follow a linking verb and refer to the subject, describing it. Here are some examples.

no doer
only describes

Garett <u>has written</u> a book. [verb]

The <u>book</u> <u>was</u> written in German. [participle]

<u>This</u> <u>is</u> a well-written book. [participle]

Principal Parts of Irregular Verbs

Present	*Past*	*Perfect Participle*
am, are, is (be)	was, were	been
arise	arose	arisen
awake, awaken	awoke, awoken	awaked, awakened
beat	beat	beaten
become	became	become
begin	began	begun

Principal Parts of Irregular Verbs *(continued)*

Present	*Past*	*Perfect Participle*
bend	bent	bent
bet	bet	bet
bid	bid	bid
bind	bound	bound
bite	bit	bitten, bit
bleed	bled	bled
blow	blew	blown
break	broke	broken
breed	bred	bred
bring	brought	brought
broadcast	broadcast	broadcast
build	built	built
burst	burst	burst
buy	bought	bought
cast	cast	cast
catch	caught	caught
choose	chose	chosen
cling	clung	clung
come	came	come
cost	cost	cost
creep	crept	crept
cut	cut	cut
deal	dealt	dealt
dig	dug	dug
*do	did	done
draw	drew	drawn
dream	dreamed, dreamt	dreamed, dreamt
*drink	drank	drunk
drive	drove	driven
eat	ate	eaten
fall	fell	fallen
feel	felt	felt
fight	fought	fought
find	found	found
flee	fled	fled
fly	flew	flown
forecast	forecast	forecast
forget	forgot	forgotten, forgot
freeze	froze	frozen
get	got	got, gotten
give	gave	given
*go	went	gone
grind	ground	ground
grow	grew	grown
hang (to suspend)	hung	hung
hang (to execute)	hanged	hanged

Principal Parts of Irregular Verbs *(continued)*

Present	*Past*	*Perfect Participle*
have	had	had
hear	heard	heard
hide	hid	hidden
hit	hit	hit
hold	held	held
hurt	hurt	hurt
keep	kept	kept
know	knew	known
*lay (to put or place)	laid	laid
lead	led	led
leave	left	left
*lend	lent	lent
let	let	let
*lie (to recline or remain)	lay	lain
lose	lost	lost
make	made	made
mean	meant	meant
meet	met	met
pay	paid	paid
prove	proved	proved, proven
put	put	put
quit	quit	quit
ride	rode	ridden
ring	rang	rung
*rise	rose	risen
run	ran	run
say	said	said
*see	saw	seen
seek	sought	sought
set	set	set
sew	sewed	sewed, sewn
shake	shook	shaken
shed	shed	shed
shine (to reflect)	shone	shone
show	showed	showed, shown
shrink	shrank, shrunk	shrunk, shrunken
*sing	sang	sung
sink	sank, sunk	sunk, sunken
sit	sat	sat
slay	slew	slain
sleep	slept	slept
slide	slid	slid
speak	spoke	spoken
spend	spent	spent
spin	spun	spun
split	split	split

Principal Parts of Irregular Verbs *(continued)*

Present	*Past*	*Perfect Participle*
spread	spread	spread
spring	sprang, sprung	sprung
stand	stood	stood
*steal	stole	stolen
stick	stuck	stuck
sting	stung	stung
stink	stank, stunk	stunk
strike	struck	struck, stricken
strive	strove	striven
string	strung	strung
swear	swore	sworn
sweep	swept	swept
*swim	swam	swum
take	took	taken
teach	taught	taught
tear	tore	torn
telecast	telecast	telecast
tell	told	told
think	thought	thought
throw	threw	thrown
thrust	thrust	thrust
wear	wore	worn
weave	wove	woven
weep	wept	wept
win	won	won
wind	wound	wound
wring	wrung	wrung
write	wrote	written

Most people make errors in their use of irregular verbs because the verbs sound right. While studying this list, you probably found some verb forms that surprised you. Noting these and referring to them from time to time will help you learn them, but it would also be helpful if you would ask close friends to tell you when you have misused a form. You may not even hear your own errors until you have worked with these for awhile.

There are three pairs of these irregular verbs that present problems related to their use in certain types of clauses. These sets are *lie–lay*, *rise–raise*, and *sit–set*. These verbs' special usages will be covered in Chapter 4.

TRY IT OUT: **Go to Exercises 3.7 and 3.8, pp. 57–58, for practice in using the irregular verbs and the six tenses.**

ACTIVE VOICE AND PASSIVE VOICE

The choice of the verb in any sentence can show either the subject's doing the action or the subject's being acted upon. This is an important distinction, and every good writer pays close attention to the verb choice in this regard.

DEFINITION The **active voice** of a verb used in a clause has an action verb with a subject that is the doer of the action.

An active voice verb sends a message that is direct, forceful, and bold; most writing should be done in this voice.

The following sentences employ active voice verbs.

doer   action
The magazine *showed* distinct pictures of the bank robbers.
doer   action
Victor *challenged* the opposing attorney to prove that the picture showed his client.

DEFINITION The **passive voice** of a verb used in a clause has the action happening to the subject; the subject is not the doer. The clause will have a linking verb followed by a past participle form of a verb used as a modifier—a participle.

Look at these examples of passive voice verbs. Linking verbs are marked *LV*.

no doer
                        LV
The bank robbers *were* shown in the picture.

attorney not
doer
                        LV
The other attorney *was* challenged to prove the whereabouts of his client.

Three Reasons to Select the Passive Voice

Although the active voice should be used in most writing, three occasions warrant the purposeful choice of passive voice.

1. The doer of the action is unknown. A common mistake is to refer to an unknown doer as *they.*

    Not:
    They said it would rain during the picnic.

    But:
    Rain is predicted for the picnic.

2. The doer of the action is unimportant or obvious.

   Not:
   The inspectors inspected each plane before takeoff.

   But:
   Each plane was inspected before takeoff.

3. The writer doesn't want to "blame" or call attention to the doer of the action.

   Not:
   Your secretary gave me the wrong directions.

   But:
   I was given wrong directions.

   There is no reason to assign blame for this error. It cannot be undone and certainly wasn't deliberate.

   Notice that each passive voice sentence contains a linking verb. This use of the linking verb removes the subject as the doer of the action.

SELF-CHECK 3–5

Rewrite each of the following sentences in the passive voice. Be ready to explain why each should be changed.

1. You did not send the order by parcel past as I requested.

2. You forgot to indicate the dress size you want when you ordered.

3. I will turn you over to my attorney if you don't pay within ten days.

4. They say you should not write most sentences in the passive voice.

5. You cannot have a charge account at this time.

Before you continue, turn to p. 172 to check your answers.

TRY IT OUT: Complete Exercise 3.9, p. 59, to check your understanding of the correct uses of the active and passive voices.

AN UNUSUAL USE OF *WERE*

Usually *was* or *were* is selected because the subject is either singular or plural. However, in certain cases *were* is used exclusively. When a sentence expresses a wish or a supposition—things contrary to fact—the verb *were* signals the reader that the idea being expressed isn't true but instead is merely a wish or is "supposing."

These clauses will either being with *if,* or the word *wish* will appear early in the clause. Notice these examples.

contrary to fact

If I were you, I would call them again. [The writer cannot be "you."]

If only it were not raining. [This shows that it _is_ raining.]

I *wish* I were finished with this report. [This sentence shows that the report is unfinished.]

Be careful that you use *were* in this manner only when the material is contrary to fact. Some clauses that start with *if* could be reporting something true. In this case, choose *was* if the subject being discussed is singular.

These *if* clauses demonstrate this situation.

If the order was late, I did not notice it. [The order may have been late, but the writer did not notice that.]

If John was at the meeting, I didn't see him. [John may have been there but wasn't seen by the writer.]

If he was in my class, I don't remember him. [He could have been in the class.]

SELF - CHECK 3-6

Decide whether the clause is contrary to reality or could be fact by choosing was *or* were *to complete it.*

1. If Mr. Erickson (was, were) more assertive, he could sell more.

2. I tried to see if it (was, were) raining outside.

3. "I wish I (was, were) President of the United States," said Justin.

4. If this bill (was, were) to be passed by the Senate, it would help industry.

5. The airline would have posted the new time if the plane (was, were) late.

Before you continue, turn to p. 172 to check your answers.

TRY IT OUT: Do Exercise 3.10, p. 59, to practice using *was* and *were*.

Incorrect verb usages can become deeply ingrained in language habits. You may have to review several areas of this chapter if correct verb usage is a weak area for you. However, if you are convinced that your errors may hinder your future job success, you will find the time for self-instruction.

Pay attention to the verb usages in your everyday reading materials. Listen to how other people speak to see how they use verbs. You should be more aware now of any misused forms. Pay attention to your own speaking and writing to monitor your verb usage. Correct yourself as you speak, if you make errors, to impress or set the correct form in your mind. Proofread your written work carefully to catch any of your mistakes. These lessons will result in improved use of Standard English.

TRY IT OUT: **Do Exercise 3.11, p. 60, to demonstrate your ability to use the active and passive voices. Exercise 3.12, p. 60, should prove to be a challenge.**

⊡ Chapter 3:   More About Verbs

●EXERCISE 3.1

Write the correct present or past tense verb or participle form on the blank in each sentence. Be sure to apply the spelling rules.

1. The city (offer) _____ the contract to Du Pont, Inc.

2. He felt that his behavior was (justify) _____.

3. The date given in the book (is, was) _____ 1941.

4. They (survey) _____ the property before marking the property lines.

5. She (wrap) _____ up the meeting before lunch.

6. We (submit) _____ a bid for the construction project.

7. My birthplace (was, is) _____ Dayton, Ohio.

8. When Mr. Gregson retired, his sons (carry) _____ on the business.

9. The plant was (equip) _____ with all new machinery.

10. He (copy) _____ the memorandum for future reference.

11. She said that generosity (is, was) _____ one of George Washington's attributes.

12. My former boss (is, was) _____ Elaine Stapleton.

13. The bright light has (ruin) _____ the prints.

14. When the list was typewritten, my name was (omit) _____.

15. He (play) _____ in a band in his spare time when he was younger.

16. Our department was (allot) _____ sixteen thousand dollars for expenses this year.

17. The new plans (embody) _____ all of the changes that we had asked for.

18. The project manager (travel) _____ 700 miles by car last week.

19. He said that he had (refer) _____ my name to Mr. Tomas.

20. I'll never know how the accident (happen) _____.

Cross out any incorrectly used verb tense, and write the correct form above it.

1. When I get to London, I will plan to see several of the famous sights. I want to see the Tower of London. I first learned about it when I studied about Henry VIII. It seems he has unfaithful wives killed there. Another sight I have always want to see is the Changing of the Guards. This took place every day of the year at Buckingham Palace. My last scheduled sight was to go to Hyde Park and see where Speaker's Corner was. Anyone who wants to can stand here and speak his or her mind, following a few rules of "good behavior." These are the three must-see sites on my list.

2. Bob drives an old car that he rebuilt himself. The car was from the fifties and is a Plymouth Fury. It came out in 1956, I believe, and comes only in gold and white. It had huge fins for back fenders. It uses regular gas and much more oil than the cars of today. When Bob's dad was younger, he always wants one of these cars, but he couldn't afford one. Of course, Bob can't afford one either brand new, but he was able to buy this used model rather cheaply. However, Bob is learning what every old-car buff knows: The original cost was just the beginning.

3. When I was a fifth grader, I went to a summer camp that is sponsored by the school system. Before the camp closed in 1978 because the school system cannot afford to run it any more, the camp's programs were designed mainly for students who show behavioral problems at school. To this day my mother said I was a prime candidate for the program. She and my dad knew the principal and the teachers so well that everyone is on a first-name basis calling each other almost weekly. While I can hardly remember what the names of my teachers were, Mom and Dad developed such closeness to them that even now many of those same educators are my parents' best friends. Although I no longer live in Pine Grove and see these people infrequently I felt uneasy around them whenever I ran into them. In spite of my behavior, I did—miraculously—graduate. One main reason was probably that my behavior did improve after I attended that summer camp session. My ex-teacher, however, were never going to let me forget my past exuberant spirits. They remind me whenever I met them of what I had hoped were forgotten incidents of unruliness. Of course, they agreed that my present profession was inevitable, given what my personality was: I am a late-night television show host—a comedian.

Name _____ Date _____ Class _____

Choose the correct verb tense to show past tense, present perfect tense, or past perfect tense, depending on the meaning of the sentence. Write the verb form on the blank in each sentence.

1. I (work) _____ here since finishing school.

2. Last year we (manufacture) _____ 12 million parts.

3. So far, he (finish) _____ one half of his route.

4. Last night he (finish) _____ his report to the Treasurer.

5. The management (try) _____ to satisfy the workers, but they went on strike.

6. Since I (arrive) _____ this morning, I (type) _____ seventeen letters.

7. Yesterday we (submit) _____ our request for a transfer.

8. He (process) _____ twelve applications already.

9. The students (apply) _____ their knowledge of the rules.

10. The secretary (stay) _____ on the job since 1972.

11. We (accept) _____ your application for a loan and will process the papers this week.

12. He (benefit) _____ from this MBA course in college.

13. The Dronman Corporation (order) _____ from us for the past twenty years.

14. As the bell rang, I (finish) _____ my report.

15. Since the mail arrived, I (file) _____ the letters.

Fill in the blanks with the proper tenses for the verbs that are indicated.

Use work *in the correct tense in these sentences.*

1. By five o'clock yesterday I _____ forty-four hours already this week.

2. Did I tell you that I _____ tomorrow?

3. Helen _____ on these notes for two hours already.

4. Mr. Longjohn _____ very hard at this job every day.

5. Before I finish this project, I _____ for twelve weeks on it.

Use expect *in the correct tense in these sentences.*

6. I _____ you to be there at noon, but you did not arrive until one o'clock.

7. Up to now, my boss _____ too much from me, but after our talk, I think he will be more realistic.

8. Do you _____ company to visit this weekend?

9. Our county _____ rain for the last three days.

10. I _____ you by six o'clock tonight.

Write the three verbs in the tenses indicated, assuming the same subject as is given in the present tense for each.

Present	he omits	they differ	she carries
Past	11. _____	16. _____	21. _____
Future	12. _____	17. _____	22. _____
Present Perfect	13. _____	18. _____	23. _____
Past Perfect	14. _____	19. _____	24. _____
Future Perfect	15. _____	20. _____	25. _____

● E X E R C I S E   3 . 5

Write the correct form of the verb for each of the following.

1. We (eliminate) _____ the problem in our next production run.

2. Your supervisor (complain) _____ about the quality of your recent work.

3. Carl Coolidge (describe) _____ his last tournament.

4. By next Tuesday I (complete) _____ my latest assignment.

5. The committee (decide) _____ on your promotion last night at the monthly meeting.

6. Tomorrow we (plan) _____ your itinerary for the upcoming sales trip.

7. The judge (adjourn) _____ the case until the prosecution could call the witness.

8. He (walk) _____ to work every day this week so far.

9. I (look) _____ everywhere for that missing file.

10. Our company (suffer) _____ a loss in revenue during the last quarter.

11. The television news reporter (forecast) _____ rain for the company picnic.

12. By this Friday you (complete) _____ your first year with the company.

13. By the time the plane landed, it (circle) _____ the airport several times.

14. The graduating student (apply) _____ for three jobs already.

15. The painter (permit) _____ the first coat of paint to dry before he (apply)

    _____ the second.

Fill in the blanks with the correct progressive (-ing) tense verb form. Remember that the verb will be at least two words long because all progressive forms must have some form of the verb be *as a helping verb.*

1. I understand that since last week you (arrange) _____ for a transfer to the Chicago office.

2. As long as two months ago Mr. Sable (try) _____ to work out the problems in his new machine.

3. Starting next week, Handle's Department Store (permit) _____ charge customers to park for no charge in the adjoining city lot.

4. The contract (lie) _____ under the folder on Elizabeth's desk.

5. Since January our branch offices (submit) _____ their reports to Mrs. Green.

6. Before we employed two new accountants, we (keep) _____ the books ourselves.

7. Ms. Travers (go) _____ on her vacation today.

8. Mr. Johnson (pay) _____ $60 per month on his account all year.

9. Mr. Deitz (hope) _____ to see your agent today, but he became ill and went home.

10. We presently (sue) _____ the contractor who did not complete the job.

11. Until the tornado hit, we (send) _____ all of the reports to the main office.

12. By next Friday the football team (play) _____ together for an entire year.

13. Yoakums' Department Store (carry) _____ both men's and women's clothes for the past 75 years.

14. Her father (study) _____ to get his high school diploma since September.

15. At this moment the pesky woodpecker (bore) _____ a hole in our garage.

■ **E X E R C I S E   3 . 7**

Fill in the missing principal parts of the following verbs.

1. drink _____ _____

2. _____ went _____

3. _____ rose _____

4. feel _____ _____

5. _____ _____ forecast

6. _____ gave _____

7. see _____ _____

8. come _____ _____

9. _____ _____ done

10. _____ lay _____

11. pay _____ _____

12. _____ sang _____

13. swim _____ _____

14. lend _____ _____

15. _____ _____ set

16. _____ burst _____

17. _____ _____ laid

18. buy _____ _____

19. bring _____ _____

20. _____ sought _____

On the blank write the correct principal part of each of the following verbs. Do not add any helping verbs.

1. She told me that she (do) _____ her homework.

2. I have (see) _____ you at the Clausing Company.

3. Before he realized it was sour, Tom had (drink) _____ some of the milk.

4. Be certain that you have (go) _____ over your letters to proofread them before you send them.

5. Have you (give) _____ all the necessary information on your application?

6. He had (pay) _____ his account in full by the first of the month.

7. The appliance manufacturer (give) _____ a one-year warranty on any of the models.

8. Be sure you have (keep) _____ all of your receipts to use when you do your taxes.

9. The bank has (lend) _____ us the full amount for our addition to the office building.

10. One of your customers has (write) _____ that she is very pleased with the service she has received.

11. Mrs. Gamble (teach) _____ herself to typewrite.

12. Have you (quit) _____ the bowling team?

13. This watch has been (wind) _____ too tightly.

14. I have (speak) _____ with Sally about her tardiness.

15. Helen said that she (see) _____ the new plant when she visited the Zenith Corporation.

• E X E R C I S E   3 . 9

Choose the better written of each pair of sentences. Be aware of the appropriate conditions for using the passive voice. Circle the letter preceding the better choice.

1. a. Henry passed the test.
    b. The test was passed by Henry.

2. a. Mr. Rutgate fired the unreliable employee.
    b. The unreliable employee was fired.

3. a. You cannot return the suit because you wore it.
    b. The suit cannot be returned because it appears to have been worn.

4. a. The President approved the new plan.
    b. The new plan was approved by the President.

5. a. Somebody said the photocopier is out of order.
    b. The photocopier is out of order.

• E X E R C I S E   3 . 1 0

Underline the correct verb in the parentheses.

1. Don't you wish it (was, were) Friday already?

2. He (was, were) planning to attend the meeting.

3. When the blackout occurred, I (was, were) surprised.

4. If only he (was, were) not so forgetful.

5. My former boss (is, was) retired and living in Florida.

6. When she (saw, seen) the review, she was delighted.

7. The weather reporter has (forecast, forecasted) snow.

8. My first-grade teacher (is, was) named Miss Horrigan.

9. When she filled in the application, she indicated that her height (is, was) 5' 8".

10. She was (hoping, hopeing) to leave early today.

11. The entertainer had (sang, sung) for two hours by ten o'clock.

12. Mr. Thomas is the highest (payed, paid) secretary in the firm.

13. He must (of, have) (gone, went) to the meeting already.

14. I (use, used) to be able to type 90 words a minute.

15. How could you have (swam, swum) in that cold water?

On other paper write ten sentences, five in the active voice and five in the passive voice. Be sure that your use of passive voice is justified.

Proofread Mr. Black's report and correct any errors in the verb usage or the spelling.

To: Mr. Harold Swanson

From: Joseph Black

Subject: Plans for the Annual Convention

I have went over the plans you give me for our convention which will have been held in Atlanta next July. You done a good job of outlineing all of the meetings and activitys that will be occuring during the week of July 19–23. If I was to have did it myself, I don't think I could of done a better job.

Your choice of Laird Koepel as the main speaker for the banquet was a good one. He had always been one of the best in his field, and he was suppose to have been excellent at the Radial Show. Our group is sure to enjoy him.

By having several of the meetings repeated during the week, you will give more people a chance to participate in them. I done that last year in Dallas and never regreted the time I spended doing so. I have never went to such a good program as in Dallas, but I think you have outdid that convention program.

The one session you have planed for Wednesday afternoon looks to be a real hit. We have been triing for years to show our dealers how to do maintenance on those models. This meeting should get them use to the way it is suppose to be did.

After I read the section on accommodations, I called the Welcome Inn to see if they would have enough rooms available for all of our people. Charles Charming was the manager and said that he can handle all of us easyly. He will reserve the rooms and prepare menus for us to approve if we want him to do so. Do you know how many members will be comeing?

I can tell that you have work on these plans very hard. You have fit all of the activitys into a tight schedule, and yet I believe it can all be accomplished in the time you have planed. You have layed out a good itinerary.

As soon as you put the final approval on these plans, I will go ahead and make the reservations. I will be wantting some more help from you as the time is getting nearer. Thanks for a job well did.

▣ Periodic Review: Chapters 1–3

Underline every prepositional phrase in the following sentences, and place commas around any that are used as interrupters, instead of as closely related modifiers.

1. Anyone with common sense knows the solution to this problem.

2. In brief the coach put the wrong quarterback into the game during the second quarter.

3. The Van Danube Award by the way carries a monetary prize of one thousand dollars.

4. After he won, Mr. Lucas headed for Las Vegas in his new car for more chances with his luck.

5. As a matter of fact I liked the pie with the crunchy top better than the one with the second crust.

Tell whether each of these verbs is action (AV), linking (LV), or either (E).

1. look   _____   6. withered   _____

2. were   _____   7. slept   _____

3. had been   _____   8. smell   _____

4. thought   _____   9. grows   _____

5. feel   _____   10. are   _____

Tell whether each phrase an infinitive (INF) or a prepositional phrase (PREP).

1. to commend   _____   6. to school   _____

2. to have been   _____   7. to the movies   _____

3. to study   _____   8. to the study   _____

4. to Newark   _____   9. to concentrate   _____

5. to convene   _____   10. to the mall   _____

Underline the verbals or complete verbal phrases in each of these sentences.

1. The man wearing the torn sweat shirt is a millionaire.

2. She went to the party store to buy favors for the gala.

3. The driver of the sulky was injured in the fall.

4. Greeting the customer at the door is a good sales practice.

5. Before he knew any better, Ted had gotten into trouble by trying to bribe the police officer.

Write the correct form of the verb, correctly spelled, to complete each of the following sentences.

1. Our choir had (sing) _____ that song for years.

2. Before he left, he (write) _____ a check for $100.

3. By Friday I (go) _____ to Texas and back home.

4. I heard last week that Tom's wife (be) _____ named Julia.

5. She (lend) _____ her brother $500 over the past six weeks.

6. Do you wish Ralph (be) _____ the head of the trust?

7. The event (occur) _____ before I was born.

8. The Simpsons were (plan) _____ to arrive at 5 p.m.

9. Sheila (do) _____ really well on the law exam.

10. After you (finish) _____ the book, call me to tell me the ending.

Choose the better written of these pairs of sentences. Do not choose the passive voice verb unless one of the conditions that would warrant it is present. Circle the letter of your choice.

1. a. This account has been found to be overdrawn and is closed.
   b. You overdrew your account so we closed it.

2. a. The highways are in bad condition this spring.
   b. They say the highways are in bad shape this year.

3. a. She reviewed the account after she completed the survey.
   b. She had completed the survey before she reviewed the account.

4. a. Before she was 65, she used to swim in the brook daily.
   b. She swam in the brook daily until her 65th birthday.

5. a. If the meeting was called off, I wasn't notified.
   b. I wasn't notified if the meeting were called off.

6. a. Our electronics area has been sold to the Japanese.
   b. Our bosses have sold the electronics area to the Japanese.

7. a. I know I would have been there if I hadn't been ill.
   b. I know I would of been there if I wasn't ill.

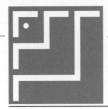

C H A P T E R 4

More About Clauses

OVERVIEW

- **Finding Subjects With Action Verbs**
- **Finding Subjects With Linking Verbs**
- **Two Types of Clauses: Independent and Dependent**
- **Three Types of Dependent Clauses**
- **The Four Clause Patterns**

Chapter 1 defined a clause as a group of words with a subject and a verb. Now that you know what is and what isn't a verb, you need to be certain that you can find the correct subjects of those verbs.

A thorough understanding of subject-verb combinations will be your foundation for more in-depth study of the clause. This chapter will examine several types of clauses and what they communicate to the reader. Finally, you'll see how four simple clause patterns provide the building blocks for an endless number of sentence variations.

FINDING SUBJECTS WITH ACTION VERBS

The subject of an action verb is, you will remember, the doer of the action. It is usually the naming word (noun) or its replacement (pronoun) that tells who or what is doing what the clause describes. Sometimes a subject takes the form of a verbal phrase (infinitive or gerund). At other times a subject can be a type of dependent clause called a noun clause, which will be described later in this chapter.

63

Locate the subject in each of the following sentences by first finding the verb and then finding the doer. The verb is in italics.

Loomis Company *sold* transistor radios. [Who or what? Loomis Company.]

Sally Fredericks, of the Personnel Office, *has been typing* those letters for Ms. Armour. [Who or what? Sally Fredericks. Were you misled by *Personnel Office*? by *Ms. Armour*? These are nouns, but not all nouns and pronouns are subjects. Subjects name the doer of the verb's action. Remember, too, that you will not find the subject in a prepositional phrase.]

Ann Logan and Jim Vance *wrote* the manual for the new washing machine. [Who or what? Ann Logan and Jim Vance a compound subject.]

Return the enclosed postcard to the Ellis Corporation today. [Who or what? The postcard can't return itself, nor is the Ellis Corporation the sender—it is the receiver. (*Ellis Corporation* is also in a prepositional phrase.) You, the reader of the sentence, are supposed to return the card. In sentences that give a command to or request an action from the reader, the subject often is not written—the subject is understood to be the word *you*. You would write this kind of subject as *(You)*. The parentheses ( ) indicate that the subject is not expressed but understood.]

To study hard now *pays* off later. [Who or what? The infinitive phrase *to study hard now* is what pays.]

┏▪ S E L F - C H E C K   4 – 1

Underline the verb twice and the subject once in each of the following sentences. Don't be misled by prepositional phrases, and be aware that the subject may be a compound or may be understood. Locate the verb first.

1. The Christmas rush begins in early November.

2. To learn more about the product, Mr. Nicholas studied the handbooks.

3. Cedar chests and cabinets sell well to new home buyers.

4. Margaret Forbes represents the Whitney Company.

5. Movies or charts help to explain new products to customers.

6. Sit next to Pete or Mary at the conference.

7. After the lecture one of the men stood to ask questions.

8. A can of pears was opened by mistake.

9. When did Susan James get her promotion to Vice President?

10. The hotel on the corner in the next block closed today.

Before you continue, turn to p. 172 to check your answers.

Next, for review, answer the questions below.

1. What is a clause?

2. How do you locate the verb in a clause?

3. How do you find the subject of an action verb?

4. What does *compound* mean in sentence structure?

5. When will you find the subject or verb of a clause in a prepositional phrase?

Before you continue, turn to p. 172 to check your answers.

TRY IT OUT: Do Exercise 4.1, p. 85, to check your skill at locating subjects of action verbs.

FINDING SUBJECTS WITH LINKING VERBS

When a clause has a linking verb instead of an action verb, the subject is the person, place, thing, or idea that the writer is saying something about. In other words, the rest of the clause describes the subject.

Study these examples.

Hardware *is* still a best seller. [Who or what *is*? Hardware.]

Some of the printing inks *were* purple. [Who or what *were*? Some. Why not inks? Not only is that word in a prepositional phrase, but not <u>all</u> were purple, only some. You can see here that (1) pronouns (replacements for nouns) can be subjects and that (2) phrases do add important information.]

On Thursday afternoons the Accounting Department and the Budget Department *are* busy with plans for the coming week. [Who or what *are*? Accounting Department and Budget Department.]

Was Ms. Homer your representative at the convention? [Who or what *was*? Ms. Homer. When looking for the verb in this clause, you will notice a peculiar thing about English grammar: To form a question, the linking verb or a helping verb is placed <u>before</u> the subject. Reversing the order would turn the question into a statement.]

Underline the subjects in the following clauses.

1. Fabric stores also stock such things as patterns and sewing supplies.

2. Baked goods and dairy products are perishable items.

3. Why was Model No. 174B in the carton with the other models?

4. In secretarial work accuracy is of tremendous importance.

5. Only one of the men has a college degree.

Before you continue, turn to p. 172 to check your answers.

TRY IT OUT: **Complete Exercise 4.2, p. 86, for additional practice in locating subjects.**

Each of the items in Self-Check 4–3 is a clause. In fact, each is a one-clause sentence. However, not every clause can stand alone as a sentence. The majority of sentences in the English language contain two or more clauses.

Why is it that most sentences have more than one clause?

1. Speech and writing would be choppy and tedious if all sentences were constructed of only one clause.

2. Not all ideas are of equal importance; thus, two types of clauses allow the writer to show different relationships between ideas.

TWO TYPES OF CLAUSES: INDEPENDENT AND DEPENDENT

Not all clauses are alike. Although each clause must have a subject and a verb, not all clauses serve the same purpose. Some clauses can, by themselves, be sentences. Some serve only as modifiers—they add extra information to the main idea, the idea that carries the important thought. These two kinds of clauses are independent and dependent.

DEFINITION An **independent clause** is a group of words that has a subject and a verb and that contains a main idea stated as a complete thought. An independent clause can be, but is not always, a sentence by itself.

Study the following clauses. The verbs are underlined twice; the subjects, once.

> When the <u>buyer</u> <u>saw</u> the new hardwood squares [Is this a clause? Yes. Is it a complete thought? No.]
>
> Because the <u>employees</u> <u>were</u> late [Is this a clause? Yes. Is it a complete thought? No.]
>
> After the new <u>machines</u> <u>were</u> installed [Is this a clause? Yes. Is it a complete thought? No.]

Although these examples are clauses—they each contain a subject and a verb—they are not independent clauses. Each lacks a mandatory element—a complete thought.

These clauses supply only some information—such as when, where, how, to what extent, or why—about a missing main idea. The clauses leave the reader with these questions.

> What happened when the buyer saw the new hardwood squares?
>
> What was the result of the employees' lateness?
>
> What resulted from the installation of the new machines?

It may be easier to understand the concept of independent clauses by first learning what is <u>not</u> an independent clause. Accordingly, look now at the definition of a dependent clause.

DEFINITION A **dependent clause** is a group of words that contains a subject and a verb but does not express a complete thought. A dependent clause cannot stand alone as a sentence but must be attached to an independent clause.

When you attach one or more of these dependent clauses to an independent clause, you are merely providing a time, place, reason, or condition for the idea expressed in the main clause. Dependent clauses can add to independent clauses in three ways; thus, there are three types of dependent clauses.

THREE TYPES OF DEPENDENT CLAUSES

Recognizing any of the three types of dependent clauses is easy. Each type of clause begins with a word or word group that causes the clause to become dependent. Without these beginning words, the clauses could be independent. Once the word or word group is added, the clause idea becomes incomplete.

Notice the beginning of this earlier example.

When the buyer saw the new hardwood squares

If the word *when* were not here, the clause would express a complete idea. It would be independent. The clause would tell that the buyer saw the new squares; this would be the main idea. Starting the clause with the word *when* changes the meaning, however. Now the clause tells only the time that something else happened. To complete the idea, another clause must be added to report the main occurrence.

> When the buyer saw the new hardwood squares, he congratulated Mr. Coney on his good choice of woods.

The other two examples could also be complete sentences without the beginning words that make them dependent. Read these clauses without the words in parentheses.

> (Because) the employees were late
>
> (After) the new machine was installed

Without the introductory words the clauses would be independent. Each could be a sentence by itself. However, once the introductory word is added, it becomes part of the clause and cannot be set apart—the clause becomes dependent and must be joined with an independent clause to form a sentence.

What then is an independent clause?

An independent clause is any clause that <u>does not</u> begin with signal words that indicate dependent clauses.

Learning the signal words will enable you to recognize clauses that are dependent and thus cannot stand alone as sentences.

Adverb Clauses

The first type of dependent clause is called an adverb clause. This modifying clause, a kind of adverb, provides the same information that other adverbs provide, as described in the following definition.

DEFINITION An **adverb clause** is a dependent clause that modifies the main clause by telling *when, where, how, how much (to what extent), or why* about the idea in the independent clause.

(*Note:* All adverbs provide the same kinds of information, but not all are clauses. You'll learn more about these adverbs in Chapter 12.)

As dependent clauses, adverb clauses begin with signal words or word groups called **subordinate conjunctions.** These signal words are called subordinate because *sub* means "beneath or less"—the idea in the adverb clause is less important than the main idea. These words are called conjunctions because they, too, act as glue, joining two clauses and indicating the relationship between the two. Clauses that begin with subordinate conjunctions are sometimes called subordinate clauses, but this text will call them adverb clauses to indicate their function in a sentence.

You can easily recognize adverb clauses if you learn this list of common signal words.

Subordinate Conjunctions

after	before	since	until
although	even though	so that	when (whenever)
as	except	supposing	where (wherever)
as long as	if	that	whether
as soon as	in case	though	while
because	provided	unless	

(*Note:* Some of these words also appear in the list of prepositions in Chapter 1. That is because they can act as either. To check whether words such as *after, since,* or *until* are prepositions or subordinate conjunctions, you must see how they are used. If they introduce phrases—no subject and verb—they are used as prepositions; if they start clauses, they are functioning as subordinate conjunctions.)

Study the following examples. Notice that a group of words with an adverb clause must contain at least two clauses for a sentence to exist. Dependent clauses cannot stand alone as sentences because they do not express complete thoughts.

                    1   2
Mr. Brown called (when) he got to the office. [In this example *when he got to the office* tells only <u>when</u> Mr. Brown called. The main idea remains that Mr. Brown called.]

              1   2
(Because) he was ill, Mr. Brown was not in the office today. [The first clause is the adverb clause because it begins with the subordinate conjunction *because.* This adverb clause tells <u>why</u> about the main clause; in other words, it tells why Mr. Brown was not in the office today.]

              1   2
(After) he ate breakfast, Mr. Hancock went to work.
(After) Mr. Hancock went to work, he ate breakfast.
[The emphasis in a sentence changes depending on which idea is placed in the main clause. In the first example Mr. Hancock's going to work is stressed. In the second, his eating breakfast is made more important. Both sentences contain exactly the same words, but the meaning and the emphasis certainly change. In both examples the adverb clause is the one that begins with *after.*]

Punctuation Points: Adverb Clauses

Chapter 7, which concentrates on using dependent clauses as a way of combining ideas, will detail the use of commas with adverb clauses. However, because you may have noticed that some of the example sentences have commas while others do not, the general principles are given here.

1. An adverb clause in its normal position (after the independent clause) does not have a comma.

2. Other adverb clauses—either before or breaking into the independent clause—are set out by commas.

Review your understanding of clauses by answering the following questions.

1. What is the difference between a phrase and a clause?

2. What is an independent clause?

3. What is a dependent clause?

4. Is a dependent clause a sentence?

5. What is a subordinate conjunction?

6. Name at least ten subordinate conjunctions.

7. What are the two general types of clauses?

8. What five things about a main clause can an adverb clause tell?

9. Why would a writer put an idea into an independent clause instead of a dependent clause?

10. Why would a writer put an idea into a dependent clause instead of an independent clause?

Before you continue, turn to p. 173 to check your answers.

TRY IT OUT: **Do Exercises 4.3 and 4.4, pp. 86–87, for practice with adverb clauses. Exercise 4.5, pp. 87–88, lets you review the difference between phrases and clauses.**

Adjective Clauses

Like other dependent clauses, adjective clauses start with signal words. These clauses open with words called **relative pronouns.** The resulting clause can be called a relative clause, although this text will call it an adjective clause because of its function.

Whereas adverb clauses modify the whole idea in an independent clause, adjective clauses modify a single noun or pronoun in the main clause. As you may know from previous study, an adjective is a word or words that modify a noun or pronoun.

Learn these signal words that can begin adjective clauses.

who	which	when
whom	that	where
whose		

The first five words are relative pronouns. *When* and *where* can act as signal words in the same way as relative pronouns; they are discussed later in the chapter.

DEFINITION An **adjective clause** is a dependent clause that immediately follows a noun or pronoun and tells more about it.

You can identify an adjective clause by noting that it (1) immediately follows a noun or pronoun and (2) begins with a relative pronoun.

Because adjective clauses are dependent—not independent—clauses, the information that they provide cannot be the main idea of the sentence. An adjective clause provides only additional information about the noun or pronoun modified, information that can be relatively unimportant or that can be absolutely necessary to complete the writer's meaning in a particular sentence.

Sentences that contain adjective clauses must, of course, have at least two clauses since dependent clauses must be added to independent clauses. Because the adjective clause must immediately follow the word or words it modifies, you may find an adjective clause in one of several positions—behind any noun or pronoun in a clause.

For every noun or pronoun in a clause, you could conceivably have an adjective clause. Although structurally correct, adding adjective clauses behind every noun would be poor writing—the sentence would become overly long and complicated. For demonstration only, look at the following to see where adjective clauses could be inserted.

> Your brother . . . flew to Boise . . . to buy a new car . . . with special steering. . . .
>
> Your brother *who lives in Idaho Falls* flew to Boise, *which is 209 miles away,* to buy a new car *that he had to order* with special steering, *which cost $495.*

You can see that this sentence loses its impact with so many added clauses, but it does show that an adjective clause can come almost anywhere within the main clause.

In the following examples two sentences containing related ideas are joined by rephrasing the lesser idea as an adjective clause. Remove the adjective clause and the more important idea remains. Note that, if you wanted to give each idea equal importance, you would leave the clauses as separate sentences. However, using one dependent clause and one independent clause gives you a way to show the relative importance of two unequal ideas.

Two Sentences:
Mr. Headley appointed a committee to study distribution. He is the President of Allied Corporation.

Adjective Clause:

     S   S V   V

Mr. Headley, *who is the President of Allied Corporation,* appointed a committee to study distribution.

The adjective clause has the less important idea

Two Sentences:
The furniture store is on Lake Street. It is having a sale.

Adjective Clause:

                    S   S   V   V
The furniture store *that is on Lake Street* is having a sale.

The sale is the important message

Two Sentences:
I talked with Mr. Hamilton. His company is interested in my plans.

Adjective Clause:

S V   S   V
I talked with Mr. Hamilton, *whose company is interested in my plans.*

The important idea remains in an independent clause

TRY IT OUT: **Exercises 4.6 and 4.7, pp. 88–89, will give you additional practice in separating phrases and clauses. Exercise 4.8, pp. 89–90, will help you to use adjective clauses.**

Notice that, in the preceding sentences, sometimes the relative pronoun is the subject of the adjective clause, and sometimes it is not. Either is correct. How you word the adjective clause will determine its subject. The subject of the adjective (ADJ) clause is underlined once in these examples.

       S   ⌐——— ADJ———⌐ V
My father, <u>who</u> <u>is</u> named Lyle, is a doctor.

       S   ⌐——— ADJ———⌐ V
My father, whose <u>name</u> <u>is</u> Lyle, is a doctor.

       S   ⌐———— ADJ————⌐ V
Dr. Carlson, <u>who</u> just <u>moved</u> to Kalamazoo, is Judy's sister.

       S   ⌐———— ADJ————⌐ V
Dr. Carlson, whose <u>car</u> <u>is</u> in the driveway, is Judy's sister.

In general, you'll know a clause is an adjective clause if it comes after a noun or pronoun and modifies it and if it starts with one of the listed signal words. This test is not foolproof, however. There are four unusual situations that provide exceptions to the rule.

First, relative pronouns can begin clauses other than adjective clauses. A question that begins with a relative pronoun is an independent clause—a sentence—rather than an adjective clause. The question "Who is named Lyle?" does not describe a noun or a pronoun in a main clause; it is a sentence.

Second, the word *that* is not always written; it can be understood. Although originally an informal spoken usage, the omission of *that* has long been commonplace in written usage as well. Either of the following is a correct sentence with an adjective clause.

             ⌐————ADJ————⌐
The man that <u>you</u> <u>saw</u> here yesterday is our new treasurer.

             ⌐————ADJ————⌐
The man <u>you</u> <u>saw</u> here yesterday is our new treasurer.

Note that this situation will occur only when the adjective has a subject other than the word *that*.

The third exception involves clauses that begin with *where* or *when*. Because they are used to begin adjective clauses in certain situations, these words were included in the list of signal words. However, they aren't actually relative pronouns. *Where* and *when* can be thought of as relative pronouns when they begin clauses that immediately follow a noun or pronoun and that really describe <u>that word or words</u>, not the entire clause as an adverbial clause would.

Meet me on an afternoon when we can spend more time on this project.   *tells which afternoon*

Let's go to a seminar where grant programs will be discussed.   *tells what kind of seminar*

Jackie showed me the place where the accident occurred.   *tells which place*

Please tell me the day when you are leaving on vacation.   *tells which day*

(*Hint: Where* and *when* signal adjective clauses when they are <u>not</u> telling time or place—the first clause already did that. You could replace these words with *and* in their adjective usages.)

The fourth exception arises when, on occasion, an adjective clause begins with a word other than the relative pronoun. The relative pronoun is the second or third word in the clause. This exceptional clause begins with an amount-telling word such as *each, several,* and so on.

John liked the hockey team, *each of whom greeted him by name.*

My coworkers, *several of whom live in Hollywood,* drive the freeway to work.

The men in the lineup, *one of whom is our suspect,* all look very much alike.

These necklaces, *any of which will retail for several thousand dollars,* must be carefully insured.

The sales representatives, *none of whom wanted the new assignment,* avoided the regional manager.

My new computer system, *part of which came from your store,* works twice as fast as my old system.

Punctuation Points: Adjective Clauses

You will find practice exercises and more examples of adjective clauses in both Chapters 6 and 7. However, the basic principles of using commas with adjective clauses are these:

1. Set off the adjective clause with commas if the idea in the clause could have been stated in a separate sentence. The idea isn't necessary to clarify the meaning in this sentence because the noun or pronoun being modified is well enough defined without the adjective clause.

2. Do not use commas with an adjective clause that is needed to limit or define the noun it is modifying. Without the adjective clause the main idea would not say what the writer intended.

Underline the adjective clause in each of the following sentences. Circle the relative pronoun that signals the beginning of the adjective clause. After you have underlined the adjective clause, read the remaining words to make certain that a clause remains. (It won't necessarily make complete sense by itself because adjective clauses sometimes add very important information to the understanding of the main clause.)

1. The person who studies each chapter carefully will be able to understand grammar and structure.

2. State Hardware, which sells everything from coops to nuts, is a great place to find appliances.

3. The desk that is in the corner belongs to Gerald Falcon.

4. At the annual dinner Mr. Campbell gave an award to Kathy Ellis, whose work has been invaluable.

5. Howard, Jenkins & Stancati is a legal firm that can handle almost anything.

Before you continue, turn to p. 173 to check your answers.

TRY IT OUT: **Exercise 4.9, pp. 90–91, will show you whether you can distinguish between adjective and adverb clauses. Do Exercise 4.10, p. 91, if you need additional practice.**

▣ Noun Clauses

The third type of dependent clause often begins with one of the same relative pronouns that begin adjective clauses. However, this type of clause does not function like an adjective clause; that is, it does not follow a noun or pronoun and describe that noun or pronoun. This third type of dependent clause <u>replaces</u> a noun in the main clause and is therefore called a noun clause.

DEFINITION A **noun clause** is a dependent clause that replaces a noun in the main clause. A clause is used because the person, place, thing, or idea under discussion cannot be expressed with a single noun or pronoun.

Although noun clauses sometimes start with other words, they most commonly start with the following signal words.

who (whoever)	whose	which (whichever)
whom (whomever)	what (whatever)	that
when (whenever)	where (wherever)	

As in an adjective clause, the relative pronoun in a noun clause sometimes is and sometimes is not the subject of its clause. Even though adjective and noun clauses have similarities, they are quite different in function.

Notice the difference between the noun clauses (Examples 1a and 2a) and the adjective clauses (1b and 2b) in the following.

no word modified by clause

1. a. <u>Whoever won the race</u> should get the prize.   *totals one clause*

   b. The man *who won the race* deserved the prize.   *two distinct clauses; one acts as a modifier*

2. a. Give the report to *whichever woman is in charge.*   *one clause is only object of preposition; totals one full idea*

   b. The leader, *whichever woman is in charge,* makes the decisions.
   two distinct clauses; one acts as modifier

Noun clauses differ from adjective clauses because (1) they don't follow and modify nouns and (2) they leave a "hole" when removed from the main clause. Read Examples 1a and 2a again. Without the noun clauses, the main clauses are incomplete. If an adjective clause is removed, as in Examples 1b and 2b, a complete clause still remains. (Of course, as mentioned before, the remaining clause may not make complete sense by itself because adjective clauses often give absolutely necessary information.)

Punctuation Point: Noun Clauses

Noun clauses are <u>never</u> set apart with commas from the remaining part of the independent clause.

SELF-CHECK 4-6

Circle the relative pronoun in each of the following sentences. Underline the noun clauses. Not every sentence will have a noun clause. Some of them will have adjective clauses. Remember that, if removed, noun clauses leave holes in main clauses.

1. Whoever wants a ride should be in front at five o'clock.

2. I saw that I was wrong.

3. Someone who wants to succeed needs stamina and tenacity.

4. You can sell a Mercedes to whoever has the interest and the money.

5. The one laid off will be the person whose job seems least necessary.

Before you continue, turn to p. 173 to check your answers.

TRY IT OUT: **Exercises 4.11 and 4.12, p. 92, will check your ability to differentiate between noun and adjective clauses; knowing the difference is important for learning correct punctuation. Exercise 4.13, p. 93, challenges you to test your ability to write all three types of dependent clauses.**

THE FOUR CLAUSE PATTERNS

Any clause, whether dependent or independent, follows a certain pattern in the way its important parts are put together. You know that each must contain a subject and verb, but many clauses have a third or even fourth element to complete the meaning. Unless you understand these patterns, you will not be able to learn to use some verbs correctly, nor will you be able to correctly select the right pronouns or choose adjectives and adverbs properly.

Your understanding of later chapters depends on your grasp of the word positions in the four patterns. Have you ever stumbled over whether to use *who* or *whom* or whether to say *I feel bad* or *I feel badly about that?* Once you determine where a troublesome word fits into its clause pattern, you can easily choose the correct form.

Pattern 1: Subject–Verb

You already know one of the four basic patterns. This pattern is used in any clause that has a verb and a subject (even an understood subject) but needs no third word to complete the meaning. The meaning comes from the other modifiers already in the clause.

This pattern is called Pattern 1: Subject–Verb.

Read the following examples to see if you can identify the two important elements, the subject and the verb. It will be helpful to place parentheses around the prepositional phrases.

Mr. Carr looked in the catalog for the picture of the duplicator. [Verb: *looked.* Subject: *Mr. Carr.*]

Feeling tired, Jill still laughed at the error. [Verb: *laughed.* Subject: *Jill.*]

Stephanie, along with the other paralegals, worked late on Thursday. [Verb: *worked.* Subject: *Stephanie.*]

From his office Jeremy watched for my taxi. [Verb: *watched.* Subject: *Jeremy.*]

The students, knowing about the visiting speaker, arrived at the classroom earlier than usual. [Verb: *arrived.* Subject: *students.*]

Carolyn returned from vacation yesterday. [Verb: *returned.* Subject: *Carolyn.*]

You'll see in the following Self-Check sentences that the verb in Pattern 1 can be either an action or a linking verb.

Underline the verb twice and the subject once in the following Pattern 1 clauses. Notice that all that remains in each sentence is modifying words and phrases.

1. The ladies' dresses sold well.

2. After graduation Helen went on vacation for two weeks.

3. The extra stationery and envelopes were in the storeroom.

4. There are 75 orders in today's mail.

5. Ms. Johnston traveled for five days to cover her territory.

Before you continue, turn to p. 173 to check your answers.

Pattern 2: Subject–Verb–Direct Object

The next pattern is used only with action verbs. That is because this pattern has a third important element, the direct object. This pattern needs an action verb because the direct object is the receiver, or "getter," of the action. The direct object may come before the subject in the clause, but normally the direct object follows both the subject and the verb.

DEFINITION A **direct object** is a noun, pronoun, or noun phrase or clause that receives the action of an action verb.

(*Note:* As you've seen in the Pattern 1 sentences, action verbs do not always need direct objects to complete their meaning.)

If you remember that the subject is the doer of an action verb, then you will see the direct object as the person, place, thing, or idea that the subject <u>does</u> the action <u>to</u>. A subject can *drive, call,* or *pitch* some item that would be the direct object, but a subject cannot *is* or *was* anything. Thus, the verb in a Pattern 2 must be an action verb, not a linking verb.

The second pattern is called Pattern 2: Subject–Verb–Direct Object.

As you study the next example sentences, you will find that, in addition to the subject and verb, there is a third element that is not in a prepositional phrase and is not simply a modifying word or phrase. The third element will be a noun or pronoun, or even a noun phrase (a verbal phrase functioning as a noun) or a noun clause.

Look for the verb first, the doer subject second, and the "getter" direct object third. Disregard the modifiers. As with subjects and verbs, direct objects are never found in prepositional phrases.

Mrs. Hendrix dictated the letter to the secretary. [Verb: *dictated*. Doer subject: *Mrs. Hendrix*. Direct object: *letter*—the secretary didn't get dictated.]

On Monday the President called a special meeting of the Board of Directors. [Verb: *called*. Doer subject: *President*. Direct object: *meeting*.]

The hard-working student learned to find direct objects. [Verb: *learned*. Doer subject: *student*. Direct object: Infinitive phrase *to find direct objects*.]

(*Note:* As with subjects, objects can be whole phrases or clauses.)

▣ Pattern 3: Subject–Verb–Indirect Object–Direct Object

Some clauses have a fourth element in addition to the subject, the action verb, and the direct object. This fourth element is also a noun or pronoun.

Called the indirect object, this fourth element remains after all phrases and modifiers are removed.

DEFINITION An **indirect object** is a noun or pronoun that indirectly benefits from the action the subject does to the direct object. The action is done <u>to</u> or <u>for</u> this person, place, thing, or idea.

Look at this sentence to see that there is an extra element after the parts of Pattern 2 are identified.

S V   DO
I read *my mother* the telegram.

The word *mother* is not in a phrase. It is not the direct object because the telegram got read, not the mother. Can you see that the mother <u>indirectly</u> received the action? This idea could have been expressed in a prepositional phrase later in the clause.

I read the telegram *to my mother*.

Thus, an indirect object is a noun or pronoun that is placed between the action verb and the direct object instead of in a prepositional phrase after the direct object. The missing, but understood, preposition will be either *to* or *for*.

A sentence with both a direct object and an indirect object follows Pattern 3: Subject–Verb–Indirect Object–Direct Object.

You can see in these illustrations that a sentence of this type could be written in either of the two ways: (1a, 2a) with an indirect object (IO) or (1b, 2b) with a prepositional phrase <u>after the direct object</u>.

1. a. Mr. Williams sold the customer a Model No. 1784 part.

    b. Mr. Williams sold a Model No. 1784 part **to** *the customer.*

S   V   IO   DO

2. a. I bought Eliza a new briefcase.

    b. I bought a new briefcase *for Eliza.*

▶ S E L F - C H E C K   4-8

Label the elements of the following sentences by writing these abbreviations above the appropriate parts: subject (S), verb (V), direct object (DO), and indirect object (IO). Not all will have indirect objects. Don't be misled by prepositional phrases. None of these elements could come in a prepositional phrase.

1. Our accountant figured the budget for the quarter.

2. Ms. Labour sent all of us to the convention.

3. Among the buyers only José Sanchez liked the new design.

4. The Acme Company sent us a proposal for a new venture.

5. Mr. Stein bought Mr. Sample lunch.

Before you continue, turn to p. 174 to check your answers.

TRY IT OUT: **Do Exercise 4.14, p. 93, to practice the word placements in clause patterns.**

Writing Hints: Troublesome Verb Pairs

Using verbs in the first three patterns is generally not a problem. You can use either action or linking verbs in Pattern 1, but you can use only action verbs in Pattern 2 and Pattern 3.

However, three sets of verbs require special consideration. Now that you're more familiar with the ability of verbs to take objects, it's a good time to look at these often-misused verbs: *sit/set, rise/raise,* and *lie/lay.* Although the verbs in each set share similar meanings, they cannot be used interchangeably. In each case, one of the verbs requires a direct object to complete its meaning, and the other takes no object.

The following table tells which verbs take direct objects and lists the forms of the verbs as they change tense.

	Present	Past	Perfect Participle	Progressive
Has No Object	sit	sat	sat	sitting
Has Object	set	set	set	setting
Has No Object	rise	rose	risen	rising
Has Object	raise	raised	raised	raising
Has No Object	lie	lay	lain	lying
Has Object	lay	laid	laid	laying

With the first pair, *sit/set,* you can see that each form is carefully chosen in these examples.

Maisy *sat* there for three hours. [past tense, no object]

Howard *set* the clock on the table. [past tense, direct object *clock*]

┌ SELF-CHECK 4–9

Complete each sentence with one of the forms of sit *or* set.

1. Will you _____ the table for dinner?

2. Yesterday I _____ in the sun for a short while.

3. We had _____ through the concert before it started to rain.

4. The papers were _____ on the desktop.

5. He _____ his mind on going to Europe.

Before you continue, turn to p. 174 to check your answers.

The next pair of verbs needing careful distinction is *rise/raise.* See how these are used in the following.

This morning I *rose* at 7:30 a.m. [past tense, no direct object]

He *raised* his eyes from his report to check the time. [past tense, direct object *eyes*]

The sun *has risen* earlier each day since spring began. [present perfect tense, no direct object]

Practice using the forms of rise *and* raise *in the following sentences. Be sure to check for direct objects.*

1. The tide will _____ again today after dinner.

2. Prices have _____ in the past six months.

3. He _____ his price on coffee again last week.

4. Can we _____ enough money for this project?

5. I can tell when I am tired because my voice _____.

Before you continue, turn to p. 174 to check your answers.

The last pair of verbs is indeed troublesome to many people. These forms are so often misused that you can't trust your ear to tell you what sounds right.

Study these forms again.

	Present	Past	Perfect Participle	Progressive
Has No Object:	lie	lay	lain	lying
Has Object:	lay	laid	laid	laying

As you look these over, one fact becomes immediately apparent: The past form of *lie* and the present form of *lay* are <u>the same word,</u> even though they are actually different forms of two separate verbs. Many people are, in fact, unaware that *laid* is not the past form of *lie*—that you cannot use *laid* unless there is a receiver of the action. Look at this first sentence. Is there a direct object? No, that is why the second sentence is actually the correct one.

Wrong:
I *laid* in the sun at the beach.
Correct:
I *lay* in the sun at the beach. [past tense of *lie*, no direct object]

A second reason that these forms are so often misused is that many people believe that *lie* means strictly "to recline." Although this is partially true, it does lead to confusion. Thinking only of reclining would lead you to envision a person, or at least an animal, as subject. However, if you think of *lie* as meaning "to recline" or "to remain in a place," you can see that inanimate objects can also be subjects of this verb. Look at these sentences.

> The old cat *lay* in the sun for warmth.
>
> The ship *lay* at anchor waiting to unload.
>
> My car keys *lay* at my feet, right where I had dropped them.

Study the examples of *lie/lay* used in these sentences, only some of which have direct objects.

> (You) *lie* down, Rover. [present tense, no direct object]
>
> Vern *laid* his papers on the credenza. [past tense, direct object *papers*]
>
> Sister, your books *have lain* on this table long enough. [present perfect tense, no object]
>
> Now I *lay* me down to sleep. [present tense, direct object *me*]

One final challenge occurs with these verb pairs in clauses written in the passive voice. You will remember that these are clauses with linking verbs. Often a linking verb is followed by a participial form of the verb, describing the subject. This form most likely reports the results of a past action—one that was shown earlier in an active voice clause. These sentences should illustrate.

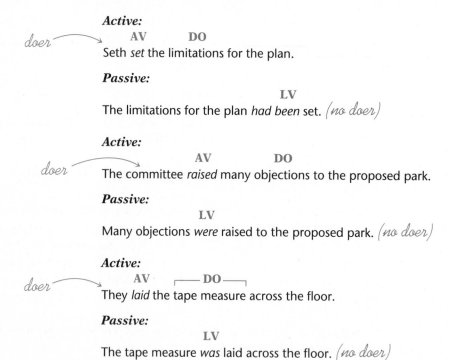

Active:

doer → AV   DO

Seth *set* the limitations for the plan.

Passive:

LV

The limitations for the plan *had been* set. *(no doer)*

Active:

doer → AV   DO

The committee *raised* many objections to the proposed park.

Passive:

LV

Many objections *were* raised to the proposed park. *(no doer)*

Active:

doer → AV — DO —

They *laid* the tape measure across the floor.

Passive:

LV

The tape measure *was* laid across the floor. *(no doer)*

Notice that in the active voice the subject is the doer of the action and, for these particular verbs, there is a direct object. In the passive voice the doer is no longer the subject, and there is no longer an action verb—or an object. The doer is left unexpressed, and the object moves to the subject position. The participle form of the second verb is used to describe this "new" subject, which is actually the receiver of the earlier action.

Practice using the forms of lie *and* lay *in these sentences. Be sure to determine whether the clause has a direct object or whether the clause is in the passive voice.*

1. Will you _____ down for a nap before dinner?

2. Will you _____ those keys over there.

3. The workers have _____ the carpet in the outer office.

4. The ship had _____ in dry dock for over two months.

5. The blame was _____ on the defective door hinge.

Before you continue, turn to p. 174 to check your answers.

TRY IT OUT: Complete Exercises 4.15 and 4.16, pp. 94–95, for practice with these troublesome verb pairs.

▣ Pattern 4: Subject–Linking Verb– Subject Complement

Pattern 1, so far, is the only pattern to use a linking verb, although it could have an action verb instead.

By contrast, Patterns 2 and 3, because they include objects, must have action verbs.

Pattern 4 <u>always</u> has a linking verb. It differs from Pattern 1 because it features a third element that completes the idea expressed in the clause. This third element cannot be called a direct object, of course, because no action is occurring. This element is called a subject complement, also known as a predicate complement, or a predicate nominative or a predicate adjective. All mean the same thing. This text will use the term *subject complement* because it is a word that "completes the subject" (see how much of the word *comple*te is in the word *comple*ment).

DEFINITION A **subject complement** is a word or word group that follows a linking verb and completes the meaning of the clause by providing more information about the subject.

A subject complement can be a noun or pronoun that renames the subject in another role, a noun phrase or clause, or an adjective that describes the subject. It can also be the participial form of a verb; in this case, the participle will describe the subject's condition.

Any clause with a subject complement follows Pattern 4: Subject–Linking Verb–Subject Complement.

Study these sentences to understand the subject complement (SC) component of Pattern 4.

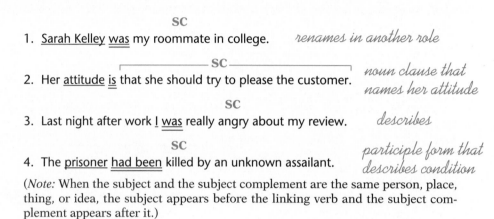

1. <u>Sarah Kelley</u> <u>was</u> my roommate in college. *renames in another role*

2. Her <u>attitude</u> <u>is</u> that she should try to please the customer. *noun clause that names her attitude*

3. Last night after work <u>I</u> <u>was</u> really angry about my review. *describes*

4. The <u>prisoner</u> <u>had been</u> killed by an unknown assailant. *participle form that describes condition*

(*Note:* When the subject and the subject complement are the same person, place, thing, or idea, the subject appears before the linking verb and the subject complement appears after it.)

SELF-CHECK 4–12

Underline the subject complements in the following sentences. Tell whether each is renaming the subject or describing the subject.

1. The overdue postage is 20 cents.

2. My favorite hobby has been skiing.

3. Peggy was elated by the news.

4. Mr. Erickson is both happy and sad to be transferred.

5. She was an active member of that organization for 30 years.

Before you continue, turn to p. 174 to check your answers.

TRY IT OUT: Do Exercises 4.17 and 4.18, pp. 95–96, for practice with clause patterns.

Chapter 4: More About Clauses

● EXERCISE 4.1

Locate the subject in each of the following sentences, and write it on the blank provided. Remember, find and underline the verb first, and then locate the doer (subject).

1. Sales for the first quarter increased 20 percent. _____

2. Following your advice, I called on the Harris Company yesterday and received an order. _____

3. Who answered the telephone just now? _____

4. Each of the sales representatives has sold over twenty thousand items this year. _____

5. March 31 marks the end of our first quarter. _____

6. Japanese electronics are selling well this year. _____

7. Purchase our stationer supplies at Houseman's. _____

8. The request from Mrs. Patterson demanded our immediate attention. _____

9. Attitude and appearance count heavily in an interview. _____

10. Several of the secretaries could take dictation at 120 words per minute. _____

11. Several secretaries typed 80 words per minute. _____

12. Minute details often determine the results of any legal case. _____

13. The Electra 200, one of our new machines, can process papers at the rate of 200 a minute. _____

14. A staff of experts will review the program. _____

15. Mr. Morales, our representative to the Board, received a promotion to Vice President. _____

Underline the complete verb (the main verb and any helping verbs) twice and the simple subject once in each of these sentences. Find the verb first.

1. The keys to the office are in the top drawer.

2. The last edition of the encyclopedia was published in 1978.

3. Will you be at our office opening?

4. One of the copies is in the Bass file.

5. Your typing is excellent.

6. Mrs. Hammer could have been President.

7. Pianos and organs are always popular items at Christmas.

8. The syllabus was typed before our change of plans.

9. Skiing is fun.

10. Mr. Jones is skiing this week in Sun Valley.

Tell whether each of the following is a dependent (D) clause or an independent (I) clause. If dependent, circle the word or words that make it dependent.

1. _____   While I was talking on the phone.

2. _____   Mr. Norton seemed to be right most of the time.

3. _____   Because he knew it.

4. _____   If you see Mrs. Bordon before I do.

5. _____   Selling vacuums, Mr. Campos met lots of new people.

6. _____   Before I take the matter into consideration.

7. _____   Please see me before noon.

8. _____   Will you settle the details by Friday?

9. _____   As long as you consider the customer first.

10. _____   Can you find a customer for this unique item?

● E X E R C I S E   4 . 4

Combine each pair of sentences by making the less important idea into an adverb clause. Reword as needed.

1. Serena liked walking in the woods. She was afraid of snakes.

    _____

    _____

2. An entrepreneur starts a business. He or she takes the risk for the sake of profit.

    _____

    _____

3. Bring the mixture to a boil. You must continue to stir it at the same time.

    _____

    _____

4. The gorilla lives in a zoo. He seems restless and bored.

    _____

    _____

5. Take care preparing the tax form. The IRS may audit you.

    _____

    _____

● E X E R C I S E   4 . 5

Tell whether each of the following is a phrase (P) or a clause (C). Remember that any word group with a subject and a verb is a clause even if it does not contain a complete meaning.

1. _____ Remember last year's figures

2. _____ He remembered last year's figures

3. _____ If he remembered last year's figures

4. _____ When I see you next

5. _____ Over the river and through the woods to Grandmother's house

6. _____ Over the river and through the woods to Grandmother's house we go

7. _____ Hurry

8. _____ To learn a great lesson from this

9. _____ Because of our difficulty with printing

10. _____ Because we had difficulty with printing

11. _____ The sales representative with the wonderful way of approaching customers

12. _____ Hidden from our view

13. _____ Since yesterday at the meeting in the boardroom

14. _____ Running the photocopier, collating the pages, and stapling them together

15. _____ She was running the ditto, collating the pages, and stapling them together

● E X E R C I S E 4 . 6

Tell whether the italicized word group is a dependent (D) or independent (I) clause or neither (N).

1. _____ Between Mr. Hanko and you, *we have a very good team.*

2. _____ *He ordered;* we delivered.

3. _____ *According to your new bylaws,* the offices of Secretary and Treasurer are now separate.

4. _____ *When you have finished the report,* please come to my office.

5. _____ The new dictating equipment was delivered *by parcel post yesterday.*

6. _____ When I hire a secretary, *I look for someone with good language skills.*

7. _____ Would you rather achieve speed with typewriting, or *would you prefer accuracy?*

8. _____ *Because we ordered too many three-piece suits,* we will have a sale after Christmas.

9. _____ Give the report to Miss Ellis, *who is the Bursar.*

10. _____ The auditor *who did our books* is from Smith and DeVries.

Tell whether the italicized word group is a dependent (D) or an independent (I) clause or neither (N).

1. _____ *Between Mr. Hanko and you,* we have a very good team.

2. _____ He ordered; *we delivered.*

3. _____ According to your new bylaws, *the offices of Secretary and Treasurer are now separate.*

4. _____ When you have finished the report, *please come to my office.*

5. _____ *The new dictating equipment was delivered* by parcel post yesterday.

6. _____ *When I hire a secretary,* I look for someone with good language skills.

7. _____ *Would you rather achieve speed with typewriting,* or would you prefer accuracy?

8. _____ Because we ordered too many three-piece suits, *we will have a sale after Christmas.*

9. _____ Give the report to Miss Ellis, *who is the Bursar.*

10. _____ *The auditor* who did our books *is from Smith and DeVries.*

Combine these sentences, making the less important idea into an adjective clause. You will have to reword as you make one sentence out of two.

1. In Greek mythology the Hydra was slain by Hercules. It had nine heads.

   _____

   _____

2. Rosella has two children. She works full time at Rosenberg's.

   _____

   _____

3. I like some power lawnmowers better than others. I prefer electric starters on lawnmowers.

_____

_____

4. Not all men are fond of athletics. Men with natural physical abilities like athletics.

_____

_____

5. A person can be called an alcoholic. A person can lose control of his or her drinking.

_____

_____

● E X E R C I S E 4 . 9

Tell whether the italicized dependent clause is adverbial (ADV) or adjective (ADJ). Hint: Adjective clauses almost always begin with relative pronouns, not subordinate conjunctions. The words when *and* where *could be exceptions.*

1. _____   On Friday our office closed at noon *because it was a holiday.*

2. _____   The man *who saw the accident* said that it was caused by the sports car.

3. _____   We had gone home *before the storm knocked out the electricity.*

4. _____   *When you have completed the balance sheet,* you should send it to the auditor for checking.

5. _____   The moment *when the rocket ignited* stunned the onlookers.

6. _____   The survey *that the Sales Department made* shows how much customers notice advertising.

7. _____   *Since you closed the books,* have you begun this year's entries?

8. _____   I saw Martha Josephson, *who used to work here,* at Knowl's last week.

9. _____   John Falmouth, *with whom you went to school,* sends his best to you.

10. _____   Close up early today *if you have finished your work.*

Go back and circle the signal words that begin each dependent clause, and then write those words on the blanks that follow. Be aware that each clause is made dependent by the word you have circled and written.

1. _____

2. _____

3. _____

4. _____

5. _____

6. _____

7. _____

8. _____

9. _____

10. _____

● E X E R C I S E   4 . 1 0

Underline the dependent clause, and tell whether it is adverbial (ADV) or adjective (ADJ).

1. _____ Someone who understands legal terminology should read this for you.

2. _____ Show me the memo that told us about this.

3. _____ If you cannot return the invoice, please send a copy.

4. _____ I met the new Treasurer, whom I had seen at last year's meeting.

5. _____ I will send a duplicate although I believe I had enclosed a copy earlier.

6. _____ As soon as you complete the application, I will call you for an interview.

7. _____ Whenever it rains, our new Cover-All will keep your golf clubs dry.

8. _____ The Ellison Company, which is located in San Diego, produces wash-and-wear clothes.

9. _____ You may, as you read the chapters, underline the important parts.

10. _____ The Iowa City branch of our company reconditions the motors that need it.

Again circle the beginning word of these dependent clauses to become more attuned to key words that signal dependent clauses. Write each word below.

1. _____

2. _____

3. _____

4. _____

5. _____

6. _____

7. _____

8. _____

9. _____

10. _____

Underline the dependent clauses in the following sentences. On the blank tell whether each is an adjective (ADJ) or a noun (N) clause. Remember that adjective clauses must follow nouns or pronouns and describe them.

1. _____ Several of the men who work in the assembly plant have been contributing new money-saving ideas.

2. _____ I saw a film that really did a good job of describing this turbosupercharger.

3. _____ The position I want to have is to be the department chairperson.

4. _____ Whichever one is chosen will be all right with me.

5. _____ I seem to like whomever I meet.

6. _____ I don't know which month contains your birthday.

7. _____ Kamala wore a sari, which is a draped garment that is wrapped around a person.

8. _____ Did you see Denine White at the conference that was held in Santa Monica?

9. _____ Please select whomever you want for the position.

10. _____ Whichever part does not shatter when it vibrates is the stronger one.

Replace each italicized noun or pronoun with a noun clause. Reword as necessary, but do not add commas.

1. I saw *someone* waving at me yesterday. _____

_____

2. *Jody* was cited for speeding on I–94. _____

_____

3. Send the memo to the *person* responsible for reservations. _____

_____

4. She gave the *winner* of the contest the award. _____

_____

5. She knows her *punishment*. _____

_____

● E X E R C I S E   4 . 1 3   CHALLENGE

On other paper write six sentences containing dependent clauses: three with clauses that begin with when *or* whenever *and three with clauses that begin with* where *or* wherever. *Each set of three should include one sentence with an adverb clause, one sentence with an adjective clause, and one sentence with a noun clause.*

● E X E R C I S E   4 . 1 4

Decide whether each of the following sentences follows a Pattern 1, 2, or 3. Put the appropriate pattern number on the blank. Hint: Underline subjects and verbs, and put parentheses around prepositional phrases.
    Pattern 1: Subject–Verb
    Pattern 2: Subject–Verb–Direct Object
    Pattern 3: Subject–Verb–Indirect Object–Direct Object

1. _____   Mr. Palmer scored a birdie on the seventh hole in the golf tournament.

2. _____   Mrs. Thomas sent the Ames Corporation an explanatory letter about the flaw in the part.

3. _____   The Treasurer has been with our firm for over twenty years.

4. _____   Mail a check for the balance by September 30.

5. _____   High-fashion models earn large salaries during their usually short careers.

6. _____   Mrs. Fisher walks to and from work every day.

7. _____   The Norris Company has sent the government ten thousand gyroscopes as part of the defense contract.

8. _____   The Oxford Motor Company has offered its customers quality service on its cars.

9. _____   Handling all loans, Mr. Burris is in charge of that area.

10. _____   On Wednesday you should mail the reminders for the meeting.

Use the correct verb form from each set of verbs specified.

Use some form of lie *or* lay *to correctly complete the following sentences.*

1. He has _____ out a plan for the remodeling.

2. The papers _____ on the shelf for months before we found them.

3. Will you _____ those typewriter ribbons on the table?

4. Petroleum products that have _____ unused for thousands of years are now being tapped.

5. New pavement has been _____ on Rush Street this week.

Use some form of sit *or* set *to correctly complete these sentences.*

6. We all _____ on the grass to listen to the speaker.

7. Will you please _____ the cartons here?

8. Those parts have been _____ in the warehouse for two weeks.

9. The sun will _____ tonight at 7:37.

10. She _____ the machine to run automatically.

Use some form of rise *or* raise *to correctly complete the following sentences.*

11. The audience _____ to its feet as the Senator came onto the platform.

12. Don't _____ your voice at me!

13. The cost of living will have _____ even more by the end of the fiscal year.

14. Have you _____ the money for the camp project you have been working on?

15. Our hopes for a successful year have _____ considerably since the unemployment figures have gone down.

● E X E R C I S E   4 . 1 6

Select the correct form of one of the pair of verbs given in each of the following sentences.

1. Before you turn on the machine, (sit/set) _____ the dial at 270°.

2. We hardly realized that the two hours had passed as we (sit/set) _____ and listened to the speaker.

3. We have had to (rise/raise) _____ the prices on our new models by 10 percent.

4. The temperature in this office must have (rise/raise) _____ at least twenty degrees this afternoon.

5. The sales representative (lie/lay) _____ her hand on the machine to demonstrate that there was no vibration.

6. Judge Fox has (sit/set) _____ on the bench for fifty years.

7. The missing compass is (lie/lay) _____ on the floor under your work table.

8. All last week during my vacation I (lie/lay) _____ around the house and read good books.

9. Our farm has (rise/raise) _____ more chickens than any other farm in the Midwest.

10. Turnko Company has been (lie/lay) _____ carpet in that apartment for three weeks.

● E X E R C I S E   4 . 1 7

These linking verb sentences follow either Pattern 1 (no third element) or Pattern 4 (with a subject complement). Identify the Pattern 4 sentences, and on the blank, tell whether each subject complement renames or describes the subject.

1. _____ The canister was located in an unauthorized dump site.

2. _____ The dictionary is outdated, not listing words from this decade.

3. _____ At least a cupful of flour should be in the bag.

4. _____ A cupful or more is left in the bag.

5. _____ Our resident manager here is Jamal Reddings.

6. _____ Jamal Reddings is our resident manager here.

7. _____ Women with political ambitions are now becoming senators and governors.

8. _____ I can become discouraged too easily by other people's criticism.

9. _____ The newspapers were under the bushes in front of the house.

10. _____ The English setter looked handsome when pointing the birds.

● E X E R C I S E 4.18

Decide whether each of the following sentences is a Pattern 1, 2, 3, or 4. Put the appropriate pattern number on the blank. Hint: Label verb as action (AV) or linking (LV).
  Pattern 1: Subject–Verb
  Pattern 2: Subject–Verb–Direct Object
  Pattern 3: Subject–Verb–Indirect Object–Direct Object
  Pattern 4: Subject–Linking Verb–Subject Complement

1. _____ Underneath all of his gruffness and despite his abruptness, Senator Forbish is really a kind person.

2. _____ Selling hosiery, Mrs. Adams called on stores in several cities.

3. _____ The old man told us long, rambling stories of the days of his sailing the seas.

4. _____ The legislators in our district have had a good record of attendance for voting.

5. _____ He can sell plants at wholesale and still make a profit of 75 percent.

6. _____ Steve Wilson is the editor of the local newspaper.

7. _____ We stock dressers and chests in the Italian style.

8. _____ Our company policy gives us eight paid holidays each year.

9. _____ The law firm representing us will be Kirk, Jones, and Hodgson.

10. _____ Good English usage will help you in your future vocation.

C H A P T E R 5

Nouns

OVERVIEW

- **Common Nouns and Proper Nouns**
- **Noun Plurals**
- **Nouns as Possessive Words**
- **Punctuation Points: Commas With Nouns**
- **Capitalization Rules—A Summary**

Clauses contain many nouns, often in several different positions: subject, subject complement, direct object, indirect object, object of preposition, and object of one of the three types of verbals. Sometimes even phrases or clauses can act as nouns, occupying these same positions.

In addition to its versatility, a noun has other qualities, too. A noun can be general or specific, can show one or more, and can indicate ownership. This chapter will look at each of these abilities, and then discuss punctuation points and capitalization.

COMMON NOUNS AND PROPER NOUNS

Every noun can be classified as one of two types, common or proper.

DEFINITION   A **common noun** is a word or words that name a general class of people, places, things, or ideas. A common noun does not name a specific person, place, thing, or idea.

DEFINITION A **proper noun** is a word or words that name a specific person, place, thing, or idea. A proper noun begins with a capital letter.

These lists should illustrate the difference between the two types.

Common	Proper
man	James
car	Chevrolet
river	Mississippi River
building	Drake Hotel
officer	Treasurer

Although in most cases a common noun consists of only one word, sometimes two or more words act together to represent one class of people, places, things, or ideas: *guinea pig, rock and roll, police officer, hole in one, hot dog.*

Later in this chapter the rules of capitalization will be covered. To be able to apply these rules, you must be able to distinguish between common and proper nouns.

NOUN PLURALS

An important quality of nouns is their ability to identify how many items are named—one or more than one. A noun that names one is said to be **singular;** a noun naming more than one is called **plural.**

English-Based Words

Several rules govern the way plurals are formed.

Spelling Rules for Forming Noun Plurals

1. Most nouns add *-s* to form the plural.

book	books
judgment	judgments
German	Germans
bookcase	bookcases
Smith	Smiths

(*Note:* Surnames should always be made plural when preceded by the word *the,* as in *the Browns* or *the Williamses.*)

2. Any noun that ends in a sibilant (hissing) sound needs an extra syllable to aid with pronunciation and, thus, adds -*es* to form the plural. The sibilant sounds come from these letters: *s, x, ch, sh,* and *z*.

boss	bosses
couch	couches
Fitz	Fitzes
Jones	Joneses
crash	crashes

3. The plurals of nouns that end in -*y* are determined by the letter preceding the -*y*. If a vowel comes before the -*y*, add -*s;* if a consonant, change the -*y* to -*i* and add -*es*.

attorney	attorneys	secretary	secretaries
journey	journeys	quantity	quantities
play	plays	city	cities
valley	valleys	duty	duties
alloy	alloys	variety	varieties

The exception is proper nouns that end in -*y*, which simply add -*s*, no matter what letter comes before the -*y*.

Henry	Henrys
Kelly	Kellys
Sally	Sallys
Fry	Frys

4. Nouns that end in -*o* preceded by a vowel usually add -*s;* those preceded by a consonant usually add -*es*.

zoo	zoos	tomato	tomatoes
radio	radios	cargo	cargoes
		hero	heroes

Exceptions to this rule are some shortened forms of longer words and musical terms.

auto	autos	piano	pianos
memo	memos	alto	altos
photo	photos	solo	solos

(*Note:* Some words that end in -*o* have two acceptable plural forms. Check the dictionary; the first form listed is the preferred spelling.)

5. Most nouns that end in -*f* add -*s* to form the plural.

staff	staffs
chief	chiefs
roof	roofs
plaintiff	plaintiffs

Some nouns that end in *-f* or *-fe* change the *-f* to *-v* and add *-es*.

wife	wives
leaf	leaves
half	halves
thief	thieves

(*Note:* Some words that end in *-f* have two acceptable plural forms. Check the dictionary to see which is listed first as the preferred spelling.)

6. Some nouns form the plural by a basic word change.

foot	feet
man	men
goose	geese
mouse	mice
person	people

7. Some nouns make no change at all when used in the plural.

deer	deer
sheep	sheep
series	series
species	species
Chinese	Chinese

(*Note:* The word *corps* is pronounced KORE; its plural, also spelled *corps*, is pronounced KORZ.)

8. Two nouns end in *-en* in the plural form.

child	children
ox	oxen

9. Some nouns always act as singular and have no plural form.

measles	ethics
news	mathematics
economics	molasses

(*Note:* The word *ethics* is considered plural if naming someone's system of behaviors.)

10. Some nouns have no singular form but are always considered plural.

pants	scissors
thanks	riches
goods	

11. Most hyphenated nouns form their plurals by making the main word of the group plural.

son-in-law	sons-in-law
editor-in-chief	editors-in-chief
court-martial	courts-martial

If there are no nouns among the word parts, usually the word forms its plural at the end.

has-been has-beens
get-together get-togethers

12. Singular words ending in *-ful* add *-s* for plural.

cupful cupfuls
handful handfuls

(*Note:* These nouns are to be distinguished from a noun with the adjective *full*, as in "Anne had several cups full of coffee ready for all of us.")

TRY IT OUT: Complete Exercises 5.1 and 5.2, pp. 119–120, to practice forming noun plurals.

Non-English–Based Words

Some words that have been adopted from other languages have retained their original spelling in the plural. These words form their plurals differently from words of English origin. Interestingly, some of these same words also have formed plurals using the English language rules and now have two plural forms. However, the non-English plural is usually the preferred spelling. As you read the following rules, notice that an -s ending tells little about whether a noun is singular or plural.

Spelling Rules for Forming Noun Plurals: Non-English–Based Words

1. Many non-English–based nouns that end in -is change the -is to -es in the plural.

parenthesis	parentheses
synthesis	syntheses
analysis	analyses
basis	bases
hypothesis	hypotheses

2. Non-English–based nouns ending in -um often change the ending to -a in the plural.

datum	data
curriculum	curricula
memorandum	memoranda
stratum	strata
referendum	referenda

3. Non-English–based nouns ending in -us often change the ending to -i for the plural form.

alumnus [male]	alumni
fungus	fungi
gladiolus	gladioli
stimulus	stimuli
radius	radii

4. Some non-English–based nouns ending in -a add -e to the base word to form the plural. (The pronunciation changes to the long e sound.)

alumna [female]	alumnae
formula	formulae
vertebra	vertebrae
fibula	fibulae
larva	larvae

5. Some nouns follow such little-used rules that they are simply listed here.

criterion	criteria
phenomenon	phenomena
bureau	bureaux
trousseau	trousseaux

What does the following ending change to when the plural of a non-English–based word is formed?

1. *-us* _____

2. *-um* _____

3. *-is* _____

4. *-a* _____

5. *-eau* _____

Before you continue, turn to p. 175 to check your answers.

TRY IT OUT: **To practice making non-English–based words plural, do Exercise 5.3, p. 121.**

NOUNS AS POSSESSIVE WORDS

Another attribute of a noun is the ability to be changed into a modifying word, thus becoming, in effect, an adjective. A noun in this usage is said to be in the possessive case.

DEFINITION The **possessive case** of a noun is an adjective formed from a noun and an apostrophe (') combined with the letter -*s*. This new form is used to indicate possession or ownership.

Having just completed the exercises in changing nouns from singular to plural, you know that you did not use apostrophes to make these plurals. You added -*s* or -*es* (or other endings for some non-English–based words) to form plurals. The apostrophe is saved for nouns used as adjectives.

These possessive case nouns act just as other adjectives do because they show a special relationship—an ownership—to nouns or pronouns that <u>closely follow</u> them. Because two nouns, or a noun and a pronoun, cannot occupy the same clause position (such as subject or object), a reader will expect that any nounlike words that come before a subject or object are only modifiers of that subject or object. In general, a reader looks for the noun to appear <u>after</u> its modifiers.

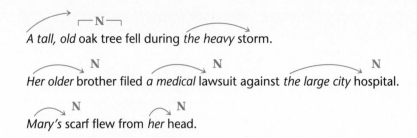

A tall, old oak tree fell during *the heavy* storm.

Her older brother filed *a medical* lawsuit against *the large city* hospital.

Mary's scarf flew from *her* head.

You can see in these examples that the adjectives (in italics) only add information to the item being talked about—the modifiers are not the nouns or pronouns. In these sentences the adjectives tell <u>which</u>, <u>what</u> <u>kind of</u>, or <u>whose</u>, referring to the nouns and pronouns that closely follow them. The ownership-type words will usually tell <u>whose</u> or <u>which</u>. As the examples show, ownership words can be pronouns (such as *her*) as well as possessive case nouns (such as *Mary's*, which tells whose scarf.) (The possessive case pronouns are discussed in Chapter 6.)

Notice these examples.

Noun + Noun	Tells	Correct Form
1. Jim hat	whose	Jim's hat
2. book cover	what kind of	book cover
		or
		book's cover
3. yesterday mail	which	yesterday's mail

Forming Possessives

Although occasionally a noun can function as an adjective without changing form (see *book* in the previous Example 2), most nouns must add an apostrophe with an -*s* to become modifiers. Examples 1 and 3 could not be possessives without the apostrophe and -*s* combinations.

Be aware that once a noun has been made possessive, it is <u>no longer a noun</u>. As discussed, the subject or object (noun or pronoun) will follow the ownership word. Look at what is <u>really</u> being named in these sentences with possessives.

<u>I</u> <u>washed</u> and <u>ironed</u> Jim's hat. *DO is the <u>hat</u>, not Jim*

<u>Margaret</u> <u>ripped</u> the book's cover, but the book is all right. *DO is the <u>cover</u>, not the whole book*

Yesterday's <u>mail</u> <u>was</u> all bills! *Subject is the <u>mail</u>, not the day*

By adding the apostrophe, you show that the word so marked has a special relationship to a noun or pronoun following it. You may have learned to call this relationship "ownership," but this word often causes a misunderstanding of possessives. How, for instance, can a book "own" a cover? How can yesterday "own" its mail? Instead, think of an apostrophe placed with a noun as showing <u>ownership</u>, <u>authorship</u>, <u>origin</u>, or <u>cause</u>, not a bought-and-paid-for ownership.

Look at these illustrations of these relationships.

Ownership: *Harold's car*
Authorship: *the author's plays*
Origin (of the color): *the rug's color*
Origin (of the pay): *two weeks' pay*
Cause (of the aftereffects): *measles' aftereffects*

This broader definition makes it clear that names of places, ideas, inanimate objects, and abstract things—as well as names of people—can be made possessive. Very often these other types of possessives are the ones to which writers fail to add apostrophes because of the mistaken idea that only people can "own" things. Now, however, you can see that the added apostrophe does not necessarily mean that one thing went out and paid for another thing.

When to Place the Apostrophe: Bird's Feathers or Birds Feather's?

How can you tell when to add an apostrophe? Whenever you come to a word that you think needs an apostrophe for possessive case, try these two tests.

1. Check to see if your word comes before a noun or pronoun that it "owns"; remember, you are trying to remove your word from being read as the item named, the subject or object. You do not want your word to be mistaken for a noun or pronoun.

2. Try to put your word after the noun with *of* or *for* between the two.

Possessive	**Prepositional**
the *men's* clothes	the clothes *for* the men
Roger's house	the house *of* Roger
a *day's* rest	rest *for* a day
the *ink's* color	the color *of* the ink
Poe's stories	the stories *of* Poe
the *students'* good grades	the good grades *of* the students
the *roses'* prickly thorns	the prickly thorns *of* the roses

If the two words can be reversed in this way, you must use an apostrophe when you choose not to relate your nouns with a preposition. The use of possessives is actually a shortcut way of showing the prepositional phrase relationship.

Notice that the last two examples show another adjective between the possessive word and the noun, a common occurrence. You should not, however, find another noun or a verb between a possessive word and the item that is owned.

Keep in mind that if you add -s but forget to add the apostrophe, you are forming only a plural noun, not a possessive.

Wrong:
Jims house is green and white. *green and white Jim or a green and white house?*

Wrong:
A days rest was what I needed. *I needed a days or I needed a rest?*

⌐ᴵ· S E L F - C H E C K 5 – 3

Using the two tests to determine the need for possessive case, underline the words in the following phrases that should have an apostrophe added. (Some phrases will not require apostrophes.)

1. Selmas old figure skates

2. a donkeys whining bray

3. the mans slippers

4. the womans reckless driving

5. the reckless driving of the woman

6. the cartons of cigarettes

7. two weeks notice of action

8. students were home

9. the series outcome

10. Mr. Rosss job description

Before you continue, turn to p. 175 to check your answers.

Where to Place the Apostrophe: Bird's Feathers or Birds' Feathers?

So far, the discussion of apostrophes has not mentioned where the apostrophes go in relation to the -s in possessive words. Although it is not difficult to use these apostrophes, many people have simplified the rules too much. These people think that the apostrophe always comes before the -s if the word is singular and comes after the -s in a plural word. This is often the case, but not always.

Read the following two sentences.

1. All of the *cats'* paws were white.
2. All of the *cat's* paws were white.

Both sentences sound exactly alike when read aloud. The problem is that you would not know how many cats are being talked about unless you could see these sentences in print. An apostrophe tells the reader not only that "ownership" occurs but also <u>how many</u> are doing the "owning."

In the examples of the paws of the cat/cats, the generalized rule does apply: *cat's* shows one cat and *cats'* shows more than one cat having white paws.

Remember, you can always tell whether the writer wanted to indicate a singular or plural word by looking in front of the apostrophe. If you do this for Example 1, you see that *cats* comes before the apostrophe. The writer intended to make the word plural—the base word was plural <u>before</u> the apostrophe was added. In Example 2 the writer added the apostrophe to the singular word *cat*, indicating that only one cat had all white paws.

You should always be able to cover the apostrophe and everything <u>after</u> it to determine whether a possessive word is singular or plural. Try that now with the two previous examples. How many cats are being named in each—one or more?

S E L F - C H E C K 5–4

Cover the apostrophe and any letter after it to decide whether the word is a singular possessive or a plural possessive. Write **S** *for singular or* **P** *for plural.*

_____ 1. the people's choice

_____ 2. The Joneses' children

_____ 3. Mrs. Jones's children

_____ 4. the window's panes

_____ 5. her sons-in-law's cars

Before you continue, turn to p. 175 to check your answers.

You know, of course, that a singular noun can "own" something that is plural (*Mrs. Jones' children*) or that a plural noun can "own" something singular (*the people's choice*). The "owned" object doesn't determine where the apostrophe goes, but the decision about how many "owners" there are, does.

Here are two simple steps to follow to decide how to add the apostrophe to possessive words.

STEP 1: Write the word out totally, in its singular or plural form, without the apostrophe.

STEP 2: Add the apostrophe.

If the noun does not end in -*s*, add -'*s* (no matter if it is singular or plural).

book	book's cover
secretary	secretary's desk
men	men's suits
people	people's opinion
Harry	Harry's dogs
sons-in-law	sons-in-law's wives

If the base word already ends in -*s* or -*es* (perhaps the -*s* or -*es* you added for plural), form the possessive from the pronunciation. If a new syllable is formed, add -'*s*. Otherwise, add only the apostrophe.

boss	boss' *or* boss's report
James	James' *or* James's report
Mr. Jones	Mr. Jones' *or* Mr. Jones's knee
the Joneses	the Joneses' house
secretaries	the secretaries' association

(*Note:* No extra -*s* can be added to the last two because they are plural, not singular.)

SELF-CHECK 5–5

Indicate whether each of the following is a singular (S) or a plural (P) possessive form. If you are unsure, cover up the apostrophe, and look at the word in front of the apostrophe. Don't be misled by the words that follow the possessive words.

_____ 1. attorney's offices   _____ 6. a girls' school

_____ 2. Thomas's office   _____ 7. children's toys

_____ 3. the Fords' children   _____ 8. the church's congregation

_____ 4. companies' offices   _____ 9. heroes' welcome

_____ 5. my Ford's engine   _____ 10. a dollar's worth of candy

Before you continue, turn to p. 175 to check your answers.

TRY IT OUT: **Fill in the blanks in Exercise 5.4, pp. 121–122, to demonstrate your understanding of the possessive forms of nouns.**

Special Usages of Possessives

Possessive forms are also used in several special situations. Be aware of the following unusual possessive case usages.

Inanimate Objects as Possessives. One type of possessive that is not readily recognized is the use of the inanimate (not living) object placed in a possessive position in a sentence. This type of possessive form is correct although some scholars suggest that the use of prepositional phrases can prevent these unusual forms.

1. a. The chair's leg is broken.
   b. The leg of the chair is broken.

2. a. The dress's belt is red.
   b. The belt of the dress is red.

3. a. The letter's signature is blurred.
   b. The signature of the letter is blurred.

If you choose to place the inanimate object before the other noun, as in Examples 1a, 2a, and 3a, remember that you must use the possessive form.

Another possessive form that is commonly missed is that showing time relationships, where a time-reporting noun comes right before another noun and must, therefore, be made possessive. Notice these examples of time words as possessives.

He was given five *days'* notice to leave his apartment.
Give me a *minute's* worth of your time, please.
We receive two *weeks'* sick pay each year.
The technician took a *year's* leave of absence to go to Iraq to work.
This *century's* progress is amazing.

Occasionally, money amounts precede other nouns and pronouns and must be made possessive.

She got her *money's* worth from that lottery ticket!
George stopped at the gas station and bought ten *dollars'* worth of gas.

If these words had not been made possessive, you could have misread the sentences. Because you are used to finding nouns in certain clause positions, you read the first noun that you come to in any of these positions as the noun intended to fill the position. In the last two examples, for instance, *money* would be assumed to be the direct object of the verb *got*, whereas it is really the value, or worth, of the money that she got; in the second sentence it would seem that George bought ten dollars, but he really purchased that value of gas.

Single or Joint Ownership. In some sentences two or more "owners" come in front of the object or objects owned. If each person or entity "owns" an item, each name needs an apostrophe. This is called **singular, or individual, ownership.**

> *Bob's* and *Fred's* cars are both restored fifties' models.
> *McGregor's* and *Brown's* stores each have their appliances on sale.
> The *administration's* and the *staff's* views are quite different.

If the compound owners share in the ownership of one or more items, only the last of the names needs an apostrophe. This type of ownership is called **joint ownership.**

> Would you give me *Smith and DeVries'* phone number.
> *Hannah and Ted's* sons are all married.
> I will take my car to *Edison and Rank's* garage for repair and repainting.

Understood Ownership. Once in a while, the item that is "owned" is not written but is understood. This situation occurs when the item is the same as the subject and is not written because it would be repetitive. The missing noun is the subject complement.

> This memorandum is Harold Grant's (memorandum).
> Ahmad's work is not as good as Lionel's (work).

When a possessive comes before a word such as *house* or *store,* the noun may be omitted if the meaning is obvious.

> If you want a name-brand item, go to Zinzer's (store).
> Next month we plan to go to Harbor's (plant) for a company tour.
> Last night I went over to Mary's (house).
>
> (*Note:* Without the apostrophes you would have only plural words in these examples. You can look back and see that these would not be correct forms.)

Possessives Before Gerunds. Another special situation arises when you place a noun or pronoun in front of a gerund, an *-ing* word acting like a noun. Any noun or pronoun "owner" of a gerund must be put into the possessive to make it into an adjective and, thus, keep the gerund in the noun position of the clause. In the sentence "I appreciate Sue's writing," if *Sue* were not made possessive, the word *Sue* would be read as a noun. The sentence would mean that <u>Sue</u> is appreciated. While that may indeed also be true, the sentence means to say that Sue's letter, her writing, is appreciated.

Note the possessives in front of the gerunds here.

I really dislike Mr. Hall's eating onions for lunch.   *I don't dislike Mr. Hall.*

The firm's advertising is old-fashioned.   *The firm is not old-fashioned.*

I don't like Frank's singing out of tune.   *I like Frank but not his singing.*

Company Names as Possessives. In current formats many companies have omitted the apostrophe from proper noun word groups that name them. Often the name is a registered trademark and should be used as the company dictates.

Consumers Power Company

Parsons Business School

Bensons Department Store

If, however, the business name uses only a *first* name, the apostrophe should remain.

Lea's Hair Styling Salon

Manny's Garage

Frank's Nursery

Abbreviations as Possessives. An abbreviation can also be possessive. If singular, the abbreviation has an apostrophe and -*s* added; if plural, an -*s* followed by an apostrophe.

Henry Ford Jr.'s book

the U.S.'s involvement

an R.N.s' meeting

(*Note:* Just like other nouns, an abbreviation functioning as a noun is made plural by adding -*s* with no apostrophe. Thus, *D.J.s* means two disc jockeys; *D.J.'s* is an adjective that tells about one disc jockey as owner.)

TRY IT OUT: **Do Exercises 5.5 and 5.6, pp. 123–126, to check your understanding of possessives.**

Change the following phrases into their possessive forms. Examples:

the window of the car = the car's window
the plan for today = today's plan

1. the leaves of the plant _____

2. the sign of the store _____

3. the footnotes of the pages _____

4. the frames of my glasses _____

5. the work for a week _____

6. the worth of a quarter _____

7. a vacation for a month _____

8. an illness of two days _____

9. the house of Beth and Fred _____

10. the separate offices of Wilson and Schriff _____

(*Note:* Did you notice that each time you changed the word order and made the phrase word possessive, the apostrophe was added to the word exactly as it appears in the original phrase? That is because the original phrase already shows the word in the correct number, singular or plural. Writing a word as it would appear in a prepositional phrase expressing ownership and <u>then</u> adding the apostrophe is another way to determine the correct form of the possessive.)

Before you continue, turn to p. 176 to check your answers.

TRY IT OUT : **Because writing possessive forms is one of the most common writing problems, you may want to complete Exercises 5.7 through 5.9, pp. 127–129, for additional practice.**

PUNCTUATION POINTS: COMMAS WITH NOUNS

Previous chapters have looked at some punctuation rules related to nouns. Nouns appear in various positions throughout sentences, and it is usually the role of the phrase or clause in which the noun appears that determines the need for punctuation.

Nouns appear in long introductory phrases, which, you'll recall from Chapter 1, may be followed with a comma. You also know that interrupting phrases are set off with commas. This section will look at some specific ways nouns are used in an "interrupting" element of a sentence. First see how a comma is used to separate ideas in a group of related nouns.

Nouns in a Series

Many times nouns are written to name several things, one after the other. These words are used in a **series.** Commas are commonly placed between the items in the list, although the comma before the conjunction is currently considered to be optional. Many writers choose to use this last comma to ensure that each of the series items gets equal emphasis.

> My brother, father, and sister will arrive today to visit for the holiday.
> You may order beef, pork, or ham.
> Chicago, Dallas, and Los Angeles have busy airports.

Do not use a comma after the last item in the series.

Commas also separate phrases and clauses in a series. Note the following illustrations.

> I plan to go shopping, to eat lunch at Harpo's, and to see a movie.
> He jumped over a rock, across the stream, and beyond the stump without getting his shoes wet.
> Norman selected a topic for research, he spent six months reading about it, and he wrote an extensive article about his discoveries.
> I washed, I dried, and I put away the dishes.

Nouns in Direct Address

While using commas in a series is one comma rule that is commonly known, the use of commas with direct address may be less familiar. Compare these two sentences.

> 1. We called Mr. Stallone to see if the book was ready.
> 2. We called, Mr. Stallone, to see if the book was ready.

Are you able to see that the two sentences, while containing exactly the same words, give quite different messages? In Example 1 the person being talked to is not known, but Mr. Stallone is being talked <u>about</u>. In Example 2 Mr. Stallone is the person being talked <u>to</u>.

Direct address means that you are speaking directly to someone and addressing him or her by name or title. Use commas to set off the name or title of the person being addressed.

Tell me, Consuelo, if you want the transfer to Selma.

Miss VanHouten, will you call the Acme Company?

I wonder, Mr. Chairman, if we have covered all of the details and are ready for a vote.

Yes, sir, I am ready to see you now.

We have, my talented teammates, won the bowling tournament.

Long Introductory Phrases

As discussed in Chapter 1, an optional comma can be used after two or more prepositional phrases or a very long phrase that comes before a clause. This comma is not required but may help your reader to interpret your intended meaning.

At the end of a long day (,) I am tired.

During an extremely long meeting (,) I need to take notes.

Nouns as Appositives

Although commas do not normally come between the subject and verb or after prepositional phrases, commas may be needed in these instances if something else comes between the subject and verb or after the phrase. Very often an explanatory phrase comes after a noun, renaming the noun. This word or word group, called an **appositive,** is the same person, place, thing, or idea as the noun it stands behind. Using an appositive helps to avoid repetition by combining two ideas into one clause. Notice how it is done in the following.

Two Sentences:
Mr. Lyle Duncan is in Altanta this week. He is the Chairman of the Board.

Appositive:
Mr. Lyle Duncan, the Chairman of the Board, is in Atlanta this week.

Two Sentences:
Florida has millions of tourists visiting each year. It is called the Sunshine State.

Appositive:
Florida, the Sunshine State, has millions of tourists visiting each year.

Writing Hints: Using Appositives to Combine

The appositive makes an excellent tool for reducing wordiness and avoiding needless repetition. The appositive also offers variety to your writing style; it replaces what could have been an adjective clause or a verbal phrase that would follow the noun and modify it.

You can see that all three of these techniques are good alternatives for writing two short separate sentences or a rather dull compound sentence. Of course, a good writer uses all techniques for variety in his or her writing.

Two Sentences:
The Mississippi River acts as drainage for several Midwestern states. It is the longest river in the United States.

Compound Sentence:
The Mississippi River acts as drainage for several Midwestern states, and it is the longest river in the United States.

Adjective Clause:
The Mississippi River, which is the United States' longest river, acts as drainage for several Midwestern states.

Adverb Clause:
Because the Mississippi River is the longest river in the United States, it can act as drainage for several Midwestern states.

Appositive:
The Mississippi River, the United States' longest river, acts as drainage for several Midwestern states.

SELF-CHECK 5–7

Underline the word or word group in the second sentence that could be an appositive if it were added to the first sentence. Rewrite the first sentence adding in the appositive.

1. Kim Lee studied law at Stanford. He is my partner.

   _____

2. The band director of the jazz band is terrific. He is named Theodore Mackle.

   _____

3. The Burton Company's product is not unusual but is selling extremely well. The company makes fiberboard tables.

   _____

4. I prefer decaffeinated tea. It is herbal tea.

   _____

5. Officer Louise Campbell has been with the police department here for three years. She is a candidate for sergeant.

   _____

Before you continue, turn to p. 176 to check your answers.

TRY IT OUT: **Combine the ideas in Exercises 5.10 and 5.11, p. 130, to practice your writing techniques.**

Nouns in Other Explanatory Phrases

In addition to appositives, there are two other forms of explanatory phrases that follow nouns and require commas. The first is a prepositional phrase that tells where the person just named comes from. The phrase will begin with the preposition *of.*

> Ms. Dorothy Daniels, of the Nashville office, will be here this Thursday.
> Mr. Larry Burns, of New Orleans, is speaking at the Directors' meeting.

Sometimes, for variety, the explanatory phrase begins with *or.* It does not offer an alternative of a different thing; it renames the <u>same</u> thing.

> Business Communications, or our letter-writing course, is offered each term.
> The first years of medical training, or pre-med, can be taken at many undergraduate schools.

More rules concerning the use of commas with nouns, such as with dates and locations or with titles, can be found in Chapter 15.

TRY IT OUT: **Practice these comma rules by doing Exercises 5.12 and 5.13, pp. 131–132.**

CAPITALIZATION RULES—A SUMMARY

You will need to consult a reference manual for the many specific rules that govern any occasional use of capital letters with nouns and noun word groups. However, following are a few of the most common usages.

1. Capitalize all proper nouns (specific items selected from the group), including proper adjectives made from proper nouns.

General	Specific
dog	Border collie
man	Freud, Freudian
country	Ireland, Irish
accounting	Payroll Accounting 211

2. Capitalize all nouns in a proper noun group.

Lawson Street	the Dark Ages
the Atlantic Ocean	Hollywood High School
Prince Company	the White House
List No. 924	Acct. No. 367–3893

3. Capitalize geographical words only if they indicate a specific place that could be located on a map, such as a section or territory.

> He drove *south* on M112. [only a direction]
>
> He was born in the *South.* [a specific part of the country]
>
> She loves the *Midwest* but is still a *Westerner* at heart. [specific parts of the country]

4. Capitalize the seasons only if they are personified (given human traits) or are a part of a proper noun group.

> I saw *Spring* in all of her glory. [The word *her* tells you that the writer meant to personify.]
>
> We have our annual *Spring Sale* in May.
>
> I plan to go to Italy in the *fall.*

5. Generally, capitalize a title with a personal name when it is part of the name or represents a high-ranking political official. Most titles do not need to be capitalized when they replace the name or follow it.

Senator Bliss	a state senator
Reverend Bundy	our priest
Dr. Jane Dill	our family doctor

In business writing it is common to capitalize a specific job title to show respect for the position: *Chairman of the Board.*

6. A family title is capitalized only when it precedes the name or when the person's name could replace the title.

> I'm sorry, Grandmother, if I offended you.
>
> She is my grandmother.
>
> Did you tell Aunt Sue about my brother?

7. Trade names are capitalized unless the name has come to represent a generic class, as has happened with *aspirin, oriental rug,* and *manhattan* (the drink). Likewise, do not capitalize generic nouns that are not part of the trade name.

a Sony television	a Xerox copy
Kleenex	Apple Macintosh

8. Words in the title of an artistic or literary work generally are capitalized. Note the following exceptions.

   a. Do not capitalize the articles *a, an,* and *the* unless the first or last word in the title.

   b. Do not capitalize prepositions and conjunctions of fewer than four letters; do capitalize if the word is an adverb.

   > *A Man for All Seasons* was a great show.
   >
   > I read the book, *The Civil War: An American Tragedy.*
   >
   > Larry Burns' new book is *I Told Off the World and Lived to Tell About It.*

TRY IT OUT: **Complete Exercises 5.14 and 5.15, p. 133, for practice with capitalization. Exercise 5.16, p. 134, is the Challenge exercise for testing possessive case usage.**

⊡ Chapter 5: Nouns

● E X E R C I S E   5 . 1

Write the plural of each of the following nouns.

1. man	_____	16. industry	_____
2. shoe	_____	17. valley	_____
3. search	_____	18. Moss	_____
4. father-in-law	_____	19. salesman	_____
5. Hix	_____	20. potato	_____
6. county	_____	21. ally	_____
7. series	_____	22. lady	_____
8. thief	_____	23. editor-in-chief	_____
9. news	_____	24. Adams	_____
10. patio	_____	25. remedy	_____
11. spoonful	_____	26. calf	_____
12. Mary	_____	27. indemnity	_____
13. deer	_____	28. motto	_____
14. box	_____	29. ratio	_____
15. copy	_____	30. turkey	_____

● E X E R C I S E   5 . 2

Write the correctly spelled plural forms of the nouns in parentheses on the blanks provided.

1. After the (attorney) _____ met, they went to look for (vacancy)

   _____ at the local hotels.

2. Several (witness) _____ said that they had seen the two (plaintiff)

   _____ arguing.

3. We held two (survey) _____ to attempt to discover which (territory)

_____ we would work.

4. A pair of (scissors) _____ can be used to cut these (pants)

_____ .

5. The (goose) _____ tried to attack the (sheep) _____ .

6. The President's (veto) _____ were not liked by the (Chinese)

_____ .

7. A few (ox) _____ were in the field when we saw the (deer)

_____ .

8. How many (casualty) _____ were there after the company (party)

_____ ?

9. Those who sang (solo) _____ wore (tuxedo)

_____ .

10. The (Fitch) _____ lived in the area near the (laboratory)

_____ .

11. Do you need (secretary) _____ for the offices at your (factory)

_____ ?

12. We ordered several (gross) _____ of pencils for the (survey)

_____ .

13. Several (studio) _____ wanted to play the recordings of the (banjo)

_____ .

14. Not many (laundry) _____ care to do (handkerchief)

_____ .

15. The (chef) _____ liked to use (tomato) _____
in their recipes.

● E X E R C I S E   5 . 3

Write the plural for each of the following non-English–based words.

1. basis _____

2. datum _____

3. fibula _____

4. stratum _____

5. alumnus _____

6. synthesis _____

7. phenomenon _____

8. gladiolus _____

9. alumna _____

10. criterion _____

11. bureau _____

12. hypothesis _____

13. radius _____

14. memorandum _____

15. fungus _____

● E X E R C I S E   5 . 4

Fill in the form of each noun as indicated. The first one is done for you as an example.

Singular	Singular Possessive	Plural	Plural Possessive
1. girl	girl's	girls	girls'
2. man			
3. chief			
4. son-in-law			
5. soprano			
6. child			
7. Harry			
8. Hess			
9. basis			
10. fox			
11. month			

12. desk   _____   _____   _____

13. glass   _____   _____   _____

14. mystery   _____   _____   _____

15. valley   _____   _____   _____

16. boss   _____   _____   _____

17. attorney general   _____   _____   _____

18. hero   _____   _____   _____

19. knife   _____   _____   _____

20. Hal Kirk Jr.   _____   _____   _____

21. lady   _____   _____   _____

22. invoice   _____   _____   _____

23. horse   _____   _____   _____

24. Jones   _____   _____   _____

25. turkey   _____   _____   _____

26. class   _____   _____   _____

27. Holtz   _____   _____   _____

28. potato   _____   _____   _____

29. ox   _____   _____   _____

30. attorney   _____   _____   _____

Name _____ Date _____ Class _____

In this and the following exercises, you have to decide what to do with the word in parentheses. It may be singular or plural; it may need an apostrophe, or it may not. Occasionally, more than one form of the word could be correct.

1. The two (sister) _____ were happy to learn of their (mother)

   _____ promotion.

2. This (week) _____ schedule calls for you to come into work at 7:30.

3. (Jim) _____ (brother) _____ car is in the

   body shop for (repair) _____ from the accident.

4. Is this a (girl) _____ or a (boy) _____ school?

5. The (hospital) _____ director ordered new (nurse)

   _____ uniforms.

6. Seven hundred (worker) _____ have been laid off from the Bangor

   (plant) _____ assembly line.

7. Several (department) _____ in this store carry (lady)

   _____ and (child) _____ clothing.

8. The (chairman) _____ duties, those for Al and Bob, were listed in the
   report.

9. The memo from the (principal) _____ office asked all of the (teacher)

   _____ to report their (student) _____
   absences by noon.

10. Her two (daughter-in-law) _____ worked at General Foods.

11. Each (secretary) _____ (duty) _____ varied
    from office to office.

12. This (Employee) _____ Dental Plan is available to all office (worker)

    _____.

13. The new building will have (office) _____ for (doctor)

    _____ and (dentist) _____.

14. These (doctor) _____ and (dentist) _____
    offices will be opened by June 1.

15. I can continue on after a few (minute) _____ rest.

16. Three (month) _____ interest on your loan is now overdue.

17. (Traveler) _____ checks are available at no cost to the (Credit Union)

    _____ customers.

18. (Lloyd) _____ and (Smith) _____ store is
    located at Colorado and Elm.

19. (Mr. Lloyd) _____ and (Mr. Smith) _____
    jewelry stores both sell Dunnigan watches. [assuming singular ownership]

20. (Shakespeare) _____ plays are still very popular in this country.

21. A few (minute) _____ preparation can save several (hour)

    _____ work.

22. Mr. (Thomas) _____ idea of a vacation is staying home to repair the

    (porch) _____ railing.

23. The old hotel had several (porch) _____ that were furnished with wicker

    (chair) _____.

24. Does that store carry (child) _____ (book)

    _____?

25. I've never liked (Lois) _____ selling our (mother)

    _____ antiques.

● E X E R C I S E   5.6

Make any changes necessary to the words in parentheses, and write the correct form on the blanks.

1. The (Fox) _____ children have been working this summer for Mr. (Fox)

   _____ father.

2. Have you seen the (Evans) _____ house since her two (brother-in-law)

   _____ sons painted it?

3. Last night we ate dinner at the (Fitch) _____ and then went to two

   (movie) _____.

4. If you put all of your best (effort) _____ into your work, you will improve

   the (company) _____ business as well as your position in it.

5. (Harry) _____ and (Jim) _____ garage can do
   the best transmission work in town.

6. Did (Nancy) _____ boss tell you that she is the (people)

   _____ favorite in their store?

7. I thought it was (Ned) _____ , but this coat is (Jim)

   _____.

8. Of the two (class) _____ papers this (class)

   _____ tests had better scores.

9. (Gus) _____ job at (Henderson) _____ plant
   is to do the time studies.

10. The (world) _____ problems could be eased by the (people)

    _____ cooperation.

11. Each (dentist) _____ patients trust that he or she will take care of their

    (child) _____ teeth.

12. Mr. (Silas) _____ house is just a (stone) _____ throw from mine.

13. The (attorney) _____ group will have its (secretary) _____ luncheon next Monday.

14. Please give 30 (day) _____ notice before breaking your (tenant) _____ lease.

15. He found the (factory) _____ warehouse at the (town) _____ edge.

16. Did you tell all of the (manager) _____ that we will close the plant for two (week) _____ vacation in July?

17. My (watch) _____ band was broken as I tried to fix the (store) _____ back door.

18. This (town) _____ government has run smoothly since (Benedict) _____ election.

19. You are covered under our (Worker) _____ Compensation Plan for any missed work due to lay (off) _____.

20. The (signature) _____ of both (defendant) _____ must accompany this notice.

• E X E R C I S E   5 . 7

Fill in the blanks with the correct form of the noun in parentheses.

1. The secretary needs two (week) _____ notice of your vacation plans.

2. The (teacher) _____ meeting was held to discuss the lack of (student)

   _____ understanding of (possessive) _____.

3. Several (attorney) _____ (case) _____ were

   delayed during the (Jones) [both Bill and Seth]_____ trial.

4. The (server) _____ (uniform) _____ were
   paid for by the restaurant.

5. The truck I saw go past is (Gerald) _____.

6. She ordered ten (dollar) _____ worth of samples.

7. Many African (country) _____ governments have changed in recent
   years.

8. My two (brother-in-law) _____ (car) _____
   have been repossessed.

9. (Mary) _____ and (Agnes) _____ apartment
   is for rent after September 1.

10. I went to (Wojak) _____ to buy several (supply)

    _____ for school.

• E X E R C I S E   5 . 8

Fill in the blanks with the correct form of the noun that is in parentheses.

1. In (today) _____ mail we received Mr. (Wilson)

   _____ (payment) _____ for March and April.

2. I saw you last night at (Steve) _____ .

3. The (editor-in-chief) _____ column discussed the (people)

   _____ concerns about the (alumnus) _____ of
   Yale for '90 and '91.

4. I went to see my (friend) _____ in New York, and I saw the (Met)

   _____ team play.

5. Our (neighbor) _____ names are the (Hiss)

   _____ and the (Jones) _____ .

6. I'll take twenty (cent) _____ worth of candy.

7. My (pant) _____ pocket is full of my (son)

   _____ marbles.

8. She has three (sister) _____ who sell (child)

   _____ clothing.

9. In two (week) _____ time we will have our (secretary)

   _____ substitutes trained.

10. The (Kendall) _____ son and the (Ross) _____
    daughter were married last Saturday in Boston.

11. She bought her watch at (J. C. Penney) _____ .

12. The (boss) _____ all met together to discuss the (employee)

    _____ (salary) _____ for the next fiscal year.

13. Your two (month) _____ grace period on your loan is over on July 1.

14. He doesn't have a (nickel) _____ worth of mechanical ability.

15. Several (man) _____ (suit) _____ were
    marked down for the two-week sale.

• E X E R C I S E   5 . 9

Fill in the blanks with the correct form of the noun that is in parentheses.

1. I wanted Mr. (Bates) _____ job, but I wasn't qualified.

2. (Dorothy) _____ and (Ann) _____ room is a mess.

3. The two (saleswoman) _____ routes were near the (state)

   _____ capital; thus, Mary and Alice didn't have far to drive.

4. We had dinner at (Mario) _____ and ate three (pizza) _____.

5. The seven (child) _____ (toothbrush) _____ had weak bristles.

6. The (scissors) _____ handle was broken.

7. The (Hess) _____ house was hit by lightning during last (year)

   _____ hurricane.

8. (Johnson & Feldman) _____ new branch office will employ 700 (worker)

   _____.

9. Give me five (dollar) _____ worth of gas and two (quart)

   _____ of oil.

10. The (datum) _____ figures were not correctly typed by my (secretary)

   _____ replacement.

Take the following two sentences, and using each of the various techniques listed, combine the ideas into one sentence. Refer to p. 114 (Writing Hints) for examples.

Sarah Henry applied for the manager's job. She has been the assistant for two years.

Compound Sentence: _____

_____

Compound Verb in Simple Sentence: _____

_____

Adjective Clause: _____

_____

Adverb Clause: _____

_____

Appositive: _____

_____

Use appositives to combine each of the following sets into one sentence.

1. Todd is an attorney. He works in the real estate office of the Burton Company.

   _____

2. The Burton Company employs more than two thousand people. It is a development company.

   _____

3. The Burton Company buys up large tracts of land for future development. The company likes to buy unused agricultural land.

   _____

4. The real estate office has eighty-four people buying land. They are well-trained environmentalists.

   _____

5. Land development is big business. It is the basis for future growth.

   _____

● E X E R C I S E   5 . 1 2

Insert any necessary commas in the following sentences. Circle any changes you make.

Items in a series

1. Good workers are seldom tardy absent without a good reason or anxious to leave work early.

2. This recipe calls for a cup of milk a cup of flour a dash of salt and three tablespoons of butter.

3. Wash cloths towels and bath mats can be found on the third floor in Housewares.

4. He is a happy warm and outgoing person.

5. My duties are to do the payroll to keep the books up to date and to prepare the billings.

Direct address

6. Tell me Sam how you managed to repair that antique machine.

7. Dr. Hendrix please report to Oncology.

8. I'm not sure I can agree to that price Mrs. Carr.

9. Oh Miss may I have more coffee?

10. "Friends Romans Countrymen lend me your ears" is a famous address from Shakespeare's *Julius Caesar.*

Explanatory phrases, including appositives

11. Our accountant the man in the green shirt has saved us thousands of dollars over the years.

12. Jordan Baylor of Boise Idaho will be here next Tuesday for the play-offs.

13. Our plant the Jorgenson Company has branches in three other locations.

14. Only one thing a dismal day will change the date of the annual picnic.

15. I plan to take this marlin's measurements and picture to a taxidermist or a person who mounts fish and makes models of them.

Add any necessary commas to the following. Remember, not all of the sentences may need commas. Circle any changes you make.

1. Ann looked for the report under her other papers in her desk drawers and behind the file cabinet.

2. Mr. Howard Dunstan of the Dallas branch designed a new product a self-starting lawn mower.

3. I ask you gentlemen if you are ready to vote on the proposal.

4. Terry's sister Martha Blount is coming to work here next week.

5. Before I agreed to buy the house the seller said he would repair the roof have the west side painted and fix the garage door.

6. Arlene will you please set up a meeting for Thursday for the entire staff of the Admissions Office.

7. Hodges and Judkins a legal firm in Reno will be handling the case.

8. *Gone With the Wind* a well-known movie was made the same year as *Wizard of Oz.*

9. Howard Hughes a well-known millionaire was a very private person.

10. Sentries or guards patrol this building all night.

11. She wanted to clean up the office and make some coffee to relax.

12. She wanted to clean up her office make some coffee and restock her supplies.

13. Please call me Mr. Kennedy when you are ready to go over the plans.

14. Robert Frost one of the best-known poets of all times wrote about his everyday life.

15. Tallahassee or the capital of Florida is growing quite rapidly.

16. I plan to move to Tallahassee or Tampa next year.

17. I can see you now Mrs. Jackson about your invention.

18. Bob Fox of Prospect Falls ordered a carton of books to be sent by postal express.

19. The brand name Lewis is well known as naming a product that is reliable.

20. To deface or disfigure public property is against the law.

● EXERCISE 5.14

Correct these sentences to include any needed capital letters. Circle any changes you make.

1. I took classes in math and french.

2. I went to see the priest and spoke to father Morales.

3. We go for drives in the fall to see the colors.

4. Jacob Sterns, our company treasurer, is from Warsaw.

5. I plan to go to college at stanford in california.

6. Washington state is located in the northwest of america.

7. My uncle fred worked for pittsburgh plate glass company.

8. The article was entitled "on christmas day we renew our family traditions of decorating and singing."

9. He won a purple heart medal in korea.

10. In his sophomore year he starred in the school play, *what in the world?*

● EXERCISE 5.15

Proofread this paragraph for proper usage of capitals, and make any necessary corrections. Circle any changes you make.

My Uncle, James Reville, is a professor in the college of law at the university of Missouri. Last winter he published a new book, *an anthology of the poems of the supreme court judges.* He has always been a Poetry Lover and has wanted to do this book for many years. We all drove North from Texas to be present for the Celebration that was held at his apartment on South Canfield street, next to the Michael Sloan memorial for world war I veterans. Not only was the College President there, but the entire Board of trustees attended too. I took my Kodak Camera to photograph the whole ceremony. It was a great day!

Correct any errors in the use of the possessive case in the following report. Circle any changes you make.

Last week Ms. Joneses' class took a field trip to the museum in Toledo to study the displays that illustrate animals' and their habitats.

The student's parents brought them to school at 8 a.m. to meet the buses. The childrens' parents were asked to return at 5 p.m. to pick them up after the days trip.

It is a two hours drive to the museum from the school. Although the poor bus drivers' ears were a bit the worse for wear, the trip to Toledo was uneventful.

The museums staff was very helpful in assisting Ms. Jones and the few parents' who had come along. The staff gave them maps and told them which exhibits would be most useful for Ms. Jone's purposes.

The class members' were attentive as they went through the exhibits, although Robert Moores behavior was not as good as it could have been. He did try to scare Susan Dugan near the snakes, but the only one that really seemed frightened was Susans mother.

As is to be expected, the class seemed to enjoy the display of dinosaurs, especially the skeletons, which showed all of the vertebrae. The students had difficulty believing that the huge bones' had really once been a dinosaurs.'

At noon the group went to the cafeteria to eat the lunches they had brought; the only lunch that had been left on the bus was Roberts. The others shared their lunch'es with him so that no one had to go all of the way back to the bus to pick up the missing lunch.

The afternoons activities' consisted of one more display section to be seen as well as a stop at the museums' souvenir shop. After that, everyone reported back to the bus for the trip home. There was a few minutes delay to wait for Robert, but once he was found in the mens' room, they were all ready.

Because of the long, hard day and Mr. Willsons good driving, all of the adults slept on the bus trip back. The classes enthusiasm never slowed, however, and there was much singing and talking during the trip. It didn't seem to affect the parents' rest.

The bus arrived back at the school at exactly five o'clock. The parents picked up their children, and after Roberts' mother arrived at 5:45, Ms. Jones went home.

Respectfully submitted by Mrs. Joy Jeffries', Roommother.

⌐·⌐ Periodic Review: Chapters 4–5

In the following sentences underline verbal phrases, and put parentheses around prepositional phrases.

1. Many of the authors of best sellers try to publish too many books by writing "formula" stories.

2. Upon hearing the good news, Norma danced around the room.

3. To like your job and to make a good living are both possible with the right position.

4. Give the framed art print to the boy hanging the other pictures in the Lough Room.

5. The doctor with the beard is an ophthalmologist specializing in cataract surgery.

Rewrite each of these passive voice sentences into active voice, having a doer subject and an action verb.

1. One of the two lots has been sold by the broker.

   _____

2. The officer was commended by the lieutenant for bravery.

   _____

3. Somebody said that the mail was delivered by a substitute.

   _____

4. Good writing techniques were learned by the students.

   _____

5. Your opinion is seldom asked for by me.

   _____

Underline the verb twice and the subject once in the following sentences.

1. Meet me after work to go shopping for the folders.

2. Until yesterday some of our officers were not sworn in.

3. An apple or an orange is not sufficient for a balanced meal.

4. Billy Joel, walking home, noticed a forced lock on the door of the hardware store.

5. Several of the staff have been talking about the robbery.

Tell whether the italicized clause is dependent (D) or independent (I). If dependent, tell whether the clause is adjective (ADJ), adverb (ADV), or noun (N).

1. _____ Someone *that gets angry easily* is probably a troubled person.

2. _____ If you are late, *we will leave without you.*

3. _____ My partner, *until I was free from my other duties,* took charge of all the cases.

4. _____ I appreciate *whoever it is* who found my wallet.

5. _____ Harold Stressor, *who retired this week,* had worked with this company for 43 years.

Indicate whether each of these is a singular (S) or plural (P) possessive.

_____ 1. my sons-in-law's cars   _____ 6. my son-in-law's car

_____ 2. a week's vacation   _____ 7. his family's history

_____ 3. Tom and Ann's son   _____ 8. his parents' mistakes

_____ 4. a heroes' welcome   _____ 9. the animals' tracks

_____ 5. a dollar's worth   _____ 10. the Joneses' house

On the blank write the proper form of the noun/pronoun in parentheses. Some could be possessive cases.

1. Our (church) _____ choir director has had a bad cold for weeks.

2. (Sue and Val) _____ apartments are not as far away from work as

   (Gladys) _____.

3. I bought five (dollar) _____ worth of kitchen (glass)

   _____ at the yard sale; I broke them.

4. Each (gardener) _____ (hose) _____ leaked.

5. The (sheep) _____ (hoof) _____ cut into the
   boards of the old wooden roadway in the field.

Tell whether each clause is a Pattern 1 (S, V); 2(S, V, DO); 3(S, V, IO, DO); or 4(S, LV, SC).

_____ 1. Telephone books are often too large for convenience.

_____ 2. Underneath the table you will find a key to the file.

_____ 3. The key for the file is underneath the table.

_____ 4. Will you please send me one of the catalogs describing the models.

_____ 5. Hand me the ratchet wrench for these lug bolts.

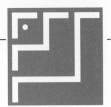

Pronouns

OVERVIEW

- **Four Aspects of Agreement**
- **Personal Pronouns**
- **Indefinite Pronouns**
- **Other Pronouns: Troublesome Usages**
- **Punctuation Points: Commas With Relative Clauses**

Without pronouns the English language would be awkward and wordy. Consider these two sentences.

> When Mr. Marr left Mr. Marr's house this morning at eight o'clock and when Mr. Marr tried to start Mr. Marr's car, Mr. Marr found that the car would not start.

> When *he* left *his* house this morning at eight o'clock, Mr. Marr found *he* could not start *his* car.

You can see from this example that using pronouns improves the clarity and smooth flow of writing as well as avoids the constant repetition that using only nouns produces. A **pronoun** is a word that replaces a noun or other pronoun. As you will learn in this chapter, there are two reasons that these replacement words are needed.

There are many different kinds of pronouns. In this chapter you will study two types—personal and indefinite—in detail. You'll then go on to examine some common grammatical errors associated with some other kinds of pronouns.

FOUR ASPECTS OF AGREEMENT

Pronouns have four aspects that you must consider in your writing.

1. **Number**—whether the pronoun refers to a singular or a plural item.

2. **Gender**—whether the pronoun refers to a male, a female, or an inanimate object.

3. **Case**—whether the pronoun acts as a subject-type word, a possessive-type word, or an object in the clause.

4. **Person**—whether the pronoun represents the speaker, the one spoken to, or the one spoken about.

The following sections will examine these aspects of personal pronouns and indefinite pronouns.

PERSONAL PRONOUNS

One type of pronoun replaces a definite person, place, thing, or idea—such as *Mr. Marr* in the example given at the start of the chapter. By using this group of pronouns, a writer prevents repeating the noun continually. These are **personal pronouns.** You may remember from previous study that *he, she, it,* and *they* are some of these pronouns.

Because a clause can contain many nouns, you must take care to clearly show which noun the pronoun refers to.

Personal pronouns are replacement words for specific nouns; people expect the pronoun to refer to the noun nearest to the pronoun. This noun is called the antecedent of the pronoun, and the pronoun must agree with it, or match it, in number, gender, case, and person.

DEFINITION The **antecedent** of a personal pronoun is the <u>nearest</u> noun or indefinite pronoun, the one the pronoun is replacing.

Read this sentence.

If your coat should lose a button, take *it* to your nearest dealer, and he or she will replace *it*.

Can you tell what you are to take to the dealer? Is it the button or the coat? Since the noun *button* is nearer to the pronoun *it*, seemingly, you are to take the button to the dealer. However, the button has been lost! Will the dealer replace the coat or the button? The final *it* is far from its antecedent, and consequently the antecedent can't be determined. Unless your pronoun is near enough to the noun to make the reference clear, you should probably not use a pronoun but should instead repeat the noun.

Nouns are the common antecedents of personal pronouns, but the indefinite pronouns can also be antecedents, as you will see later in this chapter.

An adjective <u>cannot</u> be an antecedent for a pronoun. Thus, no possessive word can serve as an antecedent. Be careful that each of your pronouns has a correct antecedent. Note the error in the first sentence that is corrected in the second.

Wrong:
I gave Mary's keys to her. [*Her* has no antecedent. *Mary's* is possessive.]

Right:
I gave Mary her keys.

When choosing the pronoun to agree in all respects with its antecedent, keep in mind that the antecedent should be the noun or indefinite pronoun closest to your pronoun. Thus, if <u>two</u> nouns are joined by *or*, your pronoun refers only to the nearer noun, not both.

Notice the pronouns chosen here to agree with the nearer antecedent.

Bill Henderson or his *boys* will give you *their* help with your move. [If you are connecting a singular and a plural with *or*, put the plural last and have the verb and pronouns agree with the plural.]

Either the sales representative or the department head will call you with *his or her* price quotation.

Each personal pronoun must agree with its antecedent in four ways—number, gender, case, and person.

Before looking at each of these aspects, you may want to review the different forms of personal pronouns.

	First Person		Second Person		Third Person	
	Singular	*Plural*	*Singular*	*Plural*	*Singular*	*Plural*
Nominative (or Subjective)	I	We	You	You	He She It	They
Objective	Me	Us	You	You	Him Her It	Them
Possessive	My Mine	Our Ours	Your Yours	Your Yours	His Her Hers Its	Their Theirs

TRY IT OUT: **Before going on, check your understanding of antecedents by doing Exercises 6.1 through 6.4, pp. 155–158.**

Number

Whether your antecedent is singular or plural will determine which of the personal pronouns you choose. There seem to be few errors with this aspect, although you might notice that there is no plural form of *you*. The same form is used for both singular and plural.

Gender

Gender is also obvious, but you will want to decide how to choose the pronoun for such generic nouns as *clerk, instructor, doctor,* and so on. Although a few writers may still use a masculine pronoun for a noun of unknown gender, the trend seems to be moving toward the use of both sex pronouns.

> ***Masculine:***
> Each Senator wrote to *his* constituents.
>
> ***Both:***
> Each Senator wrote to *his or her (his/her)* constituents. [You may use either method.]

Case

Determining the case of personal pronouns is probably the most challenging aspect of pronoun use. More errors are made here than in any other pronoun usage. However, once you have learned the clause patterns and can tell subjects from objects, very little work is left.

Case, you will remember, is the form a pronoun takes depending upon its position in a clause. The pronoun may change form in three cases.

1. **Nominative**—the form for a subject or subject complement.

2. **Objective**—the form for <u>any</u> object in a clause.

3. **Possessive**—the form for any ownership/adjective position.

See if you can choose the correct form in each of these sentences.

1. Just between you and (I, me) I think that our company is the best of its kind in town.
2. Mr. Myers took Allen and (I, me) with (he, him) to Fort Lauderdale.
3. The announcer at the contest was (she, her).
4. Seth and (she, her) left for lunch.

If you choose *me* in Example 1, *me* and *him* in 2, *she* in 3, and *she* in 4, you have no trouble choosing the correct pronoun case. However, if you missed any of these choices, you will want to learn why the answers are what they are. Misused pronouns are very obvious to most educated people, and your errors could be a handicap to you in the future.

Nominative Case

The first pronoun case is the nominative case. It consists of the following pronouns.

I, we, you, he, she, it, they

These nominative case pronouns are used in only two positions in a clause: (1) as subjects or (2) as subject complements. *You* and *it* are more flexible, but the other five pronouns <u>cannot</u> be used as any type of object. Thus, nominative case pronouns should not be used as a direct object, indirect object, or as the object of a preposition. No verbal should have one of the five nominative case pronouns as an object.

On the other hand, you must use one of the nominative case pronouns after a linking verb as the subject complement. Remember, linking verbs do not take objects; only action verbs do.

<u>Do not attempt to choose pronoun case "by ear" or by "what sounds right."</u> Unless your ear has been finely tuned by years of practice with a knowledge of the correct case usage, your ear probably needs a tune-up.

Pronoun case is determined by the position of the word in its clause. Take a look at each of the example sentences again.

#1 and #2 objects needed

```
              PREP  ┌──OBJ──┐    AV                    LV
1. Just (between you and (I, me)) I think that our company is
   the best of its kind in town.
```
I = subj. or subj. comp.
me = obj.

```
            AV  ┌──DO──┐   PREP  OBJ
2. Mr. Myers took Allen and (I, me) (with (he, him)) to Fort
   Lauderdale.
```
I, he = subj. or subj. comp.
me, him = obj.

#3 and #4 subject or subject comp. needed

```
                            LV     SC
3. The announcer at the contest was (she, her).

   ┌──────S──────┐AV
4. Seth and (she, her) left for lunch.
```
she = subj. or subj. comp.
her = obj.

You can see that the only two sentences that have clause positions requiring nominative case pronouns are Examples 3 and 4.

Most people correctly choose the nominative case pronouns to fill the subject positions in clauses but may forget that they must also choose the nominative case for subject complements.

Reviewing the fact that the subject and the subject complement are interchangeable when both name the same person, you can see why the subject complement should be the same type of pronoun as the subject. After all, the subject is not doing anything to the subject complement—it is not the object of any action.

Perhaps if you read these sentences over a few times, you can "tune up" your ear. As you read them, remind yourself that you are using the pronoun that you are because it is a subject complement, not an object.

It is I.	It was Hank and we who won.
It was he.	The people who won are they.
It might have been she.	The leaders were Jim and she.
It could have been they.	It's we at the door.
It wasn't we.	That's he whom you see.
Yes, this is she.	

Read these sentences aloud to help these usages to sound right to you. If, after all of this, you still have difficulty accepting the sound of these subject complement pronouns, don't revert to bad usages by choosing objective case words. Instead, reword your clauses so that you are using your pronouns as subjects, or create sentences that have objects, not subject complements.

Original:
The winners chosen were Yuk Ying and *he.*

As Subject:
Yuk Ying and *he* were chosen as winners.

As Object:
Lulu chose Yuk Ying and *him* as winners.

⌐ S E L F - C H E C K 6 – 1

Underline the correct form of the pronoun in parentheses after deciding whether it is a subject (S) or a subject complement (SC). Put the letters **S** *or* **SC** *on the blank.*

_____ 1. After the game Judy and (she, her) decided to get tickets for the tournament.

_____ 2. Because the dog made more noise than the cat, it was (he, him) Sarah let out first in the morning.

_____ 3. I don't know why Tom thought it might have been (they, them).

_____ 4. Even if it was (he, him), you have no reason to fire him.

_____ 5. The police officer shouted, "That's (she, her)!"

Before you continue, turn to p. 176 to check your answers.

TRY IT OUT: **Complete Exercise 6.5, p. 159, to practice using nominative case pronouns.**

Objective Case

Another pronoun case is the objective case, the case needed to fill all object positions in clauses: direct object, indirect object, object of preposition, and object of any verbal. Because there are generally more objects in clauses than either subjects or subject complements, you will use these forms of the personal pronouns more often than the nominative case forms.

> me, us, you, him, her, it, them

Note that *you* and *it* can be either nominative or objective case pronouns. However, the other five objective case forms can be used <u>only</u> as objects of one kind or another, not as subjects or subject complements.

Earlier in this section were two sentences that used objective case pronouns. Look at them again.

1. Just between you and *me* I think that our company is the best of its kind in town.
2. Mr. Myers took Allen and *me* with *him* to Fort Lauderdale.

Many people forget that *between* is a preposition and requires an object. You will hear this pronoun position misused quite often. Also, *Allen and me* may sound strange to you. For years parents have corrected children to teach them to use the other person's name first in a compound and to use the correct pronoun form <u>in the subject position</u> (*Ed and I are going out*). Thus, many people make the false assumption that any pronoun that is compounded with a name should be a nominative case pronoun. That practice is true only if the compound is used as a subject or subject complement.

Now that you know the clause patterns, you can recognize when the objective case is needed by remembering the following points.

1. If the pronoun isn't a subject or subject complement . . .

2. If it isn't in an ownership/adjective position in the clause . . .

3. It must be an object!

You really don't have to know which type of object you are looking for. You can pick your pronoun form by process of elimination.

Writing Hints: Choosing Case With Than *or* As

Sentences that compare two or more things often join them with the word *than* or *as*. When a pronoun is to be used after one of these comparative words, choosing the case can be somewhat tricky unless you understand how these comparisons work.

The confusion results because the word group following the comparative word *than* or *as* usually is not written out completely; the word group leaves several words understood because they were already stated in the first half of the sentence. You have to check back to the first part of the sentence to study the complete comparison. If that noun/pronoun occupies a subject or subject complement position, choose a nominative case pronoun; if your noun/pronoun is an object in the first half, use an objective case pronoun in the second. You can see how this occurs in these examples.

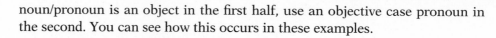

1. *Mary* is as tall as *I* (am tall). [Because *Mary* is the subject of the first part, *I* is meant to be a subject in the second.]

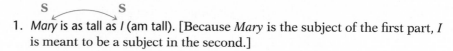

2. Your *firm* spends more money on advertising than *we* (spend). [*Firm* is the subject being compared to *we*, the subject of the understood second clause.]

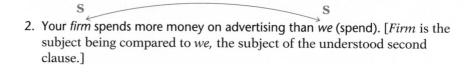

3. a. Mr. Engles chose *Wilfred* for the position rather than (Mr. Engles chose) *me*. [In this case, because *Wilfred* is the direct object of the verb, *me* is needed in the second part to let the reader know that it is meant to be compared to *Wilfred*.]

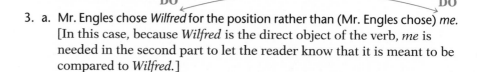

   b. *Mr. Engles* chose Wilfred for the position rather than *I* (chose Wilfred for the position.) [Using the pronoun *I* gives this sentence a meaning quite different from the one in Example 3a. The word following *than—I—* now compares to Mr. Engles, because the nominative suggests subject.]

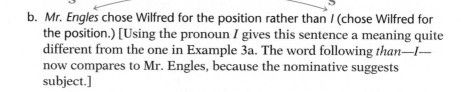

4. a. I would as soon have *Freda* for our chairperson as (have) *him*. [*Him* indicates a comparison to *Freda*, the direct object.]

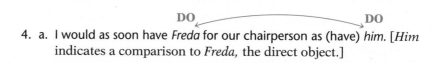

   b. *I* would as soon have Freda for our chairperson as *he* (would have Freda for our chairperson). [This sentence tells about another person's opinion—no longer the opinion of the *I* in Example 4a. *He* indicates a comparison to *I*.]

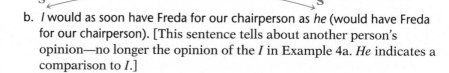

▛ SELF-CHECK 6-2

Answer these questions.

1. Can you name the five personal pronouns that are always nominative?

2. Which are the objective case pronouns?

3. Which two personal pronouns can be either nominative or objective?

4. Which clause positions use nominative case pronouns?

5. Where can you find objective case pronouns?

Before you continue, turn to p. 176 to check your answers.

TRY IT OUT: **You should now be able to select the correct pronouns in Exercises 6.6 through 6.8, pp. 159–161.**

Possessive Case

The possessive case turns pronouns into adjectives; this case does the same with nouns. The possessive case doesn't seem to cause as many usage problems as the other two cases except, perhaps, with the following two points.

1. Singular antecedents require singular pronouns.

2. The personal pronouns use no apostrophes to form the possessive. The apostrophes are saved for pronoun contractions, such as *it's* for *it is*.

   The following is a list of the pronouns in the possessive case.

my	our	your	her	its	their
mine	ours	yours	hers	his	theirs

   These sentences illustrate the use of singular possessive pronouns referring to singular antecedents. Notice that only a contraction of two words has an apostrophe, not the possessive pronouns.

   Everyone has *his or her* own way of doing things.

   You're finished with the report, aren't you?   *You're = You are*

   This company set up *its* new offices.

   These companies helped the Burris plant with *its* production plans.

   I suppose it's too soon to ask the Burris plant about *its* profits.   *it's = it is*

SELF-CHECK 6-3

Underline the correct pronoun in each of the following.

1. The dog wagged (its, it's) tail.

2. (Its, It's) a good time for us to do our inventory.

3. Tell me when (your, you're) ready to leave.

4. Give me (your, you're) name and address.

5. (Theirs, There's) a chance of a storm today.

6. These checks are (theirs, theirs').

7. The jury brought in (its, it's) verdict.

8. Each of the men gave (his, their) response.

9. Neither Ty nor his sons can find (his, their) way back to the ranch.

10. Either the patent or the copyright will protect (its, their) owner.

Before you continue, turn to p. 176 to check your answers.

TRY IT OUT: **Do Exercise 6.9, p. 162, for a short practice in deciding whether to use the form of the pronoun having an apostrophe or the form without.**

⊡ Person

The fourth aspect of all pronouns is the form dictated by the person of the pronoun, which is determined by the antecedent's person. A pronoun can be classified as showing one of three "persons."

1. **First person**—any pronoun that names the speaker or writer.

    I, me, my, mine, we, us, our, ours

2. **Second person**—any pronoun that refers to the person being addressed.

    you, your, yours

3. **Third person**—any pronoun referring to other persons, places, things, or ideas—those being spoken about.

    he, his, she, her, hers, it, its, him, they, them, their, theirs

These forms don't seem to present many difficulties except for a much too common misuse of the second person *you*. This error could be called the "vague *you*" usage because the writer or speaker shifts from the correct person to *you* even though the second person is not being considered.

Study these examples of vague *you* usage.

3rd person   *2nd*
Many people get very angry when *you* get too close to them physically. [People get angry when *anyone* gets too close, not just the reader or listener.]

1st   *2nd*
Sometimes, when I feel like dropping out of school and just giving up, *you* get discouraged. [Writer means to say "*I* get discouraged."]

As the examples show, this error really results from a faulty shift from one person to another.

TRY IT OUT: **Correct faulty pronoun shifts in Exercise 6.10, p. 162, to check your understanding of this concept.**

INDEFINITE PRONOUNS

Another type of pronoun is needed when a definite person, place, thing, or idea cannot be named. Perhaps you are generalizing about many people and cannot name each, or you may not know who or what it is that you are describing. The following sentences should help to identify this second type of pronoun, the **indefinite pronoun.**

Everybody in the class likes English usage. — *You don't need to name all 30 here.*

Someone has stolen my wallet! — *You don't know whom to name.*

Unlike a personal pronoun, which acts as a substitute after a specific noun has been named, an indefinite pronoun has no antecedent. The someone or something the pronoun refers to is unspecified. Often, the indefinite pronoun is <u>itself</u> followed by a personal pronoun. Thus, it is the indefinite pronoun and the personal pronoun that must agree in number, gender, case, and person.

◲ Number

Some indefinite pronouns are fairly easy to use because they are always plural: *both, few, many, several.*

A few others can be used as either singular or plural depending upon the writer's intent: *all, any, more, most, none, some.*

However, most indefinite pronouns are always singular. Following are the common singular indefinite pronouns.

another	everybody	no one
anybody	everyone	nothing
anyone	everything	one
anything	many a . . .	somebody
each	neither	someone
either	nobody	something
every	none	

All of the words in the list are always considered to be singular, representing only one person, place, thing, or idea. Each of these singular pronouns is used to make a general statement about someone or something: The pronoun represents the <u>typical</u> example of what is being described and is not meant to act in the plural. It is as though each is being described one at a time to better emphasize.

The sentence "Everybody has tickets to the convention" emphasizes that each and every "body" is going to the convention. Each person is as important as each other person and should not be just put into the group, as in "All of us have tickets to the convention."

Become familiar with these singular indefinite pronouns. Knowing they are singular will remind you to use a singular verb when one of these pronouns is the subject of your clause. Chapter 10 delineates the rules for the agreement of subjects and verbs.

As mentioned, a personal pronoun can refer to an indefinite pronoun. A pronoun that refers to one of these singular indefinite pronouns should also be singular, since pronouns must agree in number with the words they represent. For instance, it would be incorrect to write "Everyone should do *their* own work," because *their* is plural and *everyone* is singular.

Wrong:
Someone should see if *their* dog is barking.

Correct:
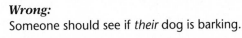
Someone should see if *his or her* dog is barking.

Wrong:
Each of the women should do *their* own knitting.

Correct:
Each of the women should do *her* own knitting.

Gender

Because the indefinite pronouns name typical or unknown items, deciding the gender can be a challenge when you are choosing another pronoun to agree in gender. If no person is referred to, *it/its* would be used for singular and *they/their/them* for plural agreement.

Either of the grains has *its* own properties.

Many of the old cars poured out *their* fumes.

If people are involved, the pronoun must carry the same sex reference. Many sentences, however, do not make this clear. In the past it was common to use masculine references (*he, him,* or *his*) if a singular unknown person were named. More recently, though, either sex is accommodated by using pronouns that refer to both sexes. Here are some examples.

Anybody needs *his or her* ego boosted.

Everyone is responsible for *himself/herself.*

Few of my classmates plan to go to *their* commencement exercises.

As you might imagine, these constructions can appear awkward, particularly in more complex sentences. Often, the solution lies in rewording the sentence to get rid of the second pronoun.

Anybody needs an ego boost.

Case

Indefinite pronouns remain in the same form whether they are subjects or objects. A form change is needed, however, to make an indefinite pronoun possessive. Only the singular indefinite pronouns can act as possessives, and because none of them ends in -*s*, they form the possessive by adding -*'s.*

Here are *somebody's* keys.
What he said is *nobody's* business.

Person

All of the indefinite pronouns refer to someone or something spoken about, not to the speaker or the person being directly addressed. Thus, personal pronouns used to replace these indefinite pronouns should be third-person pronouns that refer to other persons or things.

Wrong:
Anyone with car problems should bring *your* car to Joe's Service Station.

Correct:
Anyone with car problems should bring *his or her* car to Joe's Service Station.

Wrong:
Each of us decided to drive *our* own car.

Correct:
Each of us decided to drive *his or her* own car.

SELF-CHECK 6-4

Tell whether each statement is true (T) or false (F).

_____ 1. A pronoun is used to replace a noun.

_____ 2. An indefinite pronoun is one that replaces a known noun.

_____ 3. An indefinite pronoun is one that stands in for an unknown or typical person, place, thing, or idea.

_____ 4. With a handful of exceptions, most indefinite pronouns are singular.

_____ 5. Pronouns can be found in any noun position in a clause, such as subject, subject complement, or any object.

_____ 6. If a later pronoun refers to a singular indefinite pronoun, that second pronoun must be singular.

_____ 7. If a later pronoun refers to a singular indefinite pronoun, that second pronoun should represent both sexes, saying such things as *his or her*.

_____ 8. The person referred to by a singular indefinite pronoun is unknown and could be a man or a woman.

_____ 9. To use pronouns that refer only to men when referring to a singular indefinite pronoun is considered sexist.

_____ 10. All singular indefinite pronouns add -*'s* when put into the possessive case.

Before you continue, turn to p. 177 to check your answers.

OTHER PRONOUNS: TROUBLESOME USAGES

Sometimes other pronoun usages prove to be troublesome. A brief review of some of these should be helpful.

This/That; These/Those. When these words are used as adjectives, *this* and *that* are used to modify singular nouns; *these* and *those* are used for plural. *This* and *these* are closer, and *that* and *those* are farther away.

> This is the *way* to do this problem.
> These are the *ways* it can be done.
> This *kind* of book is easy to read.
> Those *kinds* of books are for experts only.
> I don't want that *nail* over there; I need this *one,* closer to my elbow.

(*Note: Them* is an objective case pronoun and cannot be used as an adjective to modify a noun. It would be incorrect to say, "Give me them nails over there.")

Who's/Whose. The contraction *who's* means "who is."

> *Who's* going to submit this memo under his or her name?
> I wonder *who's* going to be promoted this year.

The possessive pronoun *whose* modifies a noun, showing ownership.

> *Whose* car is that one being towed away?
> You went to *whose* office for the interview?
> The man *whose* car was hit was taken to the hospital.

Who/Whom; Whoever/Whomever; Which/That. These sets of relative pronouns often begin the noun or adjective clauses that you studied in Chapter 4. To choose one of these words for a clause, you must first decide whether the noun modified by this clause is a person, an animal, a place, or a thing.

- *Who, whoever, whom,* and *whomever* refer to people.
- *Which* refers to animals, places, or things and <u>usually</u> begins a nonrestrictive clause, one that needs commas.
- *That* can refer to anything, human or not, but the clause that begins with *that* should be restrictive, having no commas.

Although most people use *who/whom* or *that* interchangeably when referring to people, careful writers use *who/whom* when the clause modifying the "person" is telling something about the individuality of the person; *that* is used when the person is being added to a type of category of people.

My mother was a woman *who* meant business when she told me to do something.

Lincoln was the type of man *that* could be counted on to tell the truth.

The question of how to distinguish between *who* and *whom* should not be difficult now that you understand that sentences are made up of independent clauses and modifying clauses. Once you have decided that you should use *who* or *whom* because you are modifying a noun that names a person or people, you have to choose <u>between</u> *who* and *whom*.

The choice is based on the position in the clause that the word will occupy. *Who* is a nominative case pronoun and acts as a subject or a subject complement. *Whom* is objective case and acts as any object in a clause.

Note that *who* is used in all of these sentences because it is occupying a nominative position in its own clause.

Mr. Bradley, <u>who is</u> a teacher, has been here for thirteen years. [subject of adjective clause]

Do you know <u>who ate</u> the pizza I had saved? [subject of noun clause]

The <u>winner is</u> who? [subject complement of main clause]

Now look at some clauses with *whom*. These clauses already have subjects and don't need subject complements; thus, the pronoun acts as some type of object in its clause. To choose *whom* you don't have to know which object it is but would only have to determine that *whom* is <u>not acting as a subject or subject complement</u>.

I wrote the letter, "To whom <u>it may concern</u>." [Because *it* is the subject of the second clause, *whom* is an object; in this case, the object of the preposition.]

The captain of the ship is a man whom his <u>sailors trust</u>. [Because *sailors* is the subject of the verb *trust* in the clause, *whom* is an object—the direct object of *trust*.]

Alfred Gemrich, whom <u>you elected</u> to office, has a good voting record. [Because *you* is the subject of the modifying clause, *whom* is an object, the direct object of *elected*.]

You can see that isolating the relative pronoun clause from the rest of the sentence is mandatory if you are to choose correctly between *who* and *whom*.

Underline the correct pronoun in these sentences. It will be helpful to put parentheses around the clause containing the relative pronoun so that you can see how the pronoun is used in the clause.

1. Students (who, whom) work hard usually do well.

2. Mr. Reedy is a man (who, whom) everyone counts on.

3. The student (who, whom) the speaker referred to is my sister.

4. Mr. Lenderink is an insurance salesman (who, whom) represents many companies.

5. Give the data to (whoever, whomever) is in charge.

6. She will accept (whoever, whomever) we select.

7. The singer, (who, whom) all of the audience applauded, came back for an encore.

8. Marilyn Longjohn, (who, whom) majored in business in college, works for United Airlines.

9. May I ask to (who, whom) you wish to speak?

10. People (who, whom) think before they speak are seldom sorry for what they have said.

Before you continue, turn to p. 177 to check your answers.

The examples used in Self-Check 6–5, as with most relative pronoun clauses, have no interrupters that make the clause more difficult to distinguish. Sometimes, though, an extra idea is inserted into the relative pronoun clause.

$$\overset{\text{V} \quad \ulcorner \text{V} \urcorner}{}$$

He is a man (who, whom) I know will do a good job.

When more than one verb follows the *who/whom,* one of two structures is present: (1) The main clause is split by the *who/whom* clause, or (2) there are two more clauses in addition to the main clause.

The example sentence has the first clause completed *(He is a man)* before the relative pronoun. Two verbs follow the *who/whom,* and you must decide which verb goes with the relative pronoun. Are you modifying the noun *man* with the clause *I know*? In other words, are you saying he is a man *whom you know*? That could be the case, but in this particular sentence, *will do a good job* would be left over. If the *I know* were removed, the sentence would say, "He is a man who will do a good job." The *I know* is an opinion—an extra idea—inserted into the middle of the adjective clause.

The correct pronoun is *who*. Had you tried to connect the pronoun to the wrong clause, you would have chosen *whom*.

Whenever an opinion comes after the relative pronoun, be careful that you do not select it as a part of your relative clause. Watch for words such as these: *think, believe, know, feel,* and so on.

TRY IT OUT: Complete Exercises 6.11 and 6.12, pp. 163–164.

 # PUNCTUATION POINTS: COMMAS WITH RELATIVE CLAUSES

Punctuating phrases and clauses with personal and indefinite pronouns is the same as punctuating those with nouns; see Chapter 5 to review those rules.

Punctuation questions associated with pronouns usually concern the relative pronouns. The comma rules that apply to relative pronoun clauses were presented in Chapter 4. However, it would be good to review the rules and have some practice with the commas.

1. Noun clauses start with relative pronouns: No commas are used to separate the noun clause from the main clause.

2. Adjective clauses begin with relative pronouns, immediately follow nouns or pronouns, and modify them.

   a. Restrictive adjective clauses are necessary to clarify the noun for the meaning of the main clause. Use no commas to set the restrictive clause off from the main clause.

   b. Nonrestrictive adjective clauses add extra information about one of the nouns in a sentence. Because the modifying idea is not essential to the meaning of the clause, commas set off the nonessential clause from the main clause.

3. *That* clauses are considered essential to the meaning of the main clause; because they are restrictive, *that* clauses have no commas.

4. *Which* clauses are usually nonessential and thus set off by commas. The exception is the occasional situation where the writer made the clause essential.

Review your comma usage skills by adding only necessary commas to the following sentences.

1. John Wayne who starred in several movies often played the role of a cowboy.

2. This typewriter which we just purchased has a correcting tape included within it.

3. Men who beat their wives make poor husbands.

4. Please hand me the manual that is on Betty's desk.

5. No one who is a poor speller should give up with that as an excuse.

Before you continue, turn to p. 177 to check your answers.

TRY IT OUT: **Complete Exercises 6.13 and 6.14, pp. 165–166, to complete your work with pronouns. Exercise 6.15, pp. 167–168, will challenge your understanding.**

▣ Chapter 6: Pronouns

● E X E R C I S E 6.1

For each sentence write the personal pronoun(s) and the antecedent(s) in the spaces provided.

	Pronoun	Antecedent
1. Mr. Robertson plans to replace his car this year.	_____	_____
2. When they finish, the committee members will have a new plan.	_____	_____
3. The majority of the population does not make its vote count.	_____	_____
4. Tell Mr. Foster that Mr. Green will see him now.	_____	_____
5. One of the application letters showed its writer to be a qualified applicant.	_____	_____
6. Mrs. Burns has not used any of her sick days for the last five years.	_____	_____
7. The carton of books fell on its side and broke.	_____	_____
8. Those businesses that treat their personnel fairly will have very little attrition in their staffs.	_____	_____
9. Mr. Shields told Ms. Romans that he could not accept her work with so many errors.	_____	_____
10. Will each of you students please submit his or her application for the work-study opening in the Accounting Department.	_____	_____

Rewrite these sentences so that the antecedent is clearly understood.

1. Todd and Bill went to Bill's house, where he gave him the money he owed him.

   _____

   _____

2. If you have misplaced the instruction booklet that comes with the oven, just ask your dealer for a new one, and he/she will deliver it to your home.

   _____

   _____

3. When Mr. Ralston talked with Mr. Evans, he told him that he should sell his stocks while the market is high.

   _____

   _____

4. Any company that stands behind a product will find that it can't produce enough of it for its customers.

   _____

   _____

5. When I told you that I won the lottery but lost the check, I told you how upset I was by it.

   _____

   _____

● E X E R C I S E 6.3

Underline the correct pronoun in the following sentences. Be sure to locate the antecedent first and determine its number, gender, and person. Remember that your subject will not be in a prepositional phrase.

1. Has anyone bought (his or her, their) ticket for the drawing?

2. Some of the deliveries are on (its, their) way.

3. Some of the money is on (its, their) way.

4. Has one of the catalogs been through (its, their) first printing yet?

5. Each of the students hoped that (his or her, their) test scored 100 percent.

6. Won't someone please start (his or her, their) car and try to start to clear the parking lot?

7. I don't know whether Selma or Sadie remembered (her, their) program.

8. Either Ms. Samuels or her daughters will plan (her, their) vacation.

9. Mr. Thompson and Mr. Seeley plan to have (his, their) branch sale on December 10.

10. One of the customers presented (his, their) complaints to the Service Manager.

11. Whenever I have to speak in front of a group, (you, I) can feel (your, my) knees start to shake.

12. The Board of Trustees made (its, their) decision regarding the matter of raises for the administrators.

13. (You, I) never want to get too close to (your, my) neighbors because (you, I) can never tell what they might do.

14. Each and every one of the candidates had an equal chance to present (his or her, their) views.

15. If only one-half of the candidates would cast (its, their) vote, we would have a better representation of the people's feelings.

● E X E R C I S E 6.4

Fill in each blank with a pronoun that agrees with its antecedent.

1. The club wanted _____ members to vote for

   _____ choices for the Executive Committee.

2. Several people wanted _____ money returned when the show was canceled.

3. Neither of the ladies wanted _____ name to appear in the newspaper article.

4. Either of the two should notify _____ boss if

_____ cannot attend the annual meeting.

5. Many of the Senators voted the way _____ constituents wanted

_____ to.

6. Each doctor and lawyer is responsible for doing the best _____ can for

_____ patients or clients.

7. Because no one expressed _____ dissatisfaction with the plan, we will
have to report directly to Mr. George from now on.

8. Either the judge or his assistants will help us with _____ part of the
preparation for our trial.

9. A few of the women wanted _____ scores to be added to the total;

however, none of us wanted _____ scores added.

10. Everyone should send _____ scores to the Director.

11. Either of the doctors said that _____ would assist us.

12. Many a student wants to have _____ work recognized.

13. Mr. Farmer or Miss Sundry said that either _____ would be happy to

have us use _____ apartment for the party.

14. Someone left _____ lights on all night last night.

15. Some companies give _____ employees two days off for Labor Day.

16. Does anyone have _____ watch that has the correct time?

17. Could someone check _____ watch to tell me what time it is.

18. None of the tellers could get _____ receipts to balance yesterday.

19. This branch of our company always has _____ report in on time.

20. Many of the receptionists complained that _____ bosses do not give

enough instructions for _____ to deal with sensitive phone calls.

● E X E R C I S E 6.5

Underline the correct pronoun case in the following. On the blank indicate whether the pronoun is a subject (S) or a subject complement (SC).

_____ 1. Mr. Engles knew that it was (I, me) who had corrected the report.

_____ 2. Sarah Donohue and (she, her) submitted their names for promotion.

_____ 3. It was (we, us) men who had repaired the door.

_____ 4. If the winner is (he, him) be sure to call Cindy Kroeg immediately.

_____ 5. The golf team that scored the highest was Mr. Pearson and (he, him).

_____ 6. Tom declared that it could have been (he, him) who had misplaced the file.

_____ 7. The sales people who sold the most textbooks were (they, them).

_____ 8. It must have been Sally and (she, her).

_____ 9. It might be (I, me) who stays up late to study.

_____ 10. Mrs. Dickens and (he, him) went to the PTA meeting.

_____ 11. The referees for the company baseball game were Fast Eddy and (he, him).

_____ 12. Yes, it was (we, us) who called you late last night.

_____ 13. The sponsors for the show will be Walgreen's and (we, us).

_____ 14. I had hoped that Paul and (I, me) could attend the showing, but (we, us) were called out of town.

_____ 15. Several of the workers were dissatisfied with the contract, but (we, us) in data processing were happy with it.

● E X E R C I S E 6.6

Underline the pronouns that correctly complete the following sentences. Hint: An objective case pronoun is either a direct object, an indirect object, an object of a preposition, or an object of a verbal.

1. He assigned Lester and (I, me) to finish the project.

2. Give the contract to (I, me) before it is mislaid.

3. The people chosen for the play were to report to (they, them) before rehearsals.

4. To know (he, him) is to love (he, him).

CHAPTER 6 ● Pronouns   **159**

5. By asking (she, her) to do the typing, Ms. Pearson was assured of good work.

6. Helene asked (we, us) women to attend the fashion show.

7. Herb Scott wanted Shirley and (she, her) to rewrite the paper to remove sexist language.

8. If you are ready, will you please ask (we, us) to take our places in line.

9. Between you and (I, me) the last thing I want to do is work late on Friday.

10. Ms. Parker put the new secretary at a desk behind (we, us) other employees.

11. After telling (we, us) infield players that we should move in closer, the coach changed her mind.

12. We are always permitted to see any new regulations that concern (we, us) interns.

13. Jeremy, along with Tom and (I, me), attended the opening of the sales show.

14. Did Lisa want to see (she, her) and (I, me)?

15. The party was planned to honor (they, them).

● E X E R C I S E   6 . 7

Decide whether the pronoun acts as a subject or subject complement or as some type of object, and then underline the correct choices in the following sentences.

1. Mr. Sutton, Mr. Black, and (he, him) were chosen for the panel about business ethics.

2. It may have been (I, me) who left the lights on in the storeroom.

3. Please give those notes to James or (he, him).

4. Please give James or (he, him) these notes.

5. The owners of the building are the Whites and (they, them).

6. (We, us) personnel directors are planning an in-service training session for February 20.

7. During the month-end closeout the largest number of items was sold by (she, her).

8. The person responsible for balancing the books is (she, her).

9. I am surprised that (we, us) students can do so well in English grammar.

10. We sent (they, them) the memo this morning.

11. She is a better tennis player than (I, me).

12. Rafer Johnson is not so fast a runner as (he, him).

13. Ms. Heffner could as easily have chosen Alicia as (I, me).

14. Do you believe that you can sell as many items as (they, them)?

15. She could quote the price of this order as well as (I, me).

● E X E R C I S E   6 . 8

Underline the correct pronoun for each, depending on how it is used in the clause.

1. The men who will establish the new branch office are Abraham Kohn and (he, him).

2. The choice is between Mr. Morales and (he, him).

3. Two of the workers with the longest tenure are Miss Frey and (she, her).

4. We went with (they, them) to the annual flower show in Chelsea.

5. I asked Mr. Belding and (she, her) to make copies of the amendment.

6. Among (we, us) students Manuel is the one to ask for help.

7. Mary Louise Barden and (he, him) planned all of these sessions.

8. Have you asked (they, them) to do the solicitations?

9. My sister said that the winner of the drawing is (she, her).

10. We decided to settle the bill between (we, us).

11. It was (I, me) who asked you to come in early today.

12. The visitors to the plant yesterday were Mr. Bowles and (he, him).

13. As far as I know, no one but (he, him) had access to that particular folder.

14. Mr. Wu took Mr. Rutgers and (I, me) to lunch yesterday.

15. Could it have been (we, us) who were chosen to handle the Springfield account?

16. I placed the order for a new stereo with (he, him).

17. I heard him asking Mr. Towne and (she, her) to proofread the final report before it was mailed.

18. The man sitting by Ms. Courter and (she, her) is my immediate supervisor, W. J. Upjohn.

19. When he asked who was responsible for the slip-up, I had to admit that it was (I, me).

20. Do you suppose it could have been (they, them) who called you?

Underline the correct pronoun form to complete each of these.

1. (Their's, Theirs', Theirs) is the house on the left corner ahead.

2. I know (it's, its) difficult to study with so many other things happening now.

3. Is the book (her's, hers) or (your's, yours)?

4. He decided (their, they're) ready to settle the contract.

5. The panda rolled over (it's, its) offspring, but no harm was done.

6. The baseball is (our, ours'), but the bat is Jim's.

7. (There's, Theirs) no way I can handle another class this semester because (its, it's) been so busy at work that I have lots of overtime.

8. What is (you're, your) plan to solve the overcrowding that has occurred with the higher enrollments?

9. An old song begins "When (its, it's) hot, (it's, its) hot!"

10. Ms. Hui says that it is (your, you're) planning that needs more careful consideration.

Correct any pronouns that show a shift in person. Write the correct form above the incorrect one.

1. Whenever I see an accident, you get all sick to your stomach.

2. Mable said she hates to fail a student, but you have to sometimes.

3. I don't know if I will decide to replace my carpet or not, but I hope you don't have to make that decision very soon.

4. Sandy said that he loves to photograph live subjects as well as inanimate objects, but he thinks you should take special care when photographing people.

5. Mary is strict about disciplining her children and thinks you should spank your children if necessary.

● E X E R C I S E 6 . 1 1

Underline the correct pronoun.

1. Please hand me (those, them) wrenches.

2. I never did like (that, those) kinds of cars.

3. (This, These) is the type of stencil I like to use.

4. Do you have any of (those, them, that) kind of paper holders for these files?

5. A man (who, whom, which) likes his job will usually do better work than a man (who, whom) is not interested in his job.

6. Stella was the one (who, whom) we all wanted to receive the promotional award.

7. The student (who, whom) really wants to learn will put more into his or her studies than those (who, whom) just want to get a job.

8. The graduate (who, whom) has really learned his or her basic studies is sure to be able to hold the job he or she gets.

9. Mr. Toussaint is a man (who, whom) we all respect.

10. She is a member of a law firm (who, that) really cares about its clients.

11. Politicians (who, whom) the people trust are those (who, whom) are honest with their public.

12. Please give these letters to (whoever, whomever) is at the desk.

13. Several of those candidates are men (who, whom, which) the Winston Agency recommended.

14. Mrs. Stanislaus is the one to (who, whom) you should pay your deposit.

15. This contract, (who, whom, which) was signed by Mrs. Carson, will be duplicated for you right away.

16. Several of the managers (who, whom) the company fired have worked here for more than ten years.

17. I want to hire an assistant (who, whom) can spell and (who, whom) knows how to punctuate a letter.

18. He is the type of person (who, whom) people can easily talk to.

19. (Whoever, Whomever) knows how to do double-entry bookkeeping is eligible for that position.

20. Anyone (who, whom) Ms. Henry knows has a better chance for the opening than a stranger would.

Underline the correct relative pronouns in the following sentences. Be sure that you are not misled by an interrupter that simply adds an opinion to the relative pronoun clause.

1. (Who, Whom) is the person (who, whom) Mr. Sorsby believes can do the best job?

2. She is a woman (who, whom) I know is capable.

3. John is a man (who, whom) I feel will represent our firm very well in front of the Supreme Court.

4. Sally Wong is the best of all of the laboratory technicians (who, whom) the Personnel Department hired last year.

5. The sales representative from St. Louis is the woman (who, whom) Mr. Bernstein said knows the product better than the engineers.

6. She was the contestant (who, whom) everyone thought should win.

7. Mr. Ames, (who, whom) you know, is my neighbor.

8. Mr. Ames is one (who, whom) you know you can trust.

9. To (who, whom) did you want this copy to be mailed?

10. People (who, whom) have a negative attitude are not very pleasant to be around.

11. My new car, (which, that) is a sedan, is much easier to get into and out of than my sports car was.

12. Maria Elena Juarez, (who, whom) *Records* magazine lists as this year's top vocalist, has a band (which, that) is all female.

13. I saw the man (who, whom) police think robbed the corner market this afternoon.

14. I know (who, whom) to trust and (who, whom) cannot be trusted.

15. Please send these coupons to (whoever, whomever) purchased discount booklets last year.

16. I have a shy cat, (who, which) is named Oreo, that stays in the closet whenever I have company.

17. You should buy a newer, more powerful computer, (which, that) will save you lots of time.

18. The manager, (who, whom) I trust can be reached very soon, will have to deal with the insistent customer.

19. The manager is a woman (who, whom) I trust to handle this situation with grace and finesse.

20. (Whoever, Whomever) you decide to select for the promotion should be a person (who, whom) already works in the Payroll Department.

● EXERCISE 6.13

If the relative pronoun clause is nonrestrictive, use commas to set it off from the rest of the sentence. Some of these sentences will have restrictive clauses that require no commas because the clause is needed to define the noun. Circle any changes you make.

1. The clerk who waited on you rang up the sale incorrectly.

2. Yesterday I talked with John Thomas who manages the Denver office.

3. I enjoy a person who has a good attitude toward life and who is optimistic about the future.

4. Any employee who does not like the policies of his or her company should probably look for another position in another company.

5. Frank Wolfe who has taught for several years is one of the best instructors at Santa Monica College.

6. You will find that those who started at the bottom of the ladder are much more appreciative of success than those who never had to make the effort.

7. I want you to meet Janae Daniels who will be taking over Ms. Nissen's place when she retires.

8. Mrs. Hannifer about whom everyone speaks so well will tell you about her new manuscript.

9. Eileen Saxby who just returned from the Middle East is very excited about our expansion plans there.

10. The Goodman Company which just moved here from Tennessee will open its new offices in September.

11. President Martino whom you already know will be introduced to our staff at the next meeting.

12. Any person who does his or her own income tax return must be very careful to read all of the rules in the instruction booklet.

13. Several members who were dissatisfied with our insurance plan did research to find a better one.

14. I just saw Mr. Baker who has a new job at Miller and Sons.

15. Many applicants each of whom submitted a data sheet and an application letter were considered for this position.

16. I would like to meet a person who feels as strongly about this idea as I.

17. I know the Mrs. Essex who works for Brown Company but not the one who sells insurance.

18. e. e. cummings who wrote poetry used almost no capital letters.

19. The man who is wearing the trench coat is the one, Officer.

20. Bill Jacobs who is wearing the trench coat sells air compressors for Joy Manufacturing.

Add any necessary commas to the following sentences. Remember, clauses that begin with that *should be restrictive, using no commas. Circle any changes you make.*

1. Any student who really cares about his or her work's impression will study very hard while he or she has the opportunity.

2. Bruce Dannenhaur who painted his house last summer plans to refinish his dining room set this year.

3. Any employee who is not assertive cannot expect everyone else to help him or her get ahead.

4. Each person who pays for a first-class ticket is assured of a seat in the best section of the airplane, the section with more seat room.

5. Those companies that recognize the efforts of their employees will have satisfied personnel.

6. Fruit that is spoiled cannot be sold.

7. This math book which is published by Stanton and Burgess is a good one for a review of the basics.

8. Any employee who cares about the image of the company will do better than one who has no concern for its success.

9. Any plant that needs lots of sunlight will not do well in a shady spot.

10. This is Sandra Shaw who works in the Admissions area of the college.

11. Vaughn Menck who just won a million dollars in the lottery plans to retire at 35.

12. Of the two cars I prefer the one that gets 25 miles to a gallon of gasoline.

13. The train that goes to Sussex leaves at 7:33.

14. Train No. 178 which stops at Sussex leaves at 7:33.

15. We have three sons all of whom play football and tennis.

16. You may use my lighter which is on the table near you.

17. The office draperies which are made of linen are to be taken to the cleaners today.

18. You should put it on the table that is by the door.

19. Our neighbor's dog which barks all night is a beagle.

20. Our swimming pool which is built into the ground is a nice place to spend a hot afternoon.

● E X E R C I S E 6.15 CHALLENGE

Make any necessary corrections, including commas, in Mr. Hudson's memorandum. Circle any changes you make.

To: All Personnel

From: Henry Hudson

Subject: Year-end Review

All of you are aware that our company has made many changes in their staff this past year. Its been a good year for all of us and the changes seem to have helped to make it so. I am writing this memorandum to thank all of those whom has helped this transition to come about as smoothly as it has.

Mr. Jones who is head of Personnel has done much to improve the conditions of all of we employees. His work in recruiting new staff has brought us many interested people, whom want to help Atlas to get ahead. Of all of those who has done much here this past year, it's him who has done the most.

I'd like to congratulate those people on the staff of the Personnel Department who have assisted Mr. Jones in his search for employees, who would be a great addition to our company. You're canvassing of local colleges has brought many new people to us. Because we have been growing so fast in the last three years, we have had to do much more hiring than in previous years. Your new recruits seem to be of superior quality. One of our local competitors said to me recently that we seem to have had a much better pick of the candidates than him.

The changes made by we administrators in the Sales Department seem to have made a great difference. This year our sales were 25 percent better than last year. Ours' is the only one of all of the company's branches which have increased sales by so big a margin.

Your all aware, I am sure, that our President, Mack Collins, is very pleased with our progress. Anyone whose a part of the growth of this year will be rewarded. Each one of you who is part of our firm will receive a 5 percent raise in you're next paycheck.

Miss Phillips is another member of our staff whom I know deserves a word of thanks for her efforts. Mr. Jones and her have worked together on many studies to pinpoint our company's needs. Mr. Jones told me that the one to thank is her.

Its always a real pleasure to be able to write a memorandum like this. No one could be happier than me to offer you the congratulations you deserve. Someone, who is in my position, often has a memorandum of another kind to write. It is these type that I prefer. Thank you all for giving me this opportunity.

Heres to an even better year next year!

A N S W E R S   T O   S E L F - C H E C K   P R A C T I C E

Chapter 1: Phrases and Clauses

Self-Check 1–1, p. 4

1. <u>of</u> the President; <u>on</u> the second floor
2. <u>except</u> the office clerks; <u>to</u> the meeting; <u>at</u> the Regency Hotel
3. <u>without</u> Ms. Cady; <u>in</u> Dallas
4. <u>to</u> Ms. Smith and Ms. Halsted; <u>for</u> proofreading
5. <u>by</u> the window; <u>in</u> the bedroom

Self-Check 1–2, p. 6

1. Check your answers with the list on p. 5.
2. A group of related words with a preposition and an object of the preposition but which does not contain a subject or a verb.
3. No.
4. No.
5. No, only if it is a part of a phrase and has an object.

Self-Check 1–3, p. 7

1. A clause has a subject and a verb; a phrase does not.
2. No, not unless it contains a complete thought.
3. Yes, at lease one, oftentimes more than one.
4. A subject and a verb.
5. The verb.

Self-Check 1–4, p. 10

1. My boss, by the way, gave me the afternoon off.
2. No commas. The phrase *in the third drawer* tells where.
3. In other words, you cannot help me.
4. No commas. Were you fooled? This is a rare case when *in other words* tells how he tried to put it.

5. No commas! *On Monday* tells when. Don't be misled by phrases at the beginning of sentences. Do not use commas after them unless they are nonessential or very long.

6. Mr. Scott, by the way, submitted his resignation on Monday.

7. We hope, for example, to double the Snapp account.

8. No commas. The phrases *as a result of carelessness* tell why.

9. No commas. The phrases *as a rule of the association* tell why.

10. Ms. Kozlowski, as a rule, is very generous with her praise.

Chapter 2: Verbs and Verbals

Self-Check 2–1, p. 16

1. <u>shelf</u> <u>paper</u> <u>remained</u>; L
2. <u>Einstein</u> <u>proved</u>; A
3. <u>I</u> <u>tasted</u>; A
4. <u>mushroom</u> <u>tasted</u>; L
5. <u>idea</u> <u>sounds</u>; L

Self-Check 2–2, p. 20

1. to remove his tensions
2. Driving a company car
3. Flying on commercial flights; to arrive [You may include *at her meetings on time* because it completes the idea of the verbal *to arrive*.]
4. To win the account; verb = called
5. to win the account; verb = wanted
6. winding up the meeting; verb = called
7. Driving; verb = could cover
8. Called EXEL; verb = proved

Self-Check 2–3, p. 22

1. A group of related words with a subject and a verb.
2. A word that shows action or links the subject to something else in the clause.
3. Action and linking.
4. No.
5. Am, is, are, was, were, be (been, being).
6. The word's doer is the subject of the clause, and the word tells the main action.
7. An infinitive phrase contains a verblike word; a prepositional phrase has only a person, place, thing, or idea after the preposition.
8. Yes, if joined by *or, nor,* or *and.*
9. No, only if it has a helping verb and a doer subject.
10. A main verb together with any of its helping verbs.

Self-Check 2–4, p. 24

1. She was nervous, jumpy, and <u>panicky</u>.
2. Hating quiet, Theron always had the radio playing, the television set blaring, and <u>the upstairs CD player going</u>.
3. Deciding to return to school, to take a part-time job, and <u>to quit his full-time job</u>, Mark was ready for September 12 to arrive.
4. The hunters packed their guns, put the dogs in the car, and <u>stored their suitcases in the trunk</u>.
5. You may do one or the other: Take 16 credit hours next term, or <u>graduate later that you had planned</u>.

Chapter 3: More About Verbs

Self-Check 3–1, p. 35

1. Time.
2. Regular.
3. Irregular.
4. Six.
5. Permanently true.

Self-Check 3–2, p. 36

1. admitted
2. slipped
3. wearied
4. attacked
5. benefited
6. appealed
7. referred
8. offered
9. conveyed
10. permitted

Self-Check 3–3, p. 39

1. Time
2. Six
3. Will
4. Perfect participle
5. True
6. Has
7. Present
8. -s
9. -ed
10. False. *Should have studied is* correct.

Self-Check 3–4, p. 41

1. Six
2. Perfect participle
3. Has or have
4. Had
5. Will have
6. Past and now
7. Two pasts, one before the other
8. Action completed by a deadline set in the future

Self-Check 3–5, p. 48

1. The order was not sent by parcel post as suggested. [no need to blame]
2. In your order the dress size was not indicated. [no blame]
3. If payment is not made within ten days, your account will be referred to our attorney. [no blame, not to "me" for perhaps turning the account over to the attorney, nor to "you" for not making payment]
4. Most sentences should not be written in the passive voice. [unknown doer]
5. Your credit account cannot be opened at this time. [not accusing]

Self-Check 3–6, p. 49

1. were	4. were
2. was	5. were
3. were	

Chapter 4: More About Clauses

Self-Check 4–1, p. 64

1. subject = rush; verb = begins
2. subject = Mr. Nicolas; verb = studied
3. subject = Cedar chests and cabinets; verb = sell
4. subject = Margaret Forbes; verb = represents
5. subject = Movies or charts; verb = help
6. subject = (You); verb = Sit
7. subject = one; verb = stood
8. subject = can; verb = was
9. subject = Susan James; verb = get
10. subject = hotel; verb = closed

Self-Check 4–2, p. 65

1. A group of related words with a subject and a verb
2. Look for an action or a linking word
3. Find the doer of the action
4. More than one part
5. Never

Self-Check 4–3, p. 66

1. stores
2. Baked goods and dairy products
3. Model No. 174B
4. accuracy
5. one

Self-Check 4–4, p. 70

1. Each is a group of related words, but only a clause has a subject and a verb.
2. A clause that gives a complete idea.
3. A clause that does not give a complete idea because it begins with a subordinate conjunction or other word or word group that makes the clause dependent.
4. No.
5. A word or word group that begins an adverb clause and shows its relationship to another clause.
6. See the list on p. 69.
7. Dependent and independent.
8. When, where, how, how much, or why.
9. Because the idea is the important one, the one to be emphasized.
10. Because the idea is less important and only modifies or adds to the main idea.

Self-Check 4–5, p. 74

1. who studies each chapter carefully
2. which sells everything from coops to nuts
3. that is in the corner
4. whose work has been invaluable
5. that can handle almost anything

Self-Check 4–6, p. 75

1. Whoever wants a ride [This noun clause is the subject.]
2. that I was wrong [This noun clause is the direct object of the verb.]
3. who wants to succeed [Removing this adjective clause leaves an independent clause, "Someone should have good stamina and tenacity."]
4. whoever has the interest and the money [This noun clause is the object of the preposition *to*.]
5. whose job seems least necessary [Removing this adjective clause leaves "The one laid off will be the person."]

Self-Check 4–7, p. 77

1. dresses sold
2. Helen went
3. stationery and envelopes were
4. are 75 orders
5. Ms. Johnston traveled

Self-Check 4–8, p. 79

                        S   V   DO

1. Our accountant figured the budget for the quarter.

        ⌐——S——⌐   V DO

2. Ms. Labour sent all of us to the convention.

                      ⌐——S——⌐   V   DO

3. Among the buyers only José Sanchez liked the new design.

          ⌐——S——⌐ V IO   DO

4. The Acme Company sent us a proposal for a new venture.

        ⌐—S—⌐   V   ⌐—IO—⌐ DO

5. Mr. Stein bought Mr. Sample lunch.

Self-Check 4–9, p. 80

1. set; DO = table

2. sat

3. sat

4. set [as participle if "put there" is meant] or sitting [progressive form of the verb with no object]

5. set; DO = mind

Self-Check 4–10, p. 81

1. rise

2. risen or been raised [as participle]

3. raised; DO = price

4. raise; DO = money

5. rises

Self-Check 4–11, p. 83

1. lie

2. lay; DO = keep

3. laid; DO = carpet

4. lain

5. laid [participle form after linking verb in passive voice]

Self-Check 4–12, p. 84

1. 20 cents; renaming

2. skiing; renaming

3. elated; describing

4. happy (and) sad; describing

5. member; renaming

Chapter 5: Nouns

Self-Check 5–1, p. 101

1. F (proper)
2. T
3. F (Buildings)
4. F (Sallys)
5. F (Joneses)

6. F (attorneys)
7. F (a plural adjective makes it plural)
8. F (handkerchiefs)
9. F (singular)
10. F (save these for possessives)

Self-Check 5–2, p. 103

1. *-us* changes to *-i*
2. *-um* changes to *-a*
3. *-is* changes to *-es*
4. *-a* changes to *-ae* (add the *-e*)
5. *-eau* changes to *-eaux* (add the *-x*)

Self-Check 5–3, p. 106

1. Selma's
2. donkey's
3. man's
4. woman's
5. None, *of* is used.

6. None, *of* is used.
7. weeks'
8. None, the verb *were* comes between them.
9. series' [could be adjective as is, also]
10. Ross's

Self-Check 5–4, p.107

1. P
2. P
3. S
4. S
5. P

Self-Check 5–5, p. 108

1. S
2. S
3. P
4. P
5. S

6. P
7. P
8. S
9. P
10. S

Self-Check 5–6, p. 112

1. the plant's leaves
2. the store's sign
3. the pages' footnotes
4. my glasses' frames
5. a week's work
6. a quarter's worth
7. a month's vacation
8. two days' illness
9. Beth and Fred's house
10. Wilson's and Schriff's offices

Self-Check 5–7, p. 115

1. Kim Lee, <u>my partner</u>, studied law at Stanford.
2. The band director of the jazz band, <u>Theodore Mackle</u>, is terrific.
3. The Burton Company's product, <u>fiberboard tables</u>, is not unusual but is selling extremely well.
4. I prefer decaffeinated tea, <u>herbal tea</u>.
5. Officer Louise Campbell, <u>a candidate for sergeant</u>, has been with the police department here for three years.

Chapter 6: Pronouns

Self-Check 6–1, p. 142

1. S, she
2. SC, he
3. SC, they
4. SC, he
5. SC, she

Self-Check 6–2, p. 144

1. I, we, he, she, they
2. Me, us, him, her, them
3. You, it
4. Subject and subject complement
5. Any object position in the clause

Self-Check 6–3, p. 145

1. its
2. It's
3. you're
4. your
5. There's
6. theirs
7. its
8. his
9. their [antecedent is *sons*]
10. its

Self-Check 6–4, p. 149

1. T	6. T
2. F	7. T
3. T	8. T
4. T	9. T
5. T	10. T

Self-Check 6–5, p. 152

1. <u>who</u> work hard [the subject]
2. <u>whom</u> everyone counts on [the object of *on*]
3. <u>whom</u> the speaker referred to [object of *to*]
4. <u>who</u> represents many companies [subject]
5. to (<u>whoever</u> is in charge) [This clause acts like a noun; it is the object of *to*. However, you should still look inside the dependent clause itself to determine the pronoun usage. You do not use *whomever* as the object of *to* because the entire clause is the object of the preposition; *whoever* is the subject of the noun clause.]
6. <u>whomever</u> we select [Again, this entire clause acts as the object of the verb *will accept*. Within this noun clause *whomever* is the direct object of the verb *select*, which has its own subject *we*.]
7. <u>whom</u> all of the audience applauded [object of verb; *all* is the subject]
8. <u>who</u> majored in business in college [subject of *majored*]
9. to (<u>whom</u> you wish to speak) [Because *you* is the subject of *wish*, *whom* is the object.]
10. (<u>who</u> think) before they speak [Note that the adverb clause *before they speak* is very important to the meaning of the adjective clause.]

Self-Check 6–6, p. 154

1. John Wayne, who starred in several movies, often played the role of a cowboy.
2. This typewriter, which we just purchased, has a correcting tape included with it.
3. No commas or the sentence would say that men don't make good husbands.
4. No commas; remember, *that* clauses are always restrictive.
5. No commas.

U N I T   2

Constructing
Sentences

Types of Sentences

OVERVIEW

- Simple Sentences
- Compound Sentences
- Complex Sentences
- Periods, Questions Marks, and Exclamation Points

There are three types of sentences—simple, compound, and complex. The types you choose in your writing will determine the emphasis, rhythm, and even variety of style that you intend.

In this chapter you'll find out how each sentence type is put together. Then, using this knowledge, you'll learn several ways to combine simple sentences into compound and complex sentences that better convey the relationship between your ideas.

Lastly, you'll add to your study of comma usage and be introduced to three marks of end punctuation: the period, the question mark, and the exclamation point.

SIMPLE SENTENCES

The most basic type of sentence you can write is the simple sentence.

DEFINITION   A **simple sentence** is a one-clause sentence composed of one independent clause.

The clause in a simple sentence can be only one word long, such as a verb with an understood subject (*Halt!*), or it can be very long with many modifying words and phrases. Any part of the clause could be compound, such as a compound subject or a compound prepositional phrase. However, a simple sentence cannot start with either a subordinate type of conjunction or a relative pronoun type of word; such as a word would make the clause dependent, unable to stand alone as a sentence.

Notice that, although they become increasingly longer, the following are each examples of simple sentences.

The <u>dog</u> <u>howled</u>. [One subject, one verb, and one modifying word make up this sentence.]

The <u>dog</u> <u>howled</u> and <u>bayed</u> at the moon. [This simple sentence has a compound verb—joined by the conjunction *and*—a prepositional phrase, and a couple of modifiers, but it is only one clause.]

The <u>dog</u> and the <u>wolf</u> <u>howled</u> and <u>bayed</u> at the full moon. [A compound subject has been added, but there is still only one clause. There is no place to split this sentence into two parts, each part having its own subject and verb. It cannot be two separate sentences.]

Being late for work already and impatient at waiting for the train, <u>Tom</u> angrily <u>tooted</u> on the horn of his late-model, baby-blue Cadillac. [Although this sentence is long and has many modifying phrases, there is still one clause only, the subject being *Tom* and the verb *tooted*. No other part of this sentence could be separated out as a second clause.]

Thus, you can see that any sentence with only one clause is a simple sentence.

COMPOUND SENTENCES

Many times, though, the good writer wishes to join clauses to explain an idea. Limiting your writing to simple sentences—each idea in a single clause—is tiresome to read or to listen to. The rhythm is unvarying, the emphasis unchanging.

You can add variety by combining your clauses into other types of sentences, depending upon how you want your ideas to be related. If two ideas are equally important and can as easily be written as two simple sentences, you would combine them to write a compound sentence.

DEFINITION A **compound sentence** is composed of at least two independent clauses correctly joined.

What is the correct way to join these two or more independent clauses? They must have some "glue." A comma is too weak by itself to join independent clauses. Trying to glue two independent clauses with only a comma creates a very common writing problem called either a **comma splice** or a **run-on sentence.**

Unlike a comma, a semicolon is strong enough to glue two clauses together to form a compound sentence. Although correct, this method should be used sparingly. Two clauses bound by a semicolon lack a smooth transition, and, thus, don't flow together very well. The occasional use of a semicolon does add variety to your writing; it also calls attention to the equality of the two ideas being joined.

The more common way to connect two independent clauses is with a **coordinate conjunction** preceded by a comma. Coordinate conjunctions are the "connecting words" first introduced in Chapter 1: *and, but, or, nor, yet.* Sometimes *for* (meaning "because") is thought of as one of these coordinates. Some people also consider *so* as a coordinate conjunction, but many writers avoid it because *so* really shows a cause-effect relationship between two ideas, not an equality of emphasis.

Some of the coordinate conjunctions can work in pairs: *either . . . or; neither . . . nor.* The conjunction *but* can also work in a four-word combination: *Not only . . . but also.*

The following diagram should illustrate.

Compound Sentence "Glue"

INDEPENDENT CLAUSE	; / and	INDEPENDENT CLAUSE
INDEPENDENT CLAUSE,	but / or/nor / yet	INDEPENDENT CLAUSE
Either INDEPENDENT CLAUSE,	or	INDEPENDENT CLAUSE
Neither INDEPENDENT CLAUSE,	nor	INDEPENDENT CLAUSE
Not only INDEPENDENT CLAUSE,	but also	INDEPENDENT CLAUSE

Now look at some actual examples of compound sentences using the various ways to glue the clauses together. The boxes are around the glue.

1. The product was researched for six years, and then it was put on the market.
2. Mr. Nelson called the Texas plant, but he got the wrong number.
3. Actiform is recommended by many doctors; it helps to relieve headache pain.
4. Not only did the engineers figure out the problem, but they also proposed a method of production to remove it. [Note that the *but also* in the second clause does not have to be written together.]
5. Either a new product must be found, or our sales will continue to slump.

Did you notice the idea expressed in each of these clauses? In Example 1, for example, the fact that *the product was researched for six years* is given as much importance as that *it was put on the market.* Because each clause is independent, each has equal value. The conjunction that joins these independent clauses into compound sentences is called a *co*ordinate conjunction because *co-* means "equal"; neither part is less important than the other part.

When you write, you show your reader not only your ideas but also the relationship of those ideas to each other. The kind of sentence you build and the way you join clauses—the glue you choose—influence how the meaning of your sentence is communicated to your reader.

◧ SELF-CHECK 7-1

Underline the "glue" that joins the clauses in these compound sentences.

1. Neither of the men knew the answer, nor did he know how to locate it.

2. The Armada Corporation had a bad fourth quarter, yet it was in no trouble financially.

3. Corporate headquarters was in New York; it has been moved to Atlanta.

4. The sales representative and the corporate accountant were to have met today, but Mrs. Agent was called out of town.

5. Mr. Salinger not only completed the project on time, but he also published the results in *Quarterly*.

Before you continue, turn to p. 271 to check your answers.

▣ Punctuation Points: Compound Sentences

In a compound sentence with a coordinate conjunction, a comma comes at the end of the first independent clause—<u>before</u> the coordinate conjunction. Using this comma is a standard writing practice. Be sure, however, that the sentence is actually a compound sentence before you add the comma.

Don't be misled by a conjunction that joins two other equal parts, such as two subjects or two phrases. Remember that a simple sentence may have compound parts—even a compound verb. Despite the length of your sentence, you should use this comma before a coordinate conjunction <u>only</u> if your sentence has two full independent clauses.

Compare these two sentences.

no comma

no second subject

Simple Sentence: We sold several thousand dollars' worth of life insurance last month and were awarded the Branch of the Month award.

comma

with second subject

Compound Sentence: We sold several thousand dollars worth of life insurance last month, and we were awarded the Branch of the Month award.

Of course, if the two independent clauses of your compound sentence are joined by a semicolon, you will not use a coordinate conjunction and, thus, no comma. Remember, though, that a comma alone is insufficient to join or glue two independent clauses.

> ***Compound Sentence:*** <u>Jesse James</u> <u>was</u> certainly a family man ; <u>he</u> and his <u>brothers</u> even "<u>worked</u>" together.

> ***Run-On Sentence:*** <u>Jesse James</u> <u>was</u> certainly a family man , <u>he</u> and his <u>brothers</u> even "<u>worked</u>" together.

⌐ SELF-CHECK 7-2

Punctuate each of the following sentences. Decide first how many independent clauses each sentence has and whether there is a coordinate conjunction.

1. Television has been a boon to advertising it has sold thousands of items.

2. The letter was typed and mailed but it did not arrive.

3. Our rates have increased by more than 20 percent this year and have increased by more than 50 percent in the past three years.

4. I gambled and I lost.

5. A new solution must be found for this problem then there will be fewer mistakes.

Before you continue, turn to p. 271 to check your answers.

TRY IT OUT: **Complete Exercises 7.1 and 7.2, pp. 197–198, for practice punctuating sentences with compound elements.**

COMPLEX SENTENCES

The first two types of sentences have only independent clauses. The third type, the complex sentence, includes both dependent and independent clauses.

DEFINITION A **complex sentence** is one with at least one dependent clause added to at least one independent clause.

You realize, of course, why there must be at least one independent clause in a complex sentence. Phrases and dependent clauses cannot stand alone. Without an independent clause there can be no sentence.

All three types of dependent clauses presented in Chapter 4 can be found in complex sentences. Once you have added any dependent clause to an independent clause, you have created a complex sentence.

Therefore, any sentence with an adjective clause, an adverb clause, or a noun clause is a complex sentence. Sometimes a sentence can have two independent clauses <u>and</u> a dependent clause. Although some texts call this three-clause sentence compound-complex, for simplicity this text will classify it as a type of complex sentence.

Earlier in this chapter several compound sentence examples demonstrated the various types of glue for compound sentences. With compound sentences each clause idea is equally important. However, these same ideas could be combined in other ways. One way is to write complex sentences, where one idea is less important than the other.

Combining Ideas With Adverb Clauses

In Chapter 4 you learned that one kind of dependent clause is the adverb clause. Look at the example sentences that follow the compound sentence. These three different complex sentences express the same idea in slightly different ways. All three use adverb clauses. (To better illustrate, dependent clauses appear in lowercase letters, independent clauses in all capital letters.)

Compound:
THE <u>PRODUCT</u> <u>WAS</u> RESEARCHED FOR SIX YEARS, and THEN <u>IT</u> <u>WAS</u> PUT ON THE MARKET.

Complex:
After the <u>product</u> <u>was</u> researched for six years, <u>IT</u> <u>WAS</u> PUT ON THE MARKET.
Because the <u>product</u> <u>was</u> researched for six years, <u>IT</u> <u>WAS</u> READY TO PUT ON THE MARKET.
After the <u>product</u> <u>was</u> on the market for six years, <u>IT</u> <u>WAS</u> FURTHER RESEARCHED.
THE <u>PRODUCT</u> <u>WAS</u> PUT ON THE MARKET where it <u>was</u> researched further for six years.

Notice that not only do the connective words change, but sometimes the main emphasis changes also as the ideas move from dependent to independent clauses. Your careful choice of subordinate words to begin your adverb clauses will do much to point up the relationship between your ideas.

TRY IT OUT: **Do Exercise 7.3, p. 198, to practice working with these fine word-choice distinctions.**

Punctuation Points: Adverb Clauses

An adverb clause may be placed in any of three positions in relation to its independent clause. Its position determines the need for punctuation.

Comma Rules Summary: Adverb Clauses

1. Use <u>no</u> comma when an adverb clause comes after the independent clause.

2. Use <u>one</u> comma when an adverb clause comes before its independent clause.

3. Use <u>two</u> commas to set off any adverb clause placed as an interrupter of its independent clause.

These examples demonstrate each comma rule.

1. MR. BRIDGE LEFT WORK EARLY because he was ill. — *no comma, independent first*

2. Because he was ill, MR. BRIDGE LEFT WORK EARLY. — *one comma, independent second*

3. MR. BRIDGE, because he was ill, LEFT WORK EARLY. — *two commas, independent split by adverb clause*

You will see in the following example that you should use the comma after any adverb clause that precedes its independent clause, even if both come later in a sentence.

comma for adverb clause before independent

Manny forgot his tickets for the show, and even though he was late, he went back home to get them. — *comma for compound*

SELF-CHECK 7-3

Add commas as needed to these sentences with adverb clauses.

1. Whenever I get discouraged I try to remember that the present will not last forever.

2. You may if you wish use my notes to review the question.

3. He was never happy unless he had a complicated formula to compute.

4. Macy's seldom had a sale, but if there was a sale it was sure to be a good one.

5. If I feel well and if I have the extra money I hope to stay in Sarasota after the convention.

6. When you have completed that computer program will you work on this one?

7. One of the staff members when he finished the program was able to find the error in this one.

8. After the early-morning meeting the traders left for the market floor.

9. After we had an early-morning meeting we left for the trade show.

10. We left for the trade show after we had an early-morning meeting.

Before you continue, turn to pp. 271–272 to check your answers.

TRY IT OUT: **Go to Exercise 7.4, p. 199, for additional practice using commas with adverb clauses. *Hint:* Note that it is only commas that you might add to complex sentences, not semicolons. Semicolons are almost always used only with independent clauses.**

Combining Ideas With Adjective Clauses

Another type of complex sentence combines an independent clause and an adjective clause. Adjective clauses are those that begin with relative pronouns—commonly *who, whom, whose, which,* or *that*—and immediately follow and modify nouns or pronouns.

Although some adjective clauses need commas, many do not. You should decide whether or not to use commas with adjective clauses based on the intended meaning of the word modified.

Punctuation Points: Adjective Clauses

If your adjective clause adds only nonessential details, your main idea could stand without this information. The word being modified is clear enough. This added idea, then, should be set off with commas.

I saw your sister Grace, *who was at Benson's during the lunch hour.*

On the other hand, if your modified word would lose its meaning without the added definition, no commas should break into the thought. Remember, commas are inserted or omitted for structural reasons, not for "pauses for breath." For example, in the next sentence many people would pause after the word *hour.*

The woman *who was at Benson's during the lunch hour* is a suspect in the robbery.

You can see that the same adjective clause can be used in two different ways. This distinction between nonessential and essential ideas was pointed out in Chapters 4 and 6; however, a more detailed study and practice will be done here as you work to incorporate adjective clauses into your writing.

Each of the two types of adjective clauses has a name based on its intended use. Although it will help you to temporarily learn these terms for discussion purposes, the concept is the more important thing to learn.

DEFINITION A **restrictive adjective clause** is one that is absolutely necessary to the main clause because it narrows—restricts—the meaning of the noun or pronoun modified.

Study these examples of restrictive adjective clauses. *— clause needed, no commas*

STUDENTS who don't do their homework SHOULD BE SHOT AT SUNDOWN. [If you read this sentence without the adjective clause, you might agree if you were a disgruntled instructor, but as a student you would see that you would be shot no matter what.] *— clause needed, no commas*

(You) GIVE THIS TO THE CLERK who is sitting by the door. [Again, you would not get the whole meaning if the adjective clause were not here to describe which clerk should receive the item.] *— clause needed, no commas*

THE CLIENT whom you called on last week VISITED OUR OFFICE TODAY. [Without this restrictive adjective clause you would not know which of your many clients had visited.]

Often, however, an adjective clause simply adds an extra idea to the independent clause, one that could be stated in another sentence but is combined with the independent clause because it relates closely to the main idea. In addition, combining two sentences gives the writer a chance to add variety and reduce wordiness. This nonessential type of adjective clause is called a nonrestrictive clause.

DEFINITION A **nonrestrictive adjective clause** is one that is not needed to define the noun or pronoun it modifies. It simply adds an extra idea that could have been written in another clause.

These nonrestrictive clauses look just like the other adjective clauses—starting with the same relative pronouns—but they differ in function.

Consider these examples of nonrestrictive adjective clauses, and note the use of commas.

(You) *— clause not necessary, one comma*

1. SEND IT TO MRS. BERRY, who is our purchasing agent.

clause not necessary, two commas —

2. OUR FIRM, which is the largest of its kind in the Midwest, SELLS DATA-PROCESSING EQUIPMENT. *— clause not needed, two commas*

3. ELAINE NICHOLS, who is sitting in the back row, IS MY DAUGHTER'S TEACHER.

In each example of nonrestrictive adjective clauses, the independent clause could stand alone—it means the same thing with or without the added clause because the noun or pronoun modified is already <u>specific</u>, not needing the added clause to define it.

In Example 3 the clause *who is sitting in the back row* is nonrestrictive—not needed to tell which person; *Elaine Nichols* is already specific enough. Contrast that example with the use of the same word group as a restrictive adjective clause—one needed to clarify the noun and having, therefore, no commas.

clause needed, no comma

MY DAUGHTER'S <u>TEACHER</u> <u>IS</u> THE WOMAN | who | <u>is sitting</u> in the back row.

Comma Rules Summary: Adjective Clauses

1. Adjective clauses are set off with commas only when the ideas expressed are not needed to complete the idea of the independent clause.

2. Do not set off the adjective clause with commas when the independent clause would not say the same thing without it.

TRY IT OUT: **Exercises 7.5 and 7.6, pp. 200–201, will help you distinguish between restrictive and nonrestrictive adjective clauses.**

Combining Ideas With Noun Clauses

The third type of dependent clause that can be added to an independent clause to make a complex sentence is the noun clause. It is an entire clause starting with a relative pronoun type of word that functions as a noun somewhere in the independent clause. Because the main idea would lose a very important part if the noun clause were removed, noun clauses are always restrictive. As you learned in Chapter 4, noun clauses never take commas.

Look at these examples with noun clauses.

clause needed to act as subject, no comma

| What | <u>you</u> <u>learned</u> yesterday <u>HELPS</u> YOU TO LEARN EVEN MORE TODAY.

<u>ROCHELLE</u> <u>UNDERSTOOD</u> | that | <u>she</u> <u>was</u> in charge of the Finance Committee.

clause needed to act as object, no comma

Writing Hints: Choosing the Best Clause Type

You are studying this material to improve your writing style; consequently, a demonstration of the use of adjective clauses and noun clauses as careful choices to better convey meaning will be helpful.

Review the following compound sentence and then the complex sentences with adverb clauses. Then see that these ideas may also be combined in other ways using adjective and noun clauses. Independent clauses are in all capital letters. Note the subtle differences in meaning although all the combinations are based on the same ideas.

Compound:
THE <u>PRODUCT</u> <u>WAS</u> RESEARCHED FOR SIX YEARS, | and | THEN <u>IT</u> <u>WAS</u> PUT ON THE MARKET.

Complex (Adverb Clause):
| After | the <u>product</u> <u>was</u> researched for six years, <u>IT</u> <u>WAS</u> PUT ON THE MARKET.
| Because | the <u>product</u> <u>was</u> researched for six years, <u>IT</u> <u>WAS</u> READY TO PUT ON THE MARKET.
| After | the <u>product</u> <u>was</u> on the market for six years, <u>IT</u> <u>WAS</u> FURTHER RESEARCHED.
THE <u>PRODUCT</u> <u>WAS</u> PUT ON THE MARKET | where | <u>it</u> <u>was</u> researched further for six years.

Complex (Adjective Clause):
THE <u>PRODUCT</u>, | which | <u>was</u> on the market for six years, <u>WAS</u> FURTHER RESEARCHED.
THE <u>PRODUCT</u> | that | <u>was</u> researched for six years <u>WAS</u> PUT ON THE MARKET.

Complex (Noun Clause):
| That | the <u>product</u> <u>had been</u> researched for six years <u>MADE</u> IT READY FOR THE MARKET.

How you express yourself shows how you feel about a topic as well as what your knowledge of it is. Writing is an expression of both ideas and judgment. Although some of the previous sentences are probably better choices than others for the best possible writing, the number of possibilities does demonstrate how flexible the language is. This demonstration also shows how careful you should be in selecting the best structural form into which to put your ideas.

Punctuation Summary: Complex Sentences

One last note about dependent clause types: The terminology needed to distinguish between the types of clauses can seem forbidding. Although it is very true that you will not have to be able to name the different types of dependent clauses in the future, to be able to use and punctuate them correctly, you must be able to tell the differences between them. For instance, because noun and adjective clauses begin with many of the same signal words, these clauses could be thought of as interchangeable; however, as you have learned, noun clauses never take commas, whereas certain adjective clauses do. Thus, you must be able to tell the difference between them, and the terminology allows you to identify each type in discussions about style and punctuation.

The key to punctuating complex sentences is understanding how the various types of dependent clauses function in their sentences. The signal words provide excellent clues for determining comma usage, but most important is understanding how the various clauses are used.

This challenge is demonstrated in the following sentences, where the same clause is used in four different ways. The punctuation is determined by use. The writer uses punctuation to signal the reader, telling how to interpret the message.

(you)

When it will be convenient to get together, PLEASE <u>CALL</u> A MEETING. [adverb clause placed before independent]

A <u>TIME</u> when it <u>will be</u> convenient to get together <u>SHOULD BE</u> SELECTED FOR THE MEETING. [adjective, restrictive]

TODAY AT THREE, when it <u>will be</u> convenient to get together, <u>WE</u> <u>WILL HAVE</u> THE MEETING. [adjective, nonrestrictive]

When it <u>will be</u> convenient to get together <u>IS</u> GOING TO BE DIFFICULT TO DECIDE DURING THE HOLIDAY SEASON. [noun]

TRY IT OUT: Do Exercises 7.7, 7.8, and 7.9, pp. 202–204, to practice recognizing, writing, and punctuating dependent clauses. Exercise 7.10, p. 205, is the Challenge exercise.

PERIODS, QUESTION MARKS, AND EXCLAMATION POINTS

You've been using periods, question marks, and exclamation points ever since you learned to write. However, although you know how to use these punctuation marks in your everyday writing, you may be unaware of some particular uses of these marks in business letters, memorandums, and reports. Rules for these usages will be presented here along with a review of how these marks are used as end punctuation.

(Note: For formal reports or manuscripts you will want to refer to reference manuals or handbooks that give more detailed rules for the particular format chosen.)

 ## The Period

The Period as End Punctuation

1. A sentence that is a statement is called a **declarative sentence** and requires a period to end it. When typing connected matter, follow the period with two spaces.

2. Letters and memos make particular use of the **imperative sentence,** which is a sentence that makes a demand. The subjects of imperative sentences area always *you,* which is usually understood instead of written.

   (You) Mail this return post card today.

   (You) Make your reservations now.

However, because courtesy is indispensable in any communication, "demands" or "orders" are often stated as polite questions. Although the reader is asked if he or she will do something, a written or spoken response is not necessary. These polite questions are also punctuated as imperative sentences, taking a period, not a question mark.

> Will you please send your order soon.
>
> May we hear your answer by Friday.

3. Any expression that stands for a complete thought is punctuated as a sentence.

> Yes.　　No.　　Next.

The Period in Common Abbreviations

1. Place a period after an abbreviation.

   a. If the abbreviation is in lowercase letters, there are no spaces between.

   > f.o.b.　　c.o.d.

   b. Many abbreviations in all capital letters require no periods or spaces.

   > CETA　　VA　　YMCA

   c. A few capitalized abbreviations require periods but no spaces within.

   > U.S.A.　　B.A.　　P.O.

   d. If the capital letters replace names as initials, there is usually a space after each period.

   > J. C. Grundy

   e. If the abbreviation ends the sentence, use only one period and space twice if the paragraph continues.

   > I'll see you at 3 p.m. We can decide then.

2. Avoid using nonstandard abbreviations in memorandums, letters, and formal reports. A current style manual will tell you which abbreviations are standard.

   a. Be sure to use titles of respect for all names in addresses of letters. While *Mr., Mrs., Ms.,* or *Dr.* are standard abbreviations and use periods, *Miss* does not. Write out other titles, such as *Professor* or *Reverend.*

   b. Do not abbreviate such things as company names (unless that way in the official name), official titles, directions, or such words as *Street, Avenue,* or *Building* in the inside addresses of letters.

   > *Mr.* John Jones, *President*
   > Jones Insurance *Company*
   > Industrial State *Building*
   > 338 *West* Michigan *Avenue*
   > Cleveland, OH 12345

   c. In addresses use the two-letter postal abbreviations for the states. These are in capital letters and use no periods, having one space before the ZIP code. (Of course, when not used in addresses, the state is written in full.)

Add periods or other end punctuation in the following word groups.

1. Place the package on the table

2. Will you place the package on the table

3. Will you sit here

4. Will you call me with your answer

5. Will you be at the meeting

6. Yes

7. Thank you

8. NBC

9. pm

10. R A Imus

11. IBM

12. V-Pres

13. Ave

14. Miss

15. St Paul MN

Before you continue, turn to p. 272 to check your answers.

TRY IT OUT: **Complete Exercise 7.11, p. 206, for practice.**

Periods as Decimal Points

1. Use a period between the dollar and cent amounts in an uneven dollar amount.

    $27.45 $19.41 $4,729.88

2. If the dollar amount is even, use no periods, nor any zeros to indicate cents.

    $19 $2,000 $50

However, in a series or tabulation, if any of the amounts are uneven, it is common practice to use decimals and zeros with the even amounts for balance.

> The three items cost $27.00, $14.95, and $12.00.

3. Use the period as a decimal point.

> 0.3937   2.5   0.06

(Note: A zero placed before the decimal in amounts less than 1 keeps the reader from misreading the number.)

Periods in Lists

1. When a list is tabulated, use periods after each number or letter of the list.

> The three branches of the federal government are these:
> 1. Executive
> 2. Judicial
> 3. Legislative

2. If you choose to use parentheses around the number or letter, use no periods.

> The three branches of the federal government are these:
> (a) Executive
> (b) Judicial
> (c) Legislative

If your list falls within a sentence, use parentheses with no periods.

> The rules are (1) no eating, (2) no drinking, and (3) no horseplay.

3. Do not place periods at the end of the items in a tabulation except in the following instances.

a. The items are complete sentences.

> Mona had three goals in life:
> 1. She wanted to get a good education.
> 2. She wanted to help other people.
> 3. She wanted to love and be loved.

b. The items are dependent clauses or long phrases.

> He knew he would be promoted:
> 1. If he worked extra hours.
> 2. If he learned the new procedures.
> 3. If he showed initiative in his job.

c. The items are short phrases that are needed to complete the clause of introduction.

> The skills needed by a good writer are:
> 1. good organizational abilities.
> 2. a firm grasp of language skills.
> 3. pride in good workmanship.

Decide where to place periods. (The spaces in money figures indicate a separation of dollars and cents.)

1. $19 97

2. $20

3. $14 27, $19, $22 50

4. 30 percent = 30 [as a decimal]

5. Among the services at this bank are these:
   1 Passbook savings accounts
   2 Loans
   3 Certificates of Deposit

Before you continue, turn to p. 272 to check your answers.

TRY IT OUT: **Complete Exercise 7.12, p. 207, for practice.**

⊡ The Question Mark

The Question Mark After a Question

1. Use a question mark after a direct question—one that requires an answer. As with other end punctuation, type two spaces before continuing.

   > May I call you on Monday? Would one o'clock be a good time?

2. Broad questions are often used in letter and report writing to get the reader's attention and to start the reader to think about what will be discussed. Although a one-word answer could respond to this type of question, the purpose is to stimulate thoughts about the topic. Use a question mark after this type of question, which is usually written as a single paragraph.

   > Is your home insured for its true value?
   >
   > Have you thought lately about the rising costs of fuel?
   >
   > Have the newest pharmaceutical products been as carefully researched as they should have been?

3. A semicolon should not be used between independent clauses if the first clause is a question.

   > Is she here? Oh, I just saw her.
   >
   > *Not:* Is she here; oh, I just saw her.

4. Occasionally, presenting a series of questions makes an interesting writing technique. As long as the beginning of each sentence is the same, you can use a question mark, instead of a comma, after each series item. This technique avoids the repetition of completely writing each sentence, and it gets the reader's attention.

   Do you have a pen? a pencil? anything to write with?

   (Notice that two spaces separate the word groups, but no capital letters begin subsequent series items.)

The Question Mark With Quotations

Although periods and commas always are placed inside the final quotation mark, question marks can go either before or after depending on the content of the material.

1. Place the question mark inside the end quotation mark when the quotation itself requires the mark.

   "Did I hear thunder?" Mary asked.

   Stuart asked, "Would you type this for me?"

2. Place the question mark outside of the quotation mark if it relates to the entire statement, not the quoted material.

   Did he say, "I am going home"? [Notice that the stronger mark—a question mark—cancels a period or comma.]

3. If the quotation and the statement both need a question mark, keep only the first mark.

   Have you see the movie, "Who Dares To Go There?"

Unusual Situations With Questions Marks

1. Use a question mark within parentheses to show that an item of information cannot be verified.

   In 1922 (?) Mrs. Robertson left for Australia.

2. If a question ends with an abbreviation that takes a period, be sure to use the period before the question mark.

   Will you ship the item c.o.d.?

The Exclamation Point

Because the exclamation point is intended for only very emotional statements, it should be used sparingly. As with any writing technique, overuse causes a loss of impact.

The Exclamation Point as End Punctuation

1. Use an exclamation point after a statement that shows strong feeling.

   > I am so happy to be alive!
   >
   > Drive defensively!

2. You may use an exclamation point after a single word that expresses strong feeling when its acts as a complete thought.

   > Help!   Stop!

   If your exclamation is added to a sentence, use a comma after the word and an exclamation point at the end of the statement.

   > Gosh, I needed that!
   >
   > Oh, I'm so sorry!

3. The principle for placing exclamation points inside or outside of quotation marks is the same as for question marks.

   > Don't tell me "I'm sorry"!
   >
   > Mary Catherine cried, "Ouch!"

SELF-CHECK 7-6

Punctuate the following word groups.

1. Have you been feeling tired lately

2. Will you state the dress size in your order

3. Why do costs keep rising

4. Are you going to Anchorage   Why not

5. Do you feel run-down   overtired   depressed

6. She asked, "Who did this"

7. "Who did this" she asked

8. What is f.o.b.

9. Did you see the first *Star Wars*

10. Good heavens   I didn't know that

Before you continue, turn to p. 272 to check your answers.

TRY IT OUT: Complete Exercises 7.13 through 7.15, pp. 208–210, for practice with these end marks of punctuation.

▣ Chapter 7: Types of Sentences

● E X E R C I S E 7 . 1

First underline the subjects and verbs in the following sentences to determine whether the sentence is simple or compound. Then insert any needed punctuation.

1. Television is a big industry it affects millions of people.

2. Either you should send this by registered mail or you should send it by certified mail.

3. Good grammar is like any other skill it takes practice to make it perfect.

4. Tear off the enclosed coupon mail it today.

5. Helen checked on the number of cartons of envelopes left and she ordered more last week.

6. Bob checked the number of envelopes left and ordered more.

7. Several lawyers came to the regional meeting concerning new statutes several others were not able to attend.

8. Your instructor for this seminar will be Samuel Smith you'll like him very much.

9. Read no further just sign your name below.

10. Roland Wagner went to Georgia to see about a transfer and decided to move there by the first of the year.

● E X E R C I S E 7 . 2

Proofread the following letter for punctuation with the compound elements. Cross out any punctuation that is incorrectly used, and add any necessary punctuation to the compound sentences. Circle any changes you make.

Ms. Marge Stoops

1477 Nemeth Drive

Houston, TX 77002

Dear Ms. Stoops:

   Your kind comments are certainly appreciated. You said that you had enjoyed our latest copy of

Atlas you especially liked the article about Nevada.

We at *Atlas* are always pleased to learn that our readers enjoy our choice of subjects; the articles are written for you and we want you to learn as much about our great country as you can. You have shown interest in our lovely nation by subscribing to our magazine and, you should get what you have paid for.

The additional information that you requested about hotels in Las Vegas is enclosed with this letter. You will notice that the hotels with pools are starred, or are printed in italics in the brochure. The gambling casinos also have accommodations available, be sure to reserve early. The addresses of all lodgings are listed with the descriptions of the rooms and dining availability.

Nevada will be beautiful at the time of year of your planned visit. The cacti will be in bloom, the weather will be mild and sunny. You may need a sweater, or jacket in the evenings. The sun will be plenty warm during the day for using the pool. There are many scenic day trips available also.

Send your reservations in as soon as possible, and pack up, and enjoy your trip. We're happy to have had a part in helping you with your vacation plans.

Sincerely,

Clyde Croupier, Travel Agent

pam

Enclosures

● EXERCISE 7.3

For each of the following pairs, choose the sentence that better conveys the relationship between the ideas in the clauses. Circle the letter that indicates your choice.

1. a. Mr. Graham was good at driving, and he enjoyed racing his sports car on weekends.
   b. Since Mr. Graham was good at driving, he enjoyed racing his sports car on weekends.

2. a. You have not done well with this type of work; you are being transferred to another office.
   b. Because you have not done so well at this type of work, you are being transferred to another office.

3. a. Although I don't feel well, I will finish this job.
   b. Because I don't feel well, I will finish this job.

4. a. Many people want higher pay; few are willing to work harder for it.
   b. Many people want higher pay, and few are willing to work harder for it.

5. a. Mr. Frost, because he was always willing to work for the good of the company, got a raise.
   b. Mr. Frost was always willing to work for the good of the company, and he got a raise.

● **E X E R C I S E 7 . 4**

Decide whether each of these sentences has the adverb clause in the natural order. If not, add the necessary commas. Not every sentence will require commas. Look for subordinate signal words that begin adverb clauses. Circle any changes you make.

1. He planned to work on the project until he finished it.

2. As soon as we arrived at the hotel we saw the group from Davenport.

3. If you want to take advantage of our offer and if you wish to save 20 percent you must place your order by March 15.

4. You may if you have the work finished leave at four o'clock today.

5. Although he was only 17 he entered college to study business.

6. You will make fewer errors if you take your time with the project.

7. She saw the magician when she was in Colon, Michigan.

8. Before I leave remind me to sign those letters.

9. Helen when she was ready to leave remembered to check the lock on the cash drawer.

10. You are eligible for our retirement program because you have worked here for two years.

11. After you have been employed for quite a while you really appreciate the coworkers who mind their own business.

12. If I am I didn't realize that I am overly critical.

13. Although good skills are important your attitude is more important to your success in a job.

14. Your grammar has already improved since you started working with this text.

15. Without hard work you cannot unless your dad owns the company get ahead in this business.

16. The registrar as soon as enrollment data were available published the figures for full-time enrollment.

17. After lunch Miss Valdez met with the staff before she presented the report to management.

18. After she had eaten lunch Miss Valdez made her reservations for the conference in South Dakota.

19. You may take the remaining doughnuts to the coffee room because this meeting has been adjourned.

20. Even though the meter had run out an hour ago we did not receive a parking ticket.

Add commas to any of the following complex sentences with nonrestrictive clauses, those that could be left out of that particular sentence. Circle any changes you make.

1. Business owners who want to save money on raw materials shop around carefully before they buy.

2. Henry Fonda who was a well-known actor played in more than ninety films.

3. My boss is a woman who realizes the value of good workers.

4. Products that are faddish seldom have long-range sales.

5. People who live in glass houses shouldn't throw stones.

6. The President of the United States who is an elected official has a term of four years.

7. Mississippi which is a Southern state has a warmer climate than Maine which is a Northern one.

8. My boss is John Phillips who has been with this company for several years.

9. Abraham Lincoln who you all know was President served during the Civil War years.

10. This new type of china is one that is guaranteed not to crack.

11. These dishes which are chipped or cracked will not bring much money at the auction.

12. Whatever is the matter with this rotor is the thing that is causing the problem.

13. Anyone who gets good rest and who eats well probably will not get very many colds.

14. Any low lying area where there is a great deal of standing water is a prime location for mosquitoes to breed.

15. My feisty cat which is a Manx wakes me up at 6 a.m. every day.

16. The latest edition of your reference manual which just came on the market is even better than the earlier edition.

17. The canoe that passed under the bridge first went on to lose the race after overturning.

18. Edward Alvarez who directed the movie *Rainbows* is now making a film in Miami.

19. The man who directed the movie *Rainbows* is named Edward Alvarez.

20. During the storm the waves which were at least 16 feet high washed against the lighthouse.

● E X E R C I S E   7 . 6

Rewrite these sentences on the blanks provided. Use the relative pronouns—who, whom, which, that, when, where—to add another clause after each underlined word or word group. Add commas only if the added clause is nonrestrictive, that is, unneeded to define the modified word.

1. <u>Someone</u> should get some counseling.

   _____

2. My neighbor <u>Lin Wu</u> is doing very well with his English usage.

   _____

3. I have never met a <u>man</u>.

   _____

4. Any <u>son</u> will not behave in an embarrassing manner.

   _____

5. Don't plant any <u>tree</u> in this dry, hot climate.

   _____

6. <u>Anyone</u> will admire <u>Abraham Lincoln</u>.

   _____

7. This Model No. 3465–R <u>gyroscope</u> is tremendously expensive.

   _____

8. My favorite <u>restaurant</u> is named The Embers.

   _____

9. No <u>woman</u> will ever succeed in any <u>job</u>.

   _____

10. Is <u>Ramon Hector</u> the <u>Ramon Hector</u>?

   _____

Put parentheses around each dependent clause. Add necessary punctuation; then circle added punctuation.

1. The auctioneer opened the bidding when everyone was seated.

2. Until she made up her mind Sally didn't do anything about it.

3. What the lecturer said pleased the audience.

4. The hunter tried to move the stone which was heavy.

5. They thought about whether they could afford the trip.

6. Whenever the economy is uncertain people tend to be more selfish.

7. The little boy who is a nasty, spoiled brat cannot be left alone with other children.

8. Whoever wants to graduate must pass all the required courses.

9. He left early because he was tired.

10. Dale is the girl who gets there early.

On separate paper combine the following two ideas into the types of sentences listed. You may have to add words and somewhat change the wording of the statements, but try not to change the meaning. Punctuate accordingly. Hints are given to help identify the clause type.

Roberta wanted to be able to support herself well.
She attended college to get a degree.

1. A simple sentence with a compound verb element.

2. A compound sentence with a semicolon.

3. A compound sentence with a coordinate conjunction (*and, but, or, nor, yet*).

4. A complex sentence with an adverb clause in the natural order. (Uses subordinate conjunction.)

5. A complex sentence with an adverb clause before the independent clause.

6. A complex sentence with an adverb clause interrupting the independent clause.

7. A complex sentence with a restrictive adjective clause. (Uses *who, whom, whose, which, that.*)

8. A complex sentence with a nonrestrictive adjective clause.

9. A complex sentence with a noun clause. (Starts with relative pronoun.)

10. A simple sentence with one of the ideas in a prepositional phrase. The phrase will have a verblike word in it.

Name _____ Date _____ Class _____

Add any necessary punctuation to the following sales letter. Circle any changes you make.

Mr. Daniel Neptune

1440 Desert Drive

Denver, CO 09876

Dear Mr. Neptune:

You are one of the growing number of people who have decided to enjoy the warm weather with their own swimming pools. You have made a wise choice and you will enjoy many benefits from your choice.

The Algae Pool Company has been in business for eighteen years. Algae has grown from a small operation to one of the West's largest. You can depend on us to install a quality pool we stand behind our product. Remember, when you buy one of our pools, "You can be sure of Algae."

A swimming pool in your own backyard offers you a variety of benefits. You can write off the initial cost of installation because when you decide to sell you home you can count on much added value to your property. A pool adds to the decor of your yard and it surely saves you time in mowing the grass.

Because people who are health-conscious are now aware of the importance of exercise they know that a swimming pool can aid in their general health. Exercise helps to keep the body in condition and it helps to keep off those excess pounds that we all worry about. You can plan your own exercise program and consistently work off those calories. Too, you will enjoy the exercise you get when you maintain your pool each and every day.

Another plus to pool ownership is the popularity you will gain when your new pool is installed and in operation. You will see envious looks on your neighbors' faces and will renew old friendships that you hardly even remember. Your friends will just "drop in" to see you at any time of the day or night. Won't that be fun? Your children will quickly become the most popular kids in the neighborhood all of the other kids will want to be at your house to play from very early in the morning.

You may wonder about the cost of upkeep on your new investment but don't give it a thought! Because you live in the wonderful West you will have no problems. Although Denver does have some chilly weather you will hardly notice a change in your heating bills from month to month over the year. If you'd rather not pay the heating bills in the summer you will find it invigorating to swim in your unheated pool during those hot months. How refreshing!

The enclosed brochure shows you the variety of sizes and shapes that you can choose for your new pool. The kidney shape is always popular but you may want to study the plans on page 3 for our Gallbladder Galaxy which is rapidly becoming one of our best sellers. Note the economical Mini Mermaid on page 7 you can surely log lots of laps in this one!

Sam Slick, our sales representative, will call you this Friday because we don't want you to get away . . . without a super deal!

Happy Swimming!

Doreen Chlorine, Owner

jiw

Enclosure

PS   As an added incentive to help you make a decision soon, we are offering a ten percent discount to anyone who signs a pool contract by September 1st.

● **E X E R C I S E   7 . 1 0**   **CHALLENGE**

Put parentheses around each dependent clause. On the blank tell whether the clause is adjective (ADJ), adverb (ADV), or noun (N). Add and circle any necessary punctuation.

_____ 1. He knew that he had failed the test.

_____ 2. The man who fixed my furnace was here until 3 a.m.

_____ 3. Whoever wears wool clothes has to be sure to dry-clean them, not wash them.

_____ 4. I wasn't ready for the test until I had seen the tutor.

_____ 5. While you are fixing dinner please clean up the dishes.

_____ 6. Mr. Ward's only sister who is a nurse at Bronson helped keep him alive.

_____ 7. Ms. Werkle will give the book to whoever needs it most.

_____ 8. Any dessert that tastes good has lots of calories.

_____ 9. Whenever you need extra help be sure to see the tutor.

_____ 10. Our secretary as long as she knows the address will send all the letters.

_____ 11. Don't lend the book to anyone who has no library card.

_____ 12. He said that he is tired of school.

_____ 13. Whether you study or not is entirely up to you.

_____ 14. Whenever I get too tired I oversleep and don't hear the alarm clock.

_____ 15. My cousin Mary who attends Western Michigan University is studying computer programming.

_____ 16. The current phone system is undergoing a change which is supposed to improve it.

_____ 17. I don't plan to leave school early today because I have some work to catch up on.

_____ 18. I haven't received a phone call yet from whichever man is supposed to call me.

_____ 19. You may not unless you are finished with your part of the program leave before 5 p.m. today.

_____ 20. The Olympics awards with medals whoever wins the events.

Add any necessary periods to the following sentences. If there are any improper abbreviations, rewrite them. Circle any changes you make.

1. Will you please, Miss Jones, take a moment to answer these questions

2. Dr John Ellison has announced a meeting for 10:30 am

3. Mr Ted Williams, Jr, of San Antonio, Tex, is planning to come to NY next week

4. Yes

5. Frieda Goldman, of ABC television, lives at 28 N park St in Los Angeles, Calif.

6. A common abbreviation meaning "for example" is eg

7. Ms Jean Belleville, Treas

   Cunningham Sanitation Dept

   419 S Canal St

   Washington, DC 32145

8. Maynard Luscomb, PhD, has a class in Econ from 8 am to 9 am

9. Have you read anything by J D Salinger?

10. During the mo of Aug you can join the YWCA at a reduced rate

11. In the space below, write the inside address to a letter you would send to your instructor, including a title of respect and his or her job title.

● E X E R C I S E 7 . 1 2

Add necessary periods, and fix incorrectly used periods in the following. Circle any changes you make.

1. Although he charged me $20, I found out that the actual price at Sanderson's is $16.42

2. He paid me $200.00 for a used snow blower

3. When trying to find 20 percent of a number, you can multiply the number by 20

4. You may make a monthly payment of $10.00, or $30.00, depending upon the balance that is due

Punctuate these tabulations.

5. a. The following will be considered as collateral for a loan:
    1 Automobile
    2 Home
    3 Recreation vehicle

   b. You may use these as collateral for your loans:
    (a) Automobile
    (b) Home
    (c) Recreation vehicle

   c. These things would be necessary in order for you to take out a loan:
    1 You must make application 30 days in advance
    2 You must submit a completed loan application
    3 You must offer something as collateral for the money

Punctuate these short paragraphs. If a punctuation mark is misused, correct it. You may have to make changes in capitalization. Circle any changes you make.

1.   Because our new models will be coming out soon. Shouldn't you come out and take a look at the super bargains that we have available on last year's models. You can't lose, you can save!

2.   Have you ever thought that you cannot afford a swimming pool. Do you think that a pool is a luxury for those who have a great deal of money, do you use a pool only on a vacation at a motel!

3.   "Oh not again" thought Kim as her typewriter ran out of ribbon! Here it was, almost 5 pm and she had to finish that report, has this ever happened to you.

4.   Do you ever say to yourself, "I am going to study this lesson very hard tonight" Do you then do it; are you more likely to let other things get in your way? The answers to these questions should tell you a great deal about your success in learning.

5.   Have you been able to get T L Wells, Jr, on the phone, if not, try him at 849-9803. Hurry. We must tell him about the leak in the roof over his valuable book collection.

● E X E R C I S E 7.14

Add the correct end punctuation to each of these short sentences.

1. Stop

2. No

3. I did, didn't I

4. Will you please call later

5. Can you call later today

6. Why

7. He asked me if I knew

8. He asked, "Do you know"

9. A terrible accident

10. Did you send the letter

11. Will you please return the letter

12. How much

13. Was it sent c.o.d.

14. Will you come right in

15. Why not order today

Add the necessary punctuation, and correct misused punctuaiton in the following letter. Do not use semicolons. Correct any capitalizations. Circle any changes you make.

Dear Renter:

Should you be investing your money in a home rather than renting an apartment

Have you been tossing this question around lately and not reaching an answer. All of us, at one time or another, have to make a decision about this we have to decide where we are going to live.

There are certainly many things to take into consideration before making a final decision, each one of us has to decide what is best for him or her

Some people like the freedom of an apartment they don't have to do the maintenance work, they don't have to worry about the lawn work. They can move on short notice too, they can often have advantages, such as a pool or tennis courts, that they wouldn't have if they bought a home

If these are the things you are looking for. An apartment is probably the right decision for you

On the other hand, you would miss out on some of the advantages of owning your own home.

Do you enjoy privacy a sense of pride in a possession you take good care of Do you like to try unusual things in decorating Do you enjoy growing beautiful flower gardens and perhaps even your own vegetables

Are you a person who hates to see a monthly payment go out with no return in the future do you want the tax advantages that ownership may give you

If these ideas appeal to you. You should probably look further into investing your money in your own personal property

We at Roger Dodger Realty will be very happy to help you with your decision call today we will make an appointment with you immediately

Hurry, you are losing equity while you wait

Sincerely,

ROGER DODGER REALTY

Suzi Reis, Agent

◪ Periodic Review: Chapters 6–7

Underline the dependent clause in each sentence, and on the blank tell whether it is adverb (ADV), adjective (ADJ), or noun (N). Put parentheses around each prepositional phrase. Add and circle any missing punctuation.

_____ 1. I am never sure of whether or not Bob will show up for the softball games.

_____ 2. The new fax machine Mrs. Edwards purchased is certainly better than the other one.

_____ 3. Often unless the weather is stormy I take a three-mile walk on my lunch hour.

_____ 4. I have a nephew named Timothy Allan who is a skilled hockey player for the Wings.

_____ 5. Our airline reservations were canceled because that airline is cutting out its southern routes.

Write the third form (participle form) of the following verbs.

_____ 1. forecast

_____ 2. drink

_____ 3. vary

_____ 4. cut

_____ 5. lend

_____ 6. swim

_____ 7. see

_____ 8. delay

_____ 9. lie

_____ 10. rise

Rewrite each of these poorly written compound sentences by changing the underlined clause into the structure indicated.

1. <u>Eileen is my sister</u>, and she is a bus driver for the county. (adjective clause)

    _____

2. <u>I have to repair this mimeograph</u>, and then I will get to the copy machine. (adverb clause)

    _____

3. Alicia plans to scuba dive on her vacation, and <u>she is going to Bermuda</u>. (prepositional phrase)

    _____

4. I have a new high intensity lamp for my desk, and <u>it is a Bigelow lamp</u>. (adjective clause)

    _____

5. Joellen drove to the meeting, and <u>she knew how to get there</u>. (noun clause)

    _____

Use some form of lie *or* lay *in the following.*

1. Did you forget to _____ the print flat on the table to dry?

2. After he had hoed his small garden plot, he _____ down for a nap.

3. I suppose that old case study has _____ behind the files for twenty years.

4. Archie _____ his head against the cool window to get relief from the heat of his fever.

5. The new tile has been _____ in the foyer.

Underline the correct pronoun for each of the following sentences.

1. It was (I, me) who called you yesterday.

2. Behind Mel and (she, her) was a large truck, seemingly out of control.

3. The department sent Val and (I, me) to the trade show in Augusta.

4. She is a woman (who, whom) I can trust.

5. He only wanted to test (its, it's) durability.

Underline the correctly spelled form of each of the following.

1. refered, referred

2. valleys, vallies

3. gooses, geese

4. son-in-laws, sons-in-law

5. everybody's, everybodies

6. criteria, criterias

7. Fitchs, Fitches

8. lieing, lying

9. solos, soloes

10. Germen, Germans

On the blank tell whether each sentence has a direct object (DO) or a subject complement (SC).

_____ 1. Anyone can make mistakes, but, Jerry, you take the prize for the most mistakes today.

_____ 2. Yes, Jerry is definitely the winner.

_____ 3. At least Jerry has a good sense of humor.

_____ 4. He does not seem upset by our teasing.

_____ 5. Of course, I may be mistaken in my assumptions about his humor.

On the blank tell whether each sentence is simple (S), compound (CP), or complex (CX). Add and circle any missing punctuation.

_____ 1. An ibis is a large wading bird and is related to the heron.

_____ 2. Any employer who wants good workers will try to give a good benefit package and competitive wages.

_____ 3. Unless you decide otherwise I plan to leave for the football game at 4:30 p.m.

_____ 4. Not only do you have to shrink the material but you should also set the dye by washing it in warm water.

_____ 5. I never found out who had smoked in the restroom.

_____ 6. As medicine becomes more complex costs rise accordingly.

_____ 7. Whoever found that discounted price has certainly saved us some money.

_____ 8. You won; I lost.

_____ 9. If I lost however I still had a really good time playing bingo.

_____ 10. I cannot remember where I put those copies of the Valdez report.

Sentence Combining and Word Reduction

OVERVIEW

- **Verbal Phrases**
- **Other Methods of Reduction**

Besides combining your ideas into compound or complex sentences, there is another technique that will add more variety to your writing style and help to reduce wordiness. That technique is often called *reduction*. You do not have to learn this term because it is a somewhat generic term.

You might think of the term *reduction* with regards to weight loss: Used in that context reduction would mean to get rid of extra, probably unneeded, pounds. Reduction in writing simply means to employ techniques that cut out extra words, usually by turning clauses into modifying phrases. You can perform this reduction by writing any of the verbal phrases—infinitive, participial, and gerund. Two other methods of reduction are using appositives or reducing an idea to only the few words needed for a prepositional phrase.

Here are some examples of these techniques.

Original:
Asa was living in the Southwest.
He moved to Seattle so that he could get a new job.

Using a Gerund:
Moving to Seattle from the Southwest enabled Asa to get a new job.

Using a Participle:
Asa, *moving from the Southwest to Seattle,* was better able to get a job.

> ***Using an Infinitive:***
> Asa decided *to move to Seattle to get a job.*
>
> ***Using an Appositive:***
> Asa moved to Seattle, *a city with many jobs available.*
>
> ***Using a Prepositional Phrase:***
> Asa moved *to Seattle from the Southwest for a job.*

As you can see, these structures convert the less important details into modifiers, leaving the independent clauses for the major points. In this chapter you'll learn how each of these word reduction techniques can help you add variety to your writing and reduce wordiness.

VERBAL PHRASES

Look at the following two sentences.

I write in a rather unsophisticated manner.
I need new techniques for better writing.

They are closely related in idea, but the second idea is more important than the first; thus, making two simple sentences or a compound sentence would not be good writing. One alternative is to make the less important idea into a dependent clause: an adjective, an adverb, or a noun clause. Another alternative is to make the modifying idea into one of the three types of verbal phrases: an infinitive, a participial, or a gerund phrase.

The following illustrations use verbal phrases to combine these two ideas. Notice the variation in the cadence—the rhythm or flow of the words—as you read.

> ***Infinitive:***
> *To improve my rather unsophisticated writing,* I need to learn new writing techniques.
>
> ***Participle:***
> I, *not having very good writing skills,* need to learn new writing techniques.
>
> ***Gerund:***
> *Learning new writing techniques* will improve my writing a great deal.

You already know a good deal about verbals and verbal phrases. You know they're not verbs, and you've seen how they can assume various positions in the different clause patterns. In short, you can recognize the three verbal types. Your present study will give you the detail you need to use verbals comfortably in your writing.

◳ Infinitives

DEFINITION An **infinitive** is a verblike word with *to* in front of it. An infinitive does not function as a verb but as a noun or a modifier.

The verblike word in an infinitive can be either an action word or a linking word, but once the *to* comes before it, the verblike word cannot be the verb of the clause. The clause will have something else as its verb.

Some examples of simple infinitives are *to be, to ski, to sleep,* and *to withdraw*. These same infinitives could also be part of larger word groups—**infinitive phrases**—that could have other modifying words or even objects (much like prepositions having objects). In fact, infinitive phrases very often have prepositional phrases modifying them. Study these examples of various additions to simple infinitives, making infinitive phrases.

Simple Infinitive	Infinitive Phrase
to be	to be / well thought of / *modifier*
to ski	to ski / very fast / down the hill / *modifiers* *object*
to sleep	to sleep / the sleep / of the innocent / ← *modifier*
to withdraw	to withdraw / hesitatingly / his hand / from the cookie jar / *object* *modifiers*

You can see that the object of the infinitive is the item that gets the action of the verblike word in the infinitive. The infinitive and its object aren't considered verbs and direct objects because they are parts of phrases, not clauses. Infinitive phrases are not written as clauses because the writer wants to deemphasize the importance of the idea, saving the more important idea for the independent clause.

Notice the infinitive phrases in each of the following sentences. The infinitive phrases are italicized so that you can easily see the entire phrase.

He tried *to study hard.*
He wanted *to hire the secretary with experience.*
Your salesperson happened *to visit our office on Friday.*
To earn a living, Mrs. Christie often worked long hours.

Most current style and usage books still suggest that you not "split an infinitive." This means that it is better to put the modifying words after or even before the two-word infinitive, not between the word *to* and the verblike word.

Poor Usage:
I want to *thoroughly* study this technique.
Better:
I want to study this technique *thoroughly.*

Underline the infinitive phrases in the following sentences.

1. To collect stamps is my hobby.

2. She was happy to work overtime.

3. I don't like to type under pressure.

4. Would you bring that copy to me to be proofread?

5. To earn his commission, Mr. Alderman had to sell five machines a month.

Before you continue, turn to p. 273 to check your answers.

Infinitive or Preposition?

Sometimes infinitive phrases can be confused with prepositional phrases. How can you distinguish an infinitive phrase from a prepositional phrase that begins with the word *to*? The prepositional phrase <u>will not</u> have a verblike word after the word *to* but will always have an object of the preposition. The infinitive phrase <u>will</u> have a verblike word after the *to* and may or may not have an object of the infinitive. This difference is important because prepositional phrases that modify do not use commas, and infinitive phrases sometimes do, as you will soon see.

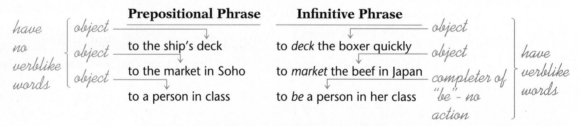

	Prepositional Phrase	**Infinitive Phrase**		
have no verblike words	*object* — to the ship's deck	to *deck* the boxer quickly — *object*	*have verblike words*
	object — to the market in Soho	to *market* the beef in Japan — *object*	
	object — to a person in class	to *be* a person in her class — *completer of "be" - no action*	

TRY IT OUT: Complete Exercise 8.1, p. 227, to check your ability to differentiate prepositional phrases from infinitive phrases.

Unusual Infinitives

When using certain infinitives, you may notice a peculiarity. The word *to* is not always written when the infinitive follows the verbs *see, hear, feel, let, help,* and *need.* You don't have to learn all of these verbs, but be aware that an infinitive doesn't always have the word *to* written out. Here are some examples.

Sheila helped Mother *prepare* the dinner last Sunday.
You need *make* a decision soon.
Did she let *go* of the account that hadn't paid?

You can recognize these unusual infinitives because the clause already has a verb, one that gives the <u>main</u> message.

Most infinitives act as modifiers to add additional information, but they can also serve as nouns—that is, the infinitive is a subject or an object.

The following examples show infinitives (italicized) in various clause positions.

To refinish furniture is my hobby.   *noun-subject*

My hobby is *to refinish furniture.*   *noun-complement*

I don't like *to work under pressure.*   *noun-direct object*

She was sad *to leave early.*   *modifier*

He ran *to catch Mrs. Christie at the door.*   *modifier*

Punctuation Points: Infinitives

You may have noticed that, in most of the example sentences with infinitive phrases, commas were not used to set off the infinitive phrases. When an infinitive or infinitive phrase acts as a noun in the main clause or when it is in its "normal" position as a modifier (at the end of the clause), <u>no</u> commas set off the phrase from the main clause. Most of the time, infinitives are used in these ways.

However, when an infinitive phrase is placed out of its natural order as a modifier, commas separate the phrase from the rest of the clause.

infinitive before its clause; use comma

infinitive phrase in natural order; no comma

To earn his commission, Mr. Alderman had to sell five machines a month.

To meet our deadline, we had to work overtime.

To get good seats for the show, we bought our tickets early. [Notice that the transposed infinitive phrase also contains a modifying prepositional phrase and that the comma is not used until the <u>end</u> of the complete infinitive modifier.]

infinitive used as noun, subject; no comma

To earn a living is all that I need. [Do you see why this beginning infinitive phrase has no comma after it? In this sentence the infinitive phrase is not a transposed modifier but acts as the subject of the main clause.]

TRY IT OUT: **Go to Exercise 8.2, pp. 227–228, to practice using commas with infinitive phrases.**

Participles

DEFINITION   A **participle** is a word that looks like a verb but acts like an adjective in the clause where it appears.

Like infinitives, participles do not always stand alone but can be part of a phrase. A participial phrase begins with the participle, can have other modifying words, and often has an object of the participle. Instead of functioning as verbs, the participles in these clauses act as adjectives, modifying a noun or a pronoun. You will find another word in the clause that is the verb.

You can see that participles have many of the same characteristics as infinitives. Keep in mind, however, that although infinitives can modify, an infinitive can also act as a noun—a subject or an object. Participles cannot be nouns, only adjectives.

Participles can also be harder to spot than infinitives because participles have more than one form. The **present participle** ends in -*ing;* the **past participle** is the third form of the verb—the perfect participle form studied in Chapter 3. Remember that this third form is used as a verb with the helping verbs *has, have,* and *had.* Many past participles come from regular verbs and end in -*ed.* However, many of them come from the irregular verbs and can be formed in any of the ways that irregular verbs are. Some examples of these irregular forms are *swum, broken,* and *brought.*

Participles have these forms because the participial phrase is actually just a short-cut adjective clause. You can see in the following examples that when the subject and helping verb are removed from the adjective clause, the result is a participial phrase. Using such a technique reduces the number of words used and offers variety in the rhythm.

Remove subject and verb and participial phrases remain

The person (who was-*leaning out the window*) fell.

Take the copy (that is-*mended with tape*).

Hortence Vickers, (who is-*running third,*) probably won't win the election.

My back left tire, (which was-*badly worn,*) had to be replaced.

Because a participle modifies a noun or a pronoun, the participle should be placed next to the word modified, unless the participle is acting as subject complement.

Placed Before:
Grinning gleefully, Maria left.

Placed After:
Maria, *grinning gleefully,* left.

Exception:

LV ⸺ SC ⸺
The dentist seems *frightening to some.*

Punctuation Points: Participles

Most participles need no commas. Only two uses of participles do require commas.

1. A transposed participle or participial phrase needs one comma after it before the main clause.

   Disappointed, Todd Stadtman returned to Mexico without the artifact.
   Edged in black, a letter would signify a death in Victorian times.

2. A participle or participial phrase placed right after the noun or pronoun modified needs to be set off with commas when it adds extra information

not needed to define that word. (These are just like the nonrestrictive adjective clauses.)

> My little sister, *looking very smug,* graduated from law school cum laude.
> We sent the data to Junior Holmes, *residing in Central Texas.*
> The Treasurer, *tired of federal regulations,* left his position to work with the homeless.

Remember that participial phrases, being only short-cut adjective clauses, are "dependent." Once the subject and verb are removed, there is no clause. The phrase that remains cannot stand alone but must be added to an independent clause.

SELF-CHECK 8-2

Add any necessary commas to the following sentences to set off participial phrases that are transposed or nonrestrictive.

1. The man winding his watch is James Carver.

2. The blue dress marked half price is only $27.

3. The annual Memorial Day parade coming around our corner passed our office building.

4. The man sitting behind Bonnie Dexter is Fred Wingo.

5. I recognized the salesperson selling Texana products.

Before you continue, turn to p. 273 to check your answers.

TRY IT OUT: **Do Exercises 8.3 and 8.4, pp. 228–229, for practice in using commas—or not using commas—with participles.**

Writing Hints: Dangling Modifiers

Read these sentences.

1. Chewing on the roof, Jack saw a squirrel.
2. Shaking hands with each other, the lions seemed to be watching Fred and Tom.
3. Arriving late for the party, the food was gone.
4. I had a friend with a glass eye named Fred.
5. To earn more money, an extra job was needed.

Do these sound pretty strange or funny to you? They do because you are accustomed to having the verbal modifiers located next to the words they modify. Therefore, when the modifiers are carelessly placed next to different nouns or pronouns, the reader assumes that they modify these nearer nouns or pronouns. Thus, it seems that Jack was chewing on the roof, that the lions were shaking hands, that the food arrived late for the party, that the glass eye is named Fred, and that the extra job is the money-earner.

Now read the examples with the modifying phrase located next to the proper word.

1. Jack saw a squirrel chewing on the roof.

   or

   The squirrel chewing on the roof was seen by Jack.

2. The lions seemed to be watching Fred and Tom shaking hands with each other.

   or

   Shaking hands with each other, Fred and Tom were watched by the two lions.

3. Arriving late for the party, we found that the food was gone.

4. My friend with a glass eye was named Fred.

5. To earn more money, I needed an extra job.

Be careful to place your participial phrases and infinitive phrases next to the words that they are meant to modify. Otherwise, these phrases are said to be dangling modifiers—misplaced modifiers. Always keep in mind when you write that your primary goal is clear communication. Using modifiers carelessly can interfere with this goal and can, as you've seen, create some amusing sentences.

DEFINITION A **dangling modifier** is one that is located next to a noun or pronoun that it does not modify.

Dangling modifiers are especially difficult to spot in transposed infinitive and participial phrases. Remember that a phrase is placed at the front of the clause because it modifies the subject of the sentence. If the modified word is not the subject of the main clause, the phrase should not be transposed, or else the main clause must be rewritten to place the correct word in the subject position.

SELF-CHECK 8-3

Underline the noun or pronoun nearest to the modifying phrase. Is it the correct person, place, or thing that the phrase is modifying? If not, rewrite the main clause so that the modifying phrase is next to the correct noun.

1. Wearing a red dress, the soldier saw his mother.

   _____

2. Hoping for rain, the farmer put in his crop today.

   _____

3. Knowing you wanted this information, this folder should help you to decide.

   _____

4. Selling 40 percent better than last year, these new items are popular with the students.

   _____

5. Lying under the other articles, we finally found the files on Thompson and Ross.

   _____

6. To learn better, more time must be spent by the student.

   _____

7. The student found a grammar error leafing through the textbook.

   _____

8. The book, lying near the candle, was covered with melted wax.

   _____

9. Invented by Edison, we are lucky to have light bulbs.

   _____

10. Ordered by the customer, these new desks are ready for shipping.

   _____

Before you continue, turn to pp. 273–274 to check your answers.

TRY IT OUT: **Complete Exercises 8.5 and 8.6, pp. 230–232, for practice with eliminating dangling modifiers.**

⊡ Gerunds

DEFINITION A **gerund** is a verblike word ending in -*ing* that functions as a noun.

Like a participle, a gerund can be either one word or the start of a phrase. A gerund can have objects and modifiers.

Also like a participle, a gerund phrase is really a short-cut clause. However, unlike a participial phrase, the gerund phrase is a short-cut <u>noun</u> clause, filling the positions of subject, complement, or some type of object. You cannot remove a gerund without leaving a "hole" in your clause.

You should have no difficulty telling present participles from gerunds when you realize that participles stand near nouns and pronouns and describe them and gerunds don't—they <u>are</u> nouns.

See how the gerunds are used in the following clauses. (Cover up the gerund and read what remains. You'll see that the clause is as incomplete without the gerund as it would be if you removed a noun clause . . . or even a noun.)

—————— S ——————, LV   SC
<u>Proofreading</u> a finished paper is a very important step.

PREP,—— OBJ——, S AV   DO   DO
From <u>tending</u> horses, I learned *<u>caring</u>* and tolerance.

S LV,—————— SC——————,
My worst character trait is *<u>putting</u> things off until tomorrow.*

S AV   INF   ,—————— OBJ of INF——————,
I tried not to notice *Mr. Gaston's <u>nodding</u> off during my speech.*

⌐· S E L F - C H E C K 8-4

Find the gerunds or gerund phrases in these sentences. Underline each, and decide which part of the clause it is filling—subject (S), object of a preposition (OP), or direct object (DO).

_____ 1. Meredith has a propensity for solving problems graciously.

_____ 2. Running in a marathon is not my idea of a fun activity.

_____ 3. The students improved their writing during this class.

_____ 4. Mr. Gephart's understanding of the problem is not clear.

_____ 5. The secretary was recording bickering among the panel members.

Before you continue, turn to p. 274 to check you answers.

Punctuation Points: Gerunds

The easy comma rule to learn for using commas with gerunds is this: Don't. That's right, just like noun clauses, gerund phrases must not be set out of their clauses.

There is one unusual exception to this general principle. When a gerund is used after a noun or pronoun as an appositive, it requires commas.

My worst shortcoming, *finding fault with others,* causes me many problems.

I have finally found a money-making hobby, *making and selling decorated cakes.*

SELF-CHECK 8-5

For review of the clause parts in the clause patterns, most of the following sentences contain verbals in subject, object, complement, or modifying positions. Underline the verbals, and determine how each is used in its clause.

Position

1. To know him is to love him. _____

2. "To be or not to be" is the question. _____

3. Selling air-conditioners is my job. _____

4. Marzella hated typing medical reports. _____

5. Good proofreading and careful typing are the marks of a good secretary. _____

6. Remembering his keys, Mr. Solomom went back to the office. _____

7. The leaves fell on the dining table. _____

8. He kept me from opening the wrong package. _____

9. Computing the payroll is an important job. _____

10. He was computing the payroll yesterday afternoon. _____

Before you continue, turn to p. 274 to check your answers.

TRY IT OUT: **Complete Exercises 8.7 and 8.8, pp. 232–233.**

OTHER METHODS OF REDUCTION

Two other ways to reduce wordiness—appositives and prepositional phrases—are not new to you. However, mentioning them here can remind you that, when you are revising your writing, you can often combine ideas through these two usages. Here are some examples.

Original:
Henry was in Eureka for twelve years. He has now moved here.

Prepositional Phrase
In Eureka for twelve years, Henry has now moved here.

Original:
Madeline needed more space in the kitchen. She moved the table and chairs to the family room.

Prepositional Phrase:
Madeline moved the table and chairs *from the kitchen to the family room for more space.*

Original:
Bubba is my second cousin. He is the president of Mississippi's largest bank.

Appositive:
Bubba, *my second cousin,* is the president of Mississippi's largest bank.

Original:
I am really interested in buying a Zimba. It is the fastest car around.

Appositive:
I am really interested in buying a Zimba, *the fastest car around.*

Again, remember that you should use all these techniques of reduction not just to remove wordiness but to improve your writing—to add variety, clarity, and emphasis.

TRY IT OUT: **Do Exercise 8.9, p. 233–234, to practice using appositives and prepositional phrases as reduction techniques. Exercise 8.10, p. 234, has two parts. In the first part you will practice the combining techniques from Chapter 7. Next, you will apply some of the reduction techniques from this chapter.**

Chapter 8: Sentence Combining and Word Reduction

Indicate on the blank whether each of the following word groups has an infinitive phrase (INF) or only a prepositional phrase (PREP). Underline the verblike word in each infinitive phrase.

_____ 1. to the other side of the street

_____ 2. to harbor a grudge against me

_____ 3. to have been in the army

_____ 4. to a person of questionable character

_____ 5. to the end of the project

_____ 6. to end the project early

_____ 7. to lend me your key to the storeroom

_____ 8. to a complete vacation from work

_____ 9. to have completed the work

_____ 10. to a purposeful, logical conclusion

Add any necessary commas to the following sentences. Remember, infinitives need commas only when they are not in their natural position. Circle any changes you make.

1. Harold Springate likes to take his dog to hunt for pheasants.

2. To assure yourself of a reservation for the convention send your order today.

3. To swim or to play tennis is a favorite summer activity.

4. To deliver this order on time we must sent it out by Friday.

5. We must send this order by Friday to deliver it on time.

6. To help us speed your order to you will you please return the enclosed card by June 12.

7. To get finished early today we should work during our lunch hour.

8. To get finished early today is what we are trying to do.

9. I hope to get finished early today.

10. To complete this exercise you will notice that you needed to add very few commas.

● E X E R C I S E 8 . 3

Place a comma after each transposed participial phrase in the following sentences. Circle any changes you make.

1. Understanding my problem Mr. Williams was very helpful in arranging a payment plan for the eyeglasses.

2. Turning on the radio we heard about the blackout in New York.

3. Writing the figures in the journal the accountant transposed two numbers.

4. Edged in red the advertisement caught my eye right away.

5. Studying your English usage will prove to be very valuable to you in the future.

6. Swimming too soon after lunch Valerie had stomach cramps.

7. Swimming too soon after lunch is thought to cause cramps.

8. Married late in life the couple seemed never to cease being newlyweds.

9. Rushing to the scene of the accident and seeing the damage the technician was surprised to find no one injured.

10. Woven in an intricate pattern the textile composition is a lovely piece of abstract art.

● E X E R C I S E   8 . 4

Add commas to any sentences that contain nonrestrictive participial phrases. Use no commas with restrictive phrases. Circle any changes you make.

1. The postal worker sorting the daily mail told me to go to the next window.

2. I gave the envelope to the woman standing next to me.

3. The car passing us now has an insignia on the right front door.

4. The station attendant washing the windows asked us if we wanted the oil checked.

5. Give this to the technician sitting near the window, not to the one washing his hands.

6. The envelope marked "Special Handling" should be taken to the post office right away.

7. Mr. Headley winding his watch said that his plane would leave in one hour.

8. The lone taxi driver waving his arm at us asked if we wanted to go into town.

9. That taxi driver waving his arm at us is Pete's brother, Harold.

10. Miss Ford working late completed the report yesterday.

11. The card attached to this letter will give you a 10-percent discount on your next purchase.

12. The bus leaving at 1:10 p.m. will arrive in Boise at 6:15 p.m.

13. Last night hearing noises I checked all of the doors and windows to make sure that they were locked.

14. The letters needing to be signed are on your desk underneath the paperweight.

15. Joann Jacobs fulfilling a dream received her M.A. degree.

16. Our project chosen for its unique plan won the award in the contest.

17. The package received this morning was damaged in the mail.

18. The sun shining brightly was overhead at noon.

19. Your umbrella lost last Thursday was found at Dimitri's.

20. The speaker concluding her address reminded us that the customer should always be our main concern.

Add a clause after each of the following transposed participial phrases. Make sure that your subject is the noun or pronoun that the phrase describes. Don't forget the comma.

1. Planning to be on time _____

   _____

2. Always elated at the team's performance _____

   _____

3. Decorated with tinsel and a star _____

   _____

4. Wondering about the results of the advertisement _____

   _____

5. Meowing in impatient anticipation _____

   _____

6. Following the twisted path into the woods _____

   _____

7. Carefully wrapped in protective paper _____

   _____

8. Considering the possible consequences of his actions _____

   _____

9. Receiving an extra twenty dollars with her change _____

   _____

10. Waking to find that the alarm had not rung _____

    _____

● EXERCISE 8.6

Rewrite the following sentences so that the transposed participial phrase modifies the correct noun or pronoun. Leave the introductory phrase as it is, at the front, and rewrite the second part. (Hint: Underline the first noun or pronoun in the main clause. Is that the correct word to be modified?) Example:

Walking to school, a car <u>crash</u> was seen by Jane.   ***Rewritten:*** Walking to school, Jane saw a car crash.

1. Swinging through the trees, the little old lady saw the gorilla.

   _____

   _____

2. Arriving late at the office, Mr. Samson's appointment was already there.

   _____

   _____

3. Dressed in a tuxedo, Mrs. Parker thought that the Senator looked very dapper.

   _____

   _____

4. Huddled in a circle, a key play was decided upon by the team.

   _____

   _____

5. Feeling sick, the doctor sent me home from work.

   _____

   _____

6. Noticing the little extras, Mr. Frank's dedication to his job was easily seen by us.

   _____

   _____

7. After going over the bids, they were sent by us to the Engineering Department for final review.

   _____

   _____

8. Typing at a rapid rate, the annual fiscal report was completed by the secretary in two days.

_____

_____

9. Rechecking the figures, the report was sent by us to the auditor for the final opinion.

_____

_____

10. Knowing about his recent problems, Mr. Hood's absences are understandable.

_____

_____

● E X E R C I S E 8.7

Add any necessary commas to the following sentences. Not all sentences, of course, will require commas. Circle any changes you make.

1. The invoice itemizing your order was sent on February 14.

2. A record book for keeping track of expenditures can be purchased at a stationery store.

3. In keeping up with inflation we have added a cost-of-living raise to this week's check.

4. Punctuating your letters and reports properly is very important to the correct reading of them.

5. Punctuating your letters and reports carefully you will see that there is less chance for a misinterpretation of them.

6. Hazel loved to go skiing at Aspen during the holidays.

7. Hazel skiing at Aspen for the holidays learned the stem-christie turn.

8. Mr. Lenderink walking to work saw the recent construction on the Miller Center.

9. The train carrying the automobiles was derailed near Portland.

10. While running errands I was caught in the torrential rains that we had last Wednesday.

11. I like running errands for the chance to get outside occasionally during the day.

12. Listening to him speak I was reminded of a teacher I once had in elementary school.

13. Warming up the engines the pilot made a final check of the instruments.

14. Our attorney listening to the arguments knew that we had a good chance to win the suit.

15. Knowing the product and understanding the prospective customer are requirements for a productive salesperson.

● E X E R C I S E 8.8

Write fifteen sentences: five with infinitive phrases, five with participial phrases, and five with gerund phrases. Underline the verbals, and add any necessary punctuation. Be prepared to tell which part of the clause each verbal is functioning as; for example, an adjective or a subject. Use other paper.

● E X E R C I S E 8.9

Practice writing prepositional phrases and appositives.

Combine the following sets of clauses by making one idea a prepositional phrase or an appositive.

1. Take this memo to Stephanie Happer. She is the head of Internal Affairs.

   _____

   _____

2. Columbus, Indiana, is an unusual town. You can see striking contemporary architecture there.

   _____

   _____

3. Try the Drake Hotel. It has a marvelous brunch every Sunday.

   _____

   _____

4. I met Claudia Dinges. She is a well-known vocalist with the Met.

   _____

   _____

5. If you need any printing done, see the Williamses. They do good work.

   _____

   _____

6. I can't wait until spring. The dogwood will bloom.

_____

_____

Write your own prepositional phrase or appositive to add to each sentence.

7. I have never met a Westerner _____.

8. That woman _____ keeps coming in here to return merchandise.

9. I like to read the type of books _____.

10. Alfonso Renatti _____ cooks a spaghetti sauce you will love.

● E X E R C I S E 8.10   CHALLENGE

Rewrite the following paragraph two times. Use other paper.

   1. *Combine any related ideas into compound or complex sentences, trying to use variety in your constructions. Try to use at least one adjective clause and one noun clause. You will probably need to add transitions to make the writing flow together.*

   2. *For this revision, use some of the verbal phrases and other techniques of reduction. Try to use at least one gerund and one appositive. You will, again, probably want to add transitions to help the writing to flow.*

    A walk in the woods can be lovely. It can be dangerous. There could be poisonous snakes in the woods in some parts of the country. The underbrush can be tangled. You could fall down. You could hurt yourself. There might be no one to hear your calls for help. A bear or other wild animal might be in the woods. There could be poison ivy or other harmful plants. The weather could change suddenly. You could lose your way. You could take a well-worn path. It could run out. You would be in a mesh of trees, bushes, roots, and plant life. It could turn dark. You couldn't see your way. You might lose any companions you were with. Any of these things could happen. None of them might happen. You could have an exhilarating time. You can take precautions to avoid most of these troubles. You should plan ahead. The risks don't outweigh the benefits of a walk in the woods.

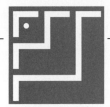

CHAPTER 9

Fragments and Run-Ons

OVERVIEW

- **Fragments**
- **Run-Ons**

Two common writing errors result from a misunderstanding of what makes a good sentence. Once you know about dependent and independent clauses and about phrases—especially verbal phrases—you can repair either of these faulty constructions. The two errors are fragments and run-ons.

FRAGMENTS

DEFINITION A **fragment** is a word group, punctuated as a sentence, that cannot stand alone because the independent clause is missing.

You could think of this writing error as "a sentence containing too little"—an incomplete idea. You can easily correct a fragment: It should probably be attached to the sentence before or after it. Most likely, the fragment is a modifying phrase or clause that is not attached to the independent clause it modifies.

Study these examples of fragments to see why each cannot stand alone. Each should be attached to the sentence written next to it. Of course, any fragment can also be repaired by being rewritten into an independent clause.

dependent adverb clause 1. Consuelo was pleased with the election. Because she received twice as many votes as the runner-up. — *past participial phrase*

Noun with present participial phrase 2. I decided to buy the convertible. Trimmed in white.

3. My head swimming with possible solutions. I couldn't make a decision. — *noun with adjective clause*

4. Joeshawn, who is employed by the post office. He has six weeks' vacation.

Introductory participial phrase 5. Worried by the heavily falling snow and the deepening drifts. I stayed overnight in Butte.

The following revisions show the repair of each fragment in two ways: (a) by attaching it to the independent clause or (b) by making it into an independent clause of its own.

1. a. Consuelo was pleased with the election because she received twice as many votes as the runner-up.

   b. Consuelo was pleased with the election. She received twice as many votes as the runner-up.

2. a. I decided to buy the convertible trimmed in white.

   b. I decided to buy the convertible. It is trimmed in white.

3. a. My head swimming with possible solutions, I couldn't make a decision.

   b. My head was swimming with possible solutions. I couldn't make a decision.

4. a. Joeshawn, who is employed by the post office, has six weeks' vacation.

   b. Joeshawn is employed by the post office. He has six weeks' vacation.

5. a. Worried by the heavily falling snow and the deepening drifts, I stayed overnight in Butte.

   b. I was worried by the heavily falling snow and the deepening drifts. I stayed overnight in Butte.

Identify the fragment by writing 1 *on the blank if the fragment is the first word group or* 2 *if the second. Repair the fragment by attaching it to the clause.*

_____ 1. Knotted and frayed. The rope was a poor one to use to tie up the boat.

_____ 2. People who care about their health. They eat properly.

_____ 3. I was used to the long hours at the restaurant. Was used to the constant change of employees.

_____ 4. While I was researching the case. I saw that Judge Kemp was the trial judge.

_____ 5. This could be a fragment. A word group that is incomplete with no independent clause.

Before you continue, turn to p. 275 to check your answers.

TRY IT OUT: **Practice repairing fragments in Exercises 9.1 and 9.2, pp. 245–246.**

RUN-ONS

DEFINITION A **run-on** is a word group made up of two or more independent clauses that are not connected by the proper glue.

This writing error was touched on in Chapter 7 in the discussion of compound sentences. A run-on could be a compound sentence, but it needs something added to form the compound correctly. A run-on could also be made into two simple sentences, punctuated separately.

Whereas a fragment contains "too little," a run-on contains "too much" for a simple sentence.

For simplicity this text will use the term *run-on* to refer to both run-on (no glue, no punctuation) and comma splice (no glue, only a comma) errors.

Look at these examples of the run-on and the comma splice.

Run-On:
Caesar transposed the figures the totals wouldn't balance.

Comma Splices:
Caesar transposed the figures, the totals wouldn't balance.
Caesar transposed the figures, hence, the totals wouldn't balance.

Repairing run-ons such as these is easy. Whichever method you choose will depend on the effect you wish to achieve.

Ways to Repair a Run-On

1. Divide the run-on into two separate sentences.

   Caesar transposed the figures. The totals wouldn't balance.

   Comment: Too many simple sentences in an essay makes for choppiness. Also, an idea written as a simple sentence draws emphasis. Having too many simple sentences confuses your reader.

2. Form a compound sentence by adding a coordinate conjunction—*and, but, or, nor, yet*—preceded by a comma.

   Caesar transposed the figures, and the totals wouldn't balance.

   Comment: Although a good choice, this method can be overused. Too many compound sentences make for a sing-song rhythm.

3. Form a compound sentence by adding a semicolon between the clauses.

   Caesar transposed the figures; the totals wouldn't balance.

   Comment: This is a good technique to add emphasis to each idea. Save this technique for that purpose. A two-clause sentence joined only by a semicolon provides an interesting stop-start rhythm, but it does not have the flow that a sentence with a conjunction provides.

4. Make a compound sentence using a transitional-type word called either an adverbial conjunction or a connective adverb. Use a semicolon at the end of the first clause.

   Caesar transposed the figures; hence, the totals wouldn't balance.

   Comment: This technique works best when a connective is needed to show the clearest relationship between the ideas. Because of the abrupt style created by the semicolon, use this method sparingly.

As you can see, each method has advantages and disadvantages. When deciding how to fix a particular run-on, think first of the message. Are the two ideas distinct and equal? Make two sentences, or add a coordinate conjunction. Do you want to contrast or balance two closely related ideas? Add a semicolon. Does the relationship between the ideas need emphasis? Add the appropriate adverbial conjunction.

Indicate on the blank whether each is a run-on (R) or a correct sentence (S). Circle the glue in the correct sentences.

1. Dairy farming is demanding work, you cannot just go off and leave the cows untended.

2. She checked the memo, and she sent it out.

3. While working, Ted saw a discrepancy in the books; he notified the auditor.

4. I talked with the man you hired.

5. I talked with that man you hired him.

6. No one can remember the date of the first contract, consequently, we had to rewrite it.

7. You are, of course, able to participate in the insurance plan, but you must provide 60 percent of the payment.

8. He insulted the customer, then he quit his job and left.

9. If you can, will you lend me your copy of the schedule; I'll give it right back.

10. He was not feeling well; consequently, he left at three o'clock.

Before you continue, turn to p. 275 to check your answers.

TRY IT OUT: **Complete Exercises 9.3 and 9.4, pp. 247–248, for practice in recognizing and repairing run-ons.**

Transitional Expressions: A Closer Look

In Chapter 1 you learned that transitional expressions can act as interrupters, breaking into a single clause. Here, you'll see transitional expressions in another role: as bridges linking two independent clauses in a compound sentence.

Adverbial Conjunctions

DEFINITION An **adverbial conjunction** is a word or word group that shows the relationship between two ideas but acts more like a transition between the two than a conjunction.

When you studied coordinate conjunctions, you learned to think of them as the glue in a compound structure. When joining two clauses, adverbial conjunctions differ from coordinate conjunctions in two ways: (1) Adverbial conjunctions are adverbs that show a specific relationship between the two ideas connected, and thus (2) they must be used with a semicolon in place of the comma in other compound sentences.

The two separate ideas can also be expressed in two sentences, with the adverbial conjunction starting off the second sentence.

Although the name *conjunction* may be misleading in the term *adverbial conjunction*, the name does show how closely in meaning the ideas are joined. The *adverbial* part of the name is effective because these connectives tell the things adverbs tell: <u>when</u>, <u>where</u>, <u>why</u>, <u>to what extent</u>, and <u>under what conditions</u>.

Study the following list of adverbial conjunctions to see what these relationships can be.

Common Adverbial Conjunctions

accordingly	however	otherwise
besides	moreover	that is
consequently	namely	then
for example	nevertheless	therefore
furthermore	on the contrary	thus
hence	on the other hand	

Punctuation Points: Adverbial Conjunctions. The important thing to keep in mind as you connect independent clauses is this: Use a semicolon instead of a comma <u>before</u> the adverbial conjunction. Whether you use a comma after a transitional expression that begins a second clause is optional, although most current usage requires one.

2 independent clauses 1. The machine seems to require a skilled worker<u>; hence,</u> our advertisement should state this fact.

2 independent clauses 2. Herman Industries manufactures high-quality clocks<u>; consequently,</u> their product is expensive.

2 independent clauses 3. Complete this letter<u>; then</u> you may leave.

Many writers omit the comma after the adverbial conjunction when the meaning of the expression is essential to the second clause—as with *then* in Example 3. The comma is used when the adverbial conjunction connects both ideas as a whole.

Decide whether to use a semicolon at the blank. Add one only if the blank comes at the point where the first independent clause ends and another begins.

1. B. J. was _____ of course, delighted to be back in the States.

2. George was born in France _____ however, he has lived in Canada for thirty years.

3. They bought the latest model but were not _____ however, impressed with the guarantee.

4. Rene felt it necessary to do volunteer work, and she was _____ for example, an award winner at the YWCA.

5. I crave vegetables _____ for example, I can't eat enough Brussels sprouts.

Before you continue, turn to p. 275 to check your answers.

TRY IT OUT: **Do Exercises 9.5 and 9.6, pp. 248–249, to practice choosing appropriate adverbial conjunctions.**

Other Transitional Expressions

In addition to connecting two independent clauses, the expressions listed on p. 240 and a number of other phrases are often used to show the reader how a train of thought is being developed. Called **transitions** when used in this manner, these expressions can help your writing flow smoothly. More importantly, these expressions also give hints to the reader about how to interpret what is being read; that is to say, transitions tell the reader to look for a comparison or contrast, a conclusion, an emphasis, a sequence, an illustration, or an indication that what is said is opinion, not fact.

Become familiar with these additional transitional expressions, grouped by their intent.

Comparison

by comparison	in the same vein	likewise
by the same token	in the same way	similarly

Contrast

at any rate	even so	incidentally
anyway	in another way	instead
by contrast	in any case	inversely
by the way	in any event	rather
conversely		

Conclusion

after all	generally speaking	on balance
all in all	in any case	on the whole
all things	in any event	ordinarily
considered	in brief	to conclude
as a result	in conclusion	to summarize
as a rule	in general	to sum up
as usual	in short	usually
by and large	in summary	
generally	in the long run	

Emphasis

also	in other words	not only that
in addition	less importantly	to emphasize
in essence	more importantly	too

Sequence

after that	first of all	in turn
afterward	for now	later on
at first	for the present	meanwhile
at the same time	for the time being	next
before that	in conclusion	second
finally	in the first place	to begin with
first	in time	to finish

Illustrations

as you can see	for instance	to give an example
for another thing	for one thing	to illustrate
for example		

Writer's Opinion

I believe	I think	one can conclude
I suppose	it seems to me	one would assume

Punctuation Points: Transitions. Any of the transitional expressions, not only those listed as adverbial conjunctions, can be placed between clauses.

If you are using the expression to connect two closely related independent clauses, place a semicolon at the end of the first clause, write the expression, and follow the transition with a comma. (See a reference manual for the less-used exceptions to this practice.)

> Axis Automotive decided it had too many models in production; consequently, the company stopped making two of the models.
>
> I really like movies; on the other hand, I find the just-released ones to be too torrid for my tastes.

Using transitions in this manner clearly calls attention to the relationship between those two clauses. Many times, though, you are moving from one larger idea to another. In these cases you will want to vary the placement of your transitional expression, following these rules of emphasis: The transitional expression placed first has greatest emphasis. Breaking into a sentence with the transition carries the second greatest emphasis. A transitional expression placed at the end carries the least emphasis.

Notice that commas are used to set off the transitional expression wherever it is placed. (In this use the expressions are the "interrupters" you studied in Chapter 1.)

in front
> *In contrast,* you do not have to redo the Brookman report, only the Harris file.
>
> I was prepared, *I think,* for any event.   *breaking into clause*
>
> We have to change our election process, *it seems to me.*   *at end*

The words and word groups listed as adverbial conjunctions can also serve as transitional words within a single clause.

> My <u>supervisor</u>, *on the other hand*, <u>will be attending</u> a different section of the meeting.   *only 1 clause*
>
> You <u>may wish</u>, *however*, to take your vacation at a different time.   *1 clause*
>
> *interrupts only 1 clause*   The new <u>program</u> <u>has</u> more up-to-date figures; the old <u>one</u>, *consequently*, <u>is</u> outdated.   *2 clauses meet here*

In summary, the key to punctuating sentences with transitional expressions is recognizing whether the expression stands between two independent clauses or interrupts one clause.

1. A transitional expression that starts the second clause of a compound sentence is preceded by a semicolon and followed with a comma.

2. A transitional expression that interrupts one clause is set off with commas.

Choose an appropriate transitional expression from the preceding lists to connect the ideas in each of the following items. Answers will vary, and more than one category of transitional expression may be appropriate in certain items.

1. Our cost estimate was fairly accurate; _____, we will have to increase the unit price by three cents.

2. First, I took off the air filter; _____, I examined the carburetor.

3. Winter offers many opportunities for outdoor sports; _____, driving can become quite hazardous.

4. Although many people are not offended by this practice, several others, _____, are very upset.

5. Hawaii offers many unusual vacation opportunities; _____, you can swim from black volcanic beaches.

6. Although some people can be cruel at times, _____, most people are kind and helpful.

7. I have studied the matter fully, and, _____, my conclusion is correct.

8. You may want to purchase a new vehicle, but, _____, be sure to study the consumers' guides.

9. The East Coast borders the Atlantic; _____, the West Coast fronts the Pacific.

10. The designer dresses cost thousands of dollars; _____, they are very expensive.

Before you continue, turn to p. 275–276 to check your answers.

TRY IT OUT: **Complete Exercises 9.7 and 9.8, pp. 249–250. Exercise 9.9, p. 250, is the Challenge exercise.**

Chapter 9: Fragments and Run-Ons

Repair these fragments by adding them to an independent clause or by supplying the missing element. (You do not have to keep the fragment first. Watch for needed punctuation.)

1. Listening for the alarm to sound

   _____

   _____

2. A test that covers things not in the class discussion

   _____

   _____

3. The envy of every man and woman in the department

   _____

   _____

4. One of the ways to detect a good candidate for the job

   _____

   _____

5. A lesson I learned the hard way

   _____

   _____

6. Terry, adept at fixing anything mechanical

   _____

   _____

7. Terry, who shudders at any scratchy sound

_____

_____

8. The bird washing himself in the clear waters of the deep, cold pond

_____

_____

9. Until I learned the importance of careful scheduling

_____

_____

10. For seven months, after having done the research for two years before that

_____

_____

● E X E R C I S E   9 . 2

Correct any fragments by adding them to the clauses they modify in each of the following paragraphs. Sometimes the fragment will belong with the sentence before it and sometimes with the sentence after it. Be careful to punctuate correctly.

1.   Working at the zoo. Was something Connie dearly loved. She really enjoyed seeing the newborns in the spring. Enjoyed the yearlings. As they played with each other. Learning how to find their places in the group. These "teenagers" would fight. But not as seriously as they might have to someday. Connie learned much. From these animals at the zoo.

2.   I used to dread going to school. Before I found a field. That I really want to learn more about. I could hardly make myself get up in the mornings. I found any excuse. To avoid classes. I was often sick. Another excuse I made for myself. Was to schedule work hours. That conflicted with the class hours. Now, however, because I know where I'm going. I attend all of my classes.

● E X E R C I S E   9 . 3

Each of the numbered items is a run-on. Repair each using one of the four methods listed on p. 238. Use each method at least once.

1. Some people want security they will go to any lengths to get it.

2. After the concert we went to dinner I had a steak.

3. Unless you have been there, you cannot judge another's reaction, you may have acted that way too.

4. Turn on the gas, quickly light the pilot.

5. Brenda, who is 24, is single, however, she is engaged.

6. The Northern Lights are remarkable they can be seen in Alaska quite often.

7. First of America is one of the largest banks in the Midwest, its assests, accordingly, are in the billions.

8. Don't capitalize the word *aspirin* it is a general term, not a specific trade name.

9. It is difficult to stick to some things to their finish you should, however, not give up.

10. Several wanted to have a picnic, others preferred a dance for the fundraiser.

● E X E R C I S E   9 . 4

Repair each of these short paragraphs by correcting the run-on sentences.

1.   Whenever you want to take a break, you should consider a vacation, some people pride themselves on never taking time off from work they just keep piling up vacation days, working longer and longer stretches at a time, they get more and more exhausted their pride starts to get really involved they get trapped into being such workaholics that they then cannot allow themselves time off, they think that they are being wonderful, admirable employees by doing this, however, studies show that this type of worker loses freshness these workers are, most likely, actually less productive than those who take time off occasionally.

2.	It always amazes me, some people take fashion so seriously, becoming slaves to the whims of designers, most of whom, I think, really don't like people, they seem to work at making most of us look absolutely ridiculous, I wonder if all of these designers are as thin as they want us to be, they put form-fitting waists in clothes, accordingly, nine-tenths of the wearers are going around not breathing and sucking in their stomachs, but fashion-fraught people buy these things, they suffer, they wear oversized jackets to hide, they diet incessantly, they beat themselves up for their failure to look like the people in the ads, this, my friends, is high-fashion slavery, a plight of first-world countries only.

● EXERCISE 9.5

Circle the letter indicating the better written sentence in each pair; that is, choose the sentence that uses the more appropriate adverbial conjunction.

1. a. A hedonist is a person given to the zealous pursuit of pleasure; hence, he/she would probably be a poor choice for a spouse.
    b. A hedonist is a person given to the zealous pursuit of pleasure; on the other hand, he/she would probably be a poor choice for a spouse.

2. a. She was afraid of heights; accordingly, she took up rock climbing.
    b. She was afraid of heights; nevertheless, she took up rock climbing.

3. a. You have several good job skills; that is, you are able to write a good sentence.
    b. You have several good job skills; for example, you are able to write a good sentence.

4. a. I like dogs; moreover, I hate cats.
    b. I like dogs; on the contrary, I hate cats.

5. a. I plan to move by December; otherwise, I would be happy to solicit for the heart fund.
    b. I plan to move by December; furthermore, I would be happy to solicit for the heart fund.

● E X E R C I S E   9 . 6

If the italicized adverbial conjunction is not appropriate, cross it out and replace it with another from the list on p. 240. Punctuate correctly.

1. Magda excelled at playing canasta, *besides,* she was not a good poker player.

2. Elaine Lasseter is an excellent salesperson, *however,* she could sell me contact lenses, and I have perfect vision!

3. Go to the bank *hence* pick up our order from from Dykman Office Supply.

4. I needed to improve my credit rating, *consequently,* I took out a small loan and made regular payments.

5. Your written English has already improved greatly in these few weeks, *otherwise,* your sentences are showing much more variety and careful style choices.

● E X E R C I S E   9 . 7

On the blanks provide any appropriate transitional expressions. Add necessary punctuation.

1. To start your homework, you should do three things. _____ you should have your books, including reference materials, ready. _____ have your study space cleared, quiet, and ready for work. _____ make sure you have such chores done as phone calls, and so on, so that you won't have constant interruptions.

2. Mae Ling can't decide what to do. She wants to finish school. _____ she wants to start her family. _____ it is a hard thing to decide. _____ her in-laws are pressuring her to have a child. _____ she will decide before the summer is over.

3. You cannot continue as you are, John. _____ you must make some change in your behavior. You have been _____ shirking your responsibilities. _____ you have ignored our suggestions for change. _____ you must make changes or leave.

On other paper write sentences using each of the following expressions as transitions: (1) before that, (2) even so, (3) for instance, (4) on the contrary, and (5) one can conclude. You will probably need to write two clauses or two separate sentences to show an appropriate context for each expression.

On other paper type or rewrite the essay below, correcting the fragments, run-ons, misused connectives, and any misused punctuation.

Once upon a time, on a planet not too far from Earth. There was a teacher. Who was named Ms. Blue. Ms. Blue loved teaching, in fact, she had no other interests in her life, of course, she assumed her students had no outside interests either. Like jobs, families, bills to pay, or even other classes.

Ms. Blue delighted in giving her students the great benefits of her complete devotion, the students were, consequently, subjected to mountains of homework, rivers of papers to write. And pools of problems to solve, hence, they were swamped.

You, dear reader, have never, of course, had a teacher like this it must be difficult for you to understand, moreover, you are probably becoming somewhat envious of these students. On this planet so near to you. Imagine having someone so devoted and selfless, try to feel the glow of knowing someone thinks enough of you to be so dedicated.

Meanwhile consider also what you might want to do for a person that unselfish. A person, who would truly be doing you a service. While you are toiling away at the seemingly endless tasks dreamed up by Ms. Blue to occupy your every waking moment (and others you hadn't planned on being awake for). Make a mental list of the possible favors you could do for Ms. Blue. Try to picture the look on her face. As she sees you coming into her classroom with her "gift." Your face, accordingly, no doubt has a glow of warmth and happiness. As you contemplate the scene, wouldn't you feel, namely, lucky to have been placed in such a situation?

Alas, it is just an imaginative situation, you aren't that lucky, you are; on the contrary, here on Earth, you are simply enrolled in a class. Headed by a mere mortal. You are, therefore, probably starved for attention, desperate for much more homework and critical review of your work; furthermore, you are probably motivated by now to seek out an academic counselor to complain. That you are being cheated.

Never fear, dear student, you may get your wish for a teacher like Ms. Blue. In fact, if you insist. Your present instructor may be willing to martyr himself/herself, you probably only have to ask.

▣ Periodic Review: Chapters 8–9

Add -ed and -ing to the following words.

1. arrange   _____

2. label   _____

3. travel   _____

4. allot   _____

5. study   _____

6. refer   _____

7. survey   _____

8. can   _____

9. offer   _____

10. omit   _____

On the blank tell whether each is a Pattern 1 (S and V); 2 (S, V, DO); 3 (S, V, IO, DO); or 4 (S, LV, SC). Write the number that indicates your choice.

_____ 1. The Essex, registered in Nantucket, was sunk by a sperm whale in 1820 during a whaling run.

_____ 2. That laptop computer is under six pounds with the capability of doing many projects.

_____ 3. During the morning the actress learned six pages of lines for the evening's practice.

_____ 4. The judge has written me a letter to respond to the criticism of the jury selection.

_____ 5. Several of the complainants had invested their savings with Mr. Stone and have lost all.

_____ 6. The Magnus Company is interested in our research into the cause of diabetes.

_____ 7. Amanda fed the llama a handful of hay.

_____ 8. Please look for my keys in the sideboard by the front door.

_____ 9. Tell me the reasons for delay in the departure of Flight 5643.

_____ 10. We were headed in the right direction at last.

From the following three clauses, write sentences that contain the elements indicated after each number. (Not all three ideas, nor the original wording, must appear in each of your sentences.)

The Dark Ages lasted from about 476 A.D. to the Eleventh Century; few people could read; there was much ignorance and poverty.

1. Independent clause modified by prepositional phrase.

   _____

   _____

2. Compound sentence.

   _____

   _____

3. Complex sentence with adverb clause in natural position.

   _____

   _____

4. Complex sentence with adjective clause.

   _____

   _____

5. Sentence with modifying participial phrase in front.

   _____

   _____

6. Sentence with infinitive phrase.

   _____

   _____

7. Sentence with gerund phrase.

   _____

   _____

8. Compound sentence with adverbial conjunction.

   _____

   _____

Fill in the blanks with the correct possessive form.

1. Save me ten (minute) _____ worth of your time later on.

2. (Baby) _____ breath is a lovely, delicate flower.

3. This new (toothbrush) _____ handle is shaped to fit easily in your hand.

4. The fault was (James) _____.

5. The (war) _____ aftermath was death and destruction.

Punctuate the following sentences, and indicate on the blank whether each is simple (S), compound (CP), or complex (CX).

_____ 1. Whoever locked up the offices yesterday forgot to turn off the coffeemaker.

_____ 2. To earn better interest on your money you may want to investigate our new municipal bonds.

_____ 3. He enjoyed classical rap and country music.

_____ 4. You should review you homeowner's insurance every year and raise the coverage as inflation occurs.

_____ 5. Angus MacDonald wearing his family tartans played the bagpipes for John Donaldson's funeral.

_____ 6. I say to you Tom Bailey you had better pay more attention to your accounts.

_____ 7. The old farmhouse derelict and forlorn seemed to cry out for someone to buy and restore it.

_____ 8. Fort Lauderdale which is near Miami has miles and miles of canals that are deep enough for large boats.

_____ 9. Although the computer can do many more things the electronic typewriters are still the choice of many.

_____ 10. Harrietta is a capable honest bank teller but she is capable of doing many other things.

_____ 11. The London Taxi a remarkable diesel with unheard-of amounts of room would be an excellent car for you.

_____ 12. Agatha Simms of Tuscaloosa Alabama has been recommended for the President's Peace Award.

_____ 13. Mr. Haroldson grabbed the telephone and placed a call to order the stock as it was rising in value.

_____ 14. Any person trained in making eyeglasses can easily find work in any part of the country.

_____ 15. By showing up and paying attention you will probably make it through life without much trouble.

Choose the correct pronouns to complete the following.

1. Anyone who has (his, their) research completed should begin the writing of the report.

2. It was (she, her) (who, whom) I know was the more qualified.

3. Between you and (I, me) I suppose the contract should go to Ralph and (he, him).

4. Did you say that (its, it's) no problem for you to show Lionel and (they, them) around the plant?

5. The money earned by Paul and (I, me) will go toward a car.

6. My sister is one of those women (who, whom) I believe always looks at the positive side of things.

7. When the winning number was announced, Marie shouted, "It's (me, I)."

8. Give the final version to LaSonya and (she, her).

9. The last laugh was (her's, hers).

10. Mr. Nestor has a dog (who, that) chases squirrels, cats, and even other dogs out of the yard.

On the blank tell whether the underlined verbal is a participle, infinitive, or gerund. Add and circle any necessary punctuation.

_____ 1. <u>Outlining a chapter</u> as you read is a good way to learn new material.

_____ 2. I like the little puppy <u>chewing on the rubber bone</u>.

_____ 3. My favorite technique for relaxing is <u>taking a hot bath</u>.

_____ 4. Mai Ling <u>filing her fingernails</u> seemed uninterested in our conversation.

_____ 5. My favorite professor at night school <u>teaching only this one semester</u> will leave in June.

_____ 6. Anyone <u>calling the hotline</u> does not have to give his or her name.

_____ 7. <u>Calling the hotline</u> is a quick way to get help.

_____ 8. The border patrol wanted <u>to finish the night's shift</u>.

_____ 9. Violet <u>to speed up her shopping</u> went to Zeke's at midnight.

_____ 10. The coroner <u>puzzled by the evidence</u> took more samples to study.

Subject and Verb Agreement

OVERVIEW

- **Determining a Verb's Number**
- **Making Subject and Verb Agree**

Agreement of subject and verb simply means this: A singular subject needs a singular verb to agree with it; a plural subject needs a plural verb.

Although you probably apply this principle in most of your sentences, you no doubt make some errors in subject-verb agreement. These errors probably occur because you (1) have misidentified the subject or (2) are unfamiliar with some of the peculiarities of the rules of the English language.

A once-through reading of the chapter will not be enough. It is not enough to "understand" the rules of subject-verb agreement. A person could understand what your name is, but would that mean he or she could use your name in the future? No, your name would have to be learned. So too these rules.

DETERMINING A VERB'S NUMBER

Examine these two examples.

The buyer call<u>s</u> on several firms.

The buyer<u>s</u> call on several firms.

As you look at these two sentences, you may notice a peculiar thing about verb number: Verbs that end in -s are <u>singular</u>. They are just the opposite of nouns. You have learned for years to add -s or -es to make a word plural, but the words made plural in this way are nouns. If the subject of your clause is a third person singular noun or pronoun, your verb should be singular and should end in -s.

Now that you are aware that verbs that end in -s are singular, you are ready to work with the rules for determining subject-verb agreement.

⌐ S E L F - C H E C K   1 0 – 1

Underline the singular verb in each of the following pairs.

1. occur, occurs

2. is, are

3. study, studies

4. has, have

5. doesn't, don't [These two words are contractions made up of *does not* and *do not*.]

Before you continue, turn to p. 276 to check your answers.

MAKING SUBJECT AND VERB AGREE

The following 14 rules will guide you past some common pitfalls writers face when making decisions about subject-verb agreement.

⊡ Subject Position

RULE 1: Don't confuse the subject complement with the subject.

With linking verbs you have to be sure you are choosing a verb that will agree with the subject of your clause, not the subject complement. Sometimes the subject and subject complement don't agree in number—one may be singular and one plural—but that is all right. However, the verb should always agree with the subject.

Notice these two examples where the subject and the complement change places.

> The traffic jam's <u>cause</u> <u>is</u> thousands of cars in L.A.
>
> <u>Thousands</u> of cars in L.A. <u>are</u> the cause of the traffic jam.

RULE 2: Watch out for unusual word order. In some sentences the subject comes <u>after</u> the verb. Such sentences usually begin with *here* or *there* but can also begin with a phrase or even an object.

Study these examples of unusual word order.

> Here <u>are</u> seven <u>volunteers</u> for the Community Chest drive.
>
> Included with these parts <u>is</u> an instruction <u>book</u> for the operation of the motor.
>
> Among the participants <u>was</u> a <u>representative</u> from the Department of Social Services.
>
> The lights <u>John</u> <u>is</u> responsible for, not the sound.
>
> Where <u>have</u> the <u>cassettes</u> disappeared?

▣ Phrases Between the Subject and the Verb

RULE 3: Do not be misled by prepositional phrases when locating the subject. (Rule 6 gives the few exceptions to this rule.)

Chapter 1 emphasized that subjects do not appear in prepositional phrases. For practice you may want to put parentheses around these phrases so that you are not confused by them when choosing the verb.

Select the correct verb for each of these sentences.

> The Director of all of the companies (is, are) attending the Open House. [Remove *of all* and *of the companies*, and you see that the <u>Director</u> <u>is</u> <u>attending</u>.]
>
> Any one of the nursing supervisors (has, have) a great deal of responsibility. [Remove *of the nursing supervisors*, and *one* <u>has</u> remains as the subject-verb.]
>
> A supply of stationery and envelopes (was, were) ordered last week. [Once *of stationery and envelopes* is removed, the subject <u>supply</u> becomes apparent, with the verb <u>was</u>.]

When proofreading your writing, you can mentally place parentheses around your prepositional phrases and more easily check the subject-verb agreement.

RULE 4: Certain other phrases act as prepositional phrases in that they add an extra idea and are not part of the subject. Disregard phrases that begin with expressions such as:

accompanied by	including
along with	plus
as well as	together with
in addition to	

These added phrases will come between the subject and the verb and will usually be set out with commas. If the nouns in the intervening phrase were meant to be as important as the subject, the writer would have made a compound subject by using a coordinate conjunction, such as *and*. By placing these nouns in this type of phrase, the writer is emphasizing the subject. You may want to use this writing technique in instances where you want to emphasize one of several who are doing something.

Locate the subjects in the following, noticing that these receive more emphasis than the people or things placed in the phrases. Then choose the verb that agrees with the subject.

Ms. Levine, as well as her associates, (was, were) present for the vote. [The important idea is that <u>Ms. Levine was</u> present. The associates are reduced in importance by being placed in the phrase. The sentence emphasizes the value of Ms. Levine's vote.]

The quote, including the most recent figures, (is, are) not thought to be unreasonable. [The important idea is that the <u>quote is</u> reasonable. Apparently, the recent figures are not very important to the idea.]

The manuscript, along with the carbon copy, (has, have) been sent to Mr. Wilson. [The important idea is that the <u>manuscript has been</u> sent.]

◢ Third Person Indefinite Pronouns

RULE 5: Third person indefinite pronouns are always singular and require singular verbs.

In Chapter 6 you learned that indefinite pronouns need singular pronouns when used as the antecedents. For review, the indefinite pronouns are listed again here.

another	everybody	no one
anybody	everyone*	nothing
anyone*	everything	one
anything	many a . . .	somebody
each	neither	someone
either	nobody	something
every		

(*Note:* In some instances *anyone* and *everyone* are each written as two words. It is easy to choose the correct spelling. If the word is followed by a phrase that begins with *of*, use two words; otherwise, use one. For example, "Everyone went home" has no phrase, but "Every one of the boys went home" does and causes *everyone* to split into two words. In either case, a singular verb is used.)

Note the singular verbs used with each of the following singular indefinite pronouns.

<u>Each</u> of the cartons <u>has</u> twenty parts in it.

<u>Everyone</u> <u>knows</u> that progress has its pitfalls.

Every <u>one</u> of the automobiles <u>comes</u> with radial tires.

<u>Nobody</u> without tickets <u>is</u> to be admitted to the show.

<u>Neither</u> of the offices <u>was</u> painted last year.

TRY IT OUT: **Do Exercise 10.1, p. 265, to practice the first five rules of subject-verb agreement.**

◨ Singular Versus Plural Meaning

RULE 6: Certain naming words convey the idea of either one whole or portion (a singular subject) or the idea of several individual items (a plural subject). These words are often tied closely in meaning to a noun in a prepositional phrase. Words in this category include the indefinite pronouns *all, any, more, most, none,* and *some;* fractions; and the words *number* and *percentage.*

These words are exceptions to the general rule that you ignore the prepositional phrase when choosing a verb to agree with the subject. In the following sentences you can see how a noun in a prepositional phrase can dictate the number of certain indefinite pronouns.

<u>Some</u> of the income <u>is</u> tax free. [one portion]

<u>Some</u> of the products <u>are</u> outdated. [several individual items]

<u>All</u> <u>is</u> well. [one whole]

<u>All</u> of the attendants <u>are wearing</u> pink. [several individuals]

<u>None</u> of the equipment <u>has had</u> a breakdown. [the equipment considered as a whole]

<u>None</u> of the questionnaires <u>have been</u> returned. [the questionnaires considered individually]

(*Note:* Because *none* can be defined as "not one," some writers always use a singular verb with it.)

Fractions, too, can be singular or plural.

<u>One half</u> of the product <u>is</u> completed.

<u>One half</u> of the questions <u>are</u> completed.

The word *number* is singular if preceded by the word *the* or *this;* otherwise it is plural. The word *percentage* is the same.

<u>The number</u> of inhabitants <u>is rising</u>.

<u>A number</u> of people <u>are moving</u> to South Dakota.

RULE 7: Subjects joined by *and* are usually plural, but occasionally the meaning will dictate a singular verb.

Most of the time the subject is plural when things are joined by the conjunction *and*.

> Mr. Small and Mr. Fong have attended the auto show.
> Good grammar and good spelling are necessary to good writing.

However, sometimes the two things joined by *and* have become one and are considered singular.

1. Smith and Westen is a company that makes guns.
2. The secretary and treasurer is an office held by one person.
3. Peanut butter and jelly is my favorite sandwich.
4. Every man and woman in the office enjoys a holiday for Martin Luther King's birthday.

(*Note: Each* and *every* will always override *and*, keeping the verb singular.)

When connecting two nouns with *and*, keep in mind that the articles—*a, an, the*—or other adjectives also indicate number. In Example 2 the word *the* does not precede *treasurer*, which indicates that it is not a separate office. If it were, the subject should have read "The secretary and *the* treasurer," which would be plural.

Here are some additional examples.

> My homeroom teacher and math teacher is Nelson Briggs.
> My homeroom teacher and my math teacher are married.
>
> A peanut butter and jelly sandwich is good.
>
> A peanut butter and a jelly sandwich are on the table for you to take your choice.

RULE 8: When two or more subjects are joined by *or* or *nor*, the subject is usually singular because the writer means one or the other, not both.

Sometimes, one of the nouns is singular and the other plural. In this case, write the plural last. When *or* and *nor* connects subjects, the verb should agree with the nearer subject.

> Sally or Althea has charge of the daily posting.
> Neither time nor trouble stops Ms. Lancaster from doing her work.
>
> *but*
> Mr. Coleman or his associates call on the Michigan clients.

Tell whether each statement is true (T) or false (F).

_____ 1. Singular verbs end in -*s*.

_____ 2. If the subject of a clause is singular, the verb should be plural.

_____ 3. The verb *reveals* is plural.

_____ 4. With a few exceptions you should ignore prepositional phrases when determining subject-verb agreement.

_____ 5. Don't be misled into using a plural verb just because a plural noun comes right before it.

_____ 6. *Does* is singular, and *do* is plural.

_____ 7. A sentence that begins, *Mary, as well as Fred,* would have a plural subject.

_____ 8. *Each* and *every* are always singular.

_____ 9. Any verb that ends in -*s* is plural.

_____ 10. *Some* is always plural.

Before you continue, turn to p. 276 to check your answers.

TRY IT OUT: Do Exercise 10.2, p. 266, for practice with the first eight rules of subject-verb agreement.

RULE 9: Sometimes a plural-sounding subject is really singular because it names one thing. This is often true of the names of books and magazines.

Note these examples.

<u>Measles</u> <u>is</u> contagious.
<u>*People*</u> <u>sells</u> very well at the newsstand.
<u>*Jaws*</u> <u>is</u> a well-known book made into a very scary movie.

RULE 10: When a subject names a single unit that can be thought of as a lump sum or mass, use a singular verb.

Notice that singular verbs are used with these subjects.

Three thousand <u>dollars</u> <u>is</u> the price on this crane.
One hundred <u>feet</u> <u>has been</u> the minimum frontage sold on Lake Claire.
Three <u>tons</u> of coal <u>was</u> delivered to the plant on North Street.

but

The three <u>tons</u> of coal <u>were</u> in separate piles at different places on the property.

TRY IT OUT: Before continuing, do Exercise 10.3, p. 267, for practice with the first ten rules of subject-verb agreement.

RULE 11: Occasionally, the subject will be a collective noun, a singular word that names a group—or collection—of people, animals, or things. These words take a singular verb if the group is acting as a single unit. The verb is plural if the members of the group are acting separately or are in disagreement.

Examine the activity of the members of each of these collectives to decide why the type of verb was chosen.

The <u>committee</u> <u>has chosen</u> a new chairperson. [acted as one, in agreement]
The <u>choir</u> <u>has performed</u> very well in tonight's concert. [all sang together]
The <u>jury</u> <u>has returned</u> a verdict of "not guilty." [came to a consensus]

In other contexts these same subjects could be considered plural.

The <u>committee</u> <u>were</u> assigned different chores. [each member doing something different]
The <u>choir</u> <u>have gone</u> to their separate homes to prepare for the concert. [not the same home for all]
The <u>jury</u> <u>have</u> not <u>agreed</u> on a verdict. [not acting as a unit but individually]

In the cases where the collective noun members are not acting as a unit, you must choose a plural verb, even if it "sounds funny" to you. You can avoid the problem by restructuring your sentence so that the subject is a plural word, not a collective noun.

The choir <u>members</u> <u>have gone</u> to their homes to get ready.

⊡ Relative Pronoun Clauses

RULE 12: Adjective clauses start with relative pronouns—*who, whom, whose, which,* or *that*—which can be either singular or plural. To decide which verb form to use, determine which word the clause is modifying and whether that word is singular or plural.

Study these illustrations of this principle.

I <u>saw</u> a man <u>who</u> (the man) <u>was</u> elected union representative.

I <u>saw</u> the men <u>who</u> (the men) <u>were</u> responsible for the new refinements in the blenders.

He <u>is</u> the person <u>that</u> (the person) <u>was</u> nominated by the Standards Board as chairperson.

They <u>are</u> the creditors <u>that</u> (the creditors) <u>are</u> able to refinance your debts.

RULE 13: Adjective clauses modify the nouns or pronouns directly in front of them with one exception: those that follow a clause that contains the words *one of those*.

In these sentences the writer is taking a subject and either <u>putting it with</u> or <u>removing it from</u> a group. If put with the group, the adjective clause will modify the whole group and have a plural verb. If separated from the group, the adjective clause will modify a single item and have a singular verb.

These sentences will illustrate this practice.

1. <u>Hernandez</u> <u>is</u> *one of those* men <u>who</u> <u>are</u> always on time.

2. <u>Hernandez</u> <u>is</u> the only *one of those* men <u>who</u> <u>is</u> always on time.

In Example 1 the *who* clause modifies *men* because Hernandez has been put into the group of men, and they are all on time.

In Example 2 Hernandez is not like the other men and has been taken out of the group. <u>The word *only* was the signal for this</u>. The *who* clause in this type of sentence is an exception because it does not modify the word in front of it; it modifies the earlier pronoun *one*. The prepositional phrase gets in the way. In all other cases the adjective clause would have been modifying the object of the preposition.

Here are two more examples.

<u>Hemingway</u> <u>was</u> *one of those* writers <u>who</u> <u>use</u> few words but <u>say</u> much. [They all do this.]

<u>Hemingway</u> <u>was</u> the only *one of those* authors <u>who</u> <u>was</u> a sport fisherman, game hunter, and tragic figure. [Note the word *only*, which set him apart from the group.]

RULE 14: A relative pronoun clause used as a subject (a noun clause) is considered singular unless it begins with *what*, in which case the meaning of the clause will determine the number. Of course, a subject could also consist of a compound of two or more noun clauses.

Here are examples of noun clause subjects.

             S

<u>Whoever eats the most pizzas</u> <u>is</u> the one most likely to get sick. [noun clause subject]

                            S

<u>What a person knows about grammar and punctuation</u> <u>is</u> very obvious to other people. [*what* clause naming one complete idea]

                        S

<u>Whatever reservations you may have about the guarantee</u> <u>are</u> sure to be satisfied by reading it thoroughly. [*what* clause with plural meaning]

               S   S

<u>Whichever one of you can get here sooner</u> and <u>whichever one of you remembers the password</u> <u>are</u> both entitled to a prize. [compound subject of two noun clauses]

SELF-CHECK 10-3

On the blank tell whether each of the following is singular (S), plural (P), or either (E).

_____ 1. each

_____ 2. several

_____ 3. the number

_____ 4. staff

_____ 5. Morse, Code & Jones

_____ 6. five hundred dollars

_____ 7. Board of Directors

_____ 8. some

_____ 9. mumps

_____ 10. Mary or Ted

Before you continue, turn to p. 276 to check your answers.

TRY IT OUT: **Exercises 10.4 and 10.5, pp. 268–269, will give you practice and review with the principles of subject-verb agreement. Before you complete these exercises, try to write the rules out in your own words to see if you really know and understand them. Exercise 10.6, p. 270, is the Challenge exercise.**

Chapter 10: Subject and Verb Agreement

Underline the correct verb in each sentence. (Remember, verbs that end in -s are singular.)

1. All of the men (is, are) going to be attending the basketball camp.

2. One of the men (is, are) going to be attending a golf class in Orlando.

3. The offices of the Salem Corporation (is, are) located in Tulsa.

4. The list of names and addresses (has, have) been put on your desk.

5. A handful of service agencies (assists, assist) us with our campaign.

6. The books for our library (needs, need) to be selected with care.

7. Your tickets for the Seattle flight (is, are) on your desk.

8. The report, as well as the copies of the charts, (was, were) printed yesterday.

9. Our treasurer, in addition to the accountants, (sends, send) statements to the auditor every three months.

10. Mr. Errol, accompanied by his wife and two children, (plans, plan) to fly to Disney World for Easter vacation.

11. Your application, as well as several others, (goes, go) to the Personnel Office for review this afternoon, Ms. Blue.

12. Everyone (is, are) invited to the office picnic.

13. Neither of the parties (have, has) filed a lawsuit yet.

14. Any one of you (know, knows) the procedure for filing this with the Securities and Exchange Commission.

15. Nobody (sell, sells) as many cars as Fred.

16. Each of the samples (was, were) packaged and shipped today.

17. Every one of our copies (comes, come) out too dark on this leased copier.

18. The phenomena of nature (is, are) marvelous.

19. (Does, Do) the analyses of the plants indicate what has caused the mutations?

20. The predominant data, as well as any new study, (seems, seem) to indicate that we are making progress.

Underline the correct verb.

1. One half of the staff (start, starts) work at 7:30 a.m.

2. Some of our trouble (begins, begin) with the quick change in the weather.

3. Every man and woman from the other departments (speaks, speak) well of Mr. Reed.

4. Anna and Frankie (tries, try) very hard to work toward perfection.

5. Edie or Lavonne (types, type) the letters each morning.

6. None of last year's models (has, have) been returned because of defects in workmanship.

7. Neither overtime work nor "Rush" assignments (seems, seem) to bother Mr. Ortega.

8. What (was, were) some of these billings sent out before the end of the month?

9. Did you know that Dalton and Cummings, Inc., (is, are) merging with Swank and Holmes?

10. Accuracy and speed (is, are) desirable but not always possible together.

11. Each nut and bolt (has, have) been checked and rechecked.

12. Mr. Paul or Mr. Peters (plans, plan) to speak at the annual dinner in May.

13. Neither of the clients (know, knows) that Mr. Ellingsworth has been transferred to Boise.

14. Every one of our accounts (has, have) to balance before we can leave today.

15. One of our representatives, along with several of your sponsors, (appears, appear) to be withholding a vote of confidence in our project.

● E X E R C I S E   10.3

Underline the correct verb.

1. Mumps (is, are) common in children.

2. Hyphens or spaces (is, are) usually used between the sets of numbers on a Social Security card.

3. Your actions, in addition to your words, (reveals, reveal) a great deal about your character.

4. Mathematics (seems, seem) harder for some people than for others.

5. Seven pounds (were, was) the weight of Mrs. Stevens' baby.

6. Every business or professional person (chooses, chose) employees carefully.

7. *U.S. News* (is, are) a periodical that (comes, come) out once a week.

8. It (doesn't, don't) make a difference how carefully you type; you must still proofread each letter several times.

9. There (has, have) been too many storms this spring for my taste.

10. One thousand dollars (is, are) the cost of our new electronic range and oven combination.

11. Here (is, are) each of the students whose names were called.

12. Ham and eggs (is, are) my favorite breakfast.

13. Either the Dearborn office or one of the Detroit offices (needs, need) a new manager.

14. The weather and the seasons (has, have) much to do with tourism in our state.

15. Included in this long list (is, are) the names of all customers who inquired about next year's model.

Underline the correct verb.

1. The public (supports, support) our new Civic Center.

2. The staff cannot agree on a place for the luncheon and (is, are) trying to decide.

3. These species of deer (lives, live) in the northern Midwest.

4. Be sure to completely erase the parenthesis that (was, were) put in the wrong place.

5. The main criterion for the meeting (is, are) well known to all of us.

6. Counsel for the defense (does, do) not agree on how to pursue the case.

7. A number of members (knows, know) for whom to vote.

8. The percentage of flaws in these items (is, are) minimal.

9. This shipment of erasers (costs, cost) $46.

10. The number of changes in these new cars (doesn't, don't) seem to be very large.

11. Sarah is a woman who (work, works) very hard.

12. Sarah is one of those women who (devotes, devote) much spare time to charitable organizations.

13. Rebecca is the only one of the women who (do, does) not give at least sixteen hours a week to volunteer work.

14. Theirs is a company that (meet, meets) the needs of small businesses.

15. That is one of several brushes that (contains, contain) pure bristles.

16. Whatever you feel is best (is, are) the best way to raise your children.

17. That he prefers peaches to all other fruits (was, were) very apparent after a few days at the resort.

18. Whoever is qualified and whomever I feel most comfortable with (is, are) those I will select to return for a second interview.

19. Whichever one of these (is, are) the stronger (seem, seems) to be the one we should select.

20. Do you see Mr. Williams as one of those people (who, whom) (relies, rely) on (his, their) assistants for the answers? [Agreement requires decisions about pronouns as well.]

● E X E R C I S E   1 0 . 5

Underline the correct verb.

1. Several parts from the machine (was, were) missing.

2. The faculty (starts, start) to work for classes long before the classes begin.

3. One hundred feet (is, are) the frontage on this lot.

4. The union steward, or our representative, (know, knows) every person in our shop.

5. The number of mistakes in your letters (depends, depend) on your attention to proofreading as well as your knowledge and skills.

6. Many a person (tries, try) to do things too quickly and (make, makes) mistakes.

7. *U.S. News* (is, are) a magazine that (help, helps) to keep you up to date with current events.

8. Here (is, are) the reports you wanted completed today.

9. Nobody among the assistants (seems, seem) to be capable of taking over while the bishop is on vacation.

10. The scissors (is, are) not sharp enough to cut this cardboard.

11. Some of the cartons (was, were) smudged and had to be reprinted.

12. Everybody in both plants (gets, get) Christmas Eve off.

13. Among a number of magazines (was, were) the copy that you were looking for.

14. Either the President or the members of this staff (takes, take) care of all inquiries sent to the main office.

15. An accountant and office manager (is, are) very busy.

16. The family (is, are) taking separate vacations this year.

17. His students, together with Mr. Arnold, (learns, learn) a great deal each term.

18. Seventy percent of these envelopes (goes, go) to Clark Valve Company.

19. We produce all of the batteries that (works, work) the hearing aids produced in the Scottsdale plant.

20. Hendrix and Weier (is, are) happy to have you as a charge customer.

Make any necessary corrections in the subject-verb agreement in the following letter.

Dear Customer:

You will be pleased to know that we at Longjohn Fashion World has just received a new shipment of fall fashions. There seems to be several very new designs available this year for everyone in your family.

The men in your household likes to feel as much a part of the fashion scene as the women. Everyone of them appreciate the new easy-to-wear sports coats and suits that feel comfortable and yet wear well. Dad, as well as older brothers, want to wear shirts that don't bind and slacks that holds their just-pressed look.

A number of our new fashions appear to have been designed with Mom in mind. The number of "dowdy" ladies' dresses have decreased in past years to keep up with the modern woman, one who not only works at home but also possibly have a job or other activities away from home. A suit or dress from our new selection are appropriate for everyday wear, whether at work or at home.

Casual clothes make up at least one half of our new shipment. These 50 percent of our fashions seems to be more comfortable than ever before. Included in this selection is a tennis outfit, a swimsuit, and a warm-up jacket for everyone. Even though fall starts cool weather, our customers don't necessarily stop sports activities.

Longjohn's are happy to report that the younger brother or sister are not left out either. With school starting soon, there is probably many things needed for the children. Shirts, slacks, and other school clothes are reasonably priced here at Longjohn's. Not only that, but there is a year's guarantee that offer a replacement garment for any of our items that show excessive wear.

To find out for yourself how you can look great while saving money, come in to Longjohn Fashion World today. Our 10 percent discount with this copy of this letter last until September 1.

A N S W E R S   T O   S E L F - C H E C K   P R A C T I C E

Chapter 7: Types of Sentences

Self-Check 7–1, p. 182

1. Neither, nor
2. yet
3. ;
4. but [The word *and* does not connect two clauses.]
5. not only . . . but . . . also

Self-Check 7–2, p. 183

1. Television has been a boon to advertising; it has sold thousands of items.
2. The letter was typed and mailed, but it did not arrive.
3. No commas; this is a simple sentence.
4. I gambled, and I lost.
5. A new solution must be found for this problem; then there will be fewer mistakes. [Because *then* is not a coordinate conjunction, a comma would not be good enough glue.]

Self-Check 7–3, p. 185–186

1. Whenever I get discouraged, I try to remember that the present will not last forever.
2. You may, if you wish, use my notes to review the question.
3. No commas; the adverb clause comes after the independent clause.
4. Macy's seldom had a sale, but if there was a sale, it was sure to be a good one. [You see that this sentence begins with an independent clause and has a coordinate conjunction. However, notice that after the first clause are <u>two</u> more clauses, an adverb clause followed by its independent clause. The second comma is still needed even though the sentence didn't start with this adverb clause.]
5. If I feel well and if I have the extra money, I hope to stay in Sarasota after the convention. [Because *and* joins dependent, not independent, clauses, there is no comma before it. The comma after *money* indicates <u>the end</u> of the dependent clauses.]

6. When you have completed that computer program, will you work on this one?

7. One of the staff members, when he finished the program, was able to find the error in this one.

8. No commas. The introductory word group is only a prepositional phrase, not an adverb clause.

9. After we had an early-morning meeting, we left for the trade show.

10. No commas when the adverb clause comes in the natural order.

Self-Check 7–4, p. 192

1. Period.
2. Period.
3. Period.
4. Period.
5. Question mark. A response is required.
6. Period.
7. Period.
8. No periods, no spaces.
9. The general usage seems to be lowercase letters with periods but no spaces (*p.m.*).
10. Periods with one space after (*R. A. Imus*).
11. No periods, no spaces.
12. Avoid. Write either *Vice President, Vice-President,* or *Vice-president.*
13. Avoid. Write out *Avenue.*
14. No period.
15. *St.* is a standard abbreviation; *MN* is the form required by post office with no periods or spaces.

Self-Check 7–5, p. 194

1. $19.97
2. $20
3. $14.27, $19.00, $22.50
4. 0.30
5. Periods after the numbers; no periods after the items.

Self-Check 7–6, p. 196

1. . . . lately?
2. . . . order.
3. . . . rising?
4. . . . Anchorage? Why not?
5. . . . down? overtired? depressed?
6. . . . this?"
7. . . . "Who did this?" she asked.
8. . . . f.o.b.?
9. . . . *Wars*?
10. Good heavens, I didn't know that!

    or

    Good heavens! I didn't know that.

Chapter 8: Sentence Combining and Word Reduction

Self-Check 8–1, p. 218

1. To collect stamps
2. to work overtime
3. to type under pressure
4. to be proofread [*to me* is a prepositional phrase]
5. To earn his commission; to sell five machines a month

Self-Check 8–2, p. 221

1. No commas; *winding his watch* is needed to tell <u>which</u> man is James Carver.
2. No commas if there is more than one blue dress because the participle would be needed to tell <u>which</u> blue dress is $27. If there is only one blue dress for sale, commas would be used before *marked* and after *half price*.
3. Commas both sides of *coming around our corner*.
4. No commas; *The man* would be too vague a noun without the participial phrase, *sitting behind Bonnie Dexter*.
5. No commas; *selling Texana products* tells <u>which</u> of all possible salespeople was seen.

Self-Check 8–3, pp. 222–223

1. *Soldier* is the wrong noun. Although there could be two ways to rewrite this, you are being asked to keep the phrase first (as in the first answer below). Even though another rewrite might make a better sentence, these answers demonstrate the practice of writing transposed phrases correctly.
   a. Wearing a red dress, his mother was seen by the soldier.
   b. The soldier saw his mother wearing a red dress.
2. *Farmer* is the correct noun.
3. *Folder* is incorrect. To find the correct noun, you have to ask yourself, "Who knows you wanted this information?" In this example the doer of the phrase is not written, but you can figure out who knows it—it would be the person sending the folder. He or she would call himself *I* or possibly *we* to represent the whole company sending the folder. Thus, the rewritten sentence should say either of these:
   a. Knowing you wanted this information, I am sending this folder to help you decide.
   b. Knowing you wanted this information, we are sending you this folder to help you decide.
4. *Items* is the correct noun modified.
5. *We* is not the correct pronoun because, obviously, "we" were not "lying under the other articles." To correct this sentence, *files* has to be modified by the phrase.
   a. Lying under the other articles, the files on Thompson and Ross were found.

b. The files on Thompson and Ross were found lying under the other articles.

6. *Time* is not the thing trying to learn better; the student is.
   a. To learn better, the student must spend more time.
   b. The student, to learn better, must spend more time.
   c. The student must spend more time to learn better. [This third choice puts the infinitive phrase next to the noun *time* again. However, because the natural position of infinitives is to fall at the end of the clause, this is considered acceptable.]

7. *Error* is closest to the infinitive phrase but is clearly not the thing doing the "leafing through the textbook." You can see here why it's often unwise to add the infinitive phrase at the end of the clause. When the meaning is so obviously wrong, the sentence should be rewritten. (It is always a good idea to keep the phrase next to the noun it modifies and away from any noun or pronoun it does not modify.)
   a. Leafing through the textbook, the student found a grammar error.
   b. The student, leafing through the textbook, found a grammar error.

8. *Book* is the modified noun. The phrase could also have been transposed to the front of the clause since *book* is the subject.

9. *We* were not invented by Edison—the light bulb was.
   a. Invented by Edison, the light bulb has made our lives easier.
   b. We are lucky to have lights, invented by Edison.

10. *Desks* is the correct noun modified by the introductory phrase.

Self-Check 8–4, p. 224

1. <u>solving problems graciously</u>, object of preposition
2. <u>running in a marathon</u>, subject
3. <u>writing</u>, direct object; *during* is a preposition
4. <u>understanding of the problem</u>, subject
5. <u>bickering</u>, direct object of the verb *was recording*. The entire gerund phrase is <u>bickering among the panel members</u>.

Self-Check 8–5, p. 225

1. <u>To know him</u>, subject; <u>to love him</u>, subject complement
2. <u>To be</u> or <u>not to be</u>, compound subject
3. <u>Selling air-conditioners</u>, subject
4. <u>typing medical reports</u>, direct object
5. <u>Good proofreading</u> and <u>careful typing</u>, compound subject
6. <u>Remembering his keys</u>, participial phrase (adjective)
7. <u>dining</u>, participle (adjective)
8. <u>opening the wrong package</u>, object of preposition *from*
9. <u>Computing the payroll</u>, subject
10. There is no verbal in this sentence; *computing* has a helping verb and a doer. Consequently, it is the verb.

Chapter 9: Fragments and Run-Ons

Self-Check 9–1, p. 237

1. 1. Knotted and frayed, the rope was a poor one to use to tie up the boat.
2. 1. People who care about their health eat properly.
3. 2. I was used to the long hours at the restaurant, was used to the constant change of employees.
4. 1. While I was researching the case, I saw that Judge Kemp was the trial judge.
5. 2. This could be a fragment, a word group that is incomplete with no independent clause.

Self-Check 9–2, p. 239

1. R. Comma after first clause (after *work*) is not good enough glue.
2. S. The glue is the coordinate conjunction *and*.
3. S. The comma after *working* is for the introductory <u>phrase</u>; the semicolon is correct between clauses.
4. S. There are two clauses here, but the second one (*you hired*) is an adjective clause with understood *that* as a connective; a run-on is two <u>independent</u> clauses without glue.
5. R. Although similar to the last sentence, in this case, the second clause is fully independent; thus, with no glue this is a run-on.
6. R. Without a semicolon before *consequently* this is a run-on.
7. S. The coordinate conjunction *but* makes this a correct compound sentence.
8. R. The word *then* is not a coordinate conjunction. Without a semicolon this is a run-on.
9. S. Because the *if* clause is dependent, the first two clauses are not a run-on. The semicolon acts as glue for the third clause.
10. S. These two clauses are correctly joined with the semicolon before the second clause.

Self-Check 9–3, p. 241

1. No semicolon. A comma would be correct because the transitional expression comes between the verb and participle in only one clause.
2. Yes, a semicolon is needed to separate these two independent clauses.
3. No, the first clause ended before *but* joined the second. A comma here would be correct to help set off the transitional expression.
4. No, just a comma. The two clauses are joined by *and*.
5. Yes, to end the first clause.

Self-Check 9–4, p. 244

1. *even so, at any rate, however*—or any other expression that shows contrast

2. *next, then, secondly*—or any other expression that shows sequence

3. *on the other hand, however, by contrast*—or any other expression that shows contrast

4. *conversely, however, by contrast*—or any other expression that shows contrast
   or
   I suppose, one would assume—or any other expression that shows illustration

5. *for instance, for example*—or any other expression that shows illustration

6. *in general, by and large*—or any other expression that shows conclusion

7. *I believe, it seems to me*—or any other expression that shows the writer's opinion

8. *in any event, even so*—or any other expression that shows contrast
   or
   first, before that—or any other expression that shows sequence

9. *by contrast, conversely*—or any other expression that shows contrast

10. *in essence, not only that, in other words*—or any other expression that shows emphasis

◘ Chapter 10: Subject and Verb Agreement

Self-Check 10–1, p. 256

1. occur<u>s</u>
2. i<u>s</u>
3. studie<u>s</u>
4. ha<u>s</u>
5. doesn't = doe<u>s</u> not

Self-Check 10–2, p. 261

1. T	6. T
2. F	7. F
3. F	8. T
4. T	9. F
5. T	10. F

Self-Check 10–3, p. 264

1. S	6. E
2. P	7. E (could act as collective)
3. S	8. E
4. E	9. S
5. S	10. S

U N I T 3

Making Word Choices

C H A P T E R   1 1

Adjectives

OVERVIEW

- Characteristics of Adjectives
- Comparative Forms of Adjectives
- Choosing the Correct Adjective
- Using the Articles
- Capitalization and Punctuation Points

This chapter will present basic principles for the correct use of one-word adjectives. You'll find out how to use adjectives to make comparisons, how to choose between similar adjectives such as *fewer* and *less*, and how to select the correct article. Finally, you'll learn capitalization and punctuation rules that apply to adjectives, including when to use hyphens.

CHARACTERISTICS OF ADJECTIVES

In this text you have already learned a number of things about adjectives. The word *adjective* should bring to mind the following attributes.

1. Adjectives modify nouns and pronouns by telling <u>which</u>, <u>what kind of</u>, <u>whose</u>, or <u>how many</u>.

2. An adjective can be a word, a phrase, or a clause.

3. Verbs have an adjective form called a participle.

4. All possessive words are adjectives.

Remember that the normal positions for adjectives are (1) in front of the word modified or (2) after the linking verb (as a subject complement). Note the position of the adjectives in each of the following examples.

Our long-range plan is *ready* for evaluation. **SC**

She was *exhausted.* **SC**

My mother's brother works in *a large unfriendly* office.

COMPARATIVE FORMS OF ADJECTIVES

As well as telling which, what kind of, whose, or how many about the words modified, adjectives can make comparisons at the same time. For example, you can say that a house is expensive and at the same time compare its cost relative to other houses.

Jim's house is *expensive.*
Jim's house is *more expensive* than Henry's.
Jim's house is the *most expensive* house on that block.

You can see adjectives used in other forms in these comparisons.

Abigail is a *happy* person.
Abigail seems *happier* than Susan.
Abigail is the *happiest* person in this office.

Did you notice the different techniques used to change the adjectives into their comparative forms? To use adjectives to compare, <u>either</u> you put *more* and *most* (or *less* and *least* if the comparison is diminished) in front of the adjective, or you add *-er* and *-est* to the base word. Notice the word *either*. Don't add both types of comparative form to the same adjective. It is incorrect to use such forms as *more tall<u>er</u>*, since that would be giving the word *tall* a double comparison.

Correctly forming comparatives depends on a few simples rules.

Rules for Forming Comparatives

1. If the adjective is a one-syllable word or a two-syllable word that ends in consonant *-y,* add *-er* to compare two things or *-est* to compare three or more.

Positive (one)	Comparative (two)	Superlative (three or more)
tall	taller	tallest
green	greener	greenest
slim	slimmer	slimmest
funny	funnier	funniest
witty	wittier	wittiest
healthy	healthier	healthiest

You can see that adjectives (and adverbs too) follow the spelling rules you learned in Chapter 3 regarding the final *-y* words and whether or not to double the final consonant when adding a suffix. You might want to review those rules on pp. 35–36.

2. With most adjectives of two or more syllables, add *more* (comparing two) or *most* (comparing three or more) in front of the base adjective.

Positive (one)	Comparative (two)	Superlative (three or more)
restful	more restful	most restful
handsome	more handsome	most handsome
complicated	more complicated	most complicated

(*Note:* Some adjectives that end in *-ble, -ple,* or *-tle* have the option of using either *-er* or *more* to form the comparative and *-est* or *most* to form the superlative. These adjectives include *gentle, simple,* and *able.*)

Positive (one)	Comparative (two)	Superlative (three or more)
gentle	gentler more gentle	gentlest most gentle

3. To make a negative comparison, add *less* or *least* in front of the base word regardless of its number of syllables.

Positive (one)	Comparative (two)	Superlative (three or more)
fat	less fat	least fat
quiet	less quiet	least quiet
pertinent	less pertinent	least pertinent

4. Certain adjectives are exceptions and do not follow the principles just outlined. You are probably already familiar with these irregular adjective forms.

Positive (one)	Comparative (two)	Superlative (three or more)
bad	worse	worst
good	better	best
little	less	least
many	more	most
much	more	most

(*Note: Little* is used to compare amounts only, not relative size. You would say *less money* to indicate an amount that is less than *a little money*. However, to compare size you would say, for example, that the *little child* has a playmate who is *smaller*. The base-word adjective would have to change.)

In no case do you add two comparative indicators to your modifying forms. Either you change the base-word ending, or you add a comparative form in front, but you do not do both.

Be certain, too, that when you want to compare things, a comparison is actually possible. If you think about the meanings of such words as *impossible, perfect, universal, complete,* or *unique,* you can see that these words already represent the extreme—there can be nothing more perfect than a perfect thing, for example.

SELF-CHECK 11-1

Answer these questions.

1. What two types of words do adjectives generally modify?

2. Besides telling <u>which</u>, what else could an adjective tell about a word it modifies? (Answer has three parts.)

3. Which adjectives add *-er* or *-est?*

4. When do you double the final consonant before adding *-er* or *-est?*

5. How would you spell *pretty* if you added *-est* to it?

6. Can there really be a *littlest* angel?

7. Would King Tut's mask be the *most unique* one ever found?

Before you continue, turn to p. 349 to check your answers.

TRY IT OUT: **Do Exercise 11.1, p. 289, for practice in locating adjectives and Exercise 11.2, p. 290, for practice in using comparatives.**

CHOOSING THE CORRECT ADJECTIVE

Errors in adjective usage commonly occur when a writer mistakes one adjective for a similar adjective, makes comparisons within a group, or misuses the superlative form.

Misused Words. Although some adjectives with similar meanings are practically interchangeable, others that appear similar actually have distinct differences. The words in the following pairs, though often mistaken for each other, are not interchangeable. Once you know their exact meanings, you'll be able to correctly use these words in your writing.

farther/farthest   a measurable distance
further/furthest   into depth

China is *farther* away from here than England.

I need *further* information about your work experience.

I plan to research this problem *further.*

later/latest   measured time
latter   the second part, used in conjunction with *former*

I will call you *later* today.

He spoke about sales in the *latter* half of his speech.

fewer   modifies plural words
less   modifies singular unit

Fewer people attended this year's meeting than came last year.

She had *fewer* opinions than most people.

I have *less* money here than I thought I had.

each other   relates two people
one another   relates three or more people

Lila and Mary tried to call *each other* at the same time.

The three salespeople talked with *one another* about the new models of cars.

Comparisons Within a Group.   Do you see what is wrong with this sentence?

Mrs. Grebe is better than any teacher in school.

If she is bett<u>er</u> (a word that compares two) than any teacher there, she is actually better than even herself since she is one of the teachers in the group.

Since this would be an impossible situation, add the word *other* after *any* so that your subject is kept out of the rest of the group.

> Mrs. Grebe is better than *any other* teacher in the school.
> Uriah is taller than *any other* boy in his class.

The same problem can occur with pronouns that end in *-thing, -body,* or *-one,* such as *anybody* or *anyone.* In these cases the addition of the word *else* after the pronoun will exclude the person or thing from the group.

> Troy can sing better than *anyone else* in the men's choir.
> If I never have *anything else,* I'd like a dishwasher.
> Please give this coupon to *somebody else* who can use it.

Inappropriate Use of the Superlative. One last caution about comparative adjectives is this: <u>Be sure to check how many things are being compared.</u> Many people use the superlative (three or more) form far too often. Do you realize what you are saying when you say, "My left eye is my *weakest* eye?" or "Put your *best* foot forward"? You have indicated three or more—three eyes? three feet?

If you have two children, you do not have an oldest, youngest, tallest, brightest, or even most loving child. These superlative forms indicate that there are at least three of the people or things being described.

▗ SELF-CHECK 11-2

Answer the following questions.

1. Which word shows a measurable distance, *farther* or *further*?

2. What does *latter* indicate?

3. Which modifies a singular entity, *fewer* or *less*?

4. Would two people talk with *one another*?

5. What is wrong with this sentence: "Jane learned to sail better than anyone in her class"?

6. When Mr. Hallet introduces you to his two children, should he say, "This is Peter, my youngest son"?

Before you continue, turn to p. 349 to check your answers.

TRY IT OUT: **Do Exercises 11.3, 11.4, and 11.5, pp. 291–292.**

USING THE ARTICLES

The articles, *a, an,* and *the* function as adjectives and have some special rules dictating their use.

1. *The* is a "definite" article, modifying a particular person, animal, place, or thing.

2. *A* and *an* are used before words that indicate a more general item in a category.

   These examples illustrate the difference.

   Please hand me *the* book.   *a certain book*

   Please get me *a* book from the library.   *any book*

   Hand me *an* apple from the bowl.   *any of the apples*

   When choosing between *a* and *an,* keep in mind these two general rules.

1. When the following word begins with a consonant sound (not necessarily spelling), use *a.* The long sound of *u* and the pronounced *h* are considered consonant sounds.

a hat	a table
a salesperson	a university

2. When the following word begins with a vowel sound, use *an.* The silent *h* and short *u* are considered vowel sounds.

an uncle	an army
an hour	an elf

SELF-CHECK 11-3

Put a *or* an *before each of the following words and groups of words.*

_____	1.	academy	_____	6.	uncle
_____	2.	house	_____	7.	person
_____	3.	honest man	_____	8.	heirloom
_____	4.	umbrella	_____	9.	horse
_____	5.	union steward	_____	10.	office manager

Before you continue, turn to p. 349 to check your answers.

Articles not only show whether the person, place, thing, or idea is definite or indefinite, but they also tell how many.

1. Today we hired *a* pilot and mechanic. [one person]
2. Today we hired *a* pilot and *a* mechanic. [two separate people]

To indicate separate individuals or items, use an article or ownership word in front of <u>each</u> noun, as in Example 2.

TRY IT OUT: **Complete Exercises 11.6 and 11.7, pp. 292–293 to practice using articles correctly.**

CAPITALIZATION AND PUNCTUATION POINTS

The most common capitalization and punctuation questions related to adjectives deal with the rules governing the use of capital letters with proper adjectives, the use of hyphens with compound adjectives, and the use of commas with consecutive adjectives.

Capitalizing

You know that proper nouns are capitalized. Sometimes proper nouns are changed into proper adjectives, and they too need to have initial capital letters.

Nouns	Adjectives
America	an American cowboy
England	an English garden
Victoria	a Victorian attitude
Freud	a Freudian slip

Some proper adjectives have come to be considered generic terms and no longer carry the capitalization: *morocco leather*, *oriental rug*, and so on.

When referring to company-named products, you will find that most often the company or brand name is capitalized, but the product isn't: *Upjohn penicillin*, a *Royal typewriter*, and so on.

It is best to consult a dictionary or a reference manual to find out whether a specific adjective of this kind is capitalized.

Forming Compound Adjectives

Although hyphenation is a matter of "style" that varies somewhat from reference manual to reference manual, most writers adhere to the following basic guidelines.

1. Generally, a compound-word adjective is hyphenated when it is located before its noun but is not hyphenated when it follows the word modified. There are some exceptions to the rule about the compound adjectives that follow the modified word, however. Use a reference manual when in doubt.

   1. a. That is an up-to-date version of our standard model.
      b. This model is up to date.

   2. a. You have produced a well-made calculator.
      b. This calculator is well made.

   Examples 1a and 2a have hyphens because the adjectives come before the words modified; Examples 1b and 2b have no hyphens because the adjectives follow the words modified.

2. Compound adjectives that have *self-* as the prefix are hyphenated whether they appear before or after the noun.

   She is very self-confident.
   This is a self-evident fact.

3. Numerical compound adjectives are always hyphenated as are spelled-out numbers between twenty-one and ninety-nine.

   Ms. Fremont is twenty-five today.
   They are celebrating their twenty-fifth anniversary.

4. When modifying a noun with two compound adjectives that share a common element, it is often unnecessary to repeat the like-words.

   We have either a two- or a three-pound box of cheese available for a gift.
   He won the 200- and 400-meter races.

   Remember that hyphens, like punctuation, serve a single purpose: to help the reader understand the written message. A hyphen helps the reader separate the modifiers from the noun modified. Thus, the sentence "I saw a man-eating snake in the Amazon" tells you that the writer saw a snake, not a man enjoying a local delicacy.

▣ Using Commas With Adjectives

1. Commas are required between adjectives in a series, and as with nouns, no comma comes after the <u>last</u> adjective in the series.

   The tall, dark, and handsome actor appeared on the stage during the second act.
   The bright, alert, and adept candidate was selected for the position.

2. Once in a while, it is a good writing technique to use two consecutive adjectives as modifiers in front of your noun. This technique adds variety and emphasizes the adjectives. When you put no conjunction between them, but the word *and* is understood to be there, place a comma there instead.

> This handy, efficient slicer will make your job easier. [handy *and* efficient]
>
> We need an experienced, capable supervisor. [experienced *and* capable]

In the preceding examples you can see that the comma replaces the word *and*—you can mentally add the word *and*, and the meaning is clear.

Sometimes, though, it is somewhat difficult to decide whether the two words are consecutive adjectives or whether the second word is part of the noun word group. In this case, reverse the two words to see if you could still add the *and*. If not, use no comma.

> Is this a difficult golf course? [not golf *and* difficult]
>
> I live in a modern apartment building. [not apartment *and* modern]

3. Another good writing technique is to place multiple adjectives <u>after</u> the noun for emphasis. Commas are used to set the adjectives off from the rest of the sentence.

> My assistant, punctual and dependable, would be very hard to replace.
>
> This furnace, clean and quiet, is a great improvement over those of earlier times.

WRITING HINT: You can see that the skillful placement of adjectives is a reduction technique that allows the writer to omit repetitive information.

> ***Weak:***
> We need a capable supervisor. He or she should have experience.
>
> ***Better:***
> We need an experienced, capable supervisor.
>
> ***Weak:***
> The moon shone on the water. It was full and bright.
>
> ***Good:***
> The moon, which was full and bright, shone on the water.
>
> ***Better:***
> The moon, full and bright, shone on the water.

Add capital letters, hyphens, or commas, as needed, to the following phrases. You may refer to a reference manual if necessary.

Capitalize any proper adjectives.

1. a new england clam bake

2. a french perfume

3. a hamburger and french fries

4. an oriental rug

Put a hyphen in any compound adjective that needs it.

5. a person that is self reliant

6. well laid plans of mice and men

7. a letter that goes first class

8. a 3 or 4 year contract

Add any necessary commas.

9. an air-conditioned office building

10. an easy quick recipe

11. the dark and hot room

12. the room dark and hot behind the heavy door

Before you continue, turn to pp. 349–350 to check your answers.

TRY IT OUT: Complete Exercises 11.8, 11.9, and 11.10, pp. 293–295, to practice using hyphens, capital letters, and commas with adjectives. Exercise 11.11, pp. 295–296, is the Challenge exercise.

▣ Chapter 11: Adjectives

● E X E R C I S E   11.1

Underline any adjectives in the following sentences.

1. Did you see the tall, skinny girl on the diving board?

2. My sister Maude is tall and skinny.

3. Seven unhappy children were crying at the overcrowded beach.

4. Having had a miserable, depressing day, I walked to the bus stop in the pouring rain.

5. After a long morning the tense, understaffed accounting group left for a much-needed lunch.

6. He is the friendliest, most sincere person I know.

7. Where is my dirty, ragged high school sweater?

8. Over the muddy river, through the spooky words, and past the old haunted house is how we get to Grandmother's house.

9. Most people don't like disorganized, boring English classes.

10. She had seventy baseball cards that were worth several dollars each.

11. Henrietta sold her greedy neighbor the map that supposedly showed a hidden buried treasure.

12. Any self-serving person is able to take advantage of honest, open, and trusting people.

13. James, I really like your brown shoes, blue pants, and black jacket together.

14. He takes a daily walk to the old farm field to see the iridescent colors of the flying pheasants.

15. Your sister's brother's boss is my former neighbor.

Write the comparative and superlative forms of any of the following adjectives that could be used to compare. The first is done as an example.

Positive	Comparative	Superlative
1. tall	taller	tallest
2. efficient		
3. good		
4. busy		
5. big		
6. little		
7. beautiful		
8. unique		
9. strong		
10. witty		
11. modern		
12. durable		
13. tan		
14. difficult		
15. merry		
16. perfect		
17. friendly		
18. successful		
19. bad		
20. competent		
21. feminine		
22. impossible		
23. sassy		
24. universal		
25. hard		

● E X E R C I S E   11.3

Underline the correct adjective to complete each of the following sentences.

1. I plan to complete this project (later, latter) in the week.

2. We send our bills according to the alphabet; you should receive yours in the (later, latter) part of the month.

3. He moved to Dallas in the (later, latter) years of his life.

4. That report is the (farthest, furthest) thing from my mind right now.

5. Let's talk about this (farther, further) into the meeting.

6. Last year I traveled (farther, further) than I ever had before.

7. Mrs. Smithers, you are (farther, further) into your pregnancy than I had thought.

8. Don't waste time, for it's (later, latter) than you think.

9. As we got (farther, further) into the problem, we saw that it was impossible to solve satisfactorily.

10. If you need any (farther, further) information, you may call us collect at 747–197–2345.

● E X E R C I S E   11.4

Underline the correct word for each sentence.

1. We prepared (less, fewer) cake and (less, fewer) cookies than we actually needed.

2. This year our county had (less, fewer) accidents than last year.

3. Ms. Fox and Mr. Krough showed (each other, one another) around their offices.

4. Several of the delegates to the convention talked over the vote with (each other, one another).

5. The examples cited by the attorney were (less, fewer) than we had hoped.

6. If two students study with (each other, one another), each one seems to learn more than if each studies alone.

7. The minimum standards of performance seem to be (less, fewer) here than at Dabos'.

8. You should now make (less, fewer) errors with these troublesome adjectives than you did before.

9. The team members seemed always to argue with (each other, one another).

10. Did you say there were more or (less, fewer) chairs there than we need?

Correct the errors in these statements that show comparisons.

1. Did any student in the class do better on his or her test than Estelle?

2. I like skiing better than anything I do.

3. He said that no candidate is more honest than Richard M. Montbaum.

4. This dictaphone works better than any machine in this office.

5. José asked me to find someone to take the second shift who could operate the forklift better than he.

6. Please look at both plans and decide which one you think is the best.

7. As he continued swimming, he discovered that his left arm seemed to be the weakest.

8. I'd like to attend both meetings, but I believe that the one on cost accounting will be the most effective.

9. Please send your order to Princeton or Los Angeles, whichever is the nearest to your office.

10. Of the two runners he is the quicker, although John always seems to finish best.

Place a *or* an *before each of the following words or word groups.*

_____ 1. honorary degree	_____ 11. historic moment	_____ 21. unusual person
_____ 2. undertaking	_____ 12. correspondent	_____ 22. skill
_____ 3. alligator	_____ 13. accountant	_____ 23. English class
_____ 4. unhappy time	_____ 14. committee	_____ 24. happy child
_____ 5. tiger	_____ 15. honor	_____ 25. opinion
_____ 6. horseshoe	_____ 16. evil person	_____ 26. universal problem
_____ 7. building	_____ 17. hotel	_____ 27. credit card
_____ 8. inventory	_____ 18. unit of time	_____ 28. organization
_____ 9. unused item	_____ 19. export business	_____ 29. orchestra
_____ 10. physician	_____ 20. honest man	_____ 30. hour

● E X E R C I S E   11.7

On the blank write the number of people, objects, or ideas named in the following.

_____ 1. the President and Vice-President

_____ 2. the Secretary and the Treasurer

_____ 3. a steel and aluminum cabinet

_____ 4. an unknown and untested product

_____ 5. the manager and sales director

_____ 6. a guide and a bus driver

_____ 7. the guide and bus driver

_____ 8. the brown and blue car

_____ 9. my sister and my friend

_____ 10. the head secretary and office manager

● E X E R C I S E   11.8

Make any corrections in the capitalization. Circle any changes you make.

1. The elizabethan Era was a productive time in the History of England.

2. Irish Linen is a very popular item for export.

3. I would love an Oriental rug, but I really can't afford one.

4. Did you say that you bought Boyer Aspirin?

5. I know he is an Indian, but I didn't know that he is a Yurok indian.

6. I like math and language classes, but I especially enjoy the latvian language.

7. Can you afford a mink coat as well as all of those dior dresses?

8. The type of cat without a tail is a manx cat.

9. An Igloo is an eskimo hut of ice built in a dome shape.

10. I decided to buy a Robbie Brooks Blouse to go with my Pendleson suit.

Hyphenate any compound adjectives in the following sentences. Circle any changes you make.

1. She finished the race in second place.

2. She won a second place ribbon.

3. He is not only self reliant, but he is also self motivated.

4. Harriet sold twenty four of those machines last week to set a company record.

5. This well made rug is well designed.

6. When I get my suit back from the cleaners, it should be well pressed.

7. A three story house is extremely hard to heat.

8. Are these data up to date?

9. Please return the self addressed envelope with your payment.

10. I played golf this week at a nine hole course in Almena.

11. We have all of our pastel colored suits and dresses on sale.

12. If Mr. Elaman is so well known, why do we even have to put together this two page list of prospects?

13. Although Peter seems to be high strung, he is really self controlled.

14. I caught a five pound bass in the little pond at the camp.

15. These are the latest up to date figures.

16. We plan to celebrate our twenty fifth anniversary with a well advertised special.

17. I have to write a two page report for tomorrow's meeting.

18. An age old problem is one that never seems to be solved.

19. Richard is a try as hard as he can person.

20. Sentence 19 is really quite unusual, but you might find something like it in your day to day reading.

Name _____ Date _____ Class _____

Add any necessary commas and hyphens to the following sentences. Also, correct any capitalization errors. Circle any changes you make.

1. Ms. Lean is a quick bright and hard working woman.

2. An efficient competent employee is an asset to any company.

3. Although this is a central American country, the main language spoken in business is English.

4. This plan practical and simple will be well accepted by the administrative staff.

5. Any well known product seems to sell more easily than one that is new.

6. Mrs. Jackson seems to promote only the younger alert employees.

7. The movie long and quite boring does not seem to be very popular, and I can see why.

8. Eileen brought me a Parker Pen for my office work, and it is a smooth easy to use pen.

9. Jason can make level headed intelligent decisions under stress.

10. His most recent decision was extremely level headed.

● E X E R C I S E   1 1 . 1 1   **CHALLENGE**

Proofread the following letter, and correct any incorrectly used adjectives. You may need to add hyphens and commas also. Circle any changes you make.

Dear Ms. Reits:

You name was given to us because your realtor said that you are one of the most unique people he knows. Mr. Terry tells us that you are apartment hunting and are looking for a tasteful well located place that is close to town but that seems to be more "in the country" than any apartment complex in town that you have already seen. We would like you to visit Greenwood Estates.

Although we are located within the city limits, Greenwood Estates is a well planned uncommonly countrified development. Careful attention was taken so that no large beautiful trees were cut, nor were any of the lovely rolling hills disturbed when we began our buildings. You will feel more freedom from city life here than you would if you actually lived out in the country, and yet you still have the convenience of living close to your work and shopping. There is no development in this city that is more prettier. Not only will you have the comfort and security of living among people with interests similar to yours, but you will also find that you can easily relate to each other.

Besides enjoying outdoor activities here, such as the indoor outdoor pool and the tennis courts, you will be included in all of our planned group events. Each year we have picnics, contests, and holiday parties, most of which include the entire families of our residents. All of the developments have less activities than we have at Greenwood.

As for your individual living unit, you will have a much better choice than anywhere. If you want a two bedroom unit, you can rent one of our lovely tri-level redwood units or buy a condominium, whichever you might like best. All of our accommodations have up to date appliances, plush carpeting, and the fashionable decorating of Mr. Armand. They are being finished in the italian motif.

Your safety is also one of our first considerations. Each unit has its own attached garage with a well lighted drive leading into it. You have no further than a few feet to walk into your own "home." You can be assured of your privacy because of the double safety locks on each door and the alarm system in each unit.

To learn more about the variety offered to you in our luxury development, simply return the enclosed postage paid card telling us when you will be available for your own private exclusive showing. Mrs. Gladys Goldstone will assist you at your convenience. You can be a resident of Greenwood within a month if you act now.

Sincerely,

Your name

◻ Periodic Review: Chapters 10–11

Rewrite these weak compound sentences by placing the less important idea into a modifying phrase or clause.

1. Miss Masters became ill at the dinner, and she went home.

   _____

   _____

2. I hurried to pack my suitcases, and I caught my plane.

   _____

   _____

3. Canadian winters are fierce, and many people go to Florida then.

   _____

   _____

4. Mr. Wong goes to my church, and he is a good employee.

   _____

   _____

5. You have learned some new techniques, and your writing should be improving.

   _____

   _____

Correct any misused verbs in these sentences by writing the correct form above the error.

1. I seen you at the contest where one of the contestants were your sister.

2. A ton of carrots are a lot of feed for the deer.

3. After Bob had drank his juice, he coughed and sputtered.

4. By tomorrow at 5 p.m. we will complete the job.

5. Two men in the ranks of the corps was commended for that.

Cross out incorrect usages in the following sentences. Write the correction above each error.

1. The mens' teams did better than the ladies' teams.

2. Please give this book to whomever you find has lost it.

3. You are definitely wrong in your directions to the farm.

4. Those two old guys have set there all day and talked.

5. Knowing your own limitations are very important.

Add any necessary commas to nonrestrictive elements in these. Circle any changes you make.

1. I presented the medal to Officer Krupky who saved a man.

2. The test that I want to take is this one which seems easy.

3. The people earning over thirty thousand dollars are those who should be paying the higher taxes.

4. Judson River a slow-moving stream is easier to canoe than the Muskegon a rapidly foaming river.

5. My only son-in-law who is a mechanic for an auto agency can fix just about anything that you give him.

Write the plural form of each of the following words or phrases.

_____ 1. Fitz

_____ 2. memorandum

_____ 3. journey

_____ 4. Chinese

_____ 5. court martial

_____ 6. photo

_____ 7. variety

_____ 8. roof

_____ 9. person

_____ 10. criterion

Underline the correct form to complete each sentence.

1. I really don't like (his, him) calling on my clients.

2. The (data, datum) is mistyped in this section.

3. Those (ladies', lady's) (shoe's, shoes) are outdated.

4. He wanted to have (bake, baked) beans at the picnic.

5. It was (they, them) (who, whom) Mrs. Soloman called.

6. The jury could not agree on (its, their) verdict.

7. Someone left (his or her, their) dogs out all night.

8. I knew Ben Johnson better than (he, him) after Ben had worked for me for ten years.

9. (Here's, Here're) your copies of the memoranda.

10. The lawyer's ethics (was, were) called into question.

11. (Everyone, Every one) of these reports has errata.

12. Was (Thomases, Thomas's) daughter elected to the Senate?

13. Was the (Thomases, Thomases') daughter arrested?

14. Here (is, are) each of the printers (who, whom) I selected.

15. Joyce and (I, me) saw Nathan and (he, him) buying the desk.

16. The (analysis, analyses) are ready for the printer.

17. We found that we had (ran, run) out of chicken by 7 p.m.

18. Any one of these watches (has, have) been cleaned and repaired.

19. The new pavement has been (lain, laid) in time for the holiday season.

20. I prefer (stretching, to stretch), running, and walking for my exercise activities.

21. I found this coat at (Jessups, Jessup's).

22. The herd (were, was) seen grazing at various sites throughout the park.

23. Please don't forget to (sit, set) the roast out to thaw.

24. The candidate, in addition to his assistants, (is, are) appearing at the Civic Center next Tuesday.

25. The understudy is (more tall, taller) than the leading man.

Decide whether each group of words below is a sentence (S), fragment (F), or a run-on (R).

_____ 1. After watering the lawn for over two hours.

_____ 2. Brendon wished he had finished college, he would have a better chance for promotion.

_____ 3. The girl who had been singing in the barbershop quartet at Old Central.

_____ 4. He preferred to drive a truck however he could do with a van if necessary.

_____ 5. Many women like to dye their hair, some find it too time-consuming to touch up the roots.

_____ 6. Someone interested in the flow of ancient rivers.

_____ 7. Tired of the constant noise and confusion, Ed retired.

_____ 8. Brent carefully prepared the reel, then he baited the hook.

_____ 9. The soda can dropped to the floor; it fizzed when it was opened.

_____ 10. When Thomas met with counsel and went over the details of the case for the court hearing.

Underline the verb that agrees in number with the subject.

1. Either of the women (is, are) responsible and mature.

2. This is one of those times that (causes, cause) gray hair.

3. Marie, along with Dina, (is, are) going to Mississippi.

4. Neither bacon nor eggs (is, are) good for you, it seems.

5. Twelve consecutive strikes (is, are) hard to get in bowling.

6. The data (was, were) published, and the staff (was, were) shocked at the final results.

7. Among our favorite clients (is, are) the Oswald Company.

8. I know a number of workers who (is, are) constantly griping.

9. Some of the profit (is, are) missing somehow.

10. The number of inhabitants (is, are) amazing.

CHAPTER 12

Adverbs

OVERVIEW

- Characteristics of Adverbs
- Locating Adverbs
- Forming Adverbs From Adjectives
- Adverbs Don't All Look Alike
- Choosing Between Adjectives and Adverbs
- Comparative Forms of Adverbs
- Often-Misused Adverbs and Adjectives

Although you have studied adverb phrases and clauses in earlier chapters, this chapter takes a closer look at one-word adverbs: how to form adverbs from adjectives, how to choose whether to use an adjective or an adverb as a modifier, how to make comparisons with adverbs, and how to select the correct forms of some often-misused modifying words.

CHARACTERISTICS OF ADVERBS

The study of adverbs naturally follows the study of adjectives because both are modifiers and both are used to compare.

You already know several characteristics of adverbs.

1. Adverbs modify action verbs, adjectives, and other adverbs.

2. Adverbs can be single words, phrases, or clauses.

3. Adverbs tell <u>when</u>, <u>where</u>, <u>how</u>, <u>how much (to what extent)</u>, or, as adverb clauses, <u>why</u>.

LOCATING ADVERBS

The clause positions of adverbs are many. When modifying an adjective or another adverb, the single-word adverb will normally be positioned directly in front of the word modified. When an adverb modifies an action verb, however, the adverb is very movable. Its natural position is to follow the verb, but such an adverb can be placed before the verb or even at the front of the clause to gain more emphasis.

Study these sentences to note the adverb position as well as to notice the type of word modified.

1. Marzella walked *quickly*. **AV**

2. Etienne *hastily* piled the dishes in the sink. **AV**

3. *Hesitantly,* Gretta confessed her ignorance about the laws regulating tax. **AV**

4. The *unfailingly* faithful setter was *extremely* tired at the end of the hunt. **ADJ** **ADJ**

5. The watches were *very quickly* sold. **ADV ADJ**

Example 4 shows an adverb modifying an adjective (*faithful*) and an adverb modifying a subject complement adjective (*tired*). In Example 5 the adverb *very*, modifies another adverb, *quickly*, which in turn modifies a subject complement adjective.

Not only do adverbs modify single words, but they also can modify any of the verbals or verbal phrases.

infinitive To study *more easily* than you do now, you might want to keep reviewing your notes each day.

participle Hanging *precariously* from the high wire, the aerialist looked for the safety net below.

gerund *Knowingly* choosing the right word will be possible with study.

FORMING ADVERBS FROM ADJECTIVES

Although not all adverbs are made from adjectives, a great many are. These adverbs end in the suffix -*ly*.

Spelling Rules for Adding -*ly*

1. To form most adverbs, you simply add -*ly* to the adjective form. If the adjective form ends in -*al*, you still add -*ly* so that your adverb will have two *l*s.

awful	awfully	accidental	accidentally
careful	carefully	critical	critically
rapid	rapidly	real	really
quick	quickly	unusual	unusually
cautious	cautiously	general	generally
unexpected	unexpectedly	official	officially
enticing	enticingly	fatal	fatally

2. If the adjective ends in -*e*, keep the -*e* and add -*ly*. (Three words are exceptions to this rule: *duly, truly, wholly.*)

like	likely
extreme	extremely
separate	separately
sincere	sincerely
false	falsely
active	actively
free	freely

3. If the adjective ends in -*le*, change the final -*e* to -*y*. Do not add an extra -*ly*.

ample	amply
considerable	considerably
noticeable	noticeably
possible	possibly
feeble	feebly
gentle	gently

4. If the adjective ends in -*y* preceded by a consonant, change the -*y* to -*i* and then add -*ly*.

busy	busily
happy	happily
satisfactory	satisfactorily
merry	merrily
scanty	scantily

Complete the following sentences.

1. Adverbs can modify _____,

_____, and _____.

2. Adverbs tell when, _____,

_____, _____, or

_____ about the words they modify.

3. _____ is the adverb form of *neat.*

4. _____ is the adverb form of *forcible.*

5. _____ is the adverb form of *natural.*

6. _____ is the adverb form of *true.*

7. _____ is the adverb form of *temporary.*

8. _____ is the adverb form of *nice.*

9. _____ is the adverb form of *sincere.*

10. _____ is the adverb form of *admirable.*

Before you continue, turn to p. 350 to check your answers.

TRY IT OUT: Complete Exercise 12.1, p. 315, to practice the rules for changing adjectives to adverbs.

ADVERBS DON'T ALL LOOK ALIKE

Do not make the common error of thinking that all words that end in *-ly* are adverbs. Look at the *-ly* words in these sentences.

    N   N   ADJ   N
Sally or *Billy* is a *lovely* singer.

             ADJ   N
He is a *friendly* man.

Remember that subject complements can be nouns, pronouns, or adjectives. In each of the preceding examples the modifier is an adjective because the subject complement is a noun. You will use an adverb to modify the subject complement only when the complement is an adjective or participle ("The pitch was forcefully delivered").

Just as all *-ly* words aren't adverbs, all adverbs do not end in *-ly*.

AV
I'll see you *soon.*

ADJ
Doctor Webster is *quite* busy with her research in the lab.

ADV   ADJ
The pamphlet was *very well* proofread, showing no mistakes.

The only sure way to choose correctly between adjectives and adverbs is by identifying the word or words modified. You cannot select your correct usage "by ear" or by "how the word ends."

TRY IT OUT: Exercise 12.2, p. 316, will help you to see adverbs modifying in different clause positions.

 # CHOOSING BETWEEN ADJECTIVES AND ADVERBS

As you speak and write, your mind is continually selecting and rejecting words. Many of these choices have to do with verb tenses. Other choices are quickly made so that you use the correct pronouns. Still other selections must be made when you are choosing the correct modifying word.

The mind is really amazing, isn't it, when you consider that you are making these varied choices without conscious effort. Your mind rapidly selects each of these usages and strings these words together into sentences, often one right after the other. Of course, you have trained your mind to select based on your understanding of English language usage.

By now, though, if you are a typical user of the language, you are finding that you had some misconceptions about certain usages. You are finding that you need to retrain your ear—and thus your mind—to make some better selections.

How do these sentences "sound" to you?

I did good on that test.

I feel badly about that.

She is real concerned about her grades.

If <u>any</u> of these sentences sounds all right to you, you need to "tune up your ear." All are examples of misused modifiers.

Studying these sentences will show you the errors.

Wrong:

AV   ADJ
I did *good* on that test.

Correct:

   ADV
I did *well* on that test.

Action verbs need adverbs as modifiers

Wrong:

LV   ADV
I feel *badly* about that.

Correct:

   ADJ
I feel *bad* about that.

Subject complements are not adverbs

Wrong:

   LV ADJ   ADJ
She is *real* concerned about her grades.

Correct:

   ADV
She is *really* concerned about her grades.

Only adverbs can modify adjectives

As you can see, when selecting a modifier, it is imperative that you check its clause position (where the word fits in its clause pattern) to determine what type of word you are modifying. Remember, the clause patterns are as follows.

Pattern 1. Subject–Verb

Pattern 2. Subject–Action Verb–Direct Object

Pattern 3. Subject–Action Verb–Indirect Object–Direct Object

Pattern 4. Subject–Linking Verb–Subject Complement

It helps, too, to ask these questions to determine which one your word answers.

Adjective: Which? What kind of? How many?

Adverb: When? Where? How? How much (to what extent)? Why?

The following two-step method will help you choose the correct modifiers.

STEP 1: Decide which form of the word is the adverb, which is the adjective.

STEP 2: Decide on the clause pattern to determine word position. The position will tell you the part of speech of the word to be modified.

Look at the following three examples to see how the two-step method works.

This first example uses one of the verbs that could be either an action verb or a linking verb.

The perfume smells (sweet, sweetly).

You know that the verb *smells* is linking because it can be replaced with a *be* verb without changing the meaning. Now follow the two steps.

1. With two like-words the *-ly* form will be the adverb. Thus, *sweetly* is the adverb, *sweet* the adjective.

2. Here the clause pattern is Pattern 4: Subject–Linking Verb–Subject Complement. With Pattern 4 you have an extra step: Is the complement a noun or pronoun, or is it an adjective? Since this complement is a describing word, you want the adjective *sweet*.

In this second example you must determine whether your modifier describes *behaved* or *child*.

Little Mac is a (good, well) behaved child.

Following the two steps gives you these answers.

1. The adjective is *good,* the adverb *well.*

2. This sentence is also a Pattern 4. In this example *child* is the complement. Working backward, *behaved* must be an adjective to modify the noun *child.* Thus, *well*—the adverb—is the correct choice because adjectives can be modified only by adverbs.

The third example contains a verb that always shows action, which should make your job of choosing the correct modifier easier.

Monty folded the clothes (neat, neatly).

1. With two like-words the *-ly* form is the adverb.

2. This sentence has an action verb and a noun, *clothes,* which receives the action; thus, this is a Pattern 2. If the unknown form came <u>before</u> the noun, it would be an adjective describing *clothes.* Coming after, the modifier must be an adverb, modifying the action—*folded.* The correct choice is *neatly.*

You should now use this same two-step method to make the correct choices in Self-Check 12–2. Don't try to make your choice based on what sounds right. That method will not retrain your mind in the selection process.

Underline the correct word choice in each sentence, and tell why you made that choice. Mark verbs AV *or* LV. *Name the clause pattern.*

1. The bread tastes (fresh, freshly).

2. She plays tennis (good, well).

3. His methods seem (extreme, extremely).

4. His methods seem (extreme, extremely) practical.

5. Paul, hide (quick, quickly)!

6. He takes pictures (bad, badly).

7. He takes (bad, badly) pictures.

8. John felt (bad, badly) about his wife's accident.

9. Burton (sure, surely) did a good job with his speech.

10. Mrs. Edison was (real, really) pleased to hear that we had captured the new account.

Before you continue, turn to p. 350 to check your answers. Be certain to check that you are identifying the clause positions correctly.

Unusual Uses of *Close* and *Near*

Generally, *close* is an adjective with *closely* as its adverb form; *near* is an adjective with *nearly* as its adverb form. However, *close* and *near* can also be used as adverbs when these two words indicate the relative position of one thing to another thing. *Closer* and *nearer* are also used as adverbs in this way.

Here are examples of *closely* and *nearly* used in their normal adverbial forms.

Elaine was *nearly* there when her car broke down.
The appraiser looked *closely* at the diamond for any flaws.

In the following examples *close* and *near* relate one thing to another in relative position—they show how far apart two things are. Because *close* and *near* are not being used to do anything but tell <u>where</u> something is located, they serve as adverbs.

I think George lives *near* to the plant.
No employee comes *close* to Erwin in dedication to this company.

The puppy cringes when anyone gets *close* to him.

Alexandra lives *closer* to work than I.

Of course, *close* and *near* are very often used as adjectives.

Keep *close* watch of the time.

A *near* miss is better than an accident, but it can be as frightening.

Take extra care when selecting *near* and *close* or *nearly* and *closely*.

TRY IT OUT: Do Exercise 12.3, p. 317, to work with choosing between adjectives and adverbs.

COMPARATIVE FORMS OF ADVERBS

Adverbs, like adjectives, are used to show comparisons as well as to modify. Basically, the same rules apply for changing the positive forms into comparative and superlative forms: You add *-er* or *-est* to one-syllable words or two-syllable words that end *-y*. Because most adverbs of two syllables have an ending of not just *-y*, but the whole syllable *-ly*, not many of the two-syllable adverbs add *-er* or *-est* to the base word. Most often, the comparative words *more* or *most* are needed.

Many people don't really realize that <u>six</u> forms of a word are possible when that word is used to compare. Look at the six forms available for describing and comparing with the word *quick*.

	Adjective	Adverb
Positive	quick	quickly
Comparative	quicker	more quickly
Superlative	quickest	most quickly

The three forms of the adjective are those used to make comparisons. Because the base word is one syllable, *-er* or *-est* is added. <u>All of these forms are still adjectives.</u>

To make an adverb from an adjective, you don't add *-er* or *-est* but add *-ly*. If you want to compare with this adverb, you place *more* or *most* in front because the word's second syllable is more than just *-y*. <u>All of these forms are still adverbs.</u>

Too often, the *-er* and *-est* forms are used for all comparisons, ignoring the rules that require adverbs to modify action verbs, adjectives, and other adverbs. Before using an *-er* or *-est* word, be careful that you check what kind of word you are modifying.

Practice this principle by using some modifying form in these sentences.

Maude Jessup is (quick, quickly, quicker) at answering questions in this board game. [A subject complement is needed, so *quickly* won't do. It is an adverb. The other two words are both adjectives, but because no comparison is stated, the simple *quick* is correct.]

This car can turn (quick, quickly). [Again, there is no comparison made. This Pattern 1 sentence has an action verb; thus, an adverb, *quickly,* is called for.]

This car on the right can turn (quicker, more quickly) than the other one. [Did you act too quickly and choose *quicker?* Is that word an adjective or an adverb? Aren't you selecting a word to modify an action verb? The comparative form that is an adverb is *more quickly.*]

Jesse swam the 100-meter race the (easiest, most easily) of anybody who was in it. [If you decided on *easiest,* you still aren't doing your work. The modifier is not modifying a noun, but it is telling how he swam; thus, an adverb, *most easily,* is needed.]

⌐ S E L F - C H E C K 1 2 – 3

For the basic modifying word in parentheses, decide which of its six forms is needed in the sentence. If it is supposed to be one of the comparative forms, the sentence should obviously make the comparison.

1. Judy, please drive (slow) _____ than you are now.

2. This new desk top feels (smooth) _____ than your old one.

3. Of the three women Ms. Thomas proofreads her work the (careful)

   _____ .

4. He is the (poor) _____ speller of the two of them.

5. This model is the (poor) _____ constructed of all of the ones in the show.

Before you continue, turn to p. 350 to check your answers.

TRY IT OUT: Complete Exercises 12.4 and 12.5, pp. 318–319, to practice selecting the correct comparative forms.

OFTEN-MISUSED ADVERBS AND ADJECTIVES

Review the following adjectives and adverbs to see whether you are familiar with the preferred usages of each.

Adjective   *good (better, best)*
Adverb   *well (better, best)*

LV
Maria's voice is *good.*

AV
She sings *well.*

Adjective   *real* (no comparative forms)
Adverb   *really* (no comparative forms)

LV
The diamond is *real.* [means "genuine"]

ADJ
He had *really* strong opinions. [means "genuinely"]

Adjective   *sure (surer, surest)*
Adverb   *surely (more surely, most surely)*

LV
He was *sure* of his facts. [means "certain"]

AV
He *surely* had a number of facts as data. [means "certainly"]

Adjective   *most* (no comparative form)
Adverb or adjective   *almost* (no comparative form)

Most men have to shave each day. [the majority]

Almost everyone attended the review. [adjective; means "nearly"]

He is *almost* always late. [adverb; means "nearly"]

Using *Only*

Two other modifiers are very often misunderstood. The first is *only,* which can be an adverb <u>or</u> an adjective. Because it can be either, you do not have to choose between *only* and another word. However, pay careful attention to the placement of this word. *Only* is used as a "selecter." It makes an exception to the general rule about whatever is modified. Thus, take care that you put it in front of the item you want to make an exception.

Only he oiled the machine. [no one else]

He *only* oiled the machine. [He did nothing else to the machine.]

He oiled *only* this machine. [no other machine]

⊡ Using *Too*

The second word that is often misunderstood is *too*. Although one meaning of the word is "also," *too* more often is used as an adverb that intensifies the word it modifies. In other words, *too* placed in front of an adjective or adverb shows an excessive amount of the item named by the word.

I hope you are not *too* tired. [overly tired]
She was *too* strongly motivated. [excessively motivated]

You can see that this adverb has a double *o*. Only the preposition *to* and the infinitive forms have the word *to* with one *o*.

⊡ One Word or Two?

Another usage question concerns those adverbs and adjectives that are sometimes written as one word and other times written as two words. This decision will depend on the writer's intended meaning.

all ready	everything is ready
already	previously
all together	everything is put together
altogether	entirely
all ways	in every way
always	at all times
all right	all correct; in good order
never one word	

⊡ Using Negative Words

The English language uses a number of words to express a negative. Many of these negative words are adverbs.

neither . . . nor	no	nobody	can't
neither	none	no one	cannot
never	not	nothing	doesn't
hardly	nor		don't
scarcely			won't
seldom			

A general principle in the English language is that two negative words together in the same clause are considered a **double negative;** this double usage is unnecessary because one of the words already makes the statement negative.

Wrong:
I *hardly never* go there anymore.

Right:
I hardly ever go there anymore.

Wrong:
I *don't* know *nothing* about the Falls' file.

Right:
I know nothing about the Falls' file.
I don't know anything about the Falls' file.

Wrong:
I *can't scarcely* see the road in this fog.

Right:
I can scarcely see the road in this fog.

SELF-CHECK 12-4

Underline the correct form in the following sentences.

1. She was (real, really) sorry that the loan could not be made.

2. Mary Lou is (all ways, always) late for the meetings.

3. I (sure, surely) do realize how difficult English can be.

4. Luke did (good, well) on his speaking tour, being booked for most locations again for next year.

5. There isn't (nothing, anything) more delicious than a hot fudge sundae with walnuts.

6. He (only) had (only) three dollars left after the meal. [Select one.]

7. The chairperson decided that we were (all ready, already) for a vote.

8. He asked me if it would be (all right, alright) to mail the order by Parcel Post.

9. I (can, can't) hardly wait for the show to begin.

10. Please don't give me (neither, either) pudding (nor, or) pie.

Before you continue, turn to p. 350 to check your answers.

Now that you have completed your study of adjectives and adverbs, you can feel more confident that you will choose correctly when you speak and write these modifying words.

TRY IT OUT: **Do Exercises 12.6, 12.7, and 12.8, pp. 320–321, to work on the careful selection of modifiers. Exercise 12.9, pp. 321–322, is the Challenge exercise.**

⊡ Chapter 12: Adverbs

● E X E R C I S E   12.1

Write the correctly spelled adverb form of these adjectives.

1. happy _____

2. separate _____

3. fine _____

4. bad _____

5. good _____

6. true _____

7. sudden _____

8. adequate _____

9. usual _____

10. merry _____

11. sincere _____

12. ordinary _____

13. due _____

14. complete _____

15. special _____

16. sole _____

17. legal _____

18. extreme _____

19. heavy _____

20. impartial _____

21. similar _____

22. like _____

23. illegible _____

24. busy _____

25. whole _____

26. noticeable _____

27. beautiful _____

28. possible _____

29. coarse _____

30. principal _____

Notice the italicized adverb in each of the following sentences. On the first blank tell which word is modified; on the second tell whether the word modified is an action verb, an adjective, or another adverb.

	Word Modified	Part of Speech
1. She was *heavily* clothed for the cold weather.		
2. I can *easily* understand how this tragedy happened.		
3. Mr. Burns was *well* prepared for the presentation.		
4. The author, Benjamin Green, is becoming *quite* well known.		
5. Amy is *busily* working on the agenda.		
6. The container of duplicating fluid is *almost* empty.		
7. One *nearly* forgotten detail proved to be very critical.		
8. Although we lost the match tonight, we played *extremely* well.		
9. The professor figured our test grades *separately*.		
10. He *hastily* added the column of figures before the tax inspector arrived.		
11. This is a *truly* lovely picture.		
12. We are *nearly* there.		
13. Our committee *wisely* decided to start the report early.		
14. The work is *completely* finished three days before it is due.		
15. He *completely* finished the work by two o'clock.		

● E X E R C I S E   1 2 . 3

On the blank write the correct adjective or adverb form. Remember first to identify the word modified to help with your choice. (Sometimes your answer will be the same as the word in parentheses.) Be prepared to explain your choice.

1. The time passed (quick) _____.

2. She is a (quick) _____ keypuncher.

3. I hope that I am (ample) _____ prepared for any questions that may arise at the meeting.

4. The soup tasted very (good) _____ to Samuel.

5. I feel (bad) _____ about arriving late for work.

6. Does our sales picture look (bad) _____ to you?

7. I was (sure) _____ pleased to learn of your luck in the drawing.

8. The work progressed (rapid) _____.

9. The production line has improved (great) _____ in the past few years.

10. He sometimes goes to (extreme) _____ measures to control his temper.

11. He tries (extreme) _____ hard to control his temper.

12. Ms. Hocevar was (skillful) _____ handling the problem.

13. Our office has been (busy) _____ preparing a new catalog for the fall season.

14. She said that she is now (ready) _____ to work with the computer.

15. He looked (longing) _____ at the deluxe model car.

16. We were seated (comfortable) _____ in the auditorium for the lecture.

17. Mary Ellen was (quiet) _____ as she took her place at the podium.

18. Mary Ellen (quiet) _____ took her place at the podium.

19. He knew he had done (bad) _____ at tennis that day.

20. However, later in the week, he did (good) _____.

Write the correct form of the word in parentheses. Before doing so, decide whether you need an adjective or an adverb, and then decide whether comparison is being made.

(strong)   1. Mr. Adams is known to be _____. He works out every day,

but his left arm seems to be the _____.

(quick)   2. Ted, run _____. You must run

_____ than Herb to win the race.

(weak)   3. When she was hurt, Mona called out _____. No one heard,

and the calls became _____ as time went by.

(busy)   4. As the convention neared, we all prepared _____. Arlene

worked _____ than Betty. Actually, Arlene seemed to be the

_____ of the two.

(careless)   5. Joan _____ did the filing so that we couldn't find the letters

and reports we needed. When we had to let one of the two clerks go, it was Joan

because she was the _____.

(easy)   6. If you organize your work, you will find that it becomes _____

than it is now. You can accomplish more work _____.

(slow)   7. Some days time seems _____. Lunch time comes

_____ than usual. Some days just seem

_____ than others.

(bright)   8. Today the sun seems _____ than usual. I wonder if it is

shining _____ because summer is so near.

(plain)   9. It is as _____ as the nose on your face. In fact, of the two

solutions it is the _____. Can't you

_____ see it?

(weary)   10. I couldn't tell who was _____ , Joe or I. We had

_____ trudged through the woods all day.

● E X E R C I S E   1 2 . 5

Proofread these sentences for misused adverbs and adjectives. Some sentences have no errors. Circle any changes you have made.

1. Of my two eyes, my right one is the weakest.

2. I did real well on this test.

3. He feels badly enough as it is without going to trial.

4. Of all of our branches this one is the poorest managed one of all.

5. He drove more slowly than Missy.

6. This car handles easier than my old one.

7. Of the two choices this one seems to be the best.

8. I swim badly, but I can dive pretty good.

9. I surely was surprised by the birthday party.

10. The whole idea sounds strange.

11. Mr. Pattison looked angry and threatened me loudly.

12. This plant grows more quicker than a cactus.

13. We can do it easier than they can.

14. This paper feels more smoother than that paper.

15. We'll just have to hurry quicker.

Underline the word or words that correctly complete each of the following sentences.

1. (Most, Almost) all of the students were ready for a vacation.

2. We (sure, surely) were surprised at the results of the election.

3. I have (most, almost) of the work finished.

4. I have (most, almost) all of the work completed.

5. (Most, Almost) people enjoy their jobs.

6. He was (real, really) sorry about his behavior.

7. Are you (sure, surely) of the ring's authenticity?

8. I thought I had given a copy to (most, almost) everyone.

9. The news about the incident looks (bad, badly).

10. She (sure, surely) can type (good, well).

Show where you would put the word only *by putting a caret (^) where the word* only *should be inserted.*

1. He was promoted yesterday. [not very long ago]

2. She planned to take one suitcase to England. [no other suitcases]

3. Ms. Ferera wanted to see glassware when she went to Gimble's. [see nothing else]

4. Mr. Gibson was fined for the speeding ticket. [no other punishment]

5. Mr. Hasborough has been to Greece before this trip. [none of us except him]

■ **E X E R C I S E   1 2 . 8**

Choose the correct word or words to complete these sentences.

1. I hope that this reservation is (all right, alright) with you.

2. This trip has been (all together, altogether) too tiring for old Mrs. Woods.

3. It was nice that we could arrive (all together, altogether).

4. We were (all ready, already) to go at 6 a.m.

5. It was (all ready, already) light by then.

6. She (all ways, always) seems to do the right thing in (all ways, always).

7. Though I am coming down with a cold, I feel (all right, alright).

8. Mr. Bradley (all ways, always) seems to be in a good mood.

9. Did you tell Mr. Wooten that we have (all ready, already) sent out the mailing?

10. He knew that everything was (all right, alright) when the President smiled and shook his hand.

■ **E X E R C I S E   1 2 . 9**   **CHALLENGE**

Please help Mr. Blue proofread his story for the newspaper. Be alert for several errors, not only those with adjectives and adverbs.

I've all ways said that nobody knows nothing about how to act in a disaster. I found out different last night when the tornado touched down in my neighborhood.

It was all ready dinner time when the funny looking clouds appeared. Me and Mrs. Blue was just getting ready to sit down to eat. We hardly had no time to sit there when there was a noise in the already dense air. The rain was coming down real hard, and there was even some hail mixed in. I had just said that we all ways have to look for the worse when this kind of weather is around.

Suddenly the noise got more loud. It sounded like a terrible roar. We looked out the kitchen window and seen huge black clouds rolling our way. They was coming closer and closer. Our dog, Spot, was whining and acting real scared. I says to Blanche, "It looks badly."

She grabbed the nearest portable radio, I grabbed Spot, and we headed for the basement. We near run into one another in our hurry. We quick got down the stairs and laid on the floor near the wall. There wasn't no windows above us.

We heard what sounded like a explosion upstairs, and Blanche and me just look at each other careful. We was both awful scared. It wasn't scarcely five minutes later that we decided that whatever it was had passed. We got up real careful and headed up to see what had happened.

Luckily, our house wasn't to bad damaged. I guess it's part because we had some of the windows open when the tornado hit. When we looked outside though, we seen alot of trees down and alot of things blowed around. We run out of the house to see if we could help any body else.

We had to move quick but careful because of all of the power lines down. We seen alot of our other neighbor's outside too, altogether to help each other. Nobody seemed to be missing, but some of us had some bad cuts and bruises. We was still real shook about the disaster.

The damage done to our houses was considerably. There was roofs off and windows smashed all over the place. Old Gracie Davis's house was hit so bad that it was about ruint. Her chickens was running all over the place clucking.

One funny thing that happened was that the wind had turned Bill Bigelow's car completely around, real neat. It didn't seem to have hurt the car at all.

We had most every one gathered altogether and had helped bandage any cuts and scrapes when the help from nearby arrived. Them guys really knew what they was doing. In no time at all, they had taken care of us all. The power company come right out and put up all the lines careful. They sure have to work slow in order not to get hurt.

It all turned out alright for us. Though I feel badly about what happened, I sure can say we all done real good in a disaster.

Word Choices

OVERVIEW

- Learning Commonly Confused Words
- Choosing the Correct Preposition
- Identifying Words Often Misspelled

When you speak, you don't have to worry about spelling or your word choices between word sets such as *holey/wholly* or *pare/pair/pear*. Unfortunately, when you write, errors in spelling and word choice become very apparent.

One problem with using a misspelled or misused word is that your message may be misinterpreted. Even more likely, though, is that your readers, seeing the errors, will become distracted by the errors and lose track of what you are saying. Not only that, but your readers may even make assumptions about your abilities in general and about your lack of attention to detail. These assumptions could interfere not only with your communication but also with the relationship or image you are trying to build with the receiver.

You may have discovered that you can find errors using computer programs that will do a spell check or a grammar check of your work. However, don't rely on these programs totally.

Although you can locate many errors this way, most programs cannot detect errors in word choice between like-words such as *accept/except*. Both are correctly spelled English words. A computer cannot check the context of the sentence to see if the word is properly used. That challenge is still up to you.

LEARNING COMMONLY CONFUSED WORDS

Of course, reference manuals and dictionaries can provide you with the correct answers, but looking up many words in a letter or report can be time-consuming. Every writer has to do some checking, but most people prefer to learn the spellings of the most common words and to learn to distinguish between most sets of confusing words. These two goals are the aim of this chapter.

This section is alphabetized for ease in future reference. Self-checks and exercises are used throughout the chapter to help you use these words enough to learn their differences. The parts of speech are listed for each entry; occasionally, other hints are given to assist you in understanding each usage.

Words Often Misused

accept (v.) to receive approvingly
except (prep.) but; (v.) to leave out or omit

Did you *accept* that proposal?

Everyone *except* Fred went home early on Friday.

Will you *except* this item from the annual budget?

adapt (v.) to change for new purposes
adept (adj.) skilled
adopt (v.) to accept something as it is

We must *adapt* this program to include the new revisions.

Mr. Benson is an *adept* management person.

I vote to *adopt* the revisions that are proposed.

addition (n.) something to be included or joined with
edition (n.) a published form (similar in form to the word *editor*)

We expect to have an *addition* to our department next week.

Which *edition* of the book did you want?

advice (n.) an opinion given
advise (v.) (pronounced ad vīz′) to give an opinion or judgment. (Do *not* use to mean *inform*.)

He gave me some good *advice* to follow.

I asked my attorney to *advise* me about the contract.

NOT: We *advise* you that your order is now ready.

affect (v.) to act upon or influence
effect (n.) the result; (v.) (seldom used as a verb) to create or bring about some result (requires a direct object)

How will this idea *affect* our new models for next year?

The recession seems to have had an *effect* on our sales.

Will you *effect* a change in policy before the new handbook is printed?

among	see *between*
anxious	(adj.) filled with worry
eager	(adj.) excited about; awaiting

He is very *anxious* about the results of his medical tests.

We are *eager* to have you place an order with us soon.

apt	see *likely*
as	see *like*
beside	(prep.) next to; at the side of
besides	(prep.) in addition to; other than

Please come and sit *beside* me.

I have asked two other board members *besides* you for an opinion about the case.

between	(prep.) a situation involving only two
among	(prep.) a situation involving three or more

The choice is *between* Arno or Beckwith.

I am the oldest one *among* the three of us.

canvas	(n.) a coarse cloth
canvass	(v.) to solicit or seek orders, opinions, votes, and so on; to take a poll

We covered the boat with a *canvas.*

Did you *canvass* the staff to see where each one would like the office party held?

capital	(adj.) main; (n.) financial resources; seat of government
capitol	(n.) the building where legislatures meet

This small invention is the *capital* reason for our success.

She has a starting *capital* of $50,000.

Lansing is the *capital* of Michigan.

We met on the steps of the *capitol* building for the photo.

cite	(v.) to refer to a source; to bring to court
sight	(v.) to see; (n.) a remarkable place or view
site	(n.) a piece of land intended for a specific purpose

I *cite* the *Federal Register* as the source of these statistics.

John Thommes was *cited* for an infraction of the law.

Columbus must have been elated to *sight* land.

This property is the *site* for our new assembly plant.

Underline the correct word for the definition given.

1. to exclude from—accept, except

2. to include with—addition, edition

3. skillful—adapt, adept, adopt

4. to give an opinion—advice, advise

5. the uncommon verb usage *to bring about*—affect, effect

6. to be desirous of—anxious, eager

7. at the side of—beside, besides

8. used in comparing three or more—between, among

9. to take a poll—canvas, canvass

10. money—capital, capitol

11. to refer to—cite, sight, site

12. in addition to—beside, besides

13. to act upon—affect, effect

14. a plot of land—cite, sight, site

15. to change—adapt, adept, adopt

Before you continue, turn to p. 351 to check your answers.

TRY IT OUT: Complete Exercise 13.1, p. 337, to practice using these words.

coarse	(adj.) rough; crude
course	(n.) method, procedure, or route

This sandpaper is very *coarse.*

His language is *coarse.*

He knew, of *course,* about the proposal.

We review your credit rating as a matter of *course.*

complement	(v.) to complete or make whole; (n.) something that completes or makes whole
compliment	(v.) to give praise; (n) an expression of praise or admiration; (n.) *compliments* or (adj.) *complimentary* can be used to mean "at no charge."

That scarf certainly *complements* your outfit.

Our scout troop now has a full *complement* of members.

After his speech he received many *compliments*.

Take these tickets with our *compliments*. [at no charge to you]

Please accept this *complimentary* copy of my new book.

confirm	(v.) to make certain
conform	(v.) to become like or in harmony with

Will you *confirm* your reservation within 48 hours?

These materials *conform* to our standards for manufacture.

continually	(adv.) repeated frequently at intervals
continuously	(adv.) going on with no interruption

My *Time* magazine has come *continually* for twenty years.

This production line works *continuously*.

council	(n.) a decision-making group
counsel	(n.) an advisor (often an attorney); (v.) to give advice
consul	(n.) a diplomat

He was elected to the Boston City *Council*.

Many people realize a need to talk with a marriage *counselor*.

I've hired Endicott, Lange & Brown to *counsel* us in this case.

Mary Beth Sterns acts as the United States *consul* in Spain.

desert	(n.) an arid land (des′ ert); (v.) to abandon (dē sert′)
dessert	(n.) an after-meal treat (dē sert′)

I would hate to be lost in a *desert*.

A captain cannot *desert* his crew or his ship.

For *dessert* we had lemon pie.

device	(n.) an invention or implement
devise	(v.) (dē vīz′) to develop, create, or adapt

This *device* will help you to slice eggs evenly.

We tried to *devise* a plan that would be satisfactory to all.

disburse	(v.) to pay out
disperse	(v.) to scatter

We *disbursed* the payment on Friday, June 11.

You must *disperse* the seed throughout a large space.

disinterested	(adj.) neutral or impartial
uninterested	(adj.) not caring about

A judge must be *disinterested* in a case, but he should not be *uninterested*.

Labor and management selected a *disinterested* person to settle their dispute.

eager	see *anxious*
edition	see *addition*
effect	see *affect*

| emigrate | (v.) to leave a country |
| immigrate | (v.) to come to a country |

The Irish had to *emigrate* because of the failure of the potato crop.

The United States regulates those who wish to *immigrate* to this country.

| eminent | (adj.) well known or outstanding |
| imminent | (adj.) impending; threatening |

Harrison Knowles is an *eminent* scientist.

A storm is *imminent;* we should close the windows.

| except | see *accept* |

| its | possessive pronoun (never uses apostrophe) |
| it's | contraction for *it is* |

The Board made *its* decision within a day after the meeting.

I know *it's* about to rain.

SELF-CHECK 13-2

Underline the correct word for the definition given.

1. a matter of procedure—coarse, course

2. to complete—complement, compliment

3. to come into harmony—confirm, conform

4. an advisor—council, counsel, consul

5. <u>s</u>omething <u>s</u>weet after a meal (note the 2 *s*'s)—desert, dessert

6. to develop—device, devise

7. neutral—disinterested, uninterested

8. outstanding—eminent, imminent

9. it is—its, it's

10. without stop—continual, continuous

11. at no cost—complementary, complimentary

12. at regular intervals—continual, continuous

13. to spread around—disburse, disperse

14. to make payment—disburse, disperse

15. to leave your home country—emigrate, immigrate

Before you continue, turn to p. 351 to check your answers.

TRY IT OUT: **Complete Exercise 13.2, p. 338.**

lead	(n.) (pronounced *led*) a mineral
led	(v.) past tense of *to lead* or conduct

My pencil *lead* is dull and needs to be sharpened.

Shanchez *led* the troops to victory.

lean	(adj.) thin; (v.) to bend
lien	(n.) a legal claim on property

The *lean* man seemed to *lean* into the wind.

Before you buy, make sure that there is no *lien* on the property.

lend	(v.) to give temporarily (the past tense is *lent*)
loan	(n.) that which is lent

We have asked the bank to *lend* us $10,000.

This *loan* has an interest rate of 10 percent.

liable	(adj.) legally bound to
libel	(n.) a statement of slander (legal)
likely	(adj.) probably
apt	(adj.) fitting; suitable; quick to learn

You will be *liable* for any damages that you may do.

An author can be sued for *libel* for damaging statements.

He is *likely* to be late for the plane.

That is an *apt* example of good writing skills.

He is an *apt* student.

like	(prep.) similar (*similar to* will easily replace it)
as	(conj.) to the same extent; since

That car is *like* mine. (could be replaced with *similar to*)

He received a promotion *as* he had done well in his sales for the last five years.

moral	(adj.) (mōr′ al) good; (n.) a lesson learned
morale	(n.) (mō rale′) spirit; mental condition

We find that the defendant has acted in a *moral* and cautious manner.

All fables have *morals*.

The *morale* in our unit is very high since the changes were made.

pair	(n.) one set of two items
pairs	(n.) more than one set of two items

I have a matched *pair* of Irish setters.

She bought two *pairs* of nylons for the trip.

passed	(v.) past tense of *to pass;* to exceed or go around or above
past	(n.) time before now; (adj.) after in time; (prep.) by;

We *passed* our quota last week, a little ahead of schedule.

Things have changed since the *past*.

Your bill is now sixty days *past* due.

He walked *past* me without saying anything to me.

personal	(adj.) individual; private
personnel	(n.) employees

He marked the letter about Ms. Menton *"Personal"* so that it would not be opened by the secretary.

If you want the position, you must apply at the *Personnel* Office before Tuesday.

precede	(v.) to come before
proceed	(v.) to move ahead; (n.) the plural *proceeds* means profit; (Note that *procedure* has only one *e* in the middle of the word.)

Did President Kennedy *precede* President Nixon?

At a caution light you may *proceed* with care after you have looked for other vehicles.

The *proceeds* from the sale will go to the recycling center.

principal	(n.) a capital sum of money; school leader; (adj.) most important
principle	(n.) a rule of conduct or a fundamental basis (Note that this word and *rule* both end in *le;* you should be able to substitute the word *rule* for this word.)

The interest on my home mortgage is higher than the *principal.*

That is the *principal* idea behind the project.

He is the *principal* of South Elementary School.

She gives herself high *principles* to live by.

It is helpful to learn the *principles* of grammar.

⌐ S E L F - C H E C K   1 3 - 3

Underline the word that is defined.

1. past tense of *to lead*—lead, led

2. a legal claim on property—lean, lien

3. the verb that shows the action of doing—lend, loan

4. probably—liable, libel, likely, apt

5. *similar to* can be substituted—like, as

6. mental attitude—moral, morale

7. one set of two—pair, pairs

8. to have gone above—passed, past

9. employees—personal, personnel

10. word for which *rule* can be substituted—principal, principle

Before you continue, turn to p. 351 to check your answers.

TRY IT OUT: **Do Exercise 13.3, p. 339.**

quiet	(adj.) silent; not noisy
quite	(adv.) rather; very

To respect the rights of others, we must sometimes be *quiet*.

She was *quite* tired after completing the tax forms for the quarter.

raise	(v.) to cause something to rise (requires a direct object)
raze	(v.) to tear down or demolish

Please *raise* the shade a little higher, will you?

We will have to *raze* the old hotel to build our offices there.

recent	(adj.) not long ago
resent	(v.) (rē zent') to feel slighted or injured

We had discussed that point at a *recent* meeting.

She *resented* having to make the coffee for everyone else.

respectfully	(adv.) with courtesy
respectively	(adv.) in a particular order

He *respectfully* refused the nomination for Treasurer.

Please do problems one, two, and five *respectively*.

shone	(v.) past tense of *to shine*
shown	(v.) demonstrated

The sun has *shone* brightly every day this week.

He has *shown* us the manner in which to proceed.

sight	see *cite*
site	see *cite*

stationary	(adj.) in one place
stationery	(n.) writing material (a le*tt*er is written on station*e*ry)

The English setter remained *stationary* after he pointed the partridge.

Be very careful with your typewriting with this expensive *stationery*.

than	(conj.) a word to show comparisons
then	(adv.) next in time

She is taller *than* I am, which is pretty tall.

He repaired the machine; *then* he tested it.

their	(pron.) personal pronoun showing ownership by *them*
there	(adv.) at that place
they're	contraction for *they are*

We sent the quotation for the order to *their* office Wednesday.

We decided to place your desk over *there.*

They're not too happy with the site selected for the plant.

to	(prep.) in a certain direction or approach
too	(adv.) also; in excess of, such as *too* hot
two	(n./adj.) 2

We went *to* Chicago after we had seen Northern Wisconsin.

Selma was included in the retirement plan, *too.*

Harold was *too* wordy in his letter of application.

I'll order *two* of those air compressors.

uninterested	see *disinterested*

weather	(n.) climate
whether	(conj.) a choice, as in *whether or not*

The *weather* conditions for the weekend look miserable.

Louis Hall didn't know *whether* he would be finished on time to attend the concert.

who's	contraction for *who is*
whose	(pron.) ownership pronoun

Who's going to lock up tonight after we all leave?

Do you know *whose* glasses these are on the table?

your	(pron.) ownership pronoun
you're	contraction of *you are*

Please put this note in *your* file on the Jensen matter.

I am not sure when *you're* leaving the country for France.

⌐ S E L F - C H E C K 1 3 - 4

Underline the word from each pair that would answer the given definition.

1. to come before—proceed, precede

2. silent—quiet, quite

3. to tear down—raise, raze

4. of late; not long ago—recent, resent

5. in order as stated—respectfully, respectively

6. demonstrated—shone, shown

7. in one place—stationary, stationery

8. next in o 1rder—than, then

9. owned by them—their, there, they're

10. excessive—to, too, two

11. of a choice—weather, whether

12. who is—who's, whose

13. you are—your, you're

14. in a complimentary close of a letter—respectfully, respectively

15. paper for writing—stationary, stationery

Before you continue, turn to p. 351 to check your answers.

TRY IT OUT: **Exercises 13.4 and 13.5, pp. 340–341, will give you practice in using these like-words.**

CHOOSING THE CORRECT PREPOSITION

Prepositions need another look in this chapter because common usage has dictated that certain ones be used with certain words to convey a specific meaning. Notice the preferred prepositions in the following usages.

accompanied	*with* an object *by* a person
	This order is accompanied <u>with</u> a description of the measurements. Mr. Selverson was accompanied <u>by</u> his assistant to the convention.
agree	*with* an opinion *to* accept terms *upon* a mutual decision
	We certainly agree *with* your idea. Our company cannot agree *to* your proposed terms. Mr. Michaels and I have agreed *upon* an itinerary for the program.
angry	*at* an inanimate thing *with* a person
	Linda became angry *at* the noise from the apartment next to hers. Ms. Parsons seems to be angry *with* me for some reason.
conform	*to* means to adapt to be like another *with* means to already be like
	We will have to conform *to* the standards before our plan will be accepted.

These appliances conform *with* the regulations for safety.

correspond   *to* means to be similar to
                   with means to write to

Your reservation dates have to correspond *to* the dates of the annual meeting.

We have been corresponding *with* Blake and Sons about the contract for over two years.

differ   *from* means to be unlike
                   with means to disagree with an opinion
                   (Do not use *than* after the word *differ.*)

This paper is different *from* the paper we have been using.

The union leader differed *with* the company representative about the insurance plans.

plan   *to* means to look to complete in the future
                   (Do not use *on* after *plan.*)

I plan *to* leave for California next Tuesday. (not "plan on leaving for")

try   *to* means to attempt to
                   (Do not use *and* after *try.*)

Will you please try *to* finish this by noon? (not "try and finish")

⌐ SELF-CHECK 13-5

Underline the correct word to complete each of the following sentences.

1. Mr. Smith's card is accompanied (by, with) a check.

2. We cannot decide whether or not to agree (with, to, upon) your demands.

3. I simply do not agree (with, to, upon) you about this matter.

4. It seems silly to get angry (with, at) this typewriter.

5. Please don't get angry (with, at) me.

6. You must conform (with, to) our standards of dress.

7. Do these figures correspond (with, to) those you have found?

8. Your answers are different (from, than) mine.

9. Does Mr. Peters plan (on going, to go) to the Roanoke conference?

10. We sincerely hope that you will try (and, to) come to our Open House on February 12.

Before you continue, turn to p. 351 to check your answers.

TRY IT OUT: **Exercise 13.6, p. 342, will check your understanding of the use of these prepositions. Exercise 13.7, pp. 343–344, is a Challenge exercise for this chapter.**

IDENTIFYING WORDS OFTEN MISSPELLED

Spelling errors in your writing are a serious problem. While not everyone may notice a misused *which* or *that* or a dangling modifier that does not immediately cause a smirk, most readers will notice even one or two spelling errors. These errors distract the reader from the content of your message and call into question your concern for accuracy.

Two underlying causes seem to contribute to frequent spelling errors. Some of you may have learned to read through a system that relied on sight recognition of words. Others of you simply may not have had a language background that included basic principles of word formation—principles that form many of the common spelling rules.

This text incorporates these rules into the study of word formations in the chapters on nouns, verbs, and modifiers. The index provides specific page references for these rules.

Some words, however, do not conform to common principles of English language spelling, probably because these words have evolved from some other language base. Other unusual words have added or lost letters over time so that these words no longer conform to basic English spelling principles. Only memorization will eliminate these misspellings and save the time necessary to verify the spellings.

As you study the following list of words commonly misspelled, look at each word for two possible considerations:

1. Does the word follow one of the common English spelling rules?
2. For words not based on common spelling principles, which part of the word causes the misspelling?

Many words will no longer be a problem once you are able to apply the spelling rules. Some problem spellings can be learned without too much difficulty if you circle the difficult part of the word and study just that part.

Some students find it helpful to write a troublesome word several times, saying the unusual spelling while writing the word. Another technique is to make flashcards for troublesome words and then to quiz yourself or ask someone to quiz you using the cards.

In addition to the words listed here, you may have your own problem words. Making your own personal "Words Often Misspelled" list and studying it in the ways suggested can improve the accuracy of your writing and avoid the negative impression that frequent spelling errors can bring. You likely will find that your confidence in your writing ability will improve with your enhanced skills.

Once you have studied the following "Words Often Misspelled" list according to your instructor's plans, you should check your spellings by completing Exercises 13.8 and 13.9, p. 344.

Words Often Misspelled

accommodate
acknowledge
allegiance
a lot
amateur
analysis
apparent
appointment
assignment
attendance
auxiliary
bankruptcy
benefited
challenge
chimney
circumstance
colonel
column
comparison
congratulate
conscience
consequently
correspondence
courteous
convenience
deceive
delicious
descend
desirable
desperately
develop
dialogue
disastrous
distinguish
eligible
embarrass
emphasize
enthusiastically
entrepreneur
essential

eventually
exaggerate
excellent
extraordinary
familiar
February
forty
government
grammar
grateful
guarantee
hesitate
hindrance
immediately
initiative
interpret
irrelevant
irresistible
judgment
library
license
lieutenant
loneliness
mischievous
mortgage
mysterious
niece
ninety
ninth
nuisance
occasion
occurrence
opportunity
parliament
particular
peculiar
permissible
possession
potato
preparation

privilege
procedure
proceed
programmed
prosperous
psychology
publicity
pursue
quantity
questionnaire
receipt
recognize
recollect
recommend
reliable
relieve
restaurant
rhythm
ridiculous
separate
sergeant
significant
similar
sincerely
sophomore
substitute
subtlety
surgeon
surprise
syllable
sympathetic
unconscious
unnecessary
vacuum
valuable
vegetable
villain
Wednesday
weird
yield

Chapter 13: Word Choices

● E X E R C I S E   13.1

Proofread the following sentences for word-usage errors. If you find an error, draw a line through it, and write the correct word above it. If there is no error, write C in front of the sentence.

1. Did the Belson Company accept our offer?

2. Everyone accept Bill was here today.

3. We must except dual-family dwellings from Zone Three.

4. A new addition of a dictionary is a must for your desk.

5. We plan to adapt your amendment in a vote at our next meeting.

6. She is very adapt at appliance repair.

7. Mr. Erickson is a good advicer.

8. I have often asked him for advice.

9. How will the change of districts effect our shipping costs?

10. Yes, it should effect some change in price.

11. What effect does the weather have on your disposition?

12. He is very anxious to go on vacation.

13. No one beside John handles this type of problem.

14. There are three people with MA degrees among our staff.

15. The two attorneys argued among themselves for several hours.

16. The United Way has its canvas each year in the fall.

17. That money is for capitol investment for next year.

18. The group went to the capitol for a tour.

19. We cannot find a building site for our warehouse close enough to the city.

20. The lawyer was able to site three previous decisions to support her position.

If you find any usage errors in these sentences, cross out each incorrect word, and write the correct one above it. If there are no errors, write C in front of the sentence.

1. In the course of a business day we see about fifty patients.

2. John and Mary compliment each other as a couple, for he is shy, and she is very outgoing.

3. Please accept this discount coupon with my compliments.

4. The team had to play the game without a full compliment of players.

5. Consulman Brown addressed the lawyer as "My dear Councilor."

6. He promised not to dessert the committee before the work is completed.

7. I really prefer to have fruit for dessert.

8. On a recent trip to Africa Ms. Thomas went to the dessert.

9. Can you devise a metal piece that will replace this broken one?

10. The correcting typewriter is a marvelous devise.

11. The umpire for the last game of the World Series was an uninterested participant.

12. The English teacher appeared uninterested in her students.

13. I am not always able to accept a complement.

14. Professor Gregory is an imminent historian, and she is often asked to present papers at meetings.

15. The threat of war was imminent before the conference was held.

16. Any time-saving devise is worth it's cost to us.

17. Did Ms. Raymond say that its her birthday today?

18. Please don't dessert me during today's talks.

19. We need an uninterested third party to help us decide this issue.

20. The City Counsel met for eight hours last Monday night.

21. The waiter gave me course ground pepper for my salad.

22. American had many immigrants in the late 1800s.

23. We disbursed over ten thousand dollars in our last pay period.

24. If you are to make the decision for all of us, you should be disinterested in the outcome.

25. I am continually having migraine headaches.

● E X E R C I S E 13.3

Proofread for any word-usage errors. Make any necessary corrections. Write C in front of any sentence with no errors.

1. Mr. Hoekzema led the recall petition drive.

2. The bank had a lean on that property until the debt was paid.

3. Jack Spratt could eat no fat; his wife could eat no lien.

4. The word *loan* should not be a verb.

5. Can you loan me $50 until we get our paychecks?

6. He loaned me enough money for the interest payment on the house.

7. It is apt to rain before the picnic starts.

8. Mr. Piper is an apt plumber.

9. An untrue statement that is deliberately intended to harm someone is considered to be liable.

10. She is libel for the damage to your fence caused by her dog's digging.

11. Lite and Lean tastes good like a yogurt should.

12. This paper is just like the other paper I had bought before.

13. Like I said before, you must proofread your work.

14. Euthanasia is a morale issue that the courts are very hesitant to make judgments about.

15. The morale of the softball team is good.

16. I bought three pair of shoes yesterday on sale.

17. Our sales have passed the record of last May.

18. I drove passed the cite to see how far along the construction work has come.

19. Your bill is now 30 days passed due.

20. I would really like to work in the Personal Department.

21. Is your payment all going toward the principle of the loan?

22. Congressperson Laird is to be the principal speaker at the banquet.

23. The principle cause of erosion is water.

24. We have established the principles of our regulations.

25. Mrs. Zwart never wavers from her basic principals.

Proofread these sentences for correct usages. Correct any errors. If no errors exist, write C in front of the sentence.

1. After Mr. Dinkins is finished, you may precede.

2. Be quite please as you proceed through the room.

3. We hope to raise funds for our annual Christmas program.

4. Did you see in the paper that the old Elevator Corporation building is being raised?

5. White-collar jobs for women are on the increase according to a resent article in the newspaper.

6. Some people resent the success of others, but they fail to realize that hard work has often been a part of that success.

7. The complementary close of the letter was, "Respectively yours."

8. The salesperson for Tuttle Wax has shone her how the finish on the bumpers has shown for weeks.

9. Aren't you ever going to change your stationery?

10. Wesley Williams is a better typist then his sister.

11. Then we went farther passed the turnoff than we had intended.

12. Their glad that they don't have to go there for the classes.

13. We went past her house on our way to their offices.

14. I knew that it was to late to do anything about my oversite.

15. We are hoping that the whether won't be too hot.

16. When your at Miniver's, please pick up some more stationary.

17. The affects of the poll were to change the election.

18. There always happy to see you at the Association meetings.

19. It was quite quiet at the library tonight.

20. Be sure too proofread to make certain that their are no errors in your report.

● E X E R C I S E   13.5

Proofread these short paragraphs and correct any usage errors that you discover.

1. Whose to blame if their are no supplies in the storeroom? I was lead to believe that when we were to

   low on stationery, for instance, Ms. Tapper was to be shone. She tends to recent it when we run low

   and she has not been told.

2. Because I had asked the bank to loan me money with my house as collateral, there is now a lean on

   the property. I am libel for any damages or decreases in the value of this property if I do not keep it up

   like I should.

3. Mr. James is quiet anxious to see his councilman about the problems he has had in his neighborhood.

   The consul has tried to adapt a new regulation concerning the problem, but a canvas of the

   representatives has not turned up enough votes between all of the members to pass it. Their seems to

   have been some bad advise from there legal counsel.

4. What affect does this devise seem to have on pollution? Auto companies are always asking themselves

   this question. The federal government is not willing to accept any automaker from the standards they

   have set. The lawmakers sight many examples of companies that have been fined for misuse of

   pollution devices. Soon, the companies themselves will be liable for infractions of the regulations.

5. Our office moral is liable to be low on a Monday. For some reason, the beginning of the week seems

   to effect everyone's attitude. We in the Personal Department try very hard to overcome this problem.

   Once Monday is over, we seem to be able to precede with the week quiet easily. By Tuesday we all

   seem to be in a better frame of mind then we were on Monday. Of coarse, they're must be a morale

   to this story, but I'm to tired to find it, and your liable to be to disinterested to care.

Underline the correct word to complete each of the following sentences.

1. Why is it that your book is different (from, than, then) mine?

2. I have tried not to become angry (at, with) you, but I am very angry (at, with) your tardiness.

3. Does that washer conform (to, with) the dimensions in the plans?

4. I want to try (to, and) work out a solution to this problem.

5. Do you plan (to go, on going) to the annual Board meeting?

6. Have the members of the Accounting Department agreed (to, with, upon) a new system of bookkeeping?

7. President Carson was accompanied (by, with) his wife of three years on the campaign.

8. Your specifications do not conform (to, with) the regulations.

9. Can you get them to conform (to, with) the federal regulations?

10. Please correspond (to, with) our Adjustments Department in the future about this matter.

11. Your program is different (from, than, then) the one that has come with my computer.

12. I shall have to differ (with, to, from) Mrs. Evans about this particular item.

13. Actually, men and women aren't very different (from, than) one another in most ways.

14. Please try (to, and) be there on time.

15. Is this brochure accompanied (by, with) a price list?

16. The President is not free to go anywhere unless accompanied (by, with) Secret Service staff.

17. Didn't you agree (to, upon, with) the company policy of employees' paying 50 percent of their insurance premium.

18. The figures you have discovered correspond (to, with) those that the accountant submitted.

19. I can hardly eat dinner any more without someone phoning my house to try (and, to) get me to buy or subscribe to something.

20. Your haircut seems different (from, than) your usual cut.

● E X E R C I S E   13.7   **CHALLENGE**

Correct any usage errors, including spelling errors, in the following.

Dear Congresswoman Butler:

Being a passed council member in our district, you are certainly aware that our new council has plans to try and push through a proposal for a solid-waste cite on Fifteenth Street in Elroy Township. The vote on this issue is eminent, but its not to late to try and change some of the votes.

Your are a woman of high principals. You have always been known as a woman who will stand up to special interest groups if what their doing is not in the best interests of the majority.

Putting that facility on that site would be harmful to many of you're local constituents. We have canvased those who live within a five-mile radius of that proposed sight, and here are their concerns:

1. The landfill would be an ugly sight for the neighbors.
2. It has been shone that there could be groundwater contamination.
3. Since Mills Creek runs passed this area, that too could become polluted.
4. One principle problem is that there might be a lien on the property, which could cause cost overuns.
5. The counsel members seem to be trying to precede too quickly before enough study has been done.
6. The quite of the neighborhood would be disturbed by the truck traffic generated.
7. The latest addition of the *Forbes Report* suggests a hold on any of these projects until new studies are completed.
8. To effect trouble-free sites, knowledgeable consultants should be employed.
9. The morales of some of the counsel members are even being called into question since the actual ownership of the property could rest with some of those members.
10. The specifications of this property don't conform with those required by law for a landfill of that size.

Because of these and other issues, we are writing to ask for your help. We hope that you could be uninterested in this issue and, thus, could offer some good advise. We don't feel you're findings will be different than ours. Please correspond to us soon about this matter.

Respectively yours,

● E X E R C I S E   13.8

Circle the letter of the correctly spelled word in each of the following pairs.

1. a. accomodate b. accommodate	6. a. enthusiasticly b. enthusiastically	11. a. dialogue b. dialouge	16. a. publisity b. publicity
2. a. immediately b. immediatly	7. a. alot b. a lot	12. a. sergeant b. sargeant	17. a. permissable b. permissible
3. a. suprise b. surprise	8. a. substatute b. substitute	13. a. opportunity b. oppertunity	18. a. sincerly b. sincerely
4. a. convience b. convenience	9. a. familiar b. familar	14. a. potatoe b. potato	19. a. nuisance b. nusance
5. a. sophomore b. sophmore	10. a. psychology b. physicalogy	15. a. quanity b. quantity	20. a. questionairre b. questionnaire

● E X E R C I S E   13.9

Proofread these short paragraphs for spelling errors. Cross out the error and write the correct form above.

1. In you're study of grammer you have no doubt learned alot for your preperation to procede to a new career. As you persue this goal, keep in mind some of these valuble lessons. You have learned to use good judgment in word choice and clause choice. You have learned how to weed out unecessary wordiness when you develope good paragraphs. The rithem of your style should be improved. You should no longer be embarassed by your speaking or writeing. You are too be congraduated on you're hard work.

2. One Wendesday in Febuary, I went to the libary to get the nineth addition of the *Agricultural Journal*. I needed to learn more about planting some of my vegtables. While there, I had an oppertunity to observe an unusual occurence. It made me greatful for what I have learned. A little girl of about nine was reading a magazine article to an old man, maybe her grandfather. He obviously couldn't read himself. What a hinderance that would be. We are priviledged to live in an age and country where we are garanteed an education—all we have to do is be in attendence to be eligable.

⚀ Periodic Review: Chapters 12–13

Tell whether the underlined part is acting as a noun, adjective, or an adverb.

_____ 1. My favorite program, <u>showing at 7 p.m. on Fridays</u>, is BERMUDA POLITICS.

_____ 2. The photograph <u>of the old fisherman</u> sold for $1200.

_____ 3. The court jester said <u>that the king had no clothes.</u>

_____ 4. She will file for bankruptcy <u>after the sale.</u>

_____ 5. In case of a tornado leave your desk and go to the basement <u>where you should be safe.</u>

_____ 6. <u>To reach Fort Wayne by noon</u>, it is necessary for us to meet Ling Wu before 10 a.m.

_____ 7. I saw Tammy, <u>who just graduated from school</u>, at the interviews for the Graham Company.

_____ 8. <u>If you get to the theater first</u>, please pick up my tickets too.

_____ 9. He is a pushover <u>for donating to a charitable cause.</u>

_____ 10. He decided <u>that he will return to school.</u>

Rewrite the following sentences, changing the underlined part into the structure indicated, using correct punctuation.

1. <u>Several of the men went to the fishing camp</u>, but they never went fishing. (adjective clause)

2. Byran Murch went to the new computer center; <u>it is located on Main Street</u>. (participial phrase)

3. She planted a garden, and <u>she wanted to grow broccoli</u>. (infinitive phrase)

4. Holography is done by lasers, and <u>it makes images appear three dimensional</u>. (adjective clause)

5. <u>Mary Beth learned to quilt as her hobby</u>, and many quilts sold at the annual hobby show. (introductory participial phrase)

Change these passive voice sentences into active voice.

1. These windows were washed just last week by Ed's Windows _____

    _____

2. Somebody said that not enough athletes were graduated by Summerfield University. _____

    _____

3. A lot of problems were caused here in the office by your report. _____

    _____

4. The issue was voted upon by the committee. _____

    _____

5. A score of over one hundred was made by the Houston Hoopers. _____

    _____

Put the proper form of the noun/pronoun on the blank; some will be possessive case.

1. It is (anybody) _____ guess how the (Giant)

    _____ ball team will do this season.

2. The (review) _____ from the movie just came in, and the (Director)

    _____ talent is apparent.

3. Did you go to your (children) _____ PTA meeting last night?

4. Our new (office) _____ are only a (stone) _____
    throw from the power plant.

5. My two (sister) _____ (son) _____ are all playing
    in Little League.

Select the correct verb form for these sentences.

1. The doctors say that mumps (is, are) a dangerous disease.

2. The percentage of fish getting to the stream (is, are) smaller than in recent years.

3. His savings of ten thousand dollars (was, were) scattered all around his house in several hiding places.

4. The Secretary and Treasurer (was, were) responsible for the Association's success.

5. Either of the candidates (is, are) a good choice.

Name _____ Date _____ Class _____

Use some form of the word smooth *in these sentences.*

1. Of the two fabrics this one feels _____.

2. She is able to handle the driving _____ than he.

3. The lake looks really _____ today.

4. I've heard many sales pitches, but this one is the _____.

5. Of all of those golfers Edwina swings the club the _____.

Underline the correct word to complete each of these.

1. Your script is (liable, likely) to be ready for lunch.

2. The (affects, effects) of acid rain are not really known.

3. The time has (past, passed) for you to pay your (past, passed) due bill; my lawyer will contact you.

4. His (principal, principle) problem is that he has too much (principal, principle) in the stock market.

5. Did we order enough (stationary, stationery) for this month?

6. You always seem to differ (from, with) me about this topic.

7. Sylvia has had problems with this lesson in the (past, passed).

8. Don't be so (anxious, eager) about how well you will perform, and you will do well.

9. The three brothers have seldom had a disagreement (among, between) them.

10. What are you planning to fix for (desert, dessert)?

Write the comparative and superlative forms of the following words.

1. trendy _____ _____

2. tan _____ _____

3. little _____ _____

4. winsome _____ _____

5. smoothly _____ _____

Correct any errors in these sentences.

1. Of the two men he is the best place kicker.

2. She drove slower after she saw the police car.

3. Frank is smarter than any boy in his class.

4. Nancy baked less cookies than Jane for the Christmas tea.

5. A unusual sight is to see two baboons grooming one another.

6. Ned folds his lab coat neater than Sally after work.

7. I love to go to the south for the perfume scented azaleas.

8. I couldn't hardly wait to call louder than he does in the pig-calling contest.

9. The soup looked good to Jim, but it tasted badly.

10. I feel badly about your losing the longest of the two races.

11. Your set of keys laid on the desk all of that time.

12. Were you all together surprised by the jury's verdict?

13. He parked the car before he walked to the theatre.

14. Isn't this plant the most perfect plant you ever saw?

15. She laid the racket on the ground and left the stadium because she was angry at herself.

16. I guess it was them whom we saw at the beach.

17. Girard became impatient with the company delaying his order.

18. The football fan just set there and criticized the team.

19. That apple is the most shiniest apple I have ever seen.

20. Every man and woman in this class know more than they did just a few weeks ago.

ANSWERS TO SELF-CHECK PRACTICE

Chapter 11: Adjectives

Self-Check 11–1, p. 281

1. Nouns and pronouns.
2. Whose, what kind of, and how many.
3. One-syllable words or two-syllable words ending in -*y*.
4. When the adjective is a one-syllable word ending in one consonant preceded by one vowel or when it is a two-syllable word ending that way with the accent on the second syllable.
5. Prettiest.
6. No, a *smallest* perhaps.
7. *Unique* cannot be compared because it means one of a kind.

Self-Check 11–2, p. 283

1. Farther.
2. The second part.
3. Less.
4. No, but to *each other*.
5. Better than herself? It should read: "Jane learned to sail better than anyone else in her class."
6. No. He should say, "This is Peter, my *younger* son."

Self-Check 11–3, p. 284

1. an	3. an	5. a	7. a	9. a
2. a	4. an	6. an	8. an	10. an

Self-Check 11–4, p. 288

1. a New England clam bake
2. a French perfume
3. No capitals.
4. No capitals.
5. self-reliant
6. well-laid
7. No hyphen; *first class* follows the noun.
8. 3- or 4-year 10. easy, quick

9. No commas. 11. No commas.

10. easy, quick 12. room, dark and hot,

Chapter 12: Adverbs

Self-Check 12–1, p. 304

1. Action verbs, adjectives, adverbs.
2. Where, how, how much (to what extent), why.
3. Neatly.
4. Forcibly.
5. Naturally.

6. Truly (one of three exceptions).
7. Temporarily.
8. Nicely
9. Sincerely.
10. Admirably.

Self-Check 12–2, p. 308

1. fresh; subject complement adjective after linking verb (Pattern 4)
2. well; adverb modifying action verb (1)
3. extreme; subject complement adjective after linking verb (4)
4. extremely; adverb modifying adjective in subject complement after linking verb (4)
5. quickly; adverb modifying action verb (1)
6. badly; adverb modifying action verb (2)
7. bad; adjective modifying action verb (2)
8. bad; subject complement adjective after linking verb (4)
9. surely; adverb modifying action verb, telling how much (2)
10. really; adverb modifying participle in subject complement after linking verb (4)

Self-Check 12–3, p. 310

1. more slowly; modifies action verb (*Slower/slowest* are unusual forms that can be adverbs also, but these words are second choice.)
2. smoother; subject complement adjective after linking verb *feels*
3. most carefully; modifies action verb
4. poorer; modifies noun subject complement
5. most poorly; modifies participle in subject complement

Self-Check 12–4, p. 313

1. really
2. always
3. surely
4. well

5. anything
6. the second *only*
7. all ready
8. all right

9. can
10. either . . . or

◻️ CHAPTER 13: Word Choices

Self-Check 13–1, p. 326

1. except	6. eager	11. cite
2. addition	7. beside	12. besides
3. adept	8. among	13. affect
4. advise	9. canvass	14. site
5. effect	10. capital	15. adapt

Self-Check 13–2, p. 328

1. course	6. devise	11. complimentary
2. complement	7. disinterested	12. continual
3. conform	8. eminent	13. disperse
4. counsel	9. it's	14. disburse
5. dessert	10. continuous	15. emigrate

Self-Check 13–3, p. 330–331

1. led	5. like	9. personnel
2. lien	6. morale	10. principle
3. lend	7. pair	
4. likely; apt	8. passed	

Self-Check 13–4, p. 332–333

1. precede	6. shown	11. whether
2. quiet	7. stationary	12. who's
3. raze	8. then	13. you're
4. recent	9. their	14. respectfully (yours)
5. respectively	10. too	15. stationery

Self-Check 13–5, p. 334

1. with	5. with	9. to go
2. to	6. to	10. to
3. with	7. to	
4. at	8. from	

U N I T   4

Connecting
Sentences

Steps to a Well-Written Paragraph

OVERVIEW

- **The Paragraph Defined**
- **Step 1: Selecting a Topic**
- **Step 2: Narrowing a Topic**
- **Step 3: Making Notes**
- **Step 4: Supporting the Topic**
- **Step 5: Writing Sentences**
- **Step 6: Revisiting the Topic**
- **Step 7: Writing the First Draft**
- **Step 8: Editing Your Writing**
- **Step 9: Preparing the Final Copy**
- **Checklist for a Well-Written Paragraph**

To write a good paragraph, you must be able to clarify your thoughts, organize them logically, and express them succinctly. In short, composing paragraphs requires the basic skills needed for every writing task.

THE PARAGRAPH DEFINED

Although any group of sentences written in a block with the first line indented may <u>look</u> like a paragraph, those sentences must have a close, logical relationship to <u>be</u> a paragraph. In this chapter you will explore the one-paragraph essay. (For simplicity, the term *paragraph* will be used throughout the chapter to refer to this particular essay type.)

DEFINITION A **one-paragraph essay** is a group of sentences that contains a limited topic, several statements of support, and an appropriate conclusion.

STEP 1: SELECTING A TOPIC

The first step in writing a paragraph is knowing where to find ideas for a topic. Consider two general areas. One, subjects of personal interest to you, might provide topics that would be easy for you to write about. These might include hobbies, pastimes, your outside activities, or your club or association memberships. Other topics of interest might be people you know, those you admire, or even those you disrespect. Your work, school, family, or career goals could lead to other pertinent topics for your paper.

Second, you might consider some broader, less personal topics. These might include current events, world problems, contemporary ethical questions, medical or scientific discoveries (present or past), or historical events or people.

SELF-CHECK 14–1

1. List five general topics from your hobbies, pastimes, or clubs.

2. List five general topics about people you know, admire, or disrespect.

3. List five topics relating to your family, work, school, or career goals.

4. List five topics from current events or world problems.

5. List five general topics about historical events or people, inventions, or discoveries.

Before you continue, turn to p. 433 to check your answers.

STEP 2: NARROWING THE TOPIC

Once you have chosen a topic about which you have plenty to say, you must decide which aspect of it you wish to focus on. The topics you listed in Self-Check 14–1 are much too broad for a one-paragraph essay.

Taking a broad topic and narrowing it to a specific aspect is probably the most important step in writing the paragraph. Without a well-defined topic your paragraph may be unfocused and try to cover too much ground. The result is often a paragraph that provides only scant support for several ideas. An effective paragraph is limited to one aspect of the topic that is clearly explained. In addition, the topic is well supported, and it convinces your reader to accept your point of view.

Since writing a paragraph is the goal of this study, a good place to begin might be with an example. Suppose you chose boxer Joe Louis as a topic. You can see that a person and his entire life is too broad a topic to attempt to describe. How can it be limited or narrowed?

List Possible Topics

Start by making a list of some of the possible aspects of Joe Louis's career or life that you might wish to describe. Your list might look like this.

Joe Louis is an American hero.
Joe Louis was a great example of a courageous man.
Joe Louis was a famous boxer.
The best heavyweight boxer of all time was Joe Louis.
Joe Louis had a tragic life.

SELF-CHECK 14-2

1. From the topic "Hobbies" list at least five possible specific subtopics.

2. List at least five subtopics from the general topic, "My mother taught me a lot."

Before you continue, turn to p. 433 to check your answers.

TRY IT OUT: **On other paper write down a general topic of interest to you and then narrow it to at least five more-specific topics about which you could write. Your instructor may ask you to hand in all of your worksheets with a completed paragraph in its final form. (See Exercise 14.1, p. 369.) Ask what you will be expected to hand in.**

Write a Tentative Topic Sentence

Once you have narrowed your topic, you are ready to write your topic sentence. As you continue this exercise, you may reword this sentence. However, it is important to write the first version now so that you can focus on the narrowed topic and develop your point of view about it.

DEFINITION A **topic sentence** is the sentence in a paragraph that states the main idea and the writer's point of view about it.

Using the example about Joe Louis, you can see that "Joe Louis was a famous boxer" would not be a good topic sentence. Although you could add support statements that would prove the topic, this sentence really doesn't pose a point of view to defend. Thus it will probably not interest your readers. If you change the topic sentence to "Joe Louis was the most famous boxer of the twentieth century," you make a statement of opinion, one that could be argued; this topic would be much more interesting.

Although the topic sentence is usually the first sentence in the paragraph, it could be placed after an introductory catchy sentence or even at the end of the paragraph. If you decide to place the topic sentence last, take care to use good transitions throughout the paragraph to allow your readers to see that they are being led to a conclusion.

Be careful, too, to avoid being as obvious as this: "I am going to write about . . . ." or "This is a paragraph about . . . ."

STEP 3: MAKING NOTES

Once you have written a preliminary topic sentence, you should jot down <u>all</u> ideas that come to mind, not in any particular order or format. These notes should not yet be fully developed sentences nor should they be in paragraph form. At this stage, you should have just a list of notes, many of which may not even be relevant to your present topic sentence. Don't worry about errors at this point.

Look at the following list of notes for the topic, "Joe Louis had a tragic life." (Deane McGovern, "Joe Louis 1914–1981," *Great Lives of the Twentieth Century*, Times Books, New York, 1988, pp. 413–418.)

(*Note:* You will learn more about the use of textnotes to recognize the sources of your quoted material in Step 9 on pages 366–367.)

- Earned $4.6 million, received $800,000
- To earn money—after retiring, boxed again, beaten by Ezzard Charles, Rocky Marciano (1951)
- Born 1914 to sharecroppers, 8th child, no money, little education
- Worked at Ford Motors before boxing
- Owed taxes of $1.25 million (deliquent)

- 1965—IRS let him be—"His earning days are over," Dana Latham, Comm. of IRS
- 60s—failed with partner—chain of food shops
- 1969 "physical breakdown" New York street
- Biography 1971, "caused by cocaine"
- 1970 5 mos. Colorado Psychiatric Hosp., family said suffering from paranoia
- Married four times, twice to first wife
- 1977 confined to wheelchair after surgery for aortic aneurysm. Had had strokes, heart problems, pacemaker
- Died, Las Vegas, April 12, 1981, Cardiac arrest, 66 yrs. old
- Louis's son compared him to Willy Loman, Arthur Miller—DEATH OF A SALESMAN—". . . started growing old and losing his customers. He was never really aware that he had lost his territory. That's the tragedy of it, just like my father's."

SELF-CHECK 14–3

1. Make a list of notes to support the topic, "A hobby is a good thing to have."

2. Make a list of notes to support the topic, "My mother taught me to stick to things, no matter what."

Before you continue, turn to pp. 433–434 to check your answers.

TRY IT OUT: **Before you continue, on a separate piece of paper make notes on the topic you have chosen, following the same technique used in the example and in the Self-Check.**

Look at your list to see if you have enough material for support. The final draft of your paragraph should have up to a dozen points of support; there may be fewer sentences, of course, as you will be combining ideas.

Generating Supporting Information

If you are having difficulty generating information to support your topic, consider using the questions journalists use to gather material for their articles: Who? What? Where? When? Why? How? Although not all of these questions are appropriate for each topic, asking them should give you several leads to pursue in your quest for interesting, illustrative support.

Remember that your readers depend on you to supply the background, reasoning, extra details, added description, and point of view that tell them what you want them to know about your topic. Each writer's essay will be different. The way you select, limit, and support the topic makes your essay original.

Consider a Clincher

Even at this early stage, you might want to look at your notes to see if you have a good way to end the paragraph. You may want to restate the topic sentence as a summary, but another choice is to add a "clincher" instead, if one would be appropriate.

DEFINITION A **clincher** is a technique for ending an essay (even a one-paragraph essay). Typical clinchers are brief quotations, short examples to illustrate, or statements that restate the writer's point of view.

The example relating to Joe Louis uses a short quotation that emphasizes the tragic aspects of his life.

STEP 4: SUPPORTING THE TOPIC

Next, study your notes to see that they provide appropriate points to support the topic. Look for these three general types of supporting statements.

1. Definitions or clarifications of terms.

2. Facts or statements by authorities (from research) that support the point of view.

3. Examples or illustrations that prove the point of the topic sentence.

Omit any ideas that do not closely relate to the point of view you are taking in your topic sentence. Even though all of the ideas may somehow relate to the general topic, some will not really support the narrowed topic sentence. Check the list of types of support to see if you are reminded of any other points that you didn't have in your first list. Add them.

Decide which ideas are most important and star (*) them. These are the ideas that you should emphasize and are the points that may require their own supporting statements.

Study the following changes in the notes that support the Joe Louis topic. Try to understand why these changes and additions were made.

- Earned $4.6 million, received $800,000   *combine with owed taxes*

too old to fight
hard to lose
- To earn money—after retirin*g*, boxed again, beaten by Ezzard Charles, * Rocky Marciano (1951)

big family
- ~~Born 1914~~ to sharecroppers, 8th child, no money, little education

- ~~Worked at Ford Motors before boxing~~

* - Owed taxes of $1.25 million (deliquent)

probably omit • 1965—IRS let him be—"His earning days are over," Dana Latham, Comm. of IRS

* • 60s—failed with partner—chain of food shops

* • 1969 "physical breakdown" New York street

  • Biography 1971, "caused by cocaine"

physical/ mental failing * • 1970 5 mos. Colorado Psychiatric Hosp., family said suffering from paranoia

  • Married four times, twice to first wife

* • 1977 confined to wheelchair after surgery for aortic aneurysm. He had strokes, heart problems, pacemaker

* • Died, Las Vegas, April 12, 1981, Cardiac arrest, 66 yrs. old

clincher • Louis's son compared him to Willy Loman, Arthur Miller—DEATH OF A SALESMAN—". . . started growing old and losing his customers. He was never really aware that he had lost his territory. That's the tragedy of it, just like my father's."

SELF-CHECK 14-4

1. In a second color revise the notes in Self-Check Answer 14–3, pp. 433–434, on the topic, "A hobby is a good thing to have." Cover up Self-Check Answer 14–4.

2. Do the same for the second topic, "My mother taught me to stick to things, no matter what."

Before you continue, turn to pp. 434–435 to check your answers.

TRY IT OUT: **Make the same additions and corrections to your own page of notes for your topic before you continue with the next step.**

STEP 5: WRITING SENTENCES

You are now ready to begin writing sentences. Don't worry yet about the order, and don't put your sentences into paragraph form. Remember that the starred items in your notes are the important points. These ideas should probably be independent clauses with the other points added as dependent clauses, appositives, and modifying phrases. Remember to use techniques of emphasis: first or last placement; an occasional <u>short</u> simple sentence; repetition, unusual sentence order (transposed or as an interrupter).

Once you have placed all of the ideas into sentences, set the paper aside for a few hours or even a whole day before continuing. That will give you time to think about the paragraph, time to see if more ideas occur to you or if your point of view changes, and time to become more objective when you return to evaluate your sentences.

Look at the preliminary sentences written in the Joe Louis example. Pay attention to the writing techniques of emphasis and subordination.

> Topic Sentence: That Joe Louis had a tragic life may not be as well known as his successful boxing record.
>
> Although he earned $4.6 million, personally receiving $800,000 of that, at the end of his career he owed $1.25 million in deliquent taxes.
>
> In his later years he struggled constantly to repay his debt and support himself and his family.
>
> This champion suffered two defeats to Ezzard Charles and, in 1951, to Rocky Marciano. He was too old to fight by then.
>
> His suffering started early when he was born the eighth child of share-croppers; his early life had little money, little schooling for the children.
>
> In his retirement, he couldn't relax but had many jobs.
>
> He and a partner failed in their attempt to set up a chain of food shops.
>
> His health deteriorated with a physical breakdown on a street in New York.
>
> Emotional damage is shown by his five-week stay in a Colorado Psychiatric Hospital; his family committed him saying he suffered from paranoia.
>
> He later wrote that these events were caused by cocaine.
>
> Four marriages (two to his first wife) had to cause many heartaches.
>
> Before he died of cardiac arrest at sixty-six, he had spent his last years in a wheelchair after strokes, heart problems, and the installation of a pacemaker.
>
> Keep quotation as is—last as clincher.

SELF-CHECK 14-5

1. From Self-Check Answer 14–4, pp. 434–435, the amended note list, write appropriate sentences for the topic on hobbies for practice in emphasis and subordination. Write in list, not paragraph, form.

2. Do the same for the "stick to it" topic.

Before you continue, turn to p. 435 to check your answers.

Now that you have studied the example and practiced sentence writing with the Self-Check examples, use your note list to compose sentences for a paragraph on your chosen topic. Although you will be rewriting, try to make these sentences demonstrate good writing principles: emphasis, subordination, variety, and so on.

Be sure to allow some time to pass before you apply the next step to your preliminary sentences.

STEP 6: REVISITING THE TOPIC

Now that you have set your paper aside for a while, reread your topic sentence and decide whether it still reflects your point of view about your topic. After a little time you may decide that you would rather take another slant toward the topic. A new direction is perfectly fine—it is probably a better-thought-out topic—but be sure that your topic sentence accurately reflects your opinion or attitude about the topic of your paragraph.

Now read each sentence from Step 5. Cross out any that no longer relate to the new or revised topic sentence. Add any sentences that might convey new support.

Next, see if you can do a better job of combining the ideas into sentences. Are there too many simple or compound sentences, making all of the support ideas sound as if they're of equal value? Is the style of your sentences varied? Label each sentence as to type—simple (S), compound (CP), or complex (CX)—and check for variety. Are there any adjective or noun clauses? Are all modifying phrases and clauses in the natural order, or have you varied the order for emphasis and variety (transposing or interrupting the main clause with the modifier)?

Make certain that you have no fragments or run-on sentences, an easy task after your labeling of sentence types. Check other possible writing errors such as nonparallel structure, misused or overused passive voice, and dangling or misplaced modifiers.

Rewrite any sentences to better achieve these techniques of good writing.

Note how these suggestions have been applied to the original support sentences on the Joe Louis topic. Notice that the material still is not in the paragraph format.

noun clause

CX   Topic Sentence: That Joe Louis had a tragic life may not be as well known as his successful boxing record.

CX   Although he earned $4.6 million, personally receiving $800,000 of that, at the end of his career he owed $1.25 million in deliquent taxes

S   In his later years he struggled constantly to repay his debt and support himself and his family.

aging, tired   *humiliating one*   *one*

S   This ⌃champion suffered two ⌃defeats ⌃to Ezzard Charles and, in 1951, ⌃to

S   Rocky Marciano. ~~He was too old to fight by then.~~

His parents, who were share-croppers, had Joe as their eighth child, allowing little money, little schooling for the children.

A failed attempt with a partner to open a chain of food shops was another tragic event.

CP { CX His suffering started early when he was born the eighth child of share-croppers; his early life had little money, little schooling for the children.

CP { S

S In his retirement, he couldn't relax but had many jobs.   *too vague*

franchise? S He and a partner tried and failed to set up a chain of food shops.

S *Soon after that* His health deteriorated with a physical breakdown on a street in New York. *tragedy = blow, shock, misfortune*

~~His~~ Emotional damage is shown by his five-week stay in a Colorado Psychi-

CP atric Hospital; his family committed him saying he suffered from paranoia. *sp?*

noun clause
CX He later wrote that these events were caused by cocaine. , *itself a sad commentary on his state of mind at the time. (trite?)*

S Four marriages (two to his first wife) had to cause many heartaches.

CX Before he died of cardiac arrest at sixty-six, he had spent his last years in a wheelchair after strokes, heart problems, and the installation of a pace-maker.

Keep quotation as is—last as clincher.

No adj clauses?   too many simple sentences

▌ S E L F - C H E C K   1 4 - 6

1. Practice your sentence writing by revising the sentences in Self-Check Answer 14–5, p. 435, for the topic on hobbies.

2. Do the same with the "stick to it" topic.

Before you continue, turn to pp. 436–437 to check your answers.

TRY IT OUT: **Now revise your sentences for your paragraph, using the hints given in Step 6 and the practice you have done as guides.**

STEP 7: WRITING THE FIRST DRAFT

The time has finally come for you to write your first draft in paragraph form. By now, much of your work is already done.

Your tasks in preparing your first draft paragraph involve guiding your reader. First, be sure that you use transitional expressions and sentences to lead your reader to your conclusions—or at least to understand how you have reached these conclusions. Second, you must make sure that the paragraph will follow one of the logical types of order.

Logical Types of Order

1. Order of Emphasis

   a. to persuade

   b. to inform

   Use appropriate transitions throughout such as *not only, importantly,* or *in addition.*

2. Chronological Order

   a. to show sequence (earliest first or moving backwards from the present time to earliest time)

   b. to make step-by-step directions

   Use appropriate transitions such as *next* or *first.* In a cause-effect situation use *consequently, therefore,* and so on.

3. Spatial Order

   a. to describe a setting, scene, or relative position

   b. to indicate direction

   Use transitions such as *near, in the next row, south of which,* and so on.

You can see the chronological order used in the paragraph about Joe Louis. The Self-Check paragraph about a hobby might also be thought of as chronological because it tries to lead step-by-step to the concluding topic sentence. However, it is actually an order-of-emphasis approach as is the Self-Check paragraph about mother's stick-to-itiveness.

Check for order and transition in the first draft that follows, noticing also that sentence rewriting is still going on, working toward the best expression possible.

That Joe Louis had a tragic life may not be as well known as his championship boxing fame. Hard times started early for Joe. His parents, who were sharecroppers, had Joe as their eighth child, allowing little money, little schooling for the children. Unskilled for other employment,

Joe took up boxing. Although he earned $4.6 million during his career, personally receiving only $800,000 after expenses, by the 1950s he owed $1.25 million in deliquent taxes and was unhappy. He struggled constantly to repay his debt and to support himself and his family. This aging champion suffered two humiliating defeats in a failed comeback attempt, one to Ezzard Charles and another to Rocky Marciano in 1951. A failed attempt to open with a partner a chain of food shops was another blow. Soon after that, his health deteriorated with a physical breakdown on a New York street followed by a five-month stay in 1970 in the Colorado Psychiatric Hospital. (He admitted in a 1971 biography that these events were caused by his cocaine use.) After four marriages, strokes, and heart problems Joe Louis died at sixty-six, his last years spent in a wheelchair. Louis' son compared him to Willy Loman in Arthur Miller's *Death of a Salesman*: ". . . started growing old and losing his customers. He was never really aware that he had lost his territory. That's the tragedy of it, just like my father's."

SELF-CHECK 14–7

1. Write a rough draft from the sentences about a hobby.

2. Write the rough draft for the topic of Mother's persistence.

Before you continue, turn to p. 437 to check your answers.

TRY IT OUT: **After practicing with the two paragraphs from the Self-Check, write the rough draft for the paragraph essay on your chosen topic.**

STEP 8: EDITING YOUR WRITING

Preferably after a period of time for more thinking about your paragraph, you should now critically read the rough draft. Check all grammar usage, punctuation, and spelling.

Next, look at your word/phrase usages and ask this question: Are any words or expressions unclear and in need of replacement?

1. Remove triteness by replacing overused expressions like *nice, fun,* or *quiet as a mouse.*

2. Remove slang or technical terms your reader may not understand, such as *awesome, aka* (which means "also known as," used for an alias or nickname), and so on.

3. Avoid euphemisms (expressions that cloud the meaning in an attempt to understate something) when the direct approach is more appropriate. An example of a euphemism is to use *peace keepers* for deadly missiles or *terminal leave* for being fired.

4. Remove any wordy phrases such as "on the day of her birth" for "on her birthday."

At the end of this chapter you will find a "Checklist for a Well-Written Paragraph." Use the checklist now to go over your rough draft once again, making any suggested changes that would improve your paragraph.

Read the entire edited paragraph (preferably aloud) to see that it flows smoothly, seems complete, and ends well.

Check your new additions and corrections for errors.

You will see fewer changes in the following version of the rough draft because many of the errors have already been corrected and much of the weak writing has been improved. Do note the changes and resulting improvements by comparing the following revision with the draft on pages 363–364.

That Joe Louis had a tragic life may not be as well known as his *[record]* championship boxing fame. *[transitional sentence]* Hard times started early for Joe. *[Joe's]* His parents, who were *[poor]* sharecroppers, had Joe as their eighth child, *[the large family]* allowing little money, little schooling for the children. Unskilled for other employment, Joe took up *[slangy?]* boxing. Although he earned $4.6 million during his career, personally receiving only $800,000 after expenses, by the 1950s he owed *[delinquent]* $1.25 million in deliquent *[sp]* taxes. He struggled constantly to repay his debt. ~~and to support himself and his family.~~ *[too obvious]* This aging champion suffered two humiliating defeats in a failed comeback attempt, one to Ezzard Charles *[too (repetitive)]* and another to Rocky Marciano in 1951. ~~A failed attempt to open with a partner~~ *[An unsuccessful venture]* a chain of food shops was another blow. Soon after that, *[Joe's]* his health *[and emotional state]* deteriorated ; ~~with a physical breakdown~~ *[1969]* *[collapse]* on a New York street *[was]* followed by a five-month stay in 1970 in the Colorado Psychiatric Hospital. *[omit: serves no good purpose]* ~~(He admitted in a 1971 biography that these events were caused by his cocaine use.)~~ After four marriages, *[several]* strokes, and heart problems Joe Louis died at sixty-six, his last years *[having been]* spent in a wheelchair. Louis's son compared him to Willy Loman in Arthur Miller's *Death of a Salesman:* ". . . started growing old and losing his customers. He was never really aware that he had lost his territory. That's the tragedy of it, just like my father's."

Can you see the improvement in this paragraph as it has gone through these steps? Can you honestly believe that a paragraph that you dash off at the last minute will show the careful attention that a conscientiously written one does?

These steps may seem overly time-consuming. At first, you may expend much effort and time, but the steps will become easier and quicker as you practice. You won't be sorry later that you have spent this time now in developing good writing skills. You will use this valuable asset in both your professional and your personal interactions.

SELF-CHECK 14-8

1. Make improvements in the rough draft of the paragraph about a hobby. You may add them to the copy on Self-Check Answer 14–7, p. 437.

2. Continue your practice by revising the rough draft on the topic of Mother's persistence.

Before you continue, turn to pp. 437–439 to check model paragraphs.

TRY IT OUT: **Now revise the rough draft of your paragraph. The practice with the Self-Check paragraphs will give you suggestions about how your paragraph can be improved.**

STEP 9: PREPARING THE FINAL COPY

This is the easy step, the one where you prepare the final copy. You may have made more than one draft as you worked with Step 8. After you are satisfied with the paragraph, key it into your computer, type it, or carefully handwrite it.

Be careful to follow your instructor's format requirements. If he or she has given no specifications, follow these general format suggestions.

Format Guidelines

1. Indent the first line.
2. Use even margins on both sides and top and bottom, usually at least one inch all around.
3. Title the paragraph with a short statement (not necessarily a sentence) that names the focus or point of view about the subject.

4. Recognize the origin of any quoted statement or of material cited by using textnotes, material in parentheses inserted within the text. See textnote for Joe Louis information on page 356.

   a. If you do not cite the source in the paragraph itself, use the complete source data.

      (Al E. Newman, "What, Me Worry?" *Glad Magazine,* July 4, 1956, p. 23.)

   b. If you mention some of the data in the paragraph, you do not need to <u>repeat</u> it in the textnote.

      . . . as Al E. Newman said. ("What, Me Worry?" *Glad Magazine,* July 4, 1956, p. 23.)

   Proofread this final copy.

Proofreading Hints

1. To check for typewriting errors, read the paragraph backwards to see each word separately. This technique helps you to avoid reading what you <u>think</u> you wrote, which can easily happen as you read from beginning to end.

2. For content, read the paragraph from the beginning to see that you haven't added extra words or left out any.

Lastly, retype or recopy the work if you have made any errors that you cannot correct <u>neatly</u>. If you are working with a computer, revise the electronic file and print a new copy. Treat each assignment as if it were going to a prospective employer as an example of your best work.

Here is the final draft of the Joe Louis paragraph. Look for the Self-Check final paragraphs on pages 438–439.

> That Joe Louis had a tragic life may not be as well known as his championship boxing record. Hard times started early. Joe's parents, who were poor sharecroppers, had Joe as their eighth child, the large family allowing little money, little schooling for the children. Unskilled for other employment, Joe undertook boxing. Although he earned $4.6 million during his career, personally receiving only $800,000 after expenses, by the 1950s he owed $1.25 million in delinquent taxes. He struggled constantly to repay his debt. This aging champion suffered two humiliating defeats in a failed comeback attempt, one to Ezzard Charles and another to Rocky Marciano in 1951. An unsuccessful venture to open a chain of food shops with a partner was another blow. Soon after that, Joe's health and emotional state deteriorated: a 1969 physical collapse on a New York street was followed by a five-month stay in 1970 in the Colorado Psychiatric Hospital. After four marriages, several strokes, and heart problems Joe Louis died at sixty-six, his last years having been spent in a wheelchair. Louis's son compared him to Willy Loman in Arthur Miller's *Death of a Salesman:* ". . . started growing old and losing his customers. He was never really aware that he had lost his territory. That's the tragedy of it, just like my father's."

TRY IT OUT: **Do Exercises 14.1 and 14.2, pp. 369–370, according to your instructor's directions.**

CHECKLIST FOR A WELL-WRITTEN PARAGRAPH

1. Have a concise topic sentence that limits the topic to specific detail and states or implies a point of view toward the topic.

2. Be sure that the topic sentence is well supported with appropriate definitions, facts, and examples.

3. Remove any sentences with only vaguely related or unrelated material.

4. Emphasize important ideas by using independent clauses, repetition, or careful placement in the paragraph.

5. Give supporting details and ideas less emphasis by placing them in modifying phrases and clauses and by having them occupy positions later in the paragraph.

6. Show variety in sentence structure with several types of structures such as adjective clauses, noun clauses, or verbal phrases.

7. Be sure that the paragraph follows one of the logical types of order.

8. Add all necessary transitional words and phrases to help the reader follow your thoughts to your conclusions.

9. Check to see that active and passive voice are used correctly.

10. Make certain that you have used parallel structure, well-placed modifiers, and correct subject-verb and pronoun agreement.

11. Check word and phrase usages to remove any slang, triteness, technical terminology, or wordiness.

12. Make sure that you have carefully chosen your closing, either a summary sentence or a "clincher" ending.

13. Proofread to make sure that all grammar usages, spelling, and punctuation are correct.

14. Look to see that the copy presents a clean, error-free appearance with an attractive format.

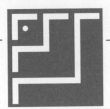

Commas

OVERVIEW

- **Comma Rules Revisited**
- **Common Uses of the Comma**
- **Other Uses of the Comma**

You have already been introduced to several of the major uses of commas. You have learned when to use commas with prepositional phrases (Chapter 1), with the three types of dependent clauses (Chapter 4), with nouns (Chapter 5), with each of the sentence types (Chapter 7), with verbals (Chapter 8), and with adjectives (Chapter 11).

In this chapter you'll be reviewing these earlier rules. You'll also become familiar with more uses of the comma that will be useful to you in letter, memo, and report writing.

Before you resume your study of commas, check your mastery of comma usage by working through the comma usage survey on the following page. The survey will provide a good test of your skill in using commas at this point. The exercises at the end of this chapter will cover both these major comma rules and the other comma uses that you'll learn in this chapter.

Using the comma rules you have already learned, decide whether or not to add commas to the following sentences.

1. I am in the first place sure of my answers.

2. On January 4 we will meet with the area representatives.

3. Hank planned to go to Sarasota but he didn't have airfare.

4. You may come to work at 7 a.m. and leave at 4 p.m. or you may arrive at 8 a.m. and leave at 5 p.m.

5. Denise has applied for a new job and has submitted her résumé.

6. The Roper Corporation has been in Seattle for seventeen years and has employed hundreds of people.

7. If you have completed the form you may leave.

8. You may if you are finished leave.

9. You may leave if you are finished.

10. Secretaries who cannot spell are not very helpful in an office.

11. Mr. Martinez who is my neighbor works for Peterson and Sons.

12. The official that signs these forms is not here right now.

13. The electrician went to the basement to look at the fuse box.

14. To earn more money Jan continued her education after graduation.

15. Talking on the phone Ms. Williams seemed to get upset.

16. She is the one talking on the phone.

17. Bryan after seeing the lot purchased the old building.

18. The woman dressed in black is my mother.

19. That house decorated in Colonial is very lovely.

20. My sister an airline hostess travels thousands of miles each year.

21. Can you see Mr. Allen why this idea is so important?

22. Did you see Mr. Allen?

23. My hobbies include reading cooking and drag racing.

24. Miss Ellingsworth is a willing capable worker.

25. A well-written reliable guidebook is a must for foreign travel.

Before you continue, turn to pp. 439–440 to check your answers.

Because you may wish to use this text as one of your references in the future, the earlier rules are restated but without explanation. The discussion of these rules includes some exceptions that were not covered earlier in this text. Also presented are rules not yet covered in this text, rules that are particularly useful in letter, memo, and report writing.

Examples follow each rule, but there are no further Self-Checks for this chapter. There are exercises at the end of the chapter incorporating the new rules as well as the ones that have already been covered.

COMMA RULES REVISITED

Commas are the most widely used—and misused—punctuation marks. As Wilson Follett, the editor of *Modern American Usage*, noted, "The comma causes trouble equally by its absence, by its presence, and by wrong placement." As you can see, it is very important in your development as a writer to master basic comma rules.

DEFINITION   A **comma** is a punctuation mark used to separate or to set off elements in a sentence.

As a careful writer, you should use commas to help your reader in these ways:

1. Grouping and separating words, phrases, and clauses.

2. Interpreting relative importance of sentence elements.

3. Providing clues for reading such as cadence and pitch.

Items in a Series

1. Separate the items in a series (words, phrases, or clauses) with commas.

> He studied law, accounting, and correspondence.
>
> Insurance is valuable for protecting your family, ensuring your possessions, and maintaining your peace of mind.
>
> Last weekend Mick planted new trees, Sunita clipped the hedges, and Joni put in our vegetable garden.

2. The comma before the conjunction is not mandatory but is helpful, especially in a series of phrases or clauses.

> The attorney acted with concern for his client, with careful attention to detail (,) and with respect for the court.

3. Be sure that you do not use a comma <u>after</u> the last item in the series, unless the continuing structure would require a comma for another reason.

Vanessa enjoys bookkeeping, math, and English, but computers are her first love. [Use a comma after *English* because it precedes the conjunction for the compound sentence.]

4. When *etc.* is at the end of your series to indicate that your list is incomplete, use a comma before *etc.* and one after it if the sentence continues. (Be sure not to use *etc.* in a series that begins with *such as* or *for example.*)

   Apples, peaches, oranges, etc., are healthful foods.

5. Do not use a comma before an ampersand (&), as in a company name.

   Johnson, Stoline & Grass is a well-known law firm.

6. If pairs of items appear in a series, use commas only to separate the series items.

   Bacon and eggs, fish and chips, and ham and beans are foods that seem to go together.

TRY IT OUT: Do Exercise 15.1, p. 385, to practice using commas with items in a series.

Direct Address

1. Use commas to set off the name of a person spoken to by name or another form of address.

   Yes, Ms. Fortino, your case is next on the docket.

2. Do <u>not</u> set off a name if the person is just talked about, not directly talked to.

   We hear next the case for Mr. Savage.

3. Use commas to set off terms of direct address that are other than names.

   Yes, gentlemen, I know about the blackout.
   I second the motion, Mr. Chairman.
   You know, fellow Americans, that I always speak the truth.

TRY IT OUT: Do Exercise 15.2, p. 386, to practice using commas in direct address.

Consecutive Adjectives

1. Use commas to separate adjectives in a series, but do not put a comma between the final adjective and the noun.

   Any gray, green, or tweed rug shows less dirt than a light-colored rug.

2. When two or more consecutive adjectives come in front of a noun, separate them with commas if *and* could be used instead.

An aged, decrepit man slowly walked past the house.

3. If adjectives immediately follow the noun they modify, set off these adjectives with commas.

The man, aged and decrepit, slowly walked past the house.

TRY IT OUT: **Do Exercise 15.3, p. 386, to practice using commas with consecutive adjectives.**

Explanatory Expressions and Appositives

1. Use commas to set off an explanatory <u>phrase</u> that clarifies the noun in front of it only if the phrase could be omitted without altering the meaning.

Helen Trend, a fashion designer from New York, will speak at our meeting.

Our net profit, the amount of profit after expenditures, was very good last year.

2. Use commas to set off a prepositional phrase starting with *of* that (1) stands behind a noun denoting a person and (2) tells <u>where</u> the person is from.

Fred Wong, of our Hollywood office, will be here by three o'clock today.

I know that Bea Strupe, of Reading and Johnson, has sold computers for twenty years.

3. Long prepositional phrases that begin with *together with, in addition to,* or *as well as* are explanatory. Use commas to set off these phrases.

Helene, as well as her friends, is a good skier.

I plan to bring a notebook, together with a pen and a legal pad.

4. An explanatory phrase could begin with *or* if the item in the phrase is a definition of the preceding noun. Use commas to set off this phrase.

An alloy, or a mixture of metals, is often stronger than any one of the metals separately.

A decennium, or a period of ten years, is also called a decade.

5. Use commas to set off any explanatory phrase that starts with *such as.*

Many homeowners, such as older couples or single parents, are moving to condominiums to avoid the problem of maintenance.

(*Note:* You will learn in Chapter 17 that any of these explanatory phrases that contain <u>their own</u> commas are set off by dashes; for instance, "Many homeowners—older couples, single parents, or widows and widowers—are moving to condominiums.")

6. Do not set off one-word explanatory expressions.

Her sister *Pearlie* is a salesperson.

I *myself* prefer this machine.

7. Do not set off words or phrases that are referred to as just that—a word or phrase. In other words, you are not using them in context but are simply referring to them as names of things.

> The trade name *Xerox* has two *x*'s.
> The expression *This is to inform you* is outdated.

TRY IT OUT: Do Exercise 15.4, p. 387, to practice using commas with explanatory phrases and appositives.

Modifying Phrases

1. Most prepositional phrases that tell <u>when</u>, <u>where</u>, <u>how</u>, or <u>what kind of</u> are closely related to the sentence. Do <u>not</u> set these phrases off by commas.

2. Some few phrases do begin with prepositions but are actually transitional expressions, not modifiers. <u>Do</u> use commas to set off this type of prepositional phrase.

> These phrases, for example, are well written.

3. Use a comma after a modifying infinitive phrase transposed to the front of its clause.

> To be on time, you should set your alarm for an extra fifteen minutes of driving time in bad weather.

4. Do not use commas with an infinitive phrase in its normal order.

> You must leave earlier *to be on time* in bad weather.

5. Use a comma after any verbal phrase transposed to the front of its clause as a modifier.

> Selling pots and pans, the clerk knew a great deal about heat transference.

6. Set off with commas participial phrases from the main clause if they are nonrestrictive and could be left out without changing the meaning of the main clause.

> The star skater, warming his hands, rested before he had to perform again.
> The United Way, counting on volunteer help, can raise funds without much overhead cost.

7. Do not use commas to set off restrictive participial phrases, as they are needed to define the nouns they modify; the meaning of the clause would not be the same without them.

> The car *painted green* is the one you should tow away.
> My boss is the woman *wearing a pant suit*.

8. Remember that *during, concerning,* and *regarding* are prepositions, not verbals; therefore, do not set off with commas phrases beginning with these words.

TRY IT OUT: Do Exercise 15.5, p. 388, to practice using commas with modifying phrases.

Adverbial Clauses

1. Use a comma after an adverbial clause placed <u>before</u> its independent clause.

> If I were you, I would get an early start.
>
> He hates homework, but he knows that if he wants to really learn something, he has to practice. [Notice that this adverbial clause occurs in the <u>second</u> part of a compound sentence.]

2. Use a pair of commas to set off an adverbial clause that breaks up the independent clause.

> Harold, because he knew better, was angry with himself for that mistake.

3. Use no commas with most complex sentences in the natural order with the adverbial clause following the independent clause.

> You should get an early start *if you want to be on time.*
>
> Please call me *as soon as you are ready.*

4. Possible exceptions to this rule are these:

   a. Adverbial clauses that begin with *as, although,* or *for* are considered to be nonrestrictive, adding nonessential material. Use a comma before each.

   > You must order by June 30, as our new models go on the market then.
   >
   > He took a course in real estate, for he planned to sell his own home.

   b. Occasionally the words *whatever* and *however* act as adverbs instead of conjunctions when they begin the second clause of a complex sentence. In these situations precede that second clause with a comma. You can recognize these situations by substituting *no matter what* for *whatever* or *no matter how* for *however.*

   > She decided to move to Arizona, whatever the job picture looked like. [no matter what]
   >
   > Mr. Preston wanted to complete the project, however long it would take. [no matter how]

   c. An adverbial clause that begins with *where* or *when* can be used differently from a normal adverbial clause that tells the time or place. Sometimes these words begin a clause that adds a <u>separate</u> idea, one that could be put in another sentence. (The first clause will already contain the time or place.) Use a comma in front of one of these unusual clauses that follows its independent clause. The *when* or *where* could be replaced with *and.*

   > You may call me on Tuesday, when I shall know the results of the tests.
   >
   > Mr. Hampstead is going to work at Toklas Bros., where he will be in charge of accounts.

   Again, if the *where* or *when* clause tells where or when about the main idea, do not use the comma.

   > I will see you when I return from Key West.
   >
   > Can you remember where we put Ms. Anson's file?

TRY IT OUT: **Do Exercise 15.6, p. 389, to practice using commas with adverbial clauses.**

Adjective Clauses

1. A nonrestrictive adjective clause is one that follows a noun and adds extra information about it. Set off these adjective clauses with commas.

    > Herb Scott, who writes poetry, teaches English at the local university.
    >
    > Margaret Coombs, whom we elected to be our treasurer, knows a great deal about accounting practice.

2. Adjective clauses that begin with *each of, all of,* or any other quantifying word are nonrestrictive. Set off these types of clauses by commas.

    > Our customers, several of whom live out of town, like our catalog service.
    >
    > These parts, twenty of which are new this year, are available now.

3. Most clauses that begin with *which* are nonessential. Set off most *which* clauses with commas.

4. Clauses that begin with *that* or *understand that* are restrictive. Use no commas.

5. Clauses that begin with *who* or *whom* can be either restrictive or nonrestrictive and must be studied to determine whether or not to be set off with commas. (See Chapters 4 and 7 for extensive examples.)

TRY IT OUT: **Do Exercise 15.7, p. 390, to practice using commas with adjective clauses.**

Compound Sentences

1. Use a comma before the coordinate conjunction (*and, but, or, nor, yet*) that connects the independent clauses in a compound sentence.

    > We purchased the building August 1, and we moved in December 15.

2. When the compound sentence is very short, ten or fewer words, the comma can be omitted.

    > He can call in the order or he can mail it.

3. When the coordinate conjunction simply adds a second verb to the original subject, the sentence is <u>not</u> compound and takes no comma. (Check behind the conjunction to see if the next verb has its own written subject.)

    > The foreman attended the meeting and learned of the new company policies.
    >
    > *but*
    >
    > The foreman attended the meeting, and *he* learned of the new company policies.

TRY IT OUT: **Do Exercise 15.8, p. 391, to practice using commas in compound sentences.**

Transitional Expressions (Sometimes Called Parentheticals or Interrupters)

1. Good writers add transitional words or phrases, or even short clauses, to sentences to help limit the meaning or express an opinion or attitude toward what is being said. Other additions show the relationships of the ideas. Set off these expressions with commas if they interrupt the flow of the main idea.

   He was, of course, happy to learn of his promotion.

   Accordingly, we have made the reservations.

   Ms. Phillips was, I believe, a corporal in the army.

   Next, I shall see Mr. Reed.

   You are, I am sure, aware of the discounts available.

   The following words, phrases, and short clauses can help you signal to your readers transitions and parenthetical interrupters.

Words

accordingly	however	otherwise
again	incidentally	personally
also	indeed	respectively
besides	moreover	still
consequently	namely	then
finally	naturally	therefore
first, second, etc.	next	too
fortunately	nevertheless	ultimately
hence	notwithstanding	unfortunately

Phrases and Clauses

after all	if any	in the long run
as a result	if necessary	in other words
as a rule	in addition	of course
as you know	in any case	on the other hand
at any rate	in brief	on the contrary
by the way	in fact	that is
for example	in conclusion	that is to say
for instance	in the first place	to be sure (certain)
I believe, know, and so on		

2. Sometimes these expressions do not act as interrupters but serve as essential modifiers of the main idea. Do <u>not</u> use commas in these instances.

   I believe what the report said.   He wore that ring *on the other hand.*

   Of course you may leave if you are ill.   *However* hard I try, I can't figure it out.

TRY IT OUT: **Do Exercise 15.9, p. 392, to practice using commas with transitional expressions.**

COMMON USES OF THE COMMA

Miscellaneous Comma Uses

1. Business writing follows this principle: Use commas to separate the digits of numbers into groups of thousands. Commas are commonly omitted in four-digit numbers unless these numbers appear with larger numbers that require commas.

   $1726   46,298   11,000,000

   The quantites sold each quarter are as follows:
First	9,864
Second	9,908
Third	10,012
Fourth	11,467

2. In a letter with mixed punctuation use a comma after the complimentary close or after an informal first-name salutation.

   Sincerely,   Yours truly,   Dear Paula,

3. Use a comma between identical verbs unless the first is a helping verb as in *had had*.

   Whoever goes, goes without my permission.

   Whatever happens, happens for the best.

   I had had trouble with the car before then. [The first *had* is a helping verb.]

4. Use a comma between words repeated for emphasis.

   Many, many errors can be avoided by proofreading.

5. Use commas to set off contrasting expressions placed after the item to be contrasted to.

   Logical thinking, not snap judgments, usually works best.

   I eat broccoli often, turnips seldom.

   We are open on Saturdays, never on Sundays.

   (*Note:* Using a contrasting idea adds emphasis to your writing.)

6. Use a comma to show that an omission has been made of a word or words that are clearly implied from the preceding clause.

   Last year we sold 16,000 television sets; this year, (we sold) 19,000.

   Julie studied to become a doctor; John, a lawyer; Marzella, a teacher.

7. Occasionally you must use a comma to avoid an incorrect reading of a sentence.

   Just before, Mel had deposited a quarter.

   Ever since, Bill has worked here.

8. When writing names in inverted order, use a comma after the surname and another after the first name if the clause continues.

> Williams, Stephen, follows Williams, Sarah, in the files.
>
> Zwart, C. F., is the last card I have.

9. Use a comma to separate volume and page numbers. Use a second comma if the clause continues.

> I looked in Volume IV, page 143, for the answer.

10. Use a comma after an exclamatory word at the beginning of a clause.

> Oh, I was so happy to hear that!

11. Use a comma after a responding word that begins a clause.

> Yes, I can see that.
>
> Well, I haven't decided what to do.

12. Use a comma to set off an added comment or question.

> You received my letter, didn't you?
>
> Will he win the contest, I wonder.

TRY IT OUT: **Do Exercise 15.10, p. 393, for more practice in miscellaneous use of commas.**

Commas With Quotations

1. Use commas to set off quotations from the rest of the sentence. Two commas are needed when the explanatory material comes in the middle of the sentence.

> "You may remember," said the speaker, "that we discussed this very problem just last year."
>
> She commented, "I've heard that before."
>
> "I don't remember that," replied Mr. Chrysler.

2. If your quotation ends with a question mark or exclamation point, do not also use a comma.

> "Who did this?" asked Ms. James.
>
> "Get out now!" he hollered.

3. A quotation within a quotation is enclosed in single quotation marks. Punctuation is the same as with double marks. There is no space between the final quotation marks.

> Mrs. Jones commented, "I was surprised when Mary Edwards said, 'I plan to resign!'"

TRY IT OUT: **Do Exercise 15.11, p. 394, to practice using commas with quotations.**

OTHER USES OF THE COMMA

Names, Addresses, and Titles

1. With mixed punctuation a title is set apart from the name in an inside address by a comma.

   > Mr. John Smyth, President
   > Acme Telephone Company
   > 316 North Pritchard Street
   > Chicago, IL 60068

   For balance this title is sometimes put on the second line, again with a comma to separate it from the other material.

   > Mr. Henry Cunningham Belson
   > Treasurer, Acme Corporation
   > 997 West Burdick Street
   > Charleston, SC 76567

2. Use no commas to set off an abbreviation—such as *Jr., Sr.,* or *Esq.*— following a name unless that person's correspondence contains those commas. If a roman numeral is part of a name, use no periods or commas.

   > John Thomas, Jr., spoke on Tuesday. [His letter's signature did have the commas.]
   > John Thomas II will be next.

   (*Note:* In alphabetic listings follow this example: Thomas, John A., Jr.)

3. Some companies use commas to separate the abbreviations *Inc.* and *Ltd.* from their names. Do so only when you know that is the preferred style for that company.

   > Langdon, Inc., will locate in the new industrial park.

4. Academic degrees and religious order abbreviations are written with periods and no spaces. Set these titles off from the name with commas.

   > Rowanda Markham, M.D., has set up new offices in the Blanford Building.
   > Seth Rhodes, Ph.D., is working on a new book.
   > The Reverend Samuel Service, D.D., will retire after Sunday's dissertation.
   > Suzanne Goodman, A.S., works at Burus Clinic.

5. When an address is part of a complete sentence, separate the elements of an address with commas.

   > You can reach Mr. Boeing at Electronics, Inc., 1313 Oak Road, Plains, GA 30704, if you send this letter today.

6. Use two commas to set off a state or country name when it identifies the city preceding it in a complete sentence.

   > Paris, France, is certainly larger, if not more exciting, than Paris, Michigan, ever hoped to be.

TRY IT OUT: **Do Exercise 15.12, p. 394, to practice using commas with names, addresses, and titles.**

Dates

1. Use a comma before and after a year when it follows a month and day.

   > July 4, 1776, was the start of our Independence Day celebrations.
   >
   > Did you know that November 22, 1963, is the date of President Kennedy's assassination?
   >
   > The ship sailed *4 June 1944* and was not seen again.

   (*Note:* United States military correspondence and most foreign usage express the date in day-month-year sequence with no commas.)

2. Use commas to set off the date from the name of the day when written together.

   > On Wednesday, March 22, out new plant in Akron opened.

3. Use no commas with a two-part date.

   > The *July 1973* issue of *National Geographic* carried the article you are looking for.
   >
   > He chose March 14 for the Grand Opening.

4. No comma is used after an introductory adverbial phrase that gives the time for the event of the clause.

   > *Last year* we handled 87,243 inquiries.
   >
   > *On January 14* we placed an order with you.

TRY IT OUT: **Do Exercise 15.13, p. 395, to practice using commas with dates.**

Article and Book Titles

Use italics—underscoring if italics is not available—to indicate the title of a complete artistic or literary work. In business communications, you may type these titles in all capital letters. These methods will indicate the titles of such things as books, pamphlets, magazines, newspapers, movies, plays, television series, and paintings or sculptures.

> *The Gregg Reference Manual* is a book used by many editors.
>
> *The Lexington Herald's* "Classified" section was seven pages long last Sunday.
>
> You will find an article on open-concept retailing in WHITE'S BUSINESS JOURNAL. [All capital letters used to show magazine title in business writing.]

1. If the title of an article or book is nonessential because the prior noun already identifies it, use commas to set off the title.

   > Have you read Margaret Mitchell's famous book, *Gone With the Wind?*
   >
   > His latest article, "Payless Paydays," is certainly an eye opener.

2. If the title contains a question mark or exclamation point, do not use the second comma to set off the title.

The first chapter, "Who Are You?" asks some very pertinent questions.

3. If the title is an essential part of the clause, use no commas.

The Jungle is one of the first books to expose gross mistreatment of people in our society.

You should read the article "Salem" in *People*.

These comma rules cover most situations you will encounter in everyday writing. You can find rules and examples for special situations in a reference manual.

TRY IT OUT: **Do Exercise 15.14, p. 395, to practice using commas with titles of articles and books. Exercise 15.15, p. 396, should prove to be a challenge.**

◘ Chapter 15: Commas

Add any necessary commas to the following sentences. Some sentences may have no commas. Circle any changes you make.

1. The new depot is a center for bus rail and other types of transportation.

2. We market refrigerators stoves dishwashers and microwave ovens.

3. I saw Helen Roberts Duane Hunt and Salena Young on the *Accent* show last night.

4. Nuts bolts screws etc. are hard items to keep in stock.

5. Mulaney Wells & Jones is a local tax firm.

6. He would prefer either a wool or a serge suit.

7. To ski to swim and to play tennis are all good exercises.

8. You may buy a 6-oz. package of cheese for $3.95 a 12-oz. package for $6.50 or a 16-oz. package for $7.95.

9. For lunch I will have bread and butter a bowl of soup and a tossed salad.

10. Most of us have to pay federal taxes state taxes and local taxes of some kind.

11. Most of us have to pay federal state and local taxes.

12. I am taking classes in math English history and science.

13. Her criticisms were presented to us tastefully tactfully and truthfully.

14. Radio television magazines newspapers etc. are ways of learning of current events.

15. The material is available in black and white red and white or green and beige.

16. The firm of Johnson Anderson & Swainson is not very well known but is well respected by those who do know it.

17. Read a sentence carefully think about what you have read put it into your own words and decide how the idea relates to the whole—these are good study techniques.

18. Africa and the Middle East are becoming places for tourist travel.

19. Students teachers parents etc. should all take an active part in educational decisions.

20. Shall we have ham turkey or a rib roast for dinner at the regular monthly meeting?

Use commas to set off any instances of direct address in the following. Remember, the person(s) must be spoken to, not spoken about. Circle any changes you make.

1. You will discover Mrs. Nelson that our branch bank near your home can give you full services.

2. You boys in the back of the room please be quiet.

3. Will you ask Mr. Fisher whether I can be of help.

4. Now fellow union members we shall take a vote on this issue.

5. Mrs. Malnight can you help me with this?

6. We will send Mr. Prince to see you next Wednesday afternoon.

7. Please place your order by Friday Ms. Green.

8. Mr. President would you like to comment on that?

9. Have you typed the letter Sue?

10. Has Sue typed the letter yet Sally?

Add any necessary commas to the following sentences. Circle any changes you make.

1. The mansion stately and old was beginning to decay.

2. The stately old mansion was beginning to decay.

3. Have you tried our new hair dryer?

4. Several brand new two-story air-conditioned apartments are available.

5. Wine is often aged in old wooden barrels.

6. An alert efficient adept employee is of great benefit to a company.

7. Ms. White just moved to a luxurious ornate home.

8. We plan to build a modern office building in the downtown area.

9. A terse derogatory remark never helps to solve a problem.

10. The golf course has broad green fairways and lush thick putting greens.

● E X E R C I S E   1 5 . 4

Use any necessary commas to separate explanatory expressions that are nonrestrictive. Not all sentences will require commas. Circle any changes you make.

1. Mr. Roy Bearer our district manager in the West will be here to discuss expansion plans.

2. Our district manager from the West Mr. Roy Bearer will be here for Monday's meeting.

3. Gerbils small desert rodents have become popular pets.

4. Edwin O'Sonner of Ireland speaks with a lovely brogue.

5. John Adams Director of Admissions and Herb Buell Director of Placement often work together.

6. I hope to see Ann Heilman of Adams Bennet & Strang at the luncheon.

7. The tarantula a large venomous spider was named that because its bite was supposed to cause an uncontrollable desire to dance (tarantism).

8. Our office staff together with our families will have our annual picnic at Hyde Park.

9. Local doctors along with other people in the health professions are encouraging everyone to have all necessary inoculations.

10. A stevedore or dockworker loads and unloads ships.

11. Public officials must be careful not to show nepotism or favoritism to relatives.

12. Several geniuses such as Einstein did not do well in school.

13. The trade name Xerox has become synonymous with copy machines.

14. Active exercise such as jogging or tennis should be avoided by those in poor health.

15. My sister Jane married my husband's brother Fred.

16. Many people misspell the word *congratulations*.

17. Macy's a large department store in New York sponsors a Christmas parade each year.

18. Sam Browne of our Boston office is being transferred to Denver.

19. Myocardial infarction a heart attack is due to arteriosclerosis.

20. Our Purchasing Agent Joan Kauffmann knows all of the latest products and prices.

Some of the following sentences need commas to set off the modifying phrases; some do not. Add only the necessary commas. Circle any changes you make.

1. To speed up delivery we have installed a computer that will expedite the order.

2. Manuel worked hard to win the scholarship.

3. Manuel to win the scholarship worked very hard.

4. We decided that it was time to start to change to our new models.

5. During the afternoon I was able to finish up the incomplete work.

6. Rachel weeding the garden discovered an old spoon from the colonial times.

7. Carrying a heavy tray the waitress hurried to the table.

8. The man looking this way seems to be lost.

9. Mrs. Adamson planning to visit three of our branch offices was careful about making her reservations.

10. The donut covered with powdered sugar is the one I want.

11. The report concerning this phase is filed under Research: Project 17.

12. To be protected against fires at night many people have installed smoke detectors.

13. The meeting to be held on Friday has been changed.

14. Sada wearing a new dress went on her first job interview.

15. While walking to the post office I saw a huge truck get stuck in an alley.

16. The man signing his name is George Edwards our new accountant.

17. George Edwards signing his name completed the application.

18. That child covered with dirt and grime couldn't be mine!

19. Sarah covered with dirt and grime came into the house after playing outside.

20. Running for President is setting a high goal for yourself.

● EXERCISE 15.6

Locate the adverbial clauses in the following, and decide whether or not to set them off with commas. Be prepared to explain why you did or did not use commas. Look for subordinate conjunctions to indicate these clauses. Circle any changes that you make.

1. After we had pitched our tent we realized that we were in a valley.

2. Please call me after you talk with Mr. Sonnefeld.

3. Madeline before she noticed it had typed the letter with the carbon paper facing the wrong way.

4. Because you will be hospitalized for your minor surgery be sure to bring your insurance card with you to the admitting office.

5. I went to Decatur because I had to see Bill Brown.

6. As long as I have worked here I have never seen anything like this.

7. When you complete the application be sure to sign it on the bottom line.

8. Please go to Room 7 when you have completed the application.

9. You can call me after 3 p.m. when I should know Ms. Judkin's schedule for next week.

10. I will not be able to attend the ceremony for I have to be in San Francisco that week.

11. Although I knew better I still tried to hurry too much with my work.

12. I made several errors in my report because I hurried although I should have known better.

13. I hope that as soon as Mr. Jeeves returns I can leave early today.

14. She is never grouchy or snappish however tired she may be.

15. I plan to go to law school whatever the difficulties may be.

16. Do you know where the Carson file is?

17. If I leave will you answer my phone for the rest of the afternoon?

18. Hatti went to Haiti when the weather was good there and when the tourist season was over.

19. Until I find that folder I cannot complete this transaction.

20. You are certainly eligible for a raise as you have been doing excellent work.

Underline the adjective clauses that need no commas; add commas to those that are nonrestrictive. Look for the signal words who, whom, whose, which, *and* that.

1. Customers who can't make up their minds can be very annoying to salespeople.

2. The medical practice that deals with the digestive tract is called gastroenterology.

3. This new dictating machine which has a memory bank will certainly help us process our paperwork.

4. The woman who called you earlier is on the phone again.

5. You had a call from Mrs. Treat who called you earlier.

6. Please tell me which one is the older one.

7. Any tree that bears cones is called coniferous.

8. This textbook which covers grammar and punctuation quite extensively should be helpful to you in the future.

9. The man who invented the cotton gin was Eli Whitney.

10. Our accountants each of whom is a CPA have prepared for years for their jobs.

11. These desks 60 percent of which are promised to Bloom, Inc. should be ready to go out next week.

12. Students who do not know the basic skills should be given extra help and encouragement.

13. Ted Jessup whom you have met before will be starting his new job as manager on Monday.

14. Everyone who needs a new deduction form should see Ted.

15. An automatic timer which can turn your lights on and off is a good thing to use when you must be gone from home for a period of time.

16. *SMASH* which is setting all kinds of records is a new television show.

17. My new drapes which are brocade material add a great deal to my living room.

18. Anyone who wants to better himself or herself should study his major subjects carefully.

19. Ezell Price whom Mrs. Johnson promoted has been with our firm for only one year.

20. The article that discusses the new trends in word processing is in *Time* magazine.

●**EXERCISE 15.8**

Place a comma before the conjunction in any of the compound sentences that follow. Not all are compound sentences. Circle any changes you make.

1. Many people are taking up skiing and many new resorts are opening up each year.

2. I saw the movie last week and didn't like it.

3. We started the project and they finished it.

4. Scientists are constantly learning new things about the universe and they believe that there are more planets in our solar system than we realize.

5. Baseball has always been America's national sport but football seems to be gaining popularity.

6. We had hoped to be able to complete the assignment yet we didn't really expect to be done on time.

7. Railroads did much to develop this country but they are not as widely used by the public as in other countries.

8. John Willson said he will give you as good a deal on your used car as anyone would or he will give you a television set as a consolation.

9. Mary Brown ran for the Senate seat that was vacated by Paul Todd and was elected in a landslide.

10. Turn in your money to Miss Ellis or send it over to the Accounting Department.

11. Whoever wants to take early retirement and whoever has accumulated 30 years with the company is eligible.

12. We were interested in investing in the annuities yet we needed to make sure that they were guaranteed.

13. The calculator used to cost close to a hundred dollars but mass production has made it available for little cost.

14. *Cliché* means either "an expression that has become trite" or it can mean "a stereotype or electrotype plate."

15. "Neither a borrower nor a lender be" is a well-known platitude.

16. Sometimes Seth liked to enter marathons but he preferred running in shorter races.

17. This report shows where our losses have occurred and when the sales figures started dropping.

18. Spring can have some lovely days but fall has not only warmth but glorious color.

19. Graphics is an exciting field to be in but a person must keep abreast of all the new technology affecting the field.

20. Business reports must be completed by a deadline and must be inclusive as well as concise.

Set off with commas any interrupting words, phrases, or clauses that stop the flow in the following sentences. Circle any changes you make.

1. She was naturally very pleased with the progress in her case.

2. Of course I have not really decided yet.

3. There are for example three dealers in this city alone.

4. Accordingly I called the committee chairperson to ask that it be included in the next handbook.

5. You are however responsible for the upkeep under this leasing plan.

6. However hard it has rained I still have no leaks in the canvas covering.

7. We were unfortunately too late to apply.

8. You may also if necessary have this shipped to another address.

9. He tried to explain it in other words.

10. I have always as you know tried to treat all of my employees fairly.

11. She was therefore unable to buy our new computer.

12. Her hair is in fact naturally curly.

13. Naturally I had hoped that he would see my side of the issue.

14. This car will in the long run be more economical than that model that costs less.

15. I think I believe him.

16. You are I believe Mr. Sallisman?

17. Besides I really do enjoy taking classes.

18. I will in any case stand behind the guarantee on this item.

19. The Joneses were fortunately away from home when the fire began.

20. First you should ask Mr. Belson and second you should go to Mrs. Bullock.

● EXERCISE 15.10

In the following sentences, add commas only where necessary. Circle any changes you make.

1. Our newest model sells for only $2468.

2. Whatever will be will be.

3. He had waited to win the lottery for a long long time.

4. Adults not children are legally responsible for their own actions.

5. Whoever wins wins a trophy.

6. I have received many many orders for our new type of folding chair.

7. I have played handball not racketball.

8. We have shipped over 300000 of these meters to our customers in foreign countries.

9. Ten years ago I wanted to be a doctor; last year an accountant.

10. Even before I knew that I wanted an antique oriental rug.

11. Ever since the last game of the year has been held on New Year's Day.

12. Larsen's Supermarket has its own butcher shop; Nobil's a bakery.

13. On June 15 I paid $50; On July 15 $20; on August 15 $50.

14. Clemens Samuel L. is where you would look in the card catalog for books by Mark Twain.

15. Aaronson Adam J. is the first name in our telephone book.

16. The *National Geographic* Volume XIV page 29 is where you will find the article about Eskimos.

17. Refer to page 267 Volume X for the quotation by French.

18. Yes I will be there.

19. My but I didn't know that!

20. That was really a good program wasn't it?

Add any necessary commas and end punctuation to these sentences. Circle any changes you make.

1. Mr. Baker said that Mrs. Fox would be in charge

2. Mr. Baker said "Ms. Foxx will be in charge"

3. "Where" asked Mr. Billingsly "could I find some more staples"

4. The article stated "The population in non-industrial nations is growing more rapidly than in industrial ones"

5. "I am shocked" exclaimed Miss Jessup

6. You may notice" he continued "several changes in our new mailing list"

7. She expressed surprise that she had been selected

8. "Why me" is a question that is futile—it really makes no difference why

9. "Consequently" said the sales manager "we must try to develop new prospects"

10. Madeline inquired "Are you taking applications for the position"

Add any necessary punctuation to the following sentences. Circle any changes you make.

1. Mr Howard Markham Jr lived in Boise Idaho for many years before he moved to 338 West Florida Street Birmingham Alabama last year.

2. Hemingway Ltd was located in London England for fifty years before it set up a branch in Chicago Illinois.

3. Have you made separate files for both Weston Jules A Sr and Weston Jules A Jr

4. Henry VIII had many wives, mostly because he wanted a male heir.

5. Alan King Jr has started his new job at Bob Moore Inc this week

6. Alaine Ingersol Ph D has started her new counseling practice at 1741 Parkview Avenue Denver Colorado

7. Fairhaven Connecticut is the new location for Bryant Inc

8. Our speakers will be Helen Jones Ph D Mark Allen M A and Sidney Greenstreet Ed D

9. Sammy Davis Jr was a very popular singer and dancer.

10. Bennet Inc has merged with the Bendix Corp

● **E X E R C I S E   1 5 . 1 3**

Insert commas where needed in these sentences containing dates. Circle any changes you make.

1. Next year we will have completed our new warehouse.

2. We received your order on October 10 for 23 hoists.

3. On October 10 we received your order for the hoists.

4. On October 10 1987 we celebrated our fifteenth year of operation.

5. Next Friday March 6 we will begin our annual spring sale.

6. By January 2014 we will have been in business for 100 years.

7. Your order will be shipped November 21 by parcel post.

8. December 7 1941 is the date of the bombing of Pearl Harbor.

9. We will see you on Wednesday August 15.

10. Last week we finally finished the Massey Report.

● **E X E R C I S E   1 5 . 1 4**

Add any necessary commas in the following sentences. Circle any changes you make.

1. Our new math textbook *Programmed Math* is designed for individual study.

2. Contrary to some students' misconceptions, *Roots* is not a book about word derivations.

3. An article about new advertising techniques "New Methods in the Media" is in this month's issue of MODERN BUSINESS.

4. Do you remember Chapter 1 "Phrases and Clauses"?

5. His most recent book *One Word of Wisdom* is autobiographical.

6. I would like to read his book about apes *An Endangered Species.*

7. Our local paper *The Daily Gazette* has much useful information about the area's activities.

8. Did you place an advertisement in the *Washington Post?*

9. Lincoln's famous speech "The Gettysburg Address" was written on a piece of brown paper while Lincoln traveled by train.

10. *Crime and Punishment* is a wonderful psychological study of a man's motivation.

Add any necessary commas to the following. Be prepared to tell why you are inserting the commas that you do add. Circle any changes you make.

If you as a student really care about yourself and your work you will want to learn to use punctuation correctly. Because commas are about the most used marks of punctuation they should be carefully studied.

Before you can really learn to use commas correctly you must "unlearn" two faulty comma rules that many students have inadvertently learned over the years.

First there is no rule that says to use a comma because there is a pause in the sentence. This idea is an overly simplified rule of thumb that does not follow the principles of structure. In many cases the correct meaning of the sentence could be lost as well as the proper flow of the language. For example notice how often a speaker will pause *after* the conjunction in a compound sentence; however the comma comes *before* the conjunction to help the reader to separate the two ideas and to note the relationship between them. Commas are placed for readers not for writers.

Second there is not a rule that says to put in a comma when the sentence becomes "too long." You will not find this rule written anywhere but sometimes it seems to be understood by some writers.

The only sure way to learn comma usage is to learn the appropriate structural places that require commas. Chapter 15 has listed those. But remember students of English usage "understanding" these rules is not enough! You can "understand" the multiplication tables but you will not be able to do math problems unless you commit these multiplication tables to memory. So it is with punctuation rules.

Of course anyone who does not understand the principles of grammar such as phrases and clauses cannot hope to learn to punctuate correctly. This person will not understand such comma usages as those dictated by a compound sentence a transposed adverbial clause or a nonrestrictive adjective clause.

If you are among those who did not immediately recall the grammatical usages just mentioned you my friend have some studying to do. On the other hand if you are a true student who has worked hard to master the skills necessary for a career you can feel confident in the product you have to sell to a potential employer. You are capable of representing yourself and that business well. You are worth that employer's time and money.

◧ Periodic Review: Chapters 14–15

Proofread these sentences and correct any usage errors.

1. Several of the criterion are clearly understood.

2. We have had to cooperate together to have lain the groundwork.

3. I appreciate you helping to effect these changes in the law.

4. Between Sarah and she Nelda is the tallest.

5. The sale of mens' pant's will start June 1.

6. After Bob started the engine, he let it run for awhile.

7. It had not occured to me to start identifying good prospects.

8. The best of the two projects is the one that can't hardly go wrong.

9. The moral of the company fell after the resent fire.

10. We were alloted five minutes and broadcasted our message.

11. Susan was a former employee of our's.

12. If he was present, he wasn't causing to much trouble.

13. I will feel badly if we have to reconvene again.

14. Emerson is the only one of the men who were canvased.

15. The data are clear that accuracy is the most important skill of the two discussed.

16. Either of the women are proud of Francesca and she.

17. I seen her at the show where she done real good.

18. A loose woven cloth is best for dessert wear.

19. Pete, whom you know is reliable, told me I am ably qualified.

20. If I was you, I wouldn't go passed that crumbling building, or you might get hurt bad, and you would be apt to be put in the nearer of our two hospitals.

Rewrite the following sentences, changing the less important idea in each into an adjective clause.

1. Marilyn is a physical education teacher because she is good at athletics.

   _____

2. The mountain air is exhilarating, and it can be cold.

   _____

3. Founded in 1645, Greenby is a well-preserved town.

   _____

4. Even though it is loaded with fat, a hamburger is still my favorite meal.

   _____

5. Job satisfaction is the most important aspect of employment, but salary is a strong consideration too.

   _____

Rewrite the following into one sentence each, making the less important idea into an adverb clause.

1. Be sure to proofread you letter. Do so after you have done the final draft.

   _____

2. Rachel completed her classes in Spanish. She plans to visit Mexico City.

   _____

3. Let's meet for dinner toinght. Let's meet at our usual meeting place, Warner's Cafe.

   _____

4. I would like to attend the Wine Festival. I have to see that Mother is well enough to be left alone.

   _____

5. I am going to marry Jack Evers; he has no money.

   _____

Name _____ Date _____ Class _____

Place an X on the blank in front of any topic that is limited enough for a one-paragraph essay.

_____ 1. My pet peeve is smoking.

_____ 2. My pet peeve is someone's cigarette smoke blowing on me during dinner.

_____ 3. My best friend Hilda is a boa constrictor.

_____ 4. The two-party system in America.

_____ 5. My very favorite movie of all time is. . . .

_____ 6. The discovery of black holes in space.

_____ 7. Several reasons why I am attending Lake College.

_____ 8. My personality trait that will be my best asset in my job is . . .

_____ 9. My aunt Melda is a nice person.

_____ 10. Earning my oun living helps my self-esteem.

Rewrite the following sentences to correct dangling modifiers. Keep the phrase as it is at the front, and rewrite the main clause.

1. After trying to call him several times, the phone number I had was incorrect I discovered.

   _____

2. To catch his limit of trout, a new lure was used by Hal.

   _____

3. Etched right into the glass, our customers can really see our new logo.

   _____

4. Hanging on the line, the sun quickly dried our clothes.

   _____

5. Located downtown, many people find our offices convenient.

   _____

Punctuate the following sentences. Add end punctuation.

1. Did you Mr. Hearns decide to go with Bickerson's plan

2. On page 365 the author asked "Who could answer that charge

3. Mackinac Island a resort island between the peninsulas of Michigan allows no vehicles except emergency vehicles

4. Was C S Stone the founder of this firm

5. The owner of this canoe a fly-tying fisherman is going to be our guide

6. Upon learning of the planned takeover our Chairman Lionel Mendelson called a quick meeting of the Board

7. You should as a rule show respect for the elderly because they have learned many things about good living

8. The wrench costing either $23.98 or $32.00 would be a fine tool to own

9. Ashville a city in North Carolina is a beautiful city that is located in the mountains and draws thousands of tourists

10. In the first place I haven't wanted to anger our clients who expect us to offer them the best price possible

11. The Verhage Corporation which is locally owned is a large company that treats its employees well

12. To corral the horses we had to have someone chase them toward us from behind

13. A traffic island a platform between the lanes is there to protect pedestrians

14. "Who goes there" asked the guard

15. My cousin a French Canadian has been in the U.S. for years

16. Your attitude not your life's condition is what will make you happy

17. Startled Jessica rushed to look out the window trying to see what had caused the noise

18. The movie well directed and well cast should win an award at Cannes where the film festival is held

19. Whoever runs runs at his or her own expense for the County Board

20. Your instructor an underappreciated overworked individual has your best interests in mind

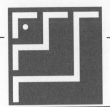

C H A P T E R   1 6

Colons and Semicolons

OVERVIEW

- **The Colon**
- **The Semicolon**

The colon and the semicolon are two marks of punctuation that are often confused. Because the names of these marks sound alike and the marks look somewhat alike, some writers use them interchangeably. Other writers don't use them at all. In this chapter you'll learn how and when to use these important punctuation marks to show the proper relationship between your ideas and to add some variety to your writing.

THE COLON

A colon is like the sounding of trumpets to announce some important event. The colon alerts the reader to pay close attention to what is to follow. The writer is indicating that something noteworthy is about to be said. For this reason the colon is often called the *mark of anticipation.*

DEFINITION   A **colon** is a punctuation mark used to direct the reader's attention to a list, explanation, or quotation that follows.

After an Independent Introductory Clause

Use a colon <u>after an independent introductory clause</u> to introduce something important. Very often, although not necessarily, the introductory clause contains such words as *this, these, thus, as follows,* or *the following,* which are included to make the introductory clause complete.

1. Use a colon to introduce a series, or list, that follows an introductory independent clause.

> The members chosen to represent us are these: Adam Smith, Estelle Jones, and Ted Hughes.

Since the introductory clause must be complete, *these* was added after the verb *are.* Without this addition the list of names would simply complete the clause as subject complements. The presence of a colon in that case would separate the subject complements from the rest of the clause.

> Please send copies of the minutes to the following departments: Personnel, Data Processing, and Accounting.

Again notice why the introductory clause has *the following departments* added. Without these words to complete the first clause, the series items would be only the objects of the preposition *to* and would follow no punctuation. Of course, the list would lose emphasis if not preceded by a colon.

> He has four favorite sporting events: tennis, field hockey, baseball, and volleyball.

Since the introductory statement is a complete clause by itself, it can stand alone, without any completing expression.

2. Use a colon after an introductory clause that precedes a famous or long quotation—one to be emphasized.

> The telegram from Mr. Libowitz said this: "Congratulations on the success of your sales program!"
>
> Patrick Henry is credited with this famous patriotic statement: "Give me liberty or give me death!"

3. Use a colon after a complete clause that introduces a major idea, one that the writer wishes to call attention to.

> The one primary goal we should always strive for is this one: Do your utmost to satisfy the customer.
>
> Probably the most remembered trait of any human is this one: kindness to others.
>
> (*Note: Do* is capitalized because it begins an independent clause after the colon. Do not capitalize the first word of anything following a colon that is less than a complete statement unless the capital letter is there for some other reason.)

Other Colon Uses

1. Use a colon after the salutation of a business letter that uses mixed punctuation style.

    Dear Ms. Halliday: Gentlemen:

2. Use a colon in the attention line or subject line of a business letter.

    ATTENTION: Miss Mary McElroy

    SUBJECT: Changes in Insurance Coverage

3. When expressing time, use a colon with no space between the hours and minutes.

    8:35   10:30

    (*Note:* Do not use a colon with a time expressed in military style, such as *2200 hours.*)

4. When writing a book title with a subtitle, use a colon between them.

    The Secretarial Handbook: An Easy Reference Guide

5. Use a colon between the volume number and page numbers of a reference source when they are not otherwise identified as such.

    You will find that article in the *American Historical Guidebook,* VII: 172–176.

6. Use a colon after a short introductory word, such as *Note, Caution,* or *Wanted.*

    Note: No Smoking Here

7. Generally, space twice after a colon and do not capitalize the next word unless the material that follows is a complete sentence or begins with a word requiring a capital letter.

    She asked for three things: accuracy, dependability, and initiative.

    Please heed the following rule: Clean up your work area before you leave for the day.

You can see from these principles that the colon is not interchangeable with the semicolon, a mark that generally combines independent clauses into compound sentences. A colon often has no independent clause following it; instead, it has a list, a quotation, or an important idea, not necessarily written in a complete clause.

Although you will most likely select the colon for its other uses more often than you select it to introduce something important, you can see that the colon is an effective mark that can help you to draw the reader's attention to a point that warrants emphasis. Using a colon may be a better choice than underlining, using an exclamation point, or using some other method to call attention.

Answer these questions about the colon.

1. The colon and semicolon are very much alike in usage. (True or False)

2. The major use of the colon is _____.

3. In a sentence the colon must be used only after a complete independent clause. (True or False)

4. You may use a colon after a verb, such as in this sentence: Our list now includes: John, Ellen, and Phil. (True or False)

5. Except for its usages in time and titles, you generally double space after a colon. (True or False)

6. You never capitalize the letter after a colon. (True or False)

7. Name the three noteworthy types of information that can be announced by a colon.

8. Where in a letter could a colon be used?

9. A colon is used in a book title with a subtitle. (True or False)

10. Colons usually come between independent clauses. (True or False)

Before you continue, turn to p. 440 to check your answers.

TRY IT OUT: **Do Exercises 16.1 and 16.2, pp. 409–410, to practice using colons. Be sure that you understand colons completely before continuing with the section on semicolons.**

THE SEMICOLON

DEFINITION   A **semicolon** is a punctuation mark that acts like a combination of a period and a comma. A semicolon indicates a stronger pause than a comma but not as strong a break in thought as a period.

A good way to understand the functions of certain marks of punctuation is to think of them as traffic signals. While a comma is like a flashing yellow caution signal and a period like a red stop light, a semicolon can be compared to a blinking red light. You must come to a full stop before continuing, but you don't have to wait as long as you would for a red light to change.

Periods show complete stops with a pause before continuing. A semicolon is often used like a period to show the break between two independent clauses, but the semicolon links the two clauses into a compound sentence.

Although this linking function is the major usage of semicolons, you will see that they can also be used to help clarify some uncommon constructions in a way that no other mark of punctuation can.

1. Semicolons are generally used to link independent clauses. Use a semicolon to replace the conjunction in a compound sentence.

> Mr. Burns is pleased with Dorothy's work; he promoted her to shift leader starting June 1.
>
> They came; they saw; they conquered.

2. A compound sentence with a coordinate conjunction can also have a semicolon instead of a comma preceding the conjunction. Use a semicolon if the sentence is long and has other commas. (This usage is optional. The comma is also acceptable.)

> We planned a trip to Yellowstone National Park for our summer vacation; and to allow us more time at the Park, we flew there and back.

3. Use a semicolon to separate the independent clauses of a compound sentence when they are connected by an adverbial conjunction such as *however*, *then*, and so on. (The semicolon is used because there is no coordinate conjunction.)

> Mr. Jacobson went to Mrs. Harris for the information; then he put together the report.
>
> Orders for the Mini-mixer were unusually large in October; consequently, our stock became depleted.
>
> The Saginaw Bureau wanted to schedule the meeting for March 15; however, there was a conflict at the convention center there.

4. Do not use a semicolon in a complex sentence to separate the adverbial clause from the independent clause.

> When you have secured their order, we will have to work overtime to complete it on time.

TRY IT OUT: **Exercise 16.3, p. 410, will help you test your understanding of the difference between using a semicolon with an adverbial conjunction and using commas around an interrupter. Complete that exercise now.**

Semicolons With Relative Clauses

1. Most adjective clauses follow immediately the nouns that they modify. Use commas to set off nonrestrictive clauses. Use no punctuation if the clause is restrictive.

> Your sister, Maude, who is my partner in bridge, is a very bright woman.
>
> Any mayor who wants to be reelected must listen to all of his constituents, not just a few.

2. An effective writing technique uses a series of adjective clauses that follow the last noun in a sentence and all modify that last noun; use semicolons in this type of series to point out the unusual structure.

> This company is made up of <u>people</u> who are devoted to the ideals of the company; who know that their contributions to the company benefit them as well; who care about the success of this firm; and who feel a part of the whole.

The word *people* is underlined to show that this is the noun modified by the four clauses that follow; notice, too, that even though the clauses are restrictive, the semicolons are still used to call attention to the unusual structure.

3. The same writing technique can be employed with noun clauses, all of which are in a series at the end of the sentence and function as the same parts of the sentence.

> We have to understand that money isn't everything; that success is not really measured in material gain; and that self-satisfaction can be the best success of all.

In this example each noun clause is an object of the infinitive *to understand*.

Other Semicolon Uses

1. Use a semicolon after an introductory clause before an idea or list if the item is preceded by one of these expressions:

for instance	as	that is
for example	namely	that is to say

Use the phrases *for instance* and *for example* to indicate that you are including only a partial list. The other four expressions point out an important idea. Although most lists or major ideas preceded by an introductory clause have a colon as introduction, these expressions introduce the list or major idea and are not actually a part of them. Use a semicolon to signal this unusual situation.

> There is one thing that should be of concern; namely, the customers' needs.

> You should work hard to learn the one skill that is essential to a career; that is to say, you must be capable of using good language practices.

> She has aptitude in several areas; for instance, manual dexterity, logical evaluation, and management of people.

Of course, if one of these expressions <u>does not</u> precede the statement or list, a colon is the appropriate mark of punctuation.

> She has aptitude in three major areas: manual dexterity, logical evaluation, and management of people.

2. Occasionally a series of items will consist of things that require commas within each item. To differentiate the series items, use semicolons. Commas separate the elements but do not show where each series item ends.

> The recent local graduates of Northern University are John Daniels, Highland Park; Fred Douglas, Bloomfield Hills; Karen Darcy, Southgate; and Hilda Maginnis, Livonia.

> Please send copies to Brown, Inc., Dayton, Ohio; Hodges and Sons, Peoria, Illinois; and Stryker Corporation, Kalamazoo, Michigan.

☞ SELF-CHECK 16-2

Answer these questions about the uses of colons and semicolons.

1. Semicolons usually come between clauses, usually independent clauses. (True or False)

2. When can a semicolon be used before a coordinate conjunction in a compound sentence?

3. Because adverbial conjunctions such as *however* have the same function as coordinate conjunctions in compound sentences, a comma is enough punctuation preceding them. (True or False)

4. Always use a semicolon to precede a list or series. (True or False)

5. Do not use a semicolon after an introductory adverbial clause. (True or False)

6. Adjective clauses at the end of an independent clause, all of which modify the last word in the main clause, are separated by commas. (True or False)

7. If your series items already have their own commas, you should use semicolons to separate the series items. (True or False)

8. List the six introductory words or phrases that could precede a list or important idea that would cause you to use a semicolon rather than a colon to precede the list.

9. Semicolons and colons are old-fashioned and out of use today. (True or False)

10. Semicolons and colons are really fairly much alike and are interchangeable. (True or False)

Before you continue, turn to p. 441 to check your answers.

TRY IT OUT: **Exercises 16.4 and 16.5, pp. 411–412, are designed to reinforce your learning about semicolons. Exercise 16.6, p. 412, has short sentences designed to help you to decide whether to use a colon or semicolon—or neither—in various situations. Exercise 16.7, p. 413, has you write your own examples. Exercise 16.8, p. 414, is the Challenge exercise that poses more difficult examples.**

▣ Chapter 16: Colons and Semicolons

● EXERCISE 16.1

Add any necessary commas and other punctuation to the following sentences. If you add any colons, be prepared to explain why. You may have to change some capitalization. There will be no semicolons. Circle any changes you make.

1. I found the article in the *Journal* IX 14–17.

2. The letter began "Gentlemen

3. *The Gossip Sheet* devotes its pages to such sensational stories as these murders catastrophes and scandals.

4. The things any writer needs are a good idea a clear understanding of the idea and a well-conceived outline to work from when writing.

5. President Kennedy said something to this effect "Ask not what your country can do for you Ask instead what you can do for your country."

6. The main advantages of this device are these low maintenance ease of use and low cost.

7. He had planned to arrive at 8 17 but did not arrive until 8 47.

8. The new book that is becoming a best seller has a title and a subtitle which are *Galaxy X Is There Life Out There?*

9. This seems to be the only thing that the company cares about profit at any expense.

10. The following people should see Dean Rand Nancy Stuart Helen Pomeroy Bruce Caldwell and Melanie Johnson.

● EXERCISE 16.2

Punctuate these sentences. Add any necessary capitals. There may be colons, but there will be no semicolons. Circle any changes you make.

1. The list should include staples carbon paper carbon ribbons and ledger sheets.

2. Among words often misspelled are *rhythm vacuum psychology* and *guarantee.*

3. Governor Brown just made this announcement there will be a tax increase this year.

4. Please send copies of this report to Mr. Gordon Brown Douglas and Sons 4016 Hazelton Avenue Tempe AZ 56789.

5. In his address the President said this "Peace will prevail."

6. Please remember this point there is no excuse for a nonchalant attitude about our clients' concerns.

7. An attention line should include a title of respect, such as this ATTENTION Mr. Howard Murphy.

8. Here is a good idea that merits some consideration yesterday is gone tomorrow has not arrived but today is here to be lived.

9. Caution bridge out ahead.

10. My favorite things as a child were my dog my best friend and a ragged teddy bear.

● E X E R C I S E 16.3

Punctuate the following sentences. Remember to use a semicolon before such words as however *only when they are acting as adverbial conjunctions between clauses; otherwise, they are probably acting as interrupters. The comma after the adverbial conjunction is optional. Circle any changes you make.*

1. All power corrupts however absolute power corrupts absolutely.

2. If you get to Dallas however be sure to see James Hanson.

3. He proved however that we are able to accomplish our goal.

4. In all of my lectures however I have stressed the importance of punctuation.

5. When Melville died in 1891 however he had not published his latest book.

6. Be sure to call me however late it is when you get home.

7. Johann worked at Link Company however he really didn't like his job.

8. The cabin cruiser however made the trip in seven hours.

9. I planned to go to England however I couldn't afford the trip.

10. I planned to go to England however expensive the trip was.

11. He had planned to purchase a new car consequently he had looked at several models.

12. He decided to keep his present car nevertheless he still looked at other models.

13. George likes to work outdoors on the other hand he enjoys his enjoys his accounting work too.

14. Send in your order then wait only two weeks for your new lounger.

15. She was pleased therefore with the service guarantee on the appliance.

16. I hope to restore this old house to its original condition whatever the cost might turn out to be.

17. The order was placed after the deadline hence we cannot assure an early delivery.

18. Just tell us the measurements of your office then we can order the new carpet and wallpaper.

19. You may pay cash of course you may also add it to your bill.

20. If you would rather not pay cash of course you may add it to your bill.

● E X E R C I S E   16.4

Add any necessary commas or semicolons to the following sentences. Circle any changes you make.

1. If you understand the types of clauses you will have little difficulty with this exercise.

2. Get lots of rest and eat good not junk foods then you should stay relatively healthy.

3. He is very intense that is he gets deeply involved in things.

4. Inflation has caused prices to rise salaries have risen too.

5. Skiing requires three things namely dexterity persistence and a love of the outdoors.

6. The three cities we visited in Europe were London England Paris France and Madrid Spain.

7. We are looking for applicants who are well trained who enjoy working who realize the value of good customer relations and who really want to work for this particular type of agency.

8. Central heating is not as common in the South as in the North however the climate is quite different.

9. You are an excellent repair person your attention to detail is very good.

10. There are several reasons for our success for example our dedicated staff and our fair management.

11. Ms. Julius was warned about her abuse of the attendance policy however it did not seem to matter to her.

12. Some people prefer ball point pens others however like the felt tip pens.

13. She was as a rule an easy-going person but she could if needed become very assertive about important things.

14. She seemed to work only under pressure that is to say only when absolutely necessary.

15. Good business people know what is important namely good customer relations and good personnel relations.

16. She was however under much pressure to complete the report by three o'clock.

17. Whenever you are late for a payment consequently your deposit will be applied instead.

18. I was famished after completing the marathon moreover I had not eaten breakfast.

19. A reservation by the way is not necessary but if you would rather not have to wait you should call ahead.

20. Our order was received late indeed we no longer had a use for it.

Add any necessary punctuation to these sentences. Circle any changes you make.

1. You have not made your remittance for May consequently you will receive your June issue only after you renew your subscription.

2. Our key people are Susan Gould Advertising Manager Horace Smothers Office Manager and Todd Simons Sales Manager.

3. We had all hoped that the annual picnic would be held at Crane Park but calling too late we found that it was already booked for July 8.

4. To perfect this machine we should run more tests and to ensure its approval we should invite the distributors to the tests.

5. Gymnastics is a sport that is very competitive that requires much training that demands extensive physical conditioning and that needs great power of concentration.

6. I would love to hear a discussion with Jacob the realist Paul the idealist and Herb the poet.

7. She was asked to work overtime accordingly she stayed at her desk until 7 30.

8. He has experience in two types of accounting that is payroll and federal tax.

9. When you have dictated those letters Ms. Adamson please let me know I will get them out today.

10. Try to think of some new advertising methods for instance billboards or skywriting.

Add any necessary punctuation to these sentences. Circle any changes you make.

1. This is a good week we have topped our October quota.

2. We listed three mattress sets for the sale regular queen and king sizes.

3. The following prices were quoted $5.98 $7.29 and $9.95.

4. Marc Anthony addressed his audience this way "Friends Romans countrymen lend me your ears."

5. We have manufactured the product the rest is up to the salespeople.

6. She was a dedicated worker however she valued her personal life more than her job.

7. If he has any one philosophy of life it is this The best defense is a good offense.

8. Danger Male Chauvinist at Work.

9. Elephants seem to be an endangered species however we are limiting import of ivory to try to stop the slaughter.

10. A budget can be a useful tool if it is used wisely it should however be flexible and realistic or it can become a weapon.

● E X E R C I S E 16.7

Write sentences that demonstrate each of these punctuation usages.

1. Write a sentence that has a colon to introduce something very important.

2. Write an attention line from a business letter.

3. Write a sentence using a colon to introduce an idea that is an independent clause.

4. Write a compound sentence with an adverbial conjunction that is preceded by a semicolon.

5. Write a compound sentence that has no coordinate conjunction, using instead a semicolon.

6. Write a sentence that ends with a series of adjective clauses, all of which modify the last noun in the main clause.

7. Write a sentence that uses a semicolon before a series that is preceded by *namely*.

8. Write a sentence that uses semicolons between series items that contain their own commas and would be confusing without the semicolons.

Add any necessary punctuation to these sentences. Watch especially for situations that require semicolons or colons. As usual, there may be sentences that require no punctuation. Circle any changes you make.

1. Please send us the following items one walnut-grain desk Model No. 4287 two desk chairs wood Model No. 1492 one fire file green Model No. 243 and one four-drawer file black Model No. 9786.

2. While trying to prepare the year-end report our accountant found an error in posting therefore she discovered why there had been a $1400 error.

3. Mr. Vance had called the Brooklyn office about the delayed order and found that it had been shipped to North Dakota not South Dakota.

4. Ms. Black frequently asks us to do research for example a recent assignment asked us to look in these magazines the *Atlantic* 214 79–84 *Senior Scholastic* 49 23-25 and *Time* 147 114–117.

5. The quartet could play these instruments Tom Ells clarinet and saxophone Bill Dodd violin and guitar Fred Snow piano and drums and Hal Brooks trombone and trumpet.

6. Before you can understand basic accounting you must learn the meanings of these terms asset liability and owner's equity.

7. This benefit package is better than most that you will find it includes life insurance health insurance dental coverage and a disability plan.

8. This item is not just a component on the contrary it is a complete unit that is self-sufficient.

9. Our last buying trip took us to New York Boston Chicago and San Francisco.

10. Engineers who wish to save time in preparation and money in estimating should consider this new system.

11. Whenever you consider a new purchase look beyond the immediate cost to such things as these durability availability of guarantees maintenance and reliability of the manufacturers.

12. Because you want your car to last longer be sure to take it to a service station for tune-ups lubrications and seasonal checks.

13. You may have studied hard and gained a good technical background but if you want to be successful in an interview you must demonstrate self-confidence.

14. Mail the enclosed card for information there is no obligation.

15. The pessimistic idea of the Peter Principle is this We all reach our levels of incompetence.

16. Mr. Emerson has admired three great people Lincoln Kennedy and M. L. King.

17. Mr. Emerson named three idols of his that is Lincoln Kennedy and M. L. King.

18. Before the Pilgrims landed at Plymouth Rock there were black men in America.

19. Ken likes a woman who is intelligent who is witty and who is self-assured.

20. Ken likes a woman who is intelligent witty and self-assured.

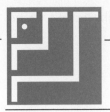

C H A P T E R   1 7

Other Marks
of Punctuation

OVERVIEW

- **Dashes**
- **Parentheses**
- **Quotation Marks**

This chapter covers the other marks of punctuation—dashes, parentheses, and quotation marks. Although these marks are used less frequently than commas and some other punctuation, they are no less important. Like the more frequently used punctuation marks, these marks can help you to make your writing clear and easy to read. As you work to make your writing style more sophisticated and varied, you will want to use some of these punctuation techniques.

DASHES

A dash may be used occasionally to replace another mark of punctuation when using the other mark would be misleading or repetitive. However, the primary use of a dash is to add emphasis.

DEFINITION A **dash** is a punctuation mark that can be used singly or in pairs to emphasize a word or phrase that interrupts the flow of a sentence.

Dashes can replace commas for either clarity or emphasis, but dashes would replace parentheses for emphasis only.

The Dash for Emphasis or Clarity

1. Use a dash to show a <u>major</u> break in thought or to insert a personal comment.

> I want—at least I think I do—to retire by the time I am forty.
>
> Queen Anne's lace—a lovely flower for arrangements—is really the wild carrot.
>
> We appealed to the judge—with what results?

2. Use the dash to emphasize an explanatory phrase or an appositive. This usage is the place where the dash is most often abused. Be very stingy with this usage, saving it for only the most important writing situations.

> Tonight we are introducing our latest development in the typewriter—the Model 1435.
>
> The Reverend Martin Luther King, Jr.—a well-known civil rights crusader—was the first in America to use passive resistance as a large-scale protest technique.

3. Use a dash before a clause that explains a series that precedes it. If the order were reversed, a colon would have come before the series.

> Honesty, understanding, and compromise—these are important traits of a politician.
>
> *but*
>
> The important traits of a politician are these: honesty, understanding, and compromise.

4. Use dashes to set off explanatory phrases that have other commas within them. With no internal commas these phrases would need only commas on either side.

> Flatfish—sole, halibut, and flounder—swim on their sides.
>
> The most effective speakers—that is, those who really capture the attention of the audience—usually use few notes and never read their speeches.

5. Use the dash after words such as *namely* or *that is* when a tabulation follows. With no tabulation, use only a comma.

> Farm prices are influenced by several things; namely—
>
> 1. the weather
> 2. foreign trade demands
> 3. parity

As you learned in Chapter 16, without the introductory words, such as *namely,* you would use a colon before the list, tabulated or not.

The Dash With Other Punctuation

1. If the dash follows an abbreviation, retain the period.

   We sent it c.o.d.—as you had so carefully asked.

2. If the material set off by dashes requires a question mark or exclamation point, keep that mark before the dash. Do not retain a period, however.

   Jane Allison—do you know her?—is the one who said that about our office.

   Jane Allison—I knew her at Emerson's—said that about our office.

3. If a closing dash would occur where otherwise a semicolon, colon, or parenthesis would be used, omit the dash and use the other mark.

   I like Sam Rosen—you know him; he lives next door to me.

   Here is a good axiom—at least, I think so: Today is the first day of the rest of your life.

SELF-CHECK 17-1

Answer these questions.

1. If a series comes <u>before</u> the summary clause, use a _____ after the series.

2. If a series comes <u>after</u> the introductory summary clause, as it usually does, use a _____.

3. Use dashes to set off an explanatory phrase or appositive when

   _____ or _____.

4. Before a tabulation use a _____ if there is an expression such as *namely* or *for example* before it.

5. Before a tabulation that has no explanatory expression such as *namely* or *that is,* the more common mark that would be used is a

   _____.

Before you continue, turn to p. 441 to check your answers.

TRY IT OUT: **Go to Exercises 17.1 and 17.2, pp. 425–426, for practice in using the dash. Type these sentences to be certain that you know the proper spacing and to practice using other punctuation with the dashes.**

PARENTHESES

Parentheses can be used in some of the same places where you would use dashes. One principle determines the differences. Material set off by dashes is generally given more emphasis than material set off by parentheses.

DEFINITION **Parentheses** are punctuation marks that work in pairs to set off words, phrases, or clauses. They add facts to a statement without increasing emphasis or essentially altering the meaning.

Parentheses With Nonessential Material

1. Use parentheses to set off words, phrases, or clauses that are not essential to the thought expressed and that need no special emphasis.

> Carver Hall (it used to be called Central Hall) is where the program will be held.
>
> We had few (four) inquiries about Model No. 14 last year.

2. Use parentheses for reference notes, dates, or instructions within another sentence.

> You will notice (see Appendix I attached) that we did a great deal of research on this product.
>
> When the Seattle branch opened (1978), we transferred Mr. Roberts to that office.
>
> The figures supporting this statement (see box, page 84) are quite impressive.

3. In formal documents where amounts are expressed in both words and figures, use parentheses to enclose the figures.

> We purchased five thousand (5000) units of this product at a cost of eight hundred dollars ($800).

4. Use parentheses to enclose letters or figures in an enumeration. If tabulated, usually no parentheses are used but only the figures or letters followed by periods.

> You would be wise to research the services of a door-to-door salesperson by (1) calling the Better Business Bureau, (2) calling the references supplied, and (3) carefully reading the contract.
>
> (*Note:* There are no periods after the numbers here because it is connected material, not a tabulation.)
>
> 1. The three branches of the federal government are (a) the executive, (b) the legislative, and (c) the judicial.
>
> (*Note:* The letters are used here because the item is already part of a numbered list.)

Parentheses With Capitalization and Other Punctuation

1. Do not capitalize the first word of a sentence in parentheses that appears in the middle of a sentence.

   > I met with Shana Williams (she is our new proofreader) at the agency Open House.

   <u>Do</u> capitalize the first word of a sentence in parentheses if it is a completely separate sentence or it begins with a word that requires capitalization.

   > I met with Shana Williams at the agency Open House. (She is our new proofreader.)

2. Do not use a period before the closing parenthesis unless it is for an abbreviation or is a totally separate sentence enclosed by parentheses.

   > The price I quoted you (f.o.b.) is the best I can do.
   >
   > *but*
   >
   > The price is f.o.b. (It is the best I can do.)

3. If the sentence containing the material in parentheses requires punctuation after the parenthetical material, place the punctuation outside the ending parenthesis.

   > If I see Billy Bob (my assistant), I will have him call you right away.
   >
   > Look in the Yellow Pages (see p. 127); you will find their business hours listed there.

4. Use a question mark or exclamation point inside the parentheses if the main sentence ends with a different mark, such as a period. If both require the same mark, use only the one at the end of the complete sentence.

   > The speaker at my session (didn't I see you there?) said that he is a self-educated man.
   >
   > Did you hear the speaker (I didn't see you at that session) say he is a self-educated man?

5. When the material in parentheses is a separate sentence altogether from the rest of the written material, it should be treated as such within the parentheses; that is, begin with a capital letter and end with closing punctuation within the parentheses.

   > Martin Luther King, Jr., was dedicated to the Civil Rights movement. (He was also a dedicated minister.) He did much to forward the cause of justice for minorities.

Double Parentheses

Use brackets to set off material needing parentheses when parentheses are already enclosing a larger section of material. This situation is similar to the principle of double and single quotation marks.

> Most Presidents age a great deal while in office. (At the end of the Civil War [1865] Abraham Lincoln looked much older than he had just a few years earlier.)

Check your knowledge of the rules governing parentheses by answering the following questions.

1. Parentheses are used to emphasize explanatory material or appositives. (True or False)

2. If an amount in formal writing is given in both words and figures, use parentheses to enclose the amount that is stated in

   _____.

3. In an enumeration in connected material rather than a tabulated enumeration, should periods be used after the numbers enclosed in parentheses? (Yes or No)

4. Usually you (would/would not) capitalize the first word of a sentence enclosed in parentheses unless it was separate from the other material.

5. You (seldom/often) use a period before the closing parenthesis when the material is part of another sentence.

6. You would not find a comma, dash, a colon, or a semicolon right before the second parenthesis in a sentence. (True or False)

7. When the material in parentheses is an entirely separate sentence

   from others, it should begin _____ and

   end _____.

8. The singular form of the word *parentheses* is spelled

   _____.

9. Instead of using another set of parentheses to enclose something

   within parentheses, you would use _____.

10. The rules governing the uses of parentheses shatter a well-known principle about using capital letters. What is it?

Before you continue, turn to p. 441 to check your answers.

TRY IT OUT: **Do Exercises 17.3 and 17.4, pp. 426–427, to practice using parentheses. Type these sentences on other paper to practice the related punctuation and capitalization rules, as well as to practice spacing.**

QUOTATION MARKS

Quotation marks are used primarily to signal to the reader that the enclosed material is taken from another speaker or writer. However, quotation marks have a few other uses that are illustrated in the following sections.

DEFINITION **Quotation marks** set off short quotations, special terms, and titles of articles, songs, television programs, chapters, and essays.

Quotation Marks With Quoted Spoken or Written Material

1. Use quotation marks around the material when using the exact words of someone else.

   > Mr. Brenner stated, "I am very pleased with the quick service your company provides us."

   > The telegram said: "Rush this order today."

   > On page 38 the author writes, "We are eternally indebted to Henry Ford for the concept of the assembly line."

2. Do <u>not</u> use quotation marks if the original statement is being reworded. Often these indirect quotations will be preceded by *that*. Contrast these examples with those in the previous rule.

   > Mr. Bunson said that he is pleased with our quick service.

   > The telegram said to rush the order today.

   > On page 38 that author writes that we owe much to Henry Ford for beginning the assembly line.

3. Use standard punctuation and capitalization rules with material in quotation marks.

   a. If the material is a complete sentence, punctuation it as such.

   > Mary replied, "I mailed it today."

   > Josh asked, "Who found that file?"

   b. When a complete quoted sentence is followed by explanatory material, use a comma to set the quotation off from the rest of the sentence unless it would require a question mark or an exclamation point.

   > "You may leave now," said the manager.

   > "Who called for me?" asked Damian.

   > "I don't care!" shouted Herb.

   c. Place periods and commas inside the closing quotation mark, but place semicolons and colons outside.

Last week you said, "I have finished this report"; however, this week you found another section incomplete.

Look for the following things in the article, "Twenty Attributes of a Good Employee": attitude, work habits, and personality.

d. Place question marks and exclamation points inside the quotation marks when they relate to the quotation; otherwise place the marks outside the quotation mark.

Mable asked, "Who is responsible for this?"

Did she say, "Hap is responsible"?

e. When a quoted sentence falls at the end of a larger sentence, do <u>not</u> use double punctuation. Use the mark that goes with the quotation unless the second mark is a question mark or an exclamation point. In a case with both of these marks being required, use both.

Why did Bill say, "Has Mr. Jordan been invited?" [The second question mark is unnecessary.]

Don't miss the article "Who Goes Home Early?"! [both marks needed]

4. If a quoted statement is broken by explanatory material, set off the explanation with commas, and do not begin the second part with a capital letter unless it is a word requiring capitalization for some other reason.

"Call me at noon," he said, "and I should have the results of your tests."

5. When writing a dialogue between two speakers, make a new paragraph for each change of speaker.

"Did you," asked Helen, "write the letter to Blake?"

"I haven't had time," answered Eloise.

6. In a quotation more than one sentence long, use the quotation marks to begin the first sentence, and place the end mark to follow the entire quotation, even if the quotation is several paragraphs long.

The article continued, "We should be sorry to see a change in the testing programs for these appliances. It seems that we need each test that we now do to assure our customers quality merchandise."

7. To enclose a quotation within another quotation, use a single mark (an apostrophe) on either side of the internal quotation.

Mr. Jepsen announced, "The President said in his address, 'I will do all I can to reduce taxes for the small businesses of this country.'"

Quotation Marks With Coined Terms

Use quotation marks around slang words, technical or trade terms, and humorously used words to show the unusual usages, but avoid overuse of any of these unusual word usages.

The first step is to "boot up" the computer.

A genuine madras print is guaranteed to "run" when washed.

Comics work just for the "pun" of it.

Quotation Marks With Titles

Use quotation marks around the titles of articles, songs, single television programs, chapters, and essays. (Underscore or use italics for the titles of complete works that have subparts.)

I really like "His Word Is True" from the album *John Chaplin's Greatest Hits.*

Did you read "Seven Returned" in this week's issue of *United States' News*?

I saw "The Revere Family" on television last night from the series *The Immigrants.*

Ellipses for Missing Words

To show an omission from a direct quotation, use **ellipses** in place of the missing words. Three dots (periods) would replace the omitted words within a sentence. Four dots indicate that the quotation's end is missing; however, should the quotation have ended with a question mark or exclamation point, that mark is used instead of the fourth dot.

The *New York Times* says of this new book, "Mr. Jones has written a book that is certainly . . . a best seller."

The song does say, "Fools rush in . . . ."

It seems that fifty times a day Mary Ellen asks, "Do you know where . . . ?"

SELF-CHECK 17-3

Answer the following questions to see if you can easily recall the basic rules for using quotation marks.

1. Direct quotations are the _____ words of someone else.

2. You must use quotation marks to recognize someone else's exact spoken or written words. (True or False)

3. Any quotation that is a complete sentence should begin with a

   _____ letter when the quotation stands separately.

4. (Do/Do not) put a period after a quoted statement unless it ends the complete sentence.

5. A _____ or a _____ is always placed inside the last quotation mark. (punctuation)

6. A _____ or a _____ is always placed outside the last quotation mark. (punctuation)

7. A question mark or an exclamation point is placed (inside/outside) the end quotation mark if it relates to the quotation itself.

8. You (often/seldom) have two end marks of punctuation when the quotation ends the sentence.

9. When a quotation consists of more than one sentence, use (one/several) set(s) of quotation marks.

10. To enclose a quotation within a quotation, use _____

_____ .

11. To indicate that a word is used as a slang word, you would use (all capital letters/quotation marks).

12. Since quotation marks are used around titles of articles or the subparts of larger things, the larger title should be

_____ or _____ .

13. Ellipses indicate _____ .

14. Four consecutive dots (periods) indicate that _____

_____ .

15. For any punctuation not covered in this textbook, you should (guess/use a reference manual).

Before you continue, turn to p. 442 to check your answers.

TRY IT OUT: **Complete Exercises 17.5 and 17.6, pp. 427–428, for practice with quoted material. You can test your understanding of the uses of dashes, parentheses, and quotation marks by writing the sentences required by Exercise 17.7, pp. 429–430. Exercise 17.8, p. 430, is a Challenge exercise that poses more difficult tasks.**

Chapter 17: Other Marks of Punctuation

Insert any necessary punctuation into these sentences. Look especially for situations requiring the use of the dash. Circle any changes you make.

1. Snow sleet wind and hail these are all expected conditions for winter in the Midwest.

2. Terrible driving conditions heavy snow sleet ice storms call for extreme caution.

3. Edward Knowles he is Mrs. Thomas' brother-in-law just won the lottery.

4. When you plan your monthly budget don't forget the most important investment your savings account.

5. Rice noodles dressing these can be welcome substitutes for that old American standby the potato.

6. The chassis in other words, the frame is the basic framework of a car.

7. A *davenport* nowadays known as a sofa is also the name used for a type of compact writing desk that was used in the cabin of a ship's captain.

8. Mr. Adams wants everyone to attend the staff meeting executives as well as support staff.

9. Television radio newspapers these are all included in the term *mass media.*

10. Isadora Duncan a very unusual lady to say the least was an imaginative dancer.

Add any necessary punctuation, including dashes. You may need a colon or semicolon in some sentences. Circle any changes you make.

1. It is only reasonable at least it seems so to me to ask that you report to work on time.

2. Please consult at least three reference works namely

    1. *Better Business Practice*
    2. *Modern Small Business*
    3. *Hogart's Guide to Merchandising*

3. Please consult these reference books

    1. *Better Business Practice*
    2. *Modern Small Business*
    3. *Hogart's Guide to Merchandising*

4. Kennedy King and Lincoln these three men are famous American heroes from recent times.

5. These three men have become heroes in the recent past in America Kennedy King and Lincoln.

6. Three men Kennedy King and Lincoln have become American heroes in the recent past.

7. The Grand Canyon you have been there haven't you is certainly a breathtaking sight.

8. We left at six that's 6 a.m. and drove for twelve hours.

9. Three sports that is football baseball and hockey are very popular spectator sports.

10. There are three popular spectator sports that is football basketball and hockey.

11. People enjoy watching these three sports football baseball and hockey.

12. In order of preference people enjoy watching three sports that is

    1. football
    2. baseball
    3. hockey

13. While learning to roller blade I took many hard and I mean hard falls.

14. Sickness poverty and despair these three often seem to occur together.

15. Probably one of the most important skills an office worker can have is one of organization being able to set priorities!

● E X E R C I S E   17.3

Add any necessary punctuation to these sentences. Use no dashes. Watch for situations that may require parentheses or changes in capitalization. Circle any changes you make.

1. The color combinations available for these drapes are 1 black and white 2 green and gold 3 red and white and 4 brown and beige.

2. Simply return the order blank it is printed on the back page of the catalog and your order will be sent to you within two weeks.

3. I agree to pay Title Bond and Mortgage Three Thousand Dollars $3000.

4. Charles Weston he is an excellent accountant will speak to us about the new tax reform bill.

5. If you pay the fee $45 you may use the facilities for two months.

6. Please have your assistant by the way who is that call me before Tuesday to arrange the seminar.

7. I will plan to see you on Friday January 19 isn't that your birthday we can settle the details then.

8. The Shakers this sect was founded 1747 in England are not a very common group here.

9. Consult the *Writer's Handbook* see page 192 to find out how to handle that problem.

10. Because your application was submitted too late for consideration the last date was July 1 we cannot consider you for the position.

● E X E R C I S E   1 7 . 4

On a separate sheet of paper, add any necessary parentheses and other punctuation or capitalization to the following sentences. Use no dashes. Circle any changes you make.

1. To relieve the symptoms you have been having you may want to do any of these things 1 reduce the prescribed amount by one-half 2 discontinue the medication or 3 continue with this medication and also take Eoprin.

2. The method of shipment you requested c.o.d. is more expensive than parcel post.

3. Please call our purchasing agent her name is Sarah Forbes she can be reached at 492-7865.

4. Fifty-five dollars $55 is the last offer we are able to make.

5. The court hearing has been postponed again this time it has been set for September 22 as I had requested from Judge Olds.

6. Did you send the letter to Harold Wilson or is it Wilton

7. I worked yesterday until 8 p.m. it seemed like 2 a.m.

8. When I last saw you wasn't that five years ago you said that you were considering a transfer to Hawaii some day.

9. His mother-in-law she's not the "typical" kind has been helping me set up a new filing system.

10. William Springer 1902–1972 founded this company he started it in his barn before any other people had even thought of an "automatic" dishwasher.

● E X E R C I S E   1 7 . 5

Add any quotation marks, end punctuation, and other necessary punctuation or capitalization to the following sentences.

1. Ralph Waite commenting on the blizzard said We have not had such a storm in this century

2. Ralph Waite said that this is the worst storm we have had in this century

3. In his recent article Professor Maine remarked Inflation is an established fact in an industrialized society

4. Who asked Ms. Black would be able to attend the United Fund annual dinner to represent our office

5. We made our quota shouted Mr. Nelson

6. Was Hamlet contemplating suicide when he said to be or not to be, that is the question

7. Stop telling me I told you so

8. Have you seen the series Century 21 on television

9. I read Women on the Move in this issue of *World News*

10. How many requests asked Bob Have we had for information about the Delta

11. Seventeen cards came in this week replied Melanie

12. Who wanted to know and asked Why do we do it this way

13. In his lecture Professor Belcoe said One great American Martin Luther King Jr. said I have a dream . . .

14. Being courteous is a must in any business transaction

15. Mr. Jasper inquired Did you mark Fragile on the package

● **EXERCISE 17.6**

Add any necessary quotation marks and other punctuation, including end punctuation, to the following sentences. Circle any changes you make.

1. The package labeled Special Handling should be mailed today

2. Mr. Krim the public accountant remarked I have not been able to find the reason for the error

3. A measurement called degree-day is used to plan heating needs for large buildings

4. Will you asked Mr. Green send these orders Rush

5. The program It's a Deal is very popular on television this year, even in reruns

6. Ms. Halloway said she was late for work today because her dog hid her car keys

7. Ms. Halloway said I was late for work because my dog hid my keys

8. Did she say I think I have the mumps

9. The author wrote America has come a long way from the days of inhumane child labor practices

10. A con man is one who tries to cheat others by deceit

11. Oh no shouted Mr Williams I forgot to enclose the application form

12. Sarah thought he was a real dweeb but she tried to show him respect anyway

13. Will you ask Emily to play the song A Forgotton Memory

14. Sorry was the only thing Tom had to say

15. Did someone here shout help

● E X E R C I S E   1 7 . 7

In the space provided, demonstrate your knowledge of the use of dashes, parentheses, and quotation marks by writing ten correctly punctuated sentences as indicated by the following.

1. Write a sentence using a dash before a tabulated list that is preceded by an explanatory clause that ends with the words *for example.*

   _____

   _____

2. Write a sentence that uses dashes around an appositive that contains its own commas.

   _____

   _____

3. Write a sentence that uses a dash before a clause that explains a series that precedes it.

   _____

   _____

4. Write a sentence that uses parentheses around an opinionated clause that is inserted within another sentence.

   _____

   _____

5. Write a sentence that uses parentheses around the letters that indicate an enumeration in connected material that is not tabulated.

   _____

   _____

6. Write three sentences, the middle of which is enclosed in parentheses because it is quite unrelated.

   _____

   _____

7. Write a direct quotation that is a question.

   _____

   _____

8. Write a direct quotation of one sentence that is interrupted by the explanation of who said it, such as *said Bob.*

   _____

   _____

9. Write a sentence that contains a quotation that is not direct but is a rewording of the speaker's words.

_____

_____

10. Write sentence that contains a direct quotation within another quotation.

_____

_____

● **EXERCISE 17.8** **CHALLENGE**

On a separate sheet of paper, add any necessary punctuation—including dashes, parentheses, and quotation marks—to these sentences. Circle any changes you make.

1. Red white and blue these are patriotic colors for Americans

2. The American flag has always had thirteen stripes these stand for the original thirteen colonies but since the 1950s has had fifty stars

3. When asked Claire did we receive the order from Byrd Co

4. People interested in ecology and there are more every day are really worried about the environment

5. Mr. Marr asked us to soft-pedal the disadvantages of the new vacation schedule

6. In Workers Choose Their Own Hours in this month's Business World the author states There is less absenteeism under this new system of varied work scheduling

7. Those students tested seventh ninth and eleventh graders showed significant improvement over last year's students

8. The song Golden Eagle is really about an independent person not an eagle

9. Malcolm Hughett he is my cousin by the way has just published a new novel that is selling well

10. The brochure see page 4 states This revolutionary new automobile sells for under ten thousand dollars $10,000

11. One dime that's right just one thin dime will enroll you in this money-saving program

12. How can you even ask Am I invited

13. When answering a business phone don't ask Who is this but say May I tell Ms. Smith who is calling

14. Omar Sharif he's a world-renowned master bridge player is probably best known for his movie roles such as that in Lawrence of Arabia

15. How does the quotation A rose by any other name end

⊡ Periodic Review: Chapters 16–17

Tell whether each of the following is a fragment (F), a run-on (RO), or a sentence (S).

_____ 1. A man who has learned about life by taking some hard knocks and surviving them to continue on.

_____ 2. The wicked witch, therefore, was punished for her bad behavior; that doesn't always happen in real life.

_____ 3. I love fairy tales, however, they don't usually reflect reality.

_____ 4. He ran for the office, he was elected.

_____ 5. Whoever wants to know the answers and whomever we select to represent us.

Write true *for each true statement or* false *for any statement not completely true.*

_____ 1. Grammar is the study of the structures of a language.

_____ 2. The word *different* should not be followed by the word *than.*

_____ 3. An adjective can be only one word, but a phrase or a clause can function as an adjective also.

_____ 4. Choosing which pronoun to use is best done by what "sounds right."

_____ 5. Most prepositional phrases are set off with commas.

_____ 6. A good writer will stick to mostly all simple or compound sentences.

_____ 7. You will often find the direct object following a linking verb.

_____ 8. The word *effect* is a verb only when the words *cause* or *bring about* could replace it in the clause.

_____ 9. Always look for the subject before you look for the verb.

_____ 10. The word *costed* is the past tense form of *cost.*

_____ 11. Always change *-y* to *-i* before adding any ending (suffix) to a base word that ends in *-y.*

_____ 12. Semicolons and colons are interchangeable marks of punctuation.

_____ 13. Some plural possessive forms end *'s.*

_____ 14. Not every clause can be a sentence by itself.

_____ 15. Parallel construction is the use of grammatically alike parts in a series.

Add all necessary punctuation to the following sentences.

1. My three goals are 1 an MBA degree 2 a high-paying job and 3 a happy family life

2. Arthur Hills a playwright loves Ireland which is verdant

3. Determined to win the horse galloped past all others which didn't seem to have the same drive

4. My office phone which is an old model has a very noisy bell which usually startles me frighteningly

5. Roger together with his department head left for San Jose California on the early flight this morning

6. I despise this haircut Jane cried in a frustrated manner

7. Three people Ogden Harold and Frank are our delegates

8. If I may I would like to take time off in July depending on other people's plans

9. She had however not mastered the rules she was unable to complete the exam

10. She had only one goal in life to marry for money

11. Tractors trucks and technicians these are what India needs

12. Raising giant vegetables seems to be a hobby for our lawyer Thad Russell who in other respects is a workaholic

13. Saving well worn well read books Gerald has had to add a room onto his house to store them

14. You should if you are unhappy search for other employment Miss Fitch

15. Vera was nevertheless a good machinist and was easygoing

16. The riel or Cambodia's monetary unit is worth very little in U S dollars

17. Whoever tore off the calendar sheet tore off two at once jumping us ahead a month too many

18. April showers along with winter snows give Wisconsin a wet climate which makes for good farming

19. In Volume III page 23 I learned something important namely the value of solar power

20. Our democracy is a form of government that encourages people to think for themselves that creates a safe climate for freethinkers to express themselves that protects any minority from the will of the majority and that has checks to guard against anarchy or totalitarianism

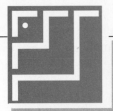

U N I T   4   **Connecting Sentences**

Chapter 14: Steps to a Well-Written Paragraph

Self-Check 14–1, p. 354 (partial lists)

1. Cooking, Parents Without Partners, model airplanes, stamp collecting, reading

2. Amil Rasch, my brother Steve, my dad, my Accounting I instructor, our minister

3. Working at Pizza Hut, juggling both work and school, employment chances in California, sharing household chores, living with a roommate

4. The two-party system, civil unrest in the Middle East, population explosion, changes in police practices, the European Common Market

5. Malcolm X, the seige of Leningrad, effects of the steam engine, the Stryker bed frame, discovery of the North Pole

Self-Check 14–2, p. 355

1. There are many types of hobbies.
   A hobby is a good thing to have.
   Everybody should have a hobby.
   My hobby is stamp collecting.
   A hobby can be very expensive.

2. My mother taught me to be kind to everybody.
   My mother taught me to respect older people.
   To be honest is what my mother stressed to me.
   My mom made me learn to stick to something without giving up.
   My mother wanted me to learn the value of other people's property and to have respect for it.

Self-Check 14–3, p. 357

1. Can provide relaxation
   Can provide outside interest, diversion, not bored
   Can be educational—learn info, learn skills
   Can meet new people
   Can travel to conventions, speciality shops, etc.
   Hobbies are lots of fun
   Can bring a family more together—include others in your interest
   Sometimes too time-consuming, you neglect other things—other people
   Can be profitable
   Can earn money by making things
   Could earn $ by teaching your skills to others

2. Was born in 1940s
   She came from a big family, hard workers. They weren't quitters.
   She herself didn't leave things undone—dishes done, beds made, etc.
   My mother is kind to everyone equally
   Worked at church, Sunday School 28 yrs.
   Tore out knitting several times untill the work satisfied her
   Followed up to see what my homework assignments were and then
      checked to see finished work <u>before</u> I could watch TV, etc.
   She sewed all of my clothes.
   When I got discouraged—I wasn't very good—wouldn't let me quit
      gymnastics. Had to finish Spring Session. "We made a committment,
      took a class space."

Self-Check 14–4, p. 359

1. ~~Can provide relaxation~~   *too "simple"*
   *Can provide outside interest, diversion, not bored
   *Can be educational—learn info, learn skills
   Can meet new people
   Can travel to conventions, specialty shops, etc.
   ~~Hobbies are lots of fun~~   *vague, not related*
   Can bring a family more together—include others in your interest
   hyphen?
   Sometimes too time-consuming, you neglect   *contrast?*
      other things—other people
   sp?
   *Can be profitable
   Can earn money be making things
   Could earn $ by teaching your skills to others

Make it the
last sent.   *(lead to the conclusion)?*
            Rewrite topic: These reasons all
                        show that a hobby can be
                        beneficial. ~~*as well as fun*~~

2. ~~Was born in 1940s~~
   ~~She came from a big family, hard workers. They~~
      ~~weren't quitters.~~
   * She herself didn't leave things undone—dishes done, beds made, etc.
   ~~My mother is kind to everyone equally~~
   volunteered
   Worked at church, Sunday School 28 yrs.   *(continuously)*   *When sewing took*
   Tore out knitting several times untill the work satisfied her   *time to fit to us—lots.*
   * Followed up to see what my homework assignments were and then
      checked to see finished work <u>before</u> I could watch TV, etc.
   She sewed all of my clothes.
   * When I got discouraged—I wasn't very good—wouldn't let me finish
      gymnastics. Had to finish Spring Session. "We made a committment,
      took a class space."

She was persistent
in her own
endeavors.

Rewrite topic? By example, and in her

teaching ⎤ ⎡*training my mother taught me*
parenting ⎦ *to be persistent.*

persistence?

others: to refuse to give up when faced with opposition
endure, prevail

~~*Always stayed up untill I got home at night.*~~

Self-Check 14–5, p. 360

1. A hobby can provide outside interests and diversions so that you won't ever be accused of being bored.

   Not only will you spend time learning about and doing your hobby, but you also can travel to conventions and/or specialty shops to find more information or materials.

   A person with a hobby can interest other family members too, causing activities in which the whole family can participate.

   You can meet new people who have your same interests.

   Some hobbies have activities that hone skills, such as woodworking, knitting, or ~~sewing~~ cooking.

   You can earn money by creating things or by teaching your acquired skills to others.

2. My mother taught me persistence not only in her instruction but also by example.

   In her own life she ~~demonstrated showed~~ was a person who didn't give up, didn't slack off.

   Her work was not left unfinished.

   She had the dishes done, beds made, and errands run.

   She returned all phone calls promptly.

   Her diligence is evident in that she volunteered as a Sunday School Teacher for 28 continuous years.

   That the knitting was flawless and that our clothes that she made fit well were important to her.

   I sometimes unwillingly, was made to endure. No television or telephone calls for me, until my homework for each class was done <u>and checked over</u> by mom.

   Discovering I wasn't an Olympic gymnast after six weeks of lessons, I wanted to quite, but because "We made a committment and took up a place in the class," I stayed to the end of that session of lessons.

bad logic—you won't face boredom since a hobby can provide ouside interests and activities.

↓

(CX) 1. A hobby can ~~provide outside interests and~~ diversions ~~so that~~ you won't ~~ever be accused of being~~ bored.

participating in

(CP) Not only will you spend time learning about and ~~doing~~ your hobby, but you also can travel to conventions and/or specialty shops to find more information or materials.

N clause? Whoever has the hobby

(CX) A person with a hobby can interest other family members too, causing activities in which the whole family can participate.

(CX) You can meet new people who have your same interests.

wrong word?

(CX) Some hobbies have activities that hone skills, such as woodworking, knitting, or ~~sewing~~ cooking.

(S) You can earn money be creating things or by teaching your acquired skills to others.

↑

Examples: sell your knitted items, cater dinners, or sell cakes; make furniture or toys.

hobby-pastime
avocation
activity
interest

weak {   *Topic sentence at end: You can see ~~from the above~~ that a hobby can be very beneficial as well as fun.*

by   even more importantly

(S) 2. My mother taught me persistence not only ~~in her~~ instruction but ~~also~~ by example.

(CX) In her own life she ~~demonstrated~~ showed was a person who didn't give up, didn't slack off. *slang*

Too many in a row 〈 (S) Her work was not left unfinished.

(S) She had the dishes done, beds made, and errands run.

(S) She returned all phone calls promptly.

all caps?

(CX) Her diligence is evident in that she volunteered as a Sunday School Teacher for 28 continuous years.

(CX) That the knitting was flawless and that our clothes that she made fit well were important to her.

awkward

(S) I sometimes unwillingly, was made to endure. *persevere*

(CX) No television or telephone calls for me, until my homework for each class

carefully completed

was done and checked over by mom.

CP/CX Discovering I wasn't an Olympic gymnast after six weeks of lessons, I

class

wanted to quite, but because "We made a committment and took up a place in the class," I stayed to the end of that session of lessons.

sp?

need CP:

She would tear out her knitting and redo it until it was, in her view, flawless; she would refit our clothes that she was sewing until they satisfied her standards.

Self-Check 14–7, p. 364

Notice that additional changes have been made in the sentences in these rough drafts, even from those in the revised sentence list in Self-Check 14–6.

1. You will not have a problem with boredom if you have a hobby. Not only will you spend time learning about your interest, but you will also travel to conventions, meets, and/or specialty shops to find more information or materials that relate to your hobby. Perhaps other family members can be involved, causing activities which the whole family can share. You can meet other people, too, who have your same interests. Some hobbies—woodworking, collecting, or knitting, etc.—teach skills that can lead to extra income; for example, you could sell furniture and toys, sell knitted items, trade and sell collectibles, or teach ~~classes~~ your acquired skills or knowledge to others in classes at hobby centers or adult education centers. All of these possibilities add up to the idea that a hobby can be a very beneficial undertaking.

2. My mother taught me persistence not only by instruction, but even more importantly, by example. In her own life, mother was a person who didn't give up, one whom others could count on. Assuming household chores, my mother made sure that her work was finished: The dishes were washed, the beds were made, all errands were run, and all phone calls returned. ~~her~~ Another sign of her diligence is that she was a Sunday School volunteer teacher for twenty-eight years continuously. Also, ~~any imperfect kni~~ she was careful with her handiwork, tearing out "imperfect" knitting, and refitting our clothes that she sewed until they satisfied her standards. My life profitted by her character trait. I, sometimes unwillingly, was made to persevere. No television or telephone use for me until my homework for each class was carefully completed <u>and</u> <u>checked over</u> by Mom. When I discovered that I wasn't an Olympic-class gymnast after six weeks of lessons and told her that I intended to quite, ~~I~~ it was made very clear to me that "We had made a commitment to the classes and had taken up a space in a sought-after class." I finished that full session of lessons. Today, though, I am glad that Mom showed me by her teaching and example that tenacity is, indeed, an important character trait.

Self-Check 14–8, p. 366

1. You ~~will~~ not have a problem with boredom if you have a hobby. Not only
   should   *Transition*

   will you spend less time learning about your ~~interest~~, but you ~~will~~ also
   activity   *can*

   travel to conventions, meets, and/or specialty shops to find more

   information or materials that relate to your hobby. Perhaps other family
   getting

members ~~can be~~ involved, *will lead to* ~~causing~~ activities ~~which~~ *that* the whole family can share. You can meet ~~other~~ *new* people, too, who have your same interests. Some hobbies—woodworking, collecting, or knitting, ~~etc.~~ *such as*—teach skills that can ~~lead to~~ *produce* extra income; for example, you could sell *handmade* furniture and toys, sell knitted items, trade and sell collectibles, or teach ~~classes~~ your acquired skills or knowledge to others in classes at hobby ~~centers~~ *stores* or adult education centers. All of these possibilities ~~add up to~~ *demonstrate* ~~the idea~~ *support* that a hobby ~~can be a very beneficial undertaking.~~ *have numerous* *benefits,* *—more than you had probably imagined.* *[trite] [conclusion]*

2. My mother taught me persistence not only by instruction, but even more importantly, by example. In her own life, mother was a person who didn't *(trans)* give up, one ~~on~~ whom others could ~~count on~~ *depend*. *Around the house* ~~Assuming household chores,~~ *each day, with our help,* my mother made sure that her work was finished: The dishes were washed, the beds were made, all errands were run, and all phone calls *were* *dried, and put away;* *early* *the* returned, ~~her~~ *promptly* *(Not || ?)* —*trans* Another sign of her diligence is that she was a Sunday School volunteer teacher for twenty-eight years ~~continuously~~ *consequitive*. ~~Also, any~~ *Another example of* ~~her care is that~~ ~~imperfect kni~~ she was ~~careful with her handiwork,~~ *painstaking* ~~tearing~~ *painstakingly tore* out "imperfect" *mother* *ed* knitting, and refitting our *handcrafted* clothes ~~that she sewed~~ *each item* until ~~they~~ satisfied her *skilled-tailor's* standards. ~~My life profitted by her character trait.~~ *trans* I, ~~sometimes~~ *often*

too many pronouns *passive?* *I, too, profited from her unflagging resolve, being,*

unwillingly, was made to persevere. No television or telephone use for me *I had carefully completed* until my homework for each class ~~was carefully completed and~~ ~~checked~~ *Mom had* *it* ~~over by Mom.~~ *(passive)* When I discovered that I wasn't an Olympic class gymnast after six weeks of lessons and told her that I intended to quit, I it was made very clear to me that *"We had"* ~~"We had~~ made a commitment to the classes," and had taken up a space in a sought-after class. I finished that full session of lessons. Today, though, I ~~am glad~~ *find that it has* ~~been~~ *benefited me in my everyday life* that Mom showed me by her teaching and example that tenacity is, indeed, an important character trait.

trite

Final Paragraphs for Self-Check 14–8, p. 366

1. You should not have a problem with boredom if you have a hobby. Not only will you spend time learning about your interest or activity, but you can also travel to conventions, meets, and/or specialty shops to find more information or materials that relate to your hobby. Perhaps getting other family members involved will lead to activities that the whole family can

share. You can meet new people, too, who have your same interests. Some hobbies—such as woodworking, collecting, or knitting—teach skills that can produce extra income; for example, you could sell handmade furniture and toys, sell knitted items, trade and sell collectibles, or teach your acquired skills or knowledge to others in classes at hobby stores or adult education centers. All of these possibilities support the conclusion that a hobby can have numerous benefits—more than you had probably imagined.

2. My mother taught me persistence not only by instruction, but even more importantly, by example. In her own life Mother was a person who didn't give up, one on whom others could depend. Around the house my mother made sure each day, with our help, that the work was finished: The dishes were washed, dried, and put away; the beds were made early; all errands were run; and all phone calls were returned promptly. Another sign of her diligence is that she was a Sunday school volunteer teacher for twenty-eight continuous years. A further example of her care is that Mother painstakingly tore out "imperfect" knitting and refitted our handcrafted clothes until each item satisfied her skilled-tailor's standards. I, too, profited from her unflagging resolve, being, often unwillingly, made to persevere. No television or telephone use for me until I had carefully completed my homework for each class and Mom had checked it over. When I discovered that I wasn't an Olympic-class gymnast after six weeks of lessons and told her that I intended to quit, it was made very clear to me that we had "made a commitment to the class" and had "taken up a space" in a sought-after class. I finished that full session of lessons. Today, though, I find that it has benefited me in my everyday life that Mom showed me by her teaching and example that tenacity is, indeed, an important character trait.

Chapter 15: Commas

Comma Usage Survey, p. 372

1. I am, in the first place, sure of my answers. [Chapter 1, phrases]
2. No commas. [Chapter 1, phrases]
3. Hank planned to go to Sarasota, but he didn't have airfare. [Chapter 7, compound sentences]
4. You may come to work at 7 a.m. and leave at 4 p.m., or you may arrive at 8 a.m. and leave at 5 p.m. [Chapter 7, compound sentences]
5. No commas. [Chapter 7, compound verbs]
6. No commas. [Chapter 7, compound verbs]
7. If you have completed the form, you may leave. [Chapter 4, adverbial clauses]
8. You may, if you are finished, leave. [Chapter 4, adverbial clauses]
9. No commas. [Chapter 4, adverbial clauses]
10. No commas. [Chapter 4, adjective clauses]
11. Mr. Martinez, who is my neighbor, works for Peterson and Sons. [Chapter 4, adjective clauses]

12. No commas. [Chapter 4, adjective clauses]

13. No commas. [Chapter 8, verbals]

14. To earn more money, Jan continued her education after graduation. [Chapter 8, verbals]

15. Talking on the phone, Ms. Williams seemed to get upset. [Chapter 8, verbals]

16. No commas. [Chapter 8, verbals]

17. Bryan, after seeing the lot, purchased the old building. [Chapter 8, verbals]

18. No commas. [Chapter 8, verbals]

19. That house, decorated in Colonial, is very lovely. [Chapter 8, verbals]

20. My sister, an airline hostess, travels thousands of miles each year. [Chapter 5, appositives]

21. Can you see, Mr. Allen, why this idea is so important? [Chapter 5, direct address]

22. No commas. [Chapter 5, nouns]

23. My hobbies include reading, cooking, and drag racing. [Chapter 5, series]

24. Miss Ellingsworth is a willing, capable worker. [Chapter 11, adjectives]

25. A well-written, reliable guidebook is a must for foreign travel. [Chapter 11, adjectives]

(*Note:* If you made any errors in these, review the punctuation section of the chapter named in parentheses.)

⊡ Chapter 16: Colons and Semicolons

Self-Check 16–1, p. 404

1. False.

2. to direct the reader's attention forward.

3. True.

4. False. If you use a colon right after the verb, you will be separating the verb from its object, in this case the direct objects. The first clause should be a complete idea.

5. True.

6. False. You do capitalize if what follows the colon is a complete clause (independent) or is a proper noun, pronoun, or adjective.

7. A quotation, a list, or a major idea.

8. In the attention line, the subject line, or the salutation.

9. True.

10. False, but semicolons usually do.

Self-Check 16–2, p. 407–408

1. True.

2. When the sentence is quite long <u>and</u> contains other commas.

3. Totally false. They do <u>not</u> have the same function. They require semicolons, not commas.

4. False. Usually a colon is used unless the list (or major idea) is preceded by an expression that somehow introduces it, such as *for instance*.

5. True, a comma is used here.

6. False, use semicolons.

7. True.

8. *for instance, for example, as, namely, that is, that is to say*.

9. False. These specialized marks of punctuation are still very much in use in all types of writing.

10. False, each mark has very specific uses.

⬛ Chapter 17: Other Marks of Punctuation

Self-Check 17–1, p. 417

1. Dash.

2. Colon at the end of the introductory clause.

3. The phrase contains commas or it needs special emphasis.

4. Dash.

5. Colon.

Self-Check 17–2, p. 420

1. False, dashes are.

2. Figures.

3. No.

4. Would not.

5. Seldom. Only for an abbreviation.

6. True.

7. With a capital letter . . . with end punctuation.

8. Parenthesis.

9. Brackets.

10. "Begin every sentence with a capital letter." This is not done for material in parentheses within another sentence.

Self-Check 17–3, p. 423–424

1. Exact.
2. True.
3. Capital.
4. Do not.
5. Period or a comma.
6. Colon or a semicolon.
7. Inside.
8. Seldom.
9. One set around all of the sentences.
10. A set of single quotation marks.
11. Quotation marks.
12. Underlined or italicized.
13. Omitted words.
14. The end of the quotation is missing.
15. Never guess, but use reference works.

INDEX